STYLES AND STRUCTURES

Alternative Approaches to College Writing

STYLES AND STRUCTURES

Alternative Approaches

to College Writing

CHARLES KAY SMITH

University of Massachusetts at Amherst

W · W · NORTON & COMPANY · INC · *New York*

52455

Published simultaneously in Canada
by George J. McLeod Limited, Toronto

Library of Congress Cataloging in Publication Data
Smith, Charles Kay.
    Styles and structures.
    Includes bibliographical references.
    1. English language—Rhetoric.   I. Title.
PE1408.S59   808'.0427   74–575
ISBN 0–393–09273–9

Printed in the United States of America
2   3   4   5   6   7   8   9   0

Design by Andrea Clark

Contents

List of Illustrations

Preface

THE premise of this book is that patterns of writing enact patterns of thinking, that by finding and practicing different ways of writing we can literally think different things. The book is designed to help people learn to do this by analyzing many diverse writing patterns and suggesting how students can practice them to achieve new ways of thinking.

On the college level the effective thinker—and writer—possesses at least the following cognitive skills:

the ability to adapt alternative descriptive and narrative techniques to different subjects and audiences;
the ability to use definitions as writing structures and tools of intellectual inquiry;
the ability to find assumptions underlying opinions in order to discover relationships and organize writing;
the ability to question conventions and generate new ideas in writing;
the ability to judge the significance of new ideas according to alternative sets of criteria.

This text encourages students to develop these abilities not as ends in themselves, but as means to becoming self-generating thinkers and writers. For example, in the first section of the book, instead of prescribing one "good" style or method of composition, several diverse methods of composition are presented and the limitations as well as advantages of each are discussed. The same manner of presentation is followed in all other sections of the text. Definition, for instance, is taught, not by prescribing any one defining structure (most rhetoric texts present only the Aristotelian definition), but by explaining several different kinds of definition. The underlying assumptions of each are made explicit, and the limitations as well as advantages of each are explained. The student is shown how to multiply these alternatives by combining two or more defining structures into new hybrid forms suitable for special purposes. Assumptions are taught in the same manner—by presenting competing alternative assumptions with a critique of their implications, and then encouraging students to combine single assumptions in order to produce whole sets of assumptions with which to organize or evaluate complex issues or events. Finally, in the last five chapters, a rhetoric of reperception is presented, which is the heart of this text because it contains generalized instruction for writing and thinking creatively in all fields. To understand the concepts in this section, and in the text as a whole, is to learn how to supercede them.

I wish to acknowledge an intellectual debt to J. V. Cunningham of Brandeis University who, among many other things, taught me how to analyze style and definition in a way that would be useful to writers, and to John Whyte who shepherded me through my first experience teaching freshman composition at Brandeis. Professors Joseph Frank, Walker Gibson, Richard Ulin, Charles Moran, Roberts French, John Clayton, and especially Robert Bagg of the University of Massachusetts all read parts of the manuscript and kindly offered me advice or encouragement, as did Professors M. H. Abrams, Robert Greenberg, Donald Gray, Brett Averitt, James Wheatley, Harold Ridlon, and Maurianne Adams.

The following colleagues who taught writing at the University of Massachusetts in the past few years used parts of the text in their classes and contributed in many and various ways to the development of the book: Floyce Alexander, Peter Alpers, Carol Angus, Jeffrey

Bartman, Rashna Batliwala, Steven Bauer, Gene Bernstein, Robert Brinkley, Ellen Broselow, Patricia Cahill, Elisa Campbell, Nancy Chinchor, Meera Clark, Fredrick Corbin, Phillip Crafts, Susan Crafts, Susan Currier, Raymond Cywinski, Lynn De Gerenday, John Foley, Roberta Gordon, Leonard Gougeon, Asheley Griffith, Marcia Hastie, Bonnie Herlihy, William Howe, R. Kevin Hughes, Andrew Jones, Christopher Jones, Bonnie Kates, R. Scott Kellner, Richard Ladd, Diedre Lannon, Monte Lorenzet, John Maclean, Barry Maid, Karen Mailler, William Mailler, Jeanne McNett, Rene Meyer, Helena Minton, Shirley Morahan, John Nordby, William Overstreet, George Ovitt, William Pasch, Leslie Perelman, Kathleen Petrisky, Bette Roberts, Kathleen Roig, Helen Roland, Lawrence Russ, Patricia Schroeder, Alexander Shishin, Edward Silver, Deborah Sitter, Betty Spence, Joyce Spencer, Wayne Ude, Margaret Walker, Gene Walz, and Bonita Wright.

My grateful thanks are also due to Peter Phelps for his intelligent editing and stimulating discussions on the subject of this book, to Carol Flechner for her expert copy editing of the text, to Andrea Clark for her excellent ideas on design, to Roy Tedoff for his efforts in expertly guiding the book into print, and to Susan Bourla for her care in researching parts of the text and illustrations.

Raymond Coppinger of Hampshire College kindly acted as a consultant on questions of natural science dealt with in the text.

I sought and received the advice of Prescott Smith, whose expertise in both education and media was an invaluable aid in choosing and arranging all the diagrams and illustrations used in the text.

I wish also to thank my mother, Grace Kay Smith, for typing parts of the manuscript.

A most profound debt is to Julie Graham, who for several years not only shared in the research but helped shape the book, generously contributing her own ideas to its development.

But by far my greatest debt is to Helen Sootin Smith whose love, research, typing, encouragement, advice, and intellectual companionship over many years contributed immeasurably to any merit this text might possess.

Shutesbury, Mass.   *Charles Kay Smith*
December, 1973

For Miranda

Part I

DESCRIPTIVE
AND
NARRATIVE STYLES

To increase writing alternatives rapidly, four different kinds of description and narration, called styles for convenience, are arranged so that the increase in complexity between one style analysis and the next is gradual enough not to dismay a new writer, but steep enough to remain challenging and interesting. Each analysis is concluded with a brief generalized diagram of the relation between the most important elements of the style. Then follows a prewriting discussion, a chapter in length, of the possibilities or problems that new writers will likely find in first using the style.

At the end of each analysis and prewriting discussion are several suggested writing exercises. These are designed to engage a new writer in discovering that stylistic structures are related to thought processes and that writing in each style demands an unusual perception of the world, distinct from any other. The student is encouraged to write, on the subject of his choice, both in the style he has just learned and in his own, and to consider the causes and effects of the difference between his own style of composition and other alternatives. The object is not for him to find fault with his own style but, on the contrary, for him to begin to inquire into the relation between his mental processes and his writing behavior. The assumption is that both his own style and the other are valid methods of composition but may aim at expressing quite different perceptions of the world in quite different ways. As a new writer becomes aware of the uniqueness of the perceptions he expresses in his writing, and at the same time learns how alternative methods of description and narration can be used to express alternative kinds of perceptions, his writing skill and intellectual identity can develop simultaneously.

The four styles used in this section represent such very great structural differences that they often seem to imply completely different perceptions of the world. Their subject matter, moreover, is diverse enough to interest new writers who will not be doing all their writing in the same field. They range in subject and period from action in the First World War (Hemingway) to a seventeenth-century sermon (Donne), from life in a modern urban ghetto (Wright) to poverty and inhumanity in eighteenth-century Ireland (Swift). If freedom is having the maximum alternatives in any situation, then to feel free to describe or narrate his own thoughts and feelings in writing a student needs at his disposal as many writing alternatives as possible. Although he may or may not use them again, involvement with these four styles will expand both the student's perceptions and his writing alternatives.

This is not a study of style in the usual sense because it will not prescribe any general rules of right or wrong in writing. Instead, it asks the reader to question the usefulness of each style, considering its disadvantages as well as its advantages. Once the several styles have been learned the emphasis will be on recombining their elements into new ways of writing that may become part of the student's own repertoire.

Because writing is so intimately related to the workings of the human mind, learning about writing can be one of the most challenging and liberating of studies. In this book we are considering writing or rhetoric not as a remedial skill but as an intellectually demanding and rewarding subject in its own right. Because we have not glossed over difficulties in the subject, some new writers may find that these chapters generally require careful study rather than casual reading. But, as in studying a text in biology, psychology, or chemistry, perseverance will result in comprehension of a new field. The new field is based on a reconception of rhetoric not as a catalogue of conventions, but as an inquiry into the relation of alternative patterns of writing to different ways of thinking and perceiving. We wish to stress the word inquiry *because the structural resources of the human intellect with respect to writing cannot be fully formalized; one can always produce new structures by combining or recombining those already known. Our interest in and explanation of structures are, therefore, not intended to formulate and perpetuate structural conventions, but rather to accelerate structural innovation by encouraging the student to use a wide range of writing structures in new combinations with virtually any subject matter the student chooses.*

"An Incident"

from A FAREWELL TO ARMS

Ernest Hemingway

AT noon we were stuck in a muddy road about, as nearly as we could figure, ten kilometres from Udine. The rain had stopped during the forenoon and three times we had heard planes coming, seen them pass overhead, watched them go far to the left and heard them bombing on the main highroad. We had worked through a network of secondary roads and had taken many roads that were blind, but had always, by backing up and finding another road, gotten closer to Udine. Now, Aymo's car, in backing so that we might get out of a blind road, had gotten into the soft earth at the side and the wheels, spinning, had dug deeper and deeper until the car rested on its differential. The thing to do now was to dig out in front of the wheels, put in brush so that the chains could grip, and then push until the car was on the road. We were all down on the road around the car. The two sergeants looked at the car and examined the wheels. Then they started off down the road without a word. I went after them.

"Come on," I said. "Cut some brush."

"We have to go," one said.

"Get busy," I said, "and cut brush."

A Farewell to Arms (New York: Charles Scribner's Sons, 1929; The Scribner Library, 1957), pp. 203–204.

"We have to go," one said. The other said nothing. They were in a hurry to start. They would not look at me.

"I order you to come back to the car and cut brush," I said. The one sergeant turned. "We have to go on. In a little while you will be cut off. You can't order us. You're not our officer."

"I order you to cut brush," I said. They turned and started down the road.

"Halt," I said. They kept on down the muddy road, the hedge on either side. "I order you to halt," I called. They went a little faster. I opened up my holster, took the pistol, aimed at the one who had talked the most, and fired. I missed and they both started to run. I shot three times and dropped one. The other went through the hedge and was out of sight. I fired at him through the hedge as he ran across the field. The pistol clicked empty and I put in another clip. I saw it was too far to shoot at the second sergeant. He was far across the field, running, his head held low. I commenced to reload the empty clip. Bonello came up.

"Let me go finish him," he said. I handed him the pistol and he walked down to where the sergeant of engineers lay face down across the road. Bonello leaned over, put the pistol against the man's head and pulled the trigger. The pistol did not fire.

"You have to cock it," I said. He cocked it and fired twice. He took hold of the sergeant's legs and pulled him to the side of the road so he lay beside the hedge. He came back and handed me the pistol.

1

How Form and Content
Work Together
in an Objective Style

YOU might begin by asking yourself a simple question about the style of this passage. What sort of sentences does the author use? You could say that you see a few very short sentences, and we would all agree, especially with regard to the dialogue: " 'Come on,' I said. 'Cut some brush.' " You might even have the impression that all the sentences are short. But this, we see, is not a fact, although perhaps it is a valuable impression just the same. Why did you think—if you did—that the sentences were all fairly short? At present we can only note that some sentences are quite short, that most are of moderate length, and that none is extremely long. But sentence length does not tell us all we need to know about style; perhaps we can learn more by examining the construction of the sentences. If we divide sentences into three types—simple (one independent clause), compound (more than one independent clause), and complex (an independent clause and one or more dependent, or subordinate, clauses)—what do we have here? A number of simple sentences occur: "The pistol did not fire." And many sentences are compound: "I missed and they both started to run." But when we look for complex sentences we experience difficulty in finding examples. We can only conclude from the preponderance of simple or compound sentences that for some reason Hemingway must be avoiding complex structures.

8

Perhaps this exclusion of complex sentences accounts for our earlier impression that his sentences are short, for he seems to use independent clauses one after another, sometimes preceding them with conjunctions and sometimes not.

How can we explain this unusual stylistic feature? Why does Hemingway prefer simple and compound sentences to complex ones? He wants, you might suggest, to achieve a simple rather than complex effect. But this explanation, this hypothesis, may be too facile and may not prove to be fruitful. A stylistic hypothesis is significant if it not only explains one structural fact, but can explain others and even lead us to see stylistic traits that we have not yet noticed. Let us see if it does, but let us be prepared to replace or modify the hypothesis if we find it less useful than some new one that may explain more facts and lead us to further inquiry.

This hypothesis is useful, you might say, because it leads us to see and relate something we have not seen before—namely, that Hemingway keeps his vocabulary simple. What precisely do we mean by this, and can we isolate any examples? This is a difficult question because simplicity is a relative concept. What we might mean by saying that Hemingway's words are simple is that his vocabulary, relative to that of other novelists we have read, is easily understandable. You might notice how few polysyllabic words appear in the passage. Then you might relate this fact to your original hypothesis and claim that Hemingway does not need any big words or difficult words because he is trying to say something quite simple.

But let's look again at Hemingway's characteristic vocabulary. His sparing use of adjectives and adverbs stands out: " 'I order you to cut brush,' I said." (Not "I said evenly" or "I said threateningly.") We are not told quite how it was said. And the only sort of adjective we see is a descriptive type. Of course, no adjective is really objective, yet most of us would agree that "soft earth" or "muddy road" represents a quite different use of adjectives than, for instance, "hostile earth" or "sinister road." In the latter cases the adjectives used are more subjective. If a road is muddy to one person it is likely to be muddy to a number of people. But a road may seem quite "sinister" to one person but "invitingly romantic" to another. Why does Hemingway avoid most adjectives and adverbs? Our earlier simple hypothesis will not help us very much here. The use or exclusion of adjectives does not make ideas simple or complex. It is perhaps time to search for a better hypothesis to explain the exclusion of adjectives and adverbs as well as the earlier traits we have already noted.

At this point you might say, "Well, if Hemingway were trying to avoid being subjective—avoid offering his own opinions or imposing his own values—he might want to exclude adjectives and adverbs." Possibly. But can you relate Hemingway's exclusion of subordinate clauses, of complex sentences, to this same hypothesis? How does a writer decide which things to subordinate to others in his work? He has to make some value judgments, you would say. He has to express an implicit opinion of what he considers more and what less important in order to subordinate in his sentences the less important information. Consider for a moment the problem of an artist painting an accurate picture of the action of Hemingway's passage. What lies in the foreground and what in the background? Wouldn't the artist have to disregard all perspective if he wished to draw an accurate picture of what Hemingway has expressed? There could be no background because Hemingway has not told us, for example, whether cocking a pistol is subordinate to shooting a man. In a painting the cocking mechanism of the pistol would have to be as clearly drawn and visible as the hole in the sergeant's head. We can now disregard our first, hasty hypothesis (that he wanted to achieve a simple effect), because this new hypothesis (that Hemingway's stylistic choices and exclusions are related to his wish to avoid making value judgments) explains two seemingly unrelater stylistic traits that could not be explained at all by our first hypothesis—the lack of subordination and avoidance of subjective adjectives and adverbs. But will this new one generate more fruitful inquiry into Hemingway's style? Let's see if it will.

If Hemingway wishes to avoid introducing any occasion for subjectivity, what other kinds of vocabulary might he use or avoid? He might avoid moral or evaluative words of any sort. Do we, in fact, find any abstract nouns like *justice, duty, mercy, cowardice, disobedience*—words that we might expect to see in such a passage if the author were not averse to making value judgments? We find no such abstract words (nonmaterial references), just as our hypothesis would have predicted. On the contrary, Hemingway evidently prefers concrete words (material references). Some pages earlier in the same novel from which the passage we are studying came, Hemingway gives his main character this plain statement of preference for concrete language and mistrust of abstractions, which he regards as based on traditional beliefs and values that no longer convey a modern man's very changed perception of the world:

> I was always embarrassed by the words sacred, glorious, and sacrifice and the expression in vain. We had heard them, sometimes standing in the rain almost out of earshot, so that only the shouted words came through, and had read them, on proclamations that were slapped up by bill-posters over other proclamations, now for a long time, and I had seen nothing sacred, and the things that were glorious had no glory and the sacrifices were like the stockyards at Chicago if nothing was done with the meat except to bury it. There were many words that you could not stand to hear and finally only the names of places had dignity. . . . Abstract words such as glory, honor, courage, or hallow were obscene beside the concrete names of villages, the numbers of roads, the names of rivers, the numbers of regiments and the dates. [*A Farewell to Arms*, pp. 184–185]

Although we said Hemingway almost always restricts himself to concrete words, these words are not always necessarily specific. To be accurate in describing the type and function of the words Hemingway uses we will have to make distinctions between abstract and concrete, general and specific nouns. An *abstract* noun refers to a quality, characteristic, or idea apart from any object—that is, *brightness, loyalty, honor*. A *concrete* noun refers to something material that can be seen, tasted, touched, smelled, or heard. We can make a further distinction between *general* and *specific* words: while a general word names a class of object or action—*child, government, nature, play*—a specific word names a member of a class—*Mary Davis, American democracy, copper beech tree, Chinese checkers.* Of course, specificity is relative: *dog* is more specific than the general term *animal*, but less specific than *Siberian husky.*

Often we find Hemingway's language is very specific, as when the speaker tells us they are "ten kilometres from Udine" or mentions that the truck rests *not* on its general underside, but on its specific "differential." There is also often a precision and arresting specificity about the very way Hemingway chooses to conceive an event. For instance, important parts of the last three paragraphs are organized around this detailed process: anyone loading an automatic pistol with a new clip of bullets will not be able to fire it until he has cocked the bolt back to pick up a bullet and shove it into the chamber ready to fire. "The pistol clicked empty and I put in another clip," the officer tells us. But Hemingway, thinking specifically about this process, chooses to let the officer and Bonello and, of course, the reader forget in the excitement of the moment this detail about loading automatic pistols. Hemingway is really laying a trap for the reader who, he calculates, will not be thinking of mechanical detail when the life of a man is at stake. Hemingway forces us to await at close range and with suspenseful horror the expected crash of a bullet into the sergeant's head. Then he springs his trap.

> Bonello leaned over, put the pistol against the man's head and pulled the trigger. The pistol did not fire.
> "You have to cock it," I said. He cocked it and fired twice.

Hemingway appears to be using a material mechanism as an organizing device to suggest that a hard, material reality is operating whether or not human beings can remember the specific details of the mechanism. By using such a detailed process in this way Hemingway has opposed a hard mechanistic reality to the very natural human feelings of shock that the reader will likely experience as this incident is described.

But just because Hemingway is often specific and detailed in his descriptions, we should not forget that his vocabulary can at other times be quite general. As a matter of fact his brilliant use of the occasional specific word or particular detail would lose effectiveness if it occurred too often. For instance, we know the sergeants by rank and talkativeness, but not by name or any specific detail of dress or appearance. Why do you think Hemingway is not more specific about these men?

Hemingway's preference for concrete, if not always specific, words, which lend themselves better to material description than to subjective value judgments, suggests that our hypothesis may now be stated in terms of inclusion as well as in terms of exclusion: Hemingway avoids those syntactical constructions or organizations or types of words (such as abstract nouns) that may allow subjective value judgments to creep in, and uses language that favors starkly material description that is often, but not always, very specific and precise.

Occasionally Hemingway seems interested in descriptive precision, and in these instances tends to pick carefully a few words to express what other writers might take many words to express. This principle of economy is related to his attempt to be objective as well as to the occasional attempt to be precise. It seems also to be related to the habit we noticed earlier of using easy words. Can we, so far, explain his preference for one- and two-syllable words? Perhaps it is time once more to consider adding to our hypothesis. We have supposed that Hemingway, in addition to avoiding evaluation, wishes to describe things materially, more or less precisely. Let us further suppose that he wishes to carry out his material description in informal language, using plain terms. This assumption might also lead us to notice that Hemingway uses mostly loose sentence structures of the common subject-verb-object type. Such sentence order causes the passage to sound more colloquial, as though it were spoken, than if the sentences were transposed into more literary, formal patterns. This is so because if you recorded an average sample of colloquial spoken English, you would discover that the incidence of loose subject-verb-object sentences was much greater than in an average sample of written literary English, where you would find more inverted, delayed, interrupted, and balanced sentences.

You might observe now that Hemingway uses many verbs, but that few of them are Latinate. Many are colloquial verb-adverb compounds: "dig out," "put in," "started off," "opened up." If Hemingway had not used "dig out in front of the wheels," for instance, he might have had to say "excavate" or "extricate." Doesn't "dig out" allow him to say informally what could have sounded rather formal? We have noted that adverbs are as rare as adjectives in the passage. But verb-adverb compounds relate adverbs to some action. In an effort to avoid subjectivity Hemingway uses chiefly adverbs that form *part* of the verb, avoiding those that modify and hence interpret. The importance of active verbs in the passage suggests the importance of action in the passage. The avoidance of the passive voice, too, suggests a further refinement of our hypothesis. We might conclude that Hemingway wishes his narrator to describe, objectively and precisely, yet colloquially, an action rather than a thought, feeling, or mood.

Consider how few figures of speech Hemingway uses. Almost no similes, metaphors, or personifications appear. Metaphors and other figures of speech provide occasions for subjectivity that we might expect him to avoid. For contrast, here is a war scene described figuratively in Shakespeare's *Hamlet,* II, ii, 499–503:

> A rouséd vengeance sets him new awork,
> And never did the Cyclops' hammers fall
> On Mars's armor, forged for proof eterne,
> With less remorse than Pyrrhus' bleeding sword
> Now falls on Priam.

Though we find none in "An Incident," Hemingway occasionally does use a simile or metaphor, and these tend to seem colorful and emphatic against the polished but plain surface of his style. Any such variation from an established norm will seem emphatic. In this passage only a few submerged metaphors occur, but these are so dead that it is difficult to think of them as metaphors at all—i.e., "roads that were *blind*."

How is the passage organized? Chronologically, you will say, and spatially, for events are described in temporal and spatial order. For instance, the narrator carefully informs us that the incident takes place at noon and at about ten kilometers from Udine. No analysis or interpretation is offered. Except on the level of routine conventions or processes ("put in brush *so that the chains could grip*," "in backing *so that we might get out of a blind road*") no cause-and-effect relation between events is provided. A few of these routine conventions or processes are explicit, but others are unstated: "Bonello leaned over, put the pistol against the man's head and pulled the trigger." We must understand that the conventions of war make desertion an offense punishable by execution. And the final act of the ritual of execution was the *coup de grâce* to put the condemned man out of his misery and seal his fate.

Hemingway tacitly structures the passage with the conventional routine behavior and rules of war that organize a soldier's life. There are, however, few trades whose rules, routines, and conventions are unusual enough to capture the interest of or unnerve the average reader. The subjects that recur in his stories, like bullfighting, deep-sea fishing, big-game hunting, and war, are all easy to make exciting without much commentary or explanation, because in each men are either killing or being killed, and sudden violent death is often imminent. Beyond the understood conventional behavior—that of war, in our passage—no explanations are given. And although the bare description of events is horrifying, the absence of any commentary leaves the reader to make of the action whatever he can. Perhaps because we are accustomed to some philosophical explanation for such violent and provocative events, Hemingway's temporal and spatial description seems laconic. We are offered a nakedly material ordering of events (which invites the reader to make his own judgments and interpretations) rather than a spiritual or philosophic order. We shall have more to say later about Hemingway's organization; the whole compass of an author's organization is not always revealed by a study of how his narrator organizes an event. In the next chapter we shall consider why the author chooses certain events and not others for his narrator to describe in the noninterpretive time-space order that we have observed. Perhaps Hemingway is doing some organizing that his narrator does not appear to be doing.

Hemingway's subject matter seems to be an incident involving an isolated ambulance detachment taking part in a general retreat and threatened by an enemy ambush. Two sergeants desert the disabled truck against orders. The officer shoots one down, and one of his men willingly administers the *coup de grâce* by shooting him twice in the head at close range. War, violent adventure, and death comprise the subject of the passage. Hemingway seems to have avoided here anything commonplace or tame.

What attitude does the narrator take toward his subject? Certainly all the structural elements of his style that we have studied so far help to determine this attitude. It is one of accurate, flat, laconic reporting. He has excluded all occasions for subjectivity and has included those elements that enable him to describe events with material accuracy, restraint, and precision.

There is much more that we could say of Hemingway's style, particularly if we were to examine some other samples of his writing. But we have inquired into his method of composing enough to have built a fairly accurate model of this small sample of his style. A "model of his style" means a kind of structural writing program that, if followed by any writer, would result in a similar pattern of inclusions or exclusions of characteristic syntactical structures, types and structures of words, figures of speech, and organizing structures. Moreover, a style or characteristic combination of writing structures such as Hemingway's, as we have seen, tends to be related to certain kinds of attitudes or processes of thought and perception of which an author may or may not be aware. Hemingway's rhetoric invites the reader to make his own interpretations because it is designed to "show" provocative action but not evaluate for the reader or "tell" him why things happen.

Here is the Hemingway style model we have just constructed expressed as a writing program in the form of a brief diagram. (When we refer to Hemingway's style, we mean his method of composition only in the specific example we analyzed. Needless to say, if we were to analyze other samples of his style we might well find him using somewhat different combinations of stylistic elements.)

Writing Program I

BRIEF DIAGRAM OF HEMINGWAY'S STYLE

Syntax:

Use simple or compound sentences. Avoid complex sentences. Use many loose or common subject-verb-object sentences. Avoid artfully contrived sentences (such as delayed, balance, inverted). Use varied-length (short to moderate) sentences. Avoid excessively long sentences.

Words:

Use concrete words. Avoid abstract words. Use informal and often specific words. Avoid subjective adjectives and adverbs.

Figures of Speech:

Use *only very rarely* a simile or metaphor. Avoid artful figures of speech such as personifications.

Organization: *

Use temporal and/or spatial order. Avoid cause-and-effect organization. Use detailed description of mechanical processes, games, or

---

* But see below, pp. 20–22, for a more subtle form of covert organization in which Hemingway guides his readers' responses by "showing" them rather than "telling" them how to respond.

ritual sequences to order an occasional paragraph. Avoid philosophical explanations or analyses as ordering principles.

Subject Matter:

Use events or emotional situations that are easy to make exciting and provocative. Avoid uneventful, emotionally relaxed, commonplace subjects that are difficult to make exciting or provocative without much explanation.

Attitudes or Ways of Thinking and Perceiving:

Use flat, laconic, reportorial, restrained attitude. Avoid subjective, interpretive, biased attitude. (Let your reader interpret the meaning of the incident.)

Exercises

1. Here are a few sentences from Edgar Allan Poe's short stories. See if you can rewrite them to fit an objective Hemingway style.

   a. "We had now reached the summit of the loftiest crag." ["A Descent into the Maelström"]
   b. "With a feeling of deep yet most singular affection I regarded my friend Morella." ["Morella"]
   c. "The thousand injuries of Fortunato I had borne as best I could; but when he ventured upon insult, I vowed revenge." ["The Cask of Amontillado"]
   d. "At Paris, just after dark one gusty evening in the autumn of 18–, I was enjoying the twofold luxury of meditation and a meerschaum, in company with my friend C. Auguste Dupin, in his little back library, or book-closet, *au troisième* [the fourth floor], No. 33, Rue Dunôt, Faubourg St. Germain." ["The Purloined Letter"]
   e. "During the whole of a dull, dark, and soundless day in the autumn of the year, when the clouds hung oppressively low

in the heavens, I had been passing alone, on horseback, through a singularly dreary tract of country, and at length found myself, as the shades of the evening drew on, within view of the melancholy House of Usher." ["The Fall of the House of Usher"]

2. Now compose a sentence of your own using Hemingway's style. Refer to the diagram for syntactical, verbal, and figurative characteristics of Hemingway's style.

3. Next compose a short paragraph using not only Hemingway's kind of sentences, but develop the paragraph according to one of his characteristic organizing patterns (temporal, spatial order, or description of a mechanical process, game, or ritual sequence).

2

Selecting, Arranging, and Organizing to Show Rather than Tell

AT the end of this section you will be encouraged to use this first style program to write on some subject matter of your own choice. When we try to write in Hemingway's style, however, two special problems arise that we can briefly discuss now before you write.

We may not be doing Hemingway justice when we confine our discussion of organization to the narrator's order of events. To leave the matter there with no further indication of control might have the effect of reducing Hemingway's artistry to that of an entry in a military report. Some difficulties arise because we are considering the passage apart from the novel as a whole. Although such isolation is useful to us at the moment, we should at least briefly indicate some of the artistic organization that makes Hemingway's fiction so different from a purely factual account of an event. The passage we are considering is part of a larger parallel structure in the novel, *A Farewell to Arms*. The hero, Lieutenant Henry, serves in our passage as prosecutor, judge, and executioner in the case of the desertion of two soldiers. He executes the one who talks the most; the other escapes. A few pages later, Henry himself will be mistakenly accused of desertion. He will wait his turn as others, similarly charged, are summarily judged and immediately shot. And Henry will run away, like the sergeant who got away from him, bidding "farewell to arms." The passage we have isolated affords a parallel to this most important later incident, which serves as a turning point in the novel.

Hemingway organizes the two parallel incidents to invite a reader to experience and consider their relation so that he can better understand the radical change that is to take place in the hero's mind and behavior when, totally disillusioned with the war, he becomes a deserter himself.

When we consider the organization of our passage from the point of view of Hemingway the author rather than that of his narrator, we realize that the author sets carefully before the reader subtle inducements to form attitudes and interpretations. For example, in reading the passage we do tend to form attitudes toward military action in war that certainly are not likely to make us anxious to go out and enlist in the army. Even though Hemingway's style does not allow him to make value judgments in the usual overt way, the situations, events, and characters that he uses provoke certain emotional responses, ideas, and evaluations. We discover these at his implicit direction. His very choice of morally freighted subjects to treat in a noncommittal style implies a certain philosophical attitude.

In other words, just because a writer employs an "objective style" does not mean that what he says is truly objective. You could, for example, write in an objective style an account of atrocities perpetrated on prisoners of war; and if you select all the prisoners from one country and all the torturers from another, you have plainly biased your reader, even if you do not use a single adjective, metaphor, subordinate clause, or abstraction, and organize only temporally and spatially. Many newspapers and magazines use an objective style much like Hemingway's. In some articles you might usefully ask yourself if an "objective" style does not mask a very biased piece of reporting.

In using an objective style a writer can communicate value judgments or interpretations by "showing" rather than "telling" his reader. By "telling" I mean the writer or narrator acts as a commentator and judges or interprets things and actions for the reader. By "showing" I mean the writer does not overtly interpret or solve things for the reader, but instead sets up a pattern of concrete objects, actions, and statements from which readers may abstract an interpretation for themselves. But it would be a mistake to assume that the writer who wishes to "show" rather than "tell" does not express an interpretation. He does so covertly, usually by careful arrangement or organization, in such a way as to suggest, but not state, certain interpretations or value judgments for the reader to feel. By covert organization I mean a kind of dramatic arrangement of a scene so that the reader can feel that he is participating with the writer by actually making his own value judgments and generally interpreting the action without feeling bullied into it, as though the writer had led him by the hand rather than by the ear. I have already explained how Hemingway has covertly organized the whole scene we read as an analogue to another desertion scene a few pages later in the novel. The effect of such an analogy is to suggest, rather than state, certain comparisons and contrasts that will lead a reader to form some judgment; the writer has arranged for the reader to make a judgment even if he has not coerced him into it.

You can practice this part of Hemingway's style by attempting to suggest to a reader that he make certain judgments by the way you arrange concrete words and actions in writing. There are many ways to do this besides setting up an analogy. How could you "show" a reader rather than "tell" him the gist of this sentence: "Mrs. Blundt was a cruel and bitter stepmother"? The problem is to communicate the ideas in the sentence to a reader by arranging a brief scene in Hemingway's style without interpreting or using abstractions or any adjectives like *cruel* and *bitter*. How well do the following sentences solve the problem? Can you think of other less exaggerated ways to do it?

> "You'll not get a bite to eat for dinner tonight. I'll see to that, and when Mr. Blundt gets here he'll thrash you," she said. "I'll tell him what you were up to. He'll take you back to the orphanage where we found you."
> Tears filled the child's eyes. "Please," he said.

> Mrs. Blundt looked into his eyes for several minutes and, still looking down into his eyes, pursed her lips. *"I* am having lemon meringue pie for dessert tonight," she said.

Notice that it seems to take more words to show than to tell. Why? Perhaps Hemingway's style is not as economical as it looks on the surface. Now see if you can set up in a few sentences a concrete scene to show a reader the judgments or interpretations we are simply told in any one of the following sentences:

1. Sarah was an existentialist, constantly seeking to define herself by her actions.
2. Ken was highly critical of even his closest friends.
3. Whether alone or in crowds, he lived in a state of alienated isolation.
4. She no longer believed that the old values made sense, or even that the world could have any meaning.
5. *David* is a powerful statue by the highly skilled artist Michelangelo.
6. He felt as if the world were crumbling when he learned he had flunked the exam.
7. John could not bridge the generation gap with his father.
8. It is unlikely that a poor family can lead a decent life in a modern urban environment.
9. He treated her with churlish contempt.
10. He had no sense of identity.
11. Carol was a hero in every sense of that word.
12. Our hearts were young and gay.

Ask a friend who has not seen the original "telling" sentence to read your "showing" sentences, and ask him for *his* interpretation of the scene. Can you rewrite the scene until, when you test it out on another friend, he will interpret it in the way you have arranged for it to be interpreted? You can improve your writing amazingly if you are willing to test out almost scientifically what you write on "naïve" readers until you find out about how readers actually react to your different arrangements of the same scene. Finally, through trial and error, you can arrive at an arrangement that works with most of your chosen readers.

But is it always better to show rather than to tell in all writing? The next problem concerns the relation of Hemingway's style to different types of subject matter. When you try to write in this style yourself, you will notice that it requires much editing, pruning, and rewriting to achieve what in the end appears artless and simple. It is not a style that lends itself to fast, unedited composing, such as occurs in a written exam. On an examination in art history, for instance, abstract words like *classical, cubist, baroque* could afford a very useful shorthand for discussing difficult concepts that might take much too long to "show." And if you tried to use Hemingway's temporal-spatial organizing with no cause-and-effect interpretation, you might seem simple-minded indeed to see no order in historical events other than their sequence in time and space. Of course, in almost any intellectual subject the avoidance of abstractions, subordination, analysis, cause and effect, and interpretation imposes a serious limitation on the writer.

This limitation is not altogether bad, however, when writing about ideas, since many of us, never having been under any restraint with respect to the use of abstractions, have allowed abstract words to dominate our vocabulary so that they have produced a vagueness in our expression, and quite possibly in our thinking. To use abstractions sparingly, and to offer concrete examples when possible, might lead us to clarify our thoughts. If your style is abstract and adjectival not because these traits allow you to communicate but simply because you have never even considered your style before, then perhaps practice with Hemingway's style might help you to effect a new balance in your own writing.

If Hemingway's whole style is difficult to use with intellectual subjects, perhaps there are certain parts of his style that could be useful to us. A possible advantage of Hemingway's style for the person who wishes to write precisely about ideas is his establishment of a norm of understatement. Because of his stylistic restraint, any figure of speech or adjective introduced will vary from that norm in such a noticeable way that it is as though a spotlight were put on it, making obvious to the reader exactly what the writer wishes to color or emphasize. A careful and meticulous writer might consider this quality of Hemingway's style a real advantage in precise communication. If Hemingway claims that a bull or a matador is "very brave," we know that the man or animal must be most extraordinarily and marvelously courageous. In a less restrained style the word *very* is only slightly intensive, as in "very truly yours" or a "very nice day."

Are there subjects other than intellectual ones that might be difficult to write on in an objective style? Try writing about an uneventful tea party in Hemingway's style. If you are not careful it might go something like this:

> "Would you care for some tea?" she said.
> "Please," he said.
> "Sugar?"
> "Just one cube," he said. She passed his cup. He stirred and began to drink it.
> "May I have some lemon?" he said.
> "Yes," she said.

This passage sounds flat and dull, and might be cleverly used to suggest the vapidity and inconsequence of these people's lives. The couple might even be used in a larger context to represent modern man in modern society. Inconsequential men and women, measuring out their lives with teaspoons, might be used to symbolize a conventional, materialistic, meaningless society.

But let us suppose that we did not want to be ironic with our tea-party passage. How could we avoid the flatness that is a constant hazard in using an objective style? Hemingway shows us one way to enliven such a scene in "The Killers," a short story in which two professional murderers have a bite to eat at a diner while awaiting their victim. The unimportant commonplaces they exchange are not dull because their flat conversation creates a contrast with their sinister purpose, which we keep always in mind. Such commonplace language would not have had the same charged effect had the two men been ordinary friends eating out before a movie. I suppose that in our own tea-party scene we could imitate Hemingway by letting the reader know that the girl had sprinkled the sugar cube with a deadly poison that causes certain, sudden, and spectacularly painful death. Only she cannot remember whether or not he takes sugar in his tea. But this sort of change has radically altered our subject matter. The first subject was a tea-party; the second, a diabolical and suspenseful murder plot that may or may not be triggered by a cube of sugar. The second subject is easy to make exciting; the first is not. We can afford to underplay the murder plot with Hemingway's style for the same reason that a startlingly beautiful woman can afford to dress with restraint.

In an objective style it is hard to show the interest in an uneventful, everyday subject. It may be easier to tell about it. Perhaps a writer could make our conventional couple at their commonplace tea-party a lively subject if he used another kind of style. In a more subjective style he could characterize them carefully with some well-chosen adjectives, give us some notion of their relationship, and let us know what they are thinking and why. Perhaps such commentary, difficult to imply in an objective style, might make the passage more interesting to read even though the physical tea-party remained as uneventful as ever. Of course, the use of a subjective, interpretive style, you might argue, would also change the subject matter—this time from drinking tea to the private thoughts and emotions of the characters, since what these people think and feel is more central, under the circumstances, than what they say and do.

If we wished to use an objective style to suggest the inner lives of the couple at the commonplace tea-party we could do it, of course, since any style can be used with any subject matter, even if in practice certain subjects and certain styles are difficult to use well together. Let us try to rewrite the passage, still in objective style, to show the couple's inner life while taking tea. Suppose that after a quarrel the night before the woman wants to be accommodating and friendly and the man rejects her attempts and remains impenetrable, and we wish to make all this implicit in their behavior rather than explicit in some commentary:

> "Would you care for some tea?" she asked.
> "I'll get it myself," he said.
> "Sugar?"
> "No," he said.
> "You always take sugar."
> "Not this morning."
> "Is it about what happened last night?" she asked.
> "I'd rather have lemon, and I'll get it myself," he said.

We have seen that, for somewhat different reasons, Hemingway's style may be hard to use well with some subjects, such as academic or uneventful ones. It may seem easiest to use with just that sort of subject about which Hemingway usually chooses to write. Bullfights, dangerous big-game hunting, and war are subjects that make his flat, understated, restrained, and laconic expression seem terribly provocative, not simply inarticulate as it might with less wild subjects. Perhaps it is too early to ask such questions, since we have considered only one style, but is it possible that a unique style lends itself best to the expression of some very particular perception of the world?

The style a writer adopts may to some extent determine his audience, his characteristic subjects, and his possible range of attitudes toward his subjects and audience. Conversely, the sorts of subjects that interest a writer, his range of attitudes toward his subject, the audience he wishes to address, and his relation to that audience will help determine the combination of rhetorical structures that he will want to use.

Exercises

1. The following sentence interprets a relationship:

   > Lee and Chris had done away with sex roles so completely that
   > as their meaningful relationship developed, you could not really
   > tell who was the man and who the woman.

   Write several paragraphs showing the development of this relationship between Lee and Chris without telling it.

2. Write several paragraphs in Hemingway's style on any subject
   that seems relevant and interesting to you. Do not use bullfights,
   deep-sea fishing, war, etc., simply because Hemingway uses
   them often enough so that they become his conventional subject
   matter. Convention is not the same as necessity. Feel free to
   adapt Hemingway's style to *your* interests. You can refresh your
   mind about the combination of writing structures that com-
   prises Hemingway's style by referring to Writing Program I on
   pp. 17–18. *Try not to parody Hemingway by repeating any of his
   actual words.*

3. Next, write a paragraph or two on the same subject as in exercise 1, but this time use your own habitual writing structures
   instead of Hemingway's. (Some people may find it easier to
   write first in their own style, and then in Hemingway's.)

4. Now write a brief discussion comparing and contrasting your
   habitual writing structures with Hemingway's. Do not under-
   rate your own style, for you may be using just as good a combination of structures that results in your perceiving the world
   in very different ways from Hemingway. Assuming that both
   your style and Hemingway's are valid, but different, combinations of structures that lend themselves to different perceptions,
   what would you say is the difference between the way you and
   a writer like Hemingway perceive the world?

"Salvation or Damnation"

from a SERMON

John Donne

LET me wither and weare out mine age in a discomfortable,
in an unwholesome, in a penurious prison, and so pay my
debts with my bones, and recompence the wastfulnesse of my
youth, with the beggery of mine age; Let me wither in a
spittle * under sharpe, and foule, and infamous diseases, and
so recompence the wantonnesse of my youth, with that loathsomnesse in mine age; yet, if God with-draw not his spirituall
blessings, his Grace, his Patience, If I can call my suffering his
Doing, my passion his Action, All this that is temporall, is but
a caterpiller got into one corner of my garden, but a mill-dew
fallen upon one acre of my Corne; The body of all, the substance of all is safe, as long as the soule is safe. But when I
shall trust to that, which wee call a good spirit, and God shall
deject, and empoverish, and evacuate that spirit, when I shall
rely upon a morall constancy, and God shall shake, and enfeeble, and enervate, destroy and demolish that constancy;
when I shall think to refresh my selfe in the serenity and sweet
ayre of a good conscience, and God shall call up the damps and

Although I refer to this paragraph as a sermon, it is really a short
extract from a sermon that Donne calls "The Second of My Prebend Sermons
upon My Five Psalmes. Preached at S. Paul's, January 29, 1625." Text from
The Sermons of John Donne, ed. Evelyn M. Simpson and George R. Potter,
10 vols. (Berkeley: University of California Press, 1953–62), VII (1954),
pp. 56–57.
    * Hospital.

The Weighing of the Souls. Fresco, Dečani Monastery (ca. 1335).

vapours of hell it selfe, and spread a cloud of diffidence, and an impenetrable crust of desperation upon my conscience; when health shall flie from me, and I shall lay hold upon riches to succour me, and comfort me in my sicknesse, and riches shall flie from me, and I shall snatch after favour, and good opinion, to comfort me in my poverty; when even this good opinion shall leave me, and calumnies and misinformations shall prevaile against me; when I shall need peace, because there is none but thou, O Lord, that should stand for me, and then shall finde, that all the wounds that I have, come from thy hand, all the arrowes that stick in me, from thy quiver; when I shall see, that because I have given my selfe to my corrupt nature, thou hast changed thine; and because I am all evill towards thee, therefore thou hast given over being good towards me; When it comes to this height, that the fever is not in the humors, but in the spirits, that mine enemy is not an imaginary enemy, fortune, nor a transitory enemy, malice in great persons, but a reall, and an irresistible, and an inexorable, and an everlasting enemy, The Lord of Hosts himselfe, The Almighty God himselfe, the Almighty God himselfe onely knowes the waight of this affliction, and except hee put in that *pondus gloriae,* that exceeding waight of an eternall glory, with his owne hand, into the other scale, we are waighed downe, we are swallowed up, irreparably, irrevocably, irrecoverably, irremediably.

3

How Form and Content Work Together in Donne's Metaphorical Prose

YOU may be surprised to see how different Donne's style is from Hemingway's. But the great contrast between them does not mean that one is good and the other bad. As you will see, Donne's style is just as effective as Hemingway's in achieving his very different goals.

First of all Donne is writing about a more abstract and intellectual subject than Hemingway; in fact, you should not be dismayed if you do not understand his sermon very well on the first reading. But can we describe the style of a piece of writing when we do not fully understand its meaning? Strange as this may seem, you will find that you can begin to identify repeated structural elements of the style even when you do not understand much of the meaning.

Some stylistic traits are immediately evident to us because they are so different from Hemingway's, such as the fact that Donne's sermon contains only two sentences, both surprisingly long and full of clauses. We can hopefully answer *why* Donne might wish to generate such unusual sentences if we first consider precisely *how* he constructs his first sentence. One of the most noticeable patterns in that first sentence is the repetition of words and syntax:

Let me wither and weare out mine age in a   discomfortable $\Big\}$
                              in an unwholesome prison
                              in a   penurious

Three phrases appear, each introduced by the same preposition "in," followed by "a" or "an," followed by a polysyllabic adjective that modifies the object which, for each prepositional phrase, is the noun "prison." (This repetition of syntactical structures is known as *parallelism,* and tripartite repetition is sometimes called a *triplet*). Occasional repetition of sounds between words also occurs (we should remember that this sermon was meant to be spoken aloud), as in "wither" and "weare" and "penurious prison." Such repetition (called *alliteration*) is usually of the initial consonant, as in these examples; but alliteration sometimes refers to any sound repetition between words. And if we look a little further into the sentence we see in the next clause a triplet of phrases:

> Let me wither in a spittle under   sharpe ⎫
>   and foule   ⎬ diseases
>   and infamous ⎭

But this time the repetitive syntactical pattern extends beyond phrases within a clause, since this entire second clause can be seen to be parallel to the first clause in construction. We notice the first three words of the first clause, "Let me wither," repeated in the second, followed again by a tripartite phrase introduced by one common preposition, "under," whose object is one noun, "diseases," modified by three different adjectives. As in the first clause there is alliteration (this time in the words "foule" and "infamous") where the repetition is not of the initial consonant in each case; in addition, there is the repetition of vowel sounds, usually called *assonance* ("wither" and "spittle").

A writer might choose to parallel one syntactical structure with another for several reasons. One of the simplest is to emphasize some relation in meaning by setting up a structural relation. A similarity of syntax often tends to coerce a reader into becoming aware of a similarity in sense that he might otherwise have overlooked. For example, in these first two clauses the unpleasant words "discomfortable," "unwholesome," and "penurious" modify the "prison" Donne offers to "wither" in, while the equally unpleasant words "sharpe," "foule," and "infa-

mous" modify the "diseases" he asks to "wither" in. Paralleling a debtor's imprisonment with a diseased old age in a hospital suggests that they are related, in this instance perhaps as
punishing experience.

Donne's clear repetition of syntactical structure is probably
not something that happened by chance, for it continues to be
one of the organizing principles of his first sentence. In the next
clauses Donne uses parallelism to help explain why he is willing to accept punishment in either a prison or a hospital, and
further elaborates on the relation between these modes of
atonement:

and so pay   my debts   with my bones

and   recompence the wastfulnesse of my youth, with the beggery
                                                    of mine age

and so recompence the wantonnesse of my youth, with that loathsomnesse
                                                    in mine age

Notice that Donne parallels word structures as well as larger
phrasal and clausal structures. "Wastfulnesse" and "wantonnesse" are rhymed with the same suffix, formed with the same
number of syllables, and alliterated as well.

The structural repetition between these clauses seems to mirror a kind of repetition of cause-and-effect subject matter—in
each case, a later unpleasant payment for an earlier excess. In
the phrase "and so pay my debts with my bones," a later unpleasant recompense seems to be exacted because of an earlier
excess (i.e., monetary debt). Remember that in Donne's day
rotting in debtor's prison was considered a just and righteous
punishment for one who had committed the shameful crime of
running into debt. Donne is here describing the only "enjoy
now, pay later" plan available to his listeners in the seventeenth
century. By the third phrase, "and so recompence the wantonnesse of my youth, with that loathsomnesse in mine age,"
Donne has moved in steps from a concrete legal exactment
(i.e., the concept of paying a debt) to a moral exactment (i.e.,
the concept of recompensing "wantonnesse" with "loathsomnesse"). Donne seems to be suggesting a parallel between a
legal (first phrase) and moral (third phrase) expiation of his

present suffering in age that balances and atones for a spiritual debt incurred by excesses in youth. In the second phrase he links this parallel through what appears to be a universal natural balance: the cares of old age follow inevitably the carelessness of youth. (In the seventeenth century as, unfortunately, in underdeveloped countries even today, the social scene presented many examples of what must have seemed an almost "natural" relation between beggary and old age.) The effect of Donne's parallelism is to mirror syntactically what he has set up conceptually as a balanced legal, natural, and moral justice: payment for debt, recompense for wastefulness, and penance for "wantonnesse."

The same kind of parallel construction occurs in the next part of Donne's first sentence:

```
      yet  /   if God with-draw not  his spirituall  blessings
           |                         his            Grace
           |                         his            Patience
   (1)     <
           |   If I can call my suffering his Doing
           \                    my passion his Action

   (2)     (  All this that is temporall,
           <  is but a caterpiller got     into  one corner of my garden
              but a mill-dew   fallen  upon one acre   of my Corne
```

But you can also see in the caterpillar and mildew metaphors of part (2) a new kind of structure that Donne uses in parallel. In a *metaphor* we think and write about one thing (a subject) in terms of another (a reference). Donne parallels metaphors by writing about one subject (physical suffering) in terms of two references that are quite different from the subject but closely related to one another: first, a single insect pest and second, an isolated patch of blight, both of which can do small damage to the crop as a whole. We have examined the paralleling within part (2), and we can see the obvious parallel "if" clause construction within part (1). Part (1) and part (2) together form a kind of structural unit. This structure involves a conceptual relation. Part (1) is the *condition,* and part (2) the *consequence* of a single assertion that can be paraphrased as:

    (1) If God's grace is with him,
    (2) then he is essentially safe (in spite of bodily suffering).

The relation between these two clauses can be abstracted and
seen even more clearly in the following paradigm of a condi-
tion/consequence structure:

If X (condition),   then Y (consequence)

Nor is this the only time in the sermon that we see Donne using
the condition/consequence relation to structure assertions.

Let us consider the rest of the first sentence:

The body   of all
the substance of all is safe

as long as the soule is safe

Even though it contains the usual internal structural repetitions,
it may not, as a whole, seem to be parallel in structure to the
clauses that just preceded it. But a little care in examining the
abstract form of the assertion being made here will show us that
it is a repetition of the same condition/consequence structure
with similar subject matter, but this time in reverse order, in
counterpoint to the clause before it, with the consequence being
presented before the statement of the condition:

(then Y)   The body   of all
the substance of all is safe

(if X)   as long as the soule is safe

The point Donne may be making is that an equilibrium exists
whichever term is placed first. One way or another, the consequence balances the condition.

Throughout this first sentence much balancing of many
kinds of structures relates ideas to one another with almost
symmetrical proportion. The speaker's present cares, as he
looks back, are balanced with the carelessness of his youth;
and, as he looks to the future, these physical cares are balanced
with the ultimate safety of his soul.

A quick look at the second sentence will indicate that
Donne's repetition of condition/consequence assertions does not
end with this first sentence. The second sentence of the paragraph is made up of a sequence, usually separated by semi-
colons, of eight parallel modifications, the first constituent of

each being an adverbial clause beginning with the subordinating conjunction "when." And much more complex (at times quite ambiguous) structural paralleling occurs between and within several of the clauses, some of which we will consider shortly.

Simplified Diagram of Condition/Consequence Clauses of Second Sentence

```
"But when I" mistakenly trust A, then God demolished that trust with Z;
    "when"                    B, then                                 Y;
    "when"                    C, then                                 X;
    "when"                    D, then                                 W;
    "when"                    E, then                                 V;
    "when"                    F, then                                 U;
    "when"                    G, then                                 T;
    "when"                    H, then "we are waighed downe
                                 we are swallowed up . . ."

        (If ["when"] he is without grace, then he is utterly lost.)
              (condition)                      (consequence)
```

Now we can see that the structural relation between sentence 1 and sentence 2 is not just syntactical parallelism, but a parallel of organization that results from the assertion of the following antithetical conditions and antithetical consequences:

```
Conditional assertion  If X (God's grace is
   of sentence 1          with him),         then Y (he is saved).
Conditional assertion  "But when" [If] not X, then Z (he is damned).
   of sentence 2
```

After this brief glance at the second sentence, let us consider it in detail. The syntactical repetitions reveal some similarity to the balanced construction of the first sentence, but some significant differences as well. It seems that Donne is using heavy polysyllabic words almost like heavy weights that serve rhetorically to put more emphasis on the consequent clause than on the condition clause:

```
But when I shall trust to that,
which wee call a good spirit ($\neq$) and God shall deject
                                      and empoverish
                                      and evacuate that spirit
```

when I shall rely upon a morall constancy ($\neq$) and God shall shake
                                                      and enfeeble
                                                      and enervate
                                                          destroy
                                                      and demolish
                                                          that constancy

Each condition/consequence unit of two clauses contains repetitions of words and syntactical structures in the consequent clause that threaten to destroy the clausal balance. In the first consequence, Donne compounds several words in a series each preceded by a conjunction (which, by the way, is a very easy but impressive sounding figure of speech called *polysyndeton*) against the speaker's trust. But the weight seems to increase when, in the second condition/consequence unit, Donne loads the balance against the speaker by five weighty words and, in addition, uses repetition of *and*s and alliteration to add emphasis to the side of the balance opposed to the speaker's safety.

It is clear in these clauses that Donne does not share Hemingway's aesthetic aim of economy in the use of words. Donne is purposely using many words with only slightly different meanings. And the same redundancy that might be wrong in Hemingway's style serves Donne's purposes well, as we will see.

In the next condition/consequence unit, the internal structure of heavy words and the repetition of three heavy phrases in the consequence clause upset the balance between clauses and throw the weight now even more decidedly against the speaker:

when I shall think to refresh my selfe in the serenity
                                          and sweet ayre of a good
                                          conscience ($\neq$)

and God shall call up the damps
                        and vapours   of hell it selfe
and   spread   a cloud   of difference
and   an impenetrable crust of desperation upon my
                                             conscience

The balanced norm Donne sets up between the clauses of the first sentence of the sermon is emphatically broken in this second sentence. We have seen in several parallel instances an inclusion of rhetorical emphasis that imbalances one clause against another. In each case, while the speaker hopefully relies on his spirit, constancy, and conscience, these are hopelessly weighed down because on the other side God will "deject," "empoverish," "evacuate," "shake," "enfeeble," "enervate," "destroy," "demolish," "call up the damps and vapours of hell it selfe," "spread a cloud of diffidence" and "an impenetrable crust of desperation." The imbalance Donne has set up against his speaker increases in the final part of the second sentence, when he recognizes that his ills are not just physical (sickness in the seventeenth century was thought to result from an imbalance of body liquids or "humors"), but spiritual (i.e., a much more serious imbalance)—"that the fever is not in the humors, but in the spirits"—and he is weighed down with the realization that without grace, God is his enemy, against him body and soul:

that mine enemy is not an imaginary enemy, fortune,
                    nor a transitory enemy,   malice in great persons, ($\neq$)

                              but a   reall
                              and an irresistible
                              and an inexorable
                              and an everlasting enemy
                                    The Lord of Hosts himselfe,
                                    The Almighty God himselfe,
                                    the Almighty God himselfe,
                    onely knowes   the waight of this   affliction

As Donne continues this sentence he makes obvious in the extended metaphor of God handling the "waight" to balance or imbalance his "scales" of judgment the relation between structural imbalance in his style and an idea of imbalance in the subject matter: "and except hee put in that *pondus gloriae,* that exceeding waight of an eternall glory, with his owne hand, into the other scale"

       (without *"pondus gloriae"*) we are waighed *downe*
                                     we are swallowed *up*
                                                irreparably
                                                irrevocably
                                                irrecoverably
                                                irremediably

The use of the words "waighed down" against "up" even suggests the operation of the scales. And once again, heavy words, like weights, throw the scales to one side: if you read this aloud you have even the tactile sensation of having your tongue overburdened and weighed down by the utterance of one polysyllabic word after another.

But why does Donne go to the trouble of setting up this almost incredible effect? Is Donne simply playing structural games with syntax and rhetoric, or is he seeking to achieve some more important writing goal? Let us consider the relation between his balanced and imbalanced structures and his subject matter.

In the two sentences, as we have seen, Donne makes condition/consequence assertions that are theological dichotomies. In the first sentence, on condition that he receive God's grace, he will be saved. To mirror this subject matter Donne's structural repetitions put all in orderly symmetrical balance. If there is any physical suffering, then it is not serious but only the product of an orderly balanced judgment that decrees as a law of nature that men suffer old age's cares in recompense for youth's carelessness.

But in the second sentence, the subject matter is the antithesis of the first sentence: on condition that God's grace is withheld, man is willy-nilly weighed down in despair to utter destruction. As in the first sentence, Donne uses structural repetitions to give life to a theological assertion. He lets us see in the image of the scales of justice, hear in his use of sound repetition, and even feel tactilely on our tongue when we read the sermon aloud, the destructive weight of damnation, expressed in numerous parallel clauses and phrases and weighty polysyllabic vocabulary. Donne is using style to make the *abstract* concept of the gift of grace and the opposite consequences of salvation or damnation perceivable to his audience's senses as well as to their intellects. We have talked of how balanced sentence structure, polysyllabic vocabulary, and emphatic compounded figures of speech are related to one another and to Donne's larger goals and aesthetic purpose. Are there any other stylistic elements that we have overlooked? How are these possibly related to the hypothetical pattern we have tentatively found?

We have seen how the central metaphor of the scales of judgment is extended and mirrored by the balance of the first half of the sermon and the imbalance of the last half. This second sentence of the paragraph also includes an organization of antonyms that is parallel to the theological antithesis of salvation versus damnation:

sweet ayre	{ [foul air] a cloud of diffidence
	{ damps and vapours of hell it selfe
riches	poverty
health	sicknesse
good opinion	calumnies and misinformations
	/ [war] arrowes that stick in me
	| wounds
peace	{ enemy
	| The Lord of Hosts
	\ The Almighty God

Each pair is a metaphorical reference for the abstract subject of good versus evil. Perhaps because many of these metaphors are concrete, they tend to make abstract theology something an audience can imaginatively experience.

These dichotomies seem to be weighted and imbalanced, like so many of the other rhetorical structures in the second sentence, toward the evil rather than the good side. They enrich by metaphor the texture of Donne's theological dichotomy between salvation and damnation, a dichotomy that is being realized in terms of stylistic imbalance, mirroring the imbalanced scales of judgment. A very similar structure of dichotomies was used in the first sentence:

wastefulness of youth————————debtors' prison in old age

careless health of youth————————sickness in old age

But the orderly balance of the dichotomies of the first half of the sermon set up an expected norm that tends to make the imbalance of the second half seem all the more noticeable.

The intricate balance and imbalance all related to the central metaphor of the "scales" is a drama in which the audience can feel and understand the importance of "that exceeding waight of an eternall glory."

There is yet another technique that Donne uses in the

second sentence that helps to dramatize and also to universalize the meaning of his sermon. Toward the end he shifts from speaking of God in the *third person* to directly addressing him as "thou, O Lord" in the *second person*. Such a sudden shift of address (a classical figure of speech called *apostrophe*) can dramatically suggest a personal and sincere change of attitude, as though the speaker has himself suddenly begun not just to understand, but to feel the importance of his meaning. Notice, too, that at the very end of his sermon Donne makes another shift, this time from the singular "I," "me," "mine" that he has used throughout to "*we* are waighed down," "*we* are swallowed up." The effect of such a shift from singular to plural at the crucial moment is to generalize the whole idea of damnation or salvation from the individual speaker to all Donne's congregation listening to the sermon.

The idea of recompense, and the weight of payment necessary to balance the weight of sin, is analagous to the theological doctrine of the redemption through Christ's suffering, which created an abundance of grace sufficient to save man. When man's sins would otherwise weigh against him, the "exceeding waight of an eternall glory" that, according to tradition, Jesus paid for with his sacrifice (Crucifixion) may, by a gift of grace, be placed in the other scale to redeem him.

Donne's aesthetic aim in this short sermon seems to be that the structures of style mirror the specific subject matter of the sermon so imaginatively that the sermon's meaning is communicated through a kind of mixed media of auditory rhythms (produced by the balance and imbalance of syntax, words, figures, and organizational structures) to amplify and illustrate the abstract assertions of the seventeenth-century Anglican conventional doctrine of the "gift of grace" and the part it plays in man's salvation or damnation. His achievement as a writer is to have enlivened feelingly and concretely what could otherwise have been merely a dry doctrinal dissertation.

Here is the Donne style model we have just constructed, expressed as a writing program in the form of a brief diagram. (When we refer to Donne's style, we mean his method of composition only in the specific example we analyzed.)

Writing Program II

Syntax:

Use a repetition of syntactical structures, sometimes phrase to phrase and sometimes clause to clause. Introduce a high proportion of adjectives and adverbs throughout (approximately one adjective to every one or two nouns used).

Words:

Parallel synonyms and antonyms. Mix concrete words with abstract words, material with spiritual. Occasionally use polysyllabic words of three or more syllables as though they were weights to be placed on either side of a grammatical parallel to either balance or throw the parallel off balance to emphasize one side. If it fits into your writing plans, use a shift of pronouns in the paragraph. (For example, you could emphasize the general nature of your particular experience by shifting near the end from a first person singular to a plural pronoun in order to suggest the inclusion of your audience in what you are saying.)

Figures of Speech:

Use alliteration and assonance. Employ many metaphors, often extended, sometimes paralleled, always related to a central metaphor, and use this metaphorical structure as the organizing principle of the paragraph. If it fits into your writing plan, use a dramatic apostrophe. (For example, set up a noun of third-person reference and then shift suddenly to second-person address.)

Organization:

Choose a central metaphor around which an entire paragraph can be organized, and that will serve to relate as many structural style characteristics as possible to whatever subject content you choose. Use different kinds of structural repetition in addition to syntactical repetition, such as repeating a type of metaphor, or a form of conceptual relation (such as condition and consequence, cause and effect, specific fact and generalization, etc.).

Subject Matter:

Choose some abstract intellectual dichotomies, such as love and hate, peace and war, etc., and often express the differences or similarities between these in concrete metaphors.

Attitudes or
Ways of Thinking
and Perceiving:

Aim at a congruence of stylistic structures with your subject matter so that these will mirror one another in the production of meaning. Using some or all of the varied stylistic techniques above, try, with congruent structure and subject, to stimulate the reader's feelings and imagination with respect to the intellectual abstract concepts you have chosen as subject matter.

Exercises

1. Write a sentence generated by repetition of grammatical structure, using as subject matter some related or opposed modern ideas that interest you (for example, peace and war, man and woman, the individual and society). Now rewrite the sentence, avoiding syntactical repetitions—without any balance. Next, rewrite the sentence imbalanced in favor of one side of the parallel. Consider the effect of meaning that each type of sentence generation produces.

2. Write a short paragraph comparing or contrasting some subject in balanced style, and then try to write a few sentences using, as nearly as possible, the same comparison and contrast but this time in Hemingway's style. Try to consider precisely the relation of the specific stylistic techniques that you used to their effect on the meaning that you intended to convey in each case. Which paragraph is more effective? Why?

3. Write a paragraph of a few sentences in Hemingway's style, but break Hemingways' norm of no parallelism with some struc-

tural repetition whenever you think it would help you reinforce or clarify your meaning.

4. Now consider how you could use an extended metaphor as a structure around which to organize a whole paragraph. Pick what you think could be a strong central metaphor (expansion or growth, for example, or pollution and decay); then either extend your metaphor and build a paragraph around the extended structure, or perhaps relate some other metaphors to this central metaphor and use the structure of the metaphorical relations to organize a paragraph.

4

Using Metaphors
and Parallel Constructions

Now that we have constructed a rhetorical model of Donne's style, we can seriously consider how we might use it today—what may need modification in modern writing.

We saw that one of Donne's techniques was to organize his paragraph around a central metaphor rather than a topic sentence. Dichotomies referring to a number of different areas, such as peace and war, health and disease, had as their subject good and evil, not just in a physical but in a spiritual sense. And Donne related all of these to the central scales metaphor, in which he sees himself balanced and finally judged either saved or lost. But perhaps it is not so easy to learn from this one specific example the general principles of metaphorical structuring so that you could organize the subject matter that interests you with your own pattern of metaphors.

Many of the metaphors that Donne used to organize his sermon were not original but were repeated in sermons for centuries before he was born. In fact, they were at least a millennium and a half old since they were taken from the Bible. In your own writing you will likely reuse many more metaphors than you originate; so let us first discuss how to steal metaphors skillfully, and later consider the bolder art of coining our own.

How is it that Donne can vividly resurrect comatose metaphors that in the hands of another writer might have seemed dead? Whether a worn metaphor can still serve must not depend so much on its age as on the way you treat it. (Remember that in making a metaphor we think and write of one thing [a subject] in terms of another [a reference].) The tired metaphor dies on the page for the writer who, in using it, forgets that every metaphor has a reference and supposes that what was once a metaphor has become simply a colorless word that stands for a subject. There seems to be a tendency in all writers when they use a metaphor over and over again to grow so insensitive to its reference that they become unaware that they are using a metaphor at all.

This natural tendency toward a weakening of the reference of every used metaphor has, in fact, determined much of the growth of vocabulary in all languages. It is surprising how many of our words started out as metaphors and gradually lost their original references. If you were to label something either a *masterpiece* or a *phony* you would most likely be unaware that both words were metaphors. *Phony* probably came from an earlier word, *fawney,* that meant "[finger] ring." The fawney man traveled the countryside selling gold rings that too often were not really gold. Calling something fawney or phony originally had reference to a misrepresented ring. The reference of the word *masterpiece* is also almost forgotten. A candidate for the rank of master craftsman was required to produce on his own (often locked in a single room with food, water, and tools) a piece that required all his skill—like a candidate for a master of arts degree today, who must produce a thesis. If he were a furniture maker, the piece might have been a lady's inlaid jewel cabinet, or, for a silversmith, an elaborate salt cellar.

Each of these two words (*phony* and *masterpiece*) is a fossil metaphor whose reference has decayed until only antiquarian reconstruction can give museum interest to what long ago may have been a vivid metaphor. Quite a few metaphors (such as *chair arm*) are almost, but not quite, fossils because such meta-

phors, even though all but extinct, can occasionally be seen
still alive. The term *chair arm* is used so much that it is easy to
forget that its reference is to a part of the human anatomy.

No doubt many words that were once metaphors are now
safer left dead. Yet we all rely on the service of used metaphors
that can sometimes awaken at the most inopportune moment
during a writing operation. For instance, when a writer uses
more than one worn metaphor in the same sentence without
being aware of any of their references, these may clash so
shockingly or ridiculously that it makes the reader fully conscious of the writer's lack of awareness. Here is an example:
"He was such a marvelous teacher that whenever he recognized a spark of genius you could be sure he'd water it." Such
mixed metaphor is not always a writing fault. It can occasionally be well used as long as you are aware of the clashing
references and purposely juxtapose them for unusual effect.
For instance, the mixed metaphor of the teacher who waters
sparks of genius might have been used shrewdly to convey sar-
casm. And when Shakespeare mixes his metaphor in this example from *Hamlet*—"to take arms against a sea of troubles"—
he effectively conveys a sense of how overwhelming Hamlet's
problems seem by reference to the futility of trying to hold the
sea back with a sword.

We have been speaking of worn metaphors that are revived,
perhaps unexpectedly, when they are mixed; but even without
a clash of clichés, sometimes a clash between a single, worn
metaphor and the context will be enough to wake up its reference. This possibility was realized in 1968 by Mrs. Philip Blai-
berg over international TV when reporters asked her how her
husband had reacted to the news that he was to receive one of
the world's first heart transplants. "I want it with all *my heart,*"
she reported he had said. And then as the cliché came to life for
her, she added nervously, "and—uh—soul." Notice that only
after the speaker became aware of the unfortunate anatomical
reference did she shift that reference from the material essence
of man ("heart") to the spiritual essence ("soul"), which was
more comfortable considering the context.

An important first step in writing well with used metaphors

seems to be, in all the cases we have met so far, to resist consciously our natural tendency to think only of the *subject* while quite forgetting about the reference we are using. The trouble with a writer's lack of awareness of the reference of a metaphor is his consequent inability to judge whether or not such a reference is appropriate to the context in which he is about to use it. You are not free to use with discrimination a metaphor of which you are only half aware. Only after a writer is fully aware of a metaphor's reference can he take the next, more important step of judging how well that metaphor fits what he is trying to express. Used metaphors will tend to keep your writing dull and conformist until, by practicing these two steps, you can set yourself free to control metaphors that convey the precise thoughts and feelings you as an individual choose to express.

To become more aware of areas of reference in metaphors, try underlining all the metaphors in any sample of writing. How many seem to have originated with the writer, and how many were borrowed? Of those borrowed, how many are used without making sure that the reference actually is appropriate to the context?

Suppose that in an example of your writing—a humorous essay that touched on the subject of love—you had used the worn metaphor "to fall in love" without being aware of its reference or whether its reference really expressed what you wanted to say. How could you refurbish this used metaphor? You might take a lesson from Donne and use these methods of refurbishing. Sometimes he retains the area of reference but freshens it by extending it. For instance, he takes the warlike metaphor of the Almighty God as a Lord of Hosts (armies) and extends God to a warrior shooting a quiver full of arrows into poor John Donne. You might, for instance, freshen "falling" to "free-falling" in parachute jumps, and perhaps extend your metaphor something like this: "Their love was prolonged free fall, until she finally got scared of reality rushing toward her and opened the question of marriage." Another technique Donne uses is to modulate to a new, but related, area of reference, as he shifts reference from caterpillar to mildew. Can you think of a way to modulate from the cliché "falling" in love to some new but related area of reference (e.g., rocking, tripping) in order to refurbish this tired metaphor?

Though you will probably be borrowing more metaphors than you originate, often there is no other way to express precisely what you have in mind except to make up a new metaphor. How do we learn to be producers rather than simply consumers of metaphor? It is not at all hard to do. For instance, you might try thinking of the subject of memory in terms of nature. You might come up with something like "the sea of memory." Or perhaps you perceive your memory as not so deep and huge as the sea but narrower, its contents more swiftly changing like a rushing mountain stream. If you wish, you could extend your metaphor a little, as in this sentence: "Memory is a swift stream I sometimes fish in."

Once fusion into metaphor takes place it is really quite artificial, though perhaps useful, to distinguish between the subject and the reference. Each original metaphor that you might fuse by combining two or more known ideas introduces some new idea into the world. Producing an original metaphor is, therefore, a small creative act. A reference to fishing in a stream or fishing in the sea probably did not yield an entirely satisfactory metaphor to convey your own thoughts about memory. Practice creating at least ten metaphors to express your own feelings on the subject of memory (or try the subjects loneliness, utopia, community), with reference to each of the following areas:

reference areas	sample metaphors
1. sensations of taste, touch, etc.	memory is bitter
2. sports or games	memory is an umpire
3. technology	memory is a computer bank
4. science (biology, medicine, etc.)	memory is the fossil of our personal evolution
5. pop culture (TV, movies, music)	memory is a strobe light into our past
6. economics	memory collects the diminishing returns on life
7. philosophy or religion	memory is a tin god

8. politics   memory is a caucus we hold with ourselves to nominate a candidate for consciousness

9. art   memory is a poorly lighted museum, containing works of uneven quality

10. nature   memory is a weeded garden of sweet flowers through which I sometimes tiptoe

Obviously this list of general reference areas could be greatly extended.

The kind of reference a writer fuses with his subject to produce a metaphor often reflects the range or limitations of his thoughts. Each writer tends to originate his metaphors by reference to certain areas of knowledge rather than others. Which ones do you tend to use when you make up metaphors —sports? pop culture? The areas from which a person consistently chooses his references may reveal his limitations or freedom as a writer. The student who cannot make metaphors without referring to baseball, for example, can be seriously limited in many kinds of writing. In writing narration it is easy to suggest much about your narrator or one of your characters simply by controlling the metaphor reference areas that you allow him to use. You can tell quite a lot about a person's mental life by becoming aware of the particular areas from which he tends to choose his metaphors. Notice how flexible Donne is in choosing from diverse areas of reference. In fact, one of the principles of Donne's use of metaphor seems to be to effect the relation of abstract subjects erence into one metaphor. For example, of those ten reference by mixing many areas of concrete reference. There is really no reason why you could not combine different areas of reference areas above you might combine areas 1 and 10 to produce a possible metaphor like this one: "Memory is feeling with your hand in the ice-cold sea to find something lost in its depths." Now consider how you could use an extended metaphor like this one as a structure around which to organize a whole paragraph. Here is an example of how you might proceed from

Dylan Thomas, who, like Donne, is very good at metaphorical organizing. He has constructed a metaphorical organization similar to the "ice-cold sea" combined metaphor to convey to the reader the operation of his own memory in trying later in life to recreate his experience of Christmas in Wales as a child:

> All the Christmases roll down the hill towards the Welsh-speaking sea, like a snowball growing whiter and bigger and rounder, like a cold and headlong moon bundling down the sky that was our street; and they stop at the rim of the ice-edged, fish-freezing waves, and I plunge my hands in the snow and bring out whatever I can find; holly or robins or pudding, squabbles and carols and oranges and tin whistles, and the fire in the front room, and bang go the crackers, and holy, holy, holy, ring the bells, and the glass bells shaking on the tree, and Mother Goose. . . .
>
> In goes my hand into that wool-white bell-tongued ball of holidays resting at the margin of the carol-singing sea, and out come . . .

Metaphorical organizations, especially when they are made very dense with a bold metaphor or two in every sentence as in Donne or Thomas, can be exciting and also confusing unless the relation of each subordinate metaphor to a central metaphor or two is kept very simple and clear. There is a fine line between complexity and confusion that only experimenting on a real audience will give you a feeling for.

The technique of metaphor has been used in many ways by various writers. To some, fresh metaphors are necessary to clarify experience. It is almost impossible to talk about any working of the mind or emotions without resorting to metaphor. Try writing about how loneliness feels without using some metaphors. Original metaphors are often more accurate and appropriate because they are created to fit precisely the context in which they are used. How could you express a unique personal feeling or perception without making up your own metaphors? Some writers hang metaphors like ornaments while others more responsibly regard metaphors as hypothetical models of reality for which the writer can be held accountable. Then, too, metaphor can be used to make writing more compact and economical by saying in a word what might take a paragraph or more of explanation and even then perhaps not convey the same meaning.

Clearly, a subject as important in writing as metaphor can barely be introduced in these few pages. In almost every succeeding chapter we will be learning more about the functions of metaphor.

Using Structural Repetition

Donne's sermon is frankly an extreme of style, and yet such an intentional exaggeration of balance and imbalance is peculiarly instructive, since it allows you to see very plainly the paralleling of syntactical structure with idea that was and is still widely used. Listen to almost any public speech, for instance, and you will hear it. Balance seems to be even more effective as an auditory structure than as a visual and mental structure. And so the effectiveness of balance is most in evidence when you read aloud rather than silently speed-read. Try reading Donne's sermon aloud and see how spoken rhythms exaggerate the parallels and antitheses. But Donne's balance is something more than simply a rhythmic device used to give emphasis to related ideas; his balance and imbalance are related to a whole philosophy, a particular world view.

Donne, like many writers of his time, seems to have used symmetry and proportion as the counterparts in style to an orderly universe that he considered fundamentally just, reasonable, and providentially determined. And because parallelism was so often used by writers, particularly those of the eighteenth century, who perceived their world as essentially justly ordered and duly proportioned, some modern critics have made an absolute out of an aesthetic convention and would now insist that only if the subject is orderly and proportioned should structural repetitions be stylistically used. This insistence, however, relies on two questionable assumptions. The first is that style must always be an imitation or a mirror of subject matter. The second is that a structurally repetitive style must always suggest order and proportion. Writers, especially modern ones who no longer perceive their world as essentially justly ordered and duly proportioned, far from seeking to mirror style and content, might even put them in opposition. We have all seen this done in movies, even though you may not have noticed it in modern writing. The getaway after a bloody, realistic murder, for instance, might be filmed in the style of a humorous Keystone Kops chase. Gay country banjo music or saccharine love songs might be

What do you think might be the philosophy behind the structural repetitions in Stonehenge?

used to determine the beat for a bombing scene. A television show might have a scene of police beating and Macing young girls and boys and bystanders, narrated by a "sincere" voice singing jubilantly about what a "wonderful town" he lives in. Here is an earlier example in writing of style played against subject and situation. Winston Churchill used parallelism to try to pull together what was, in fact, a chaotic and disintegrating military position at the retreat of Dunkirk. Churchill, by using structural repetition, helps suggest the ideal stages of an orderly disintegration and symmetrical rout of the entire British forces as each subsequent defensive position crumbles: "We shall fight on the beaches, we shall fight on the landing grounds, we shall fight in the fields and in the streets, we shall fight in the hills; we shall never surrender" (House of Commons, June 4, 1940). Far from trying to imitate the disorderly situation with an irregular style, he tries desperately to give courage to those who, if they were to stay sane, had to suppose they were still in reasonable control of a predictable world.

The Churchill example suggests that, contrary to the first commonly held assumption, style may effectively be played against subject matter rather than necessarily mirror it. But an analysis of what Churchill is doing seems to confirm the second assumption: that parallelism must always suggest orderly relation and due proportion. Though Churchill is using parallelism to convey this traditional suggestion of order and proportion, this is not the only way parallelism can be used. Here is an example of a very different use, from Dylan Thomas's "A Visit to America," in which the effect of Thomas's word and syntax repetition is directly opposed to Donne's since it tends to emphasize not order and symmetry, but a general chaos of gross juxtapositions:

> Across the United States of America, from New York to California and back, glazed, again, for many months of the year, there streams and sings for its heady supper a dazed and prejudiced procession of European lecturers, scholars, sociologists, economists, writers, authorities on this and that

and even, in theory, on the United States of America. And, breathlessly, between addresses and receptions, in planes and trains and boiling hotel bedroom ovens, many of these attempt to keep journals and diaries.

At first, confused and shocked by shameless profusion and almost shamed by generosity, unaccustomed to such importance as they are assumed, by their hosts, to possess, and up against the barrier of a common language, they write in their notebooks like demons, generalizing away, on character and culture and the American political scene. But, towards the middle of their middle-aged whisk through middle-western clubs and universities, the fury of the writing flags; their spirits are lowered by the spirit with which they are everywhere strongly greeted and which, in ever increasing doses, they themselves lower; and they begin to mistrust themselves, and their reputations—for they have found, too often, that an audience will receive a lantern-lecture on, say, Ceramics, with the same uninhibited enthusiasm that it accorded the very week before to a paper on the Modern Turkish Novel. And, in their diaries, more and more do such entries appear as, "No way of escape!" or "Buffalo" or "I am beaten," until at last they cannot write a word. And, twittering all over, old before their time, with eyes like rissoles in the sand, they are helped up the gangway of the home-bound liner by kind bosom friends (of all kinds and bosoms) who boister them on the back, pick them up again, thrust bottles, sonnets, cigars, addresses, into their pockets, have a farewell party in their cabin, pick them up again, and, snickering and yelping, are gone: to wait at the dockside for another boat from Europe and another batch of fresh, green lecturers.

There they go, every spring, from New York to Los Angeles: exhibitionists, polemicists, histrionic publicists, theological rhetoricians, historical hoddy-doddies, balletomanes, ulterior decorators, windbags and bigwigs and humbugs, men in love with stamps, men in love with steaks, men after millionaires' widows, men with elephantiasis of the reputation (huge trunks and teeny minds), authorities on gas, bishops, best-sellers, editors looking for writers, writers looking for publishers, publishers looking for dollars, existentialists, serious physicists with nuclear missions, men from the B.B.C. who

> speak as though they had the Elgin Marbles in their mouths, potboiling philosophers, professional Irishmen (very lepricorny), and, I am afraid, fat poets with slim volumes.

Like Donne, Thomas is using very long sentences generated by repetitive structuring and the compounding of polysyllabic words often bound together by alliteration. Just as Donne relates with structural repetition prison, hospital, youth, age, caterpillar, mildew, peace, war, sickness, health, sin, grace, etc., so Thomas links with structural repetition seemingly unrelated or opposite realms of knowledge, things, people, ideas, places, attitudes, subjects, all of which conveys to the reader, trying to keep up with the writer and take it all in, the unmistakeable impression of what it must feel like for a foreigner to give lecture after lecture to audience after audience in all climates from one end of America to the other and back again—repetitive chaos, parallel disorder.

If you thought that Donne seemed old-fashioned, you cannot now think that his whole style is responsible for the impression, since we see Thomas using a similar style yet achieving some very modern-sounding prose. It seems that the subject matter and attitudes we choose and the particular pattern into which we combine writing structures are far more important determinants of modernity than the mere use of any isolated element of style. Until you are more practiced at thinking of style structurally, with a particular subject matter as only one of its possible variables rather than its necessary constant, you might tend to identify Donne's balanced style with sermonlike subject matter, and it may not be so easy to see that its application is much wider. In fact, the use of any style is restricted to any subject only by the limitations of our imagination and ingenuity.

To suggest how a replica of the structural characteristics of Donne's style can be used with the most unlikely modern subject matter, consider this example, which is sometimes so close to Donne's original that it seems more like parody than imitation:

When I am loose and free, if I am turned on and tuned in, then the bleak streets, and concrete, the gray faces are overgrown with green grass and flowers and picnicking people, then the catatonic crowds, the contracted life flow into oceans of daisies and daffodils, they bloom into blossoms of spindrift and joy, if only I am free and turned on. Now if I am turned off and tuned out, when I am fettered and unfree, then my life in my native land is shriveled, diminished and malignant; if I act out a nonviolent revolt from the contract America has taken out in my name, then I am branded and gassed, gouged, beaten, and bloodied; if I feel small and alone in a crowded country then I am from all sides further diminished by bureaucratic decisions that plan my obsolescence, by computerized industrialization and mobilization of my remaining energies; if I try to feel, even that is presumably only a rationalization; like America, Amerika— we are not even human without your expansion—consciousness expansion, like, unless our minds can grow blow blossom and expand, we are all shriveled, contracted, and diminished technologically, technocratically, technocentrically.

There is another difficulty with using structural repetition: when it is too noticeable it can seem artificial. Even Donne was not often so noticeable in his use of parallelism as he is in this sermon. Though Donne's sermon is an unforgettable example of balance, and imitating it could be a useful exercise, you will probably find few occasions when such very obvious use of structural repetition can occur without making your writing seem so cleverly contrived that your sincerity might be questioned. Modern audiences generally share a tradition that for many years has tended to admire and cultivate the appearance, if not always the fact, of plain sincerity and natural spontaneity. On the other hand, a modern master of the structurally repetitive style such as Martin Luther King, Jr., can use it in just as noticeable a way as Donne and achieve marvelous effectiveness and sincerity.

Note that, as in Donne, there is the paralleling of two metaphors with similar subjects (the creation of something beautiful out of raw chaos), one with a reference to sculpting and the other with a reference to composing music:

> This is our hope. This is the faith with which I return to the South. With this faith we will be able to hew out of the mountain of despair a stone of hope. With this faith we will be able to transform the jangling discords of our nation into a beautiful symphony of brotherhood. With this faith we will be able to work together, to pray together, to struggle together, to go to jail together, to stand up for freedom together, knowing that we will be free one day.

Perhaps you will choose not to use structural repetition too often in your own writing. But it may be useful to know how to generate even an occasional sentence or two by grammatically balancing the expression of certain related ideas. To put two ideas that you wish your reader to relate intellectually into parallel grammatical construction is to cause him to experience a relation linguistically as well as intellectually. Such linguistic emphasis of intellectual relations helps weld together the connections you are suggesting to the reader.

In the beginning of Lincoln's second inaugural address, he balances "with malice toward none, with charity for all." Consider how much he would have lost in clarity and emphasis if he had not used parallelism and had said, "with charity for all, and being devoid of any malicious feelings whatsoever."

But now consider the possibility of expressing quite unrelated ideas in parallel construction: "with charity for all, with ice cream for some." This may be upsetting to a traditionalist or it may be taken as satirical, because we have suggested by syntactical symmetry that the reader seriously consider the relation between charity and ice cream. This last example of parallelism is the technique Dylan Thomas uses so effectively (when he talks, for instance, of "authorities on gas, bishops, best-sellers") and that we found peculiarly modern because it relates the exalted and trivial just as these are so often juxtaposed in our modern world. Characteristically a TV interview with the secretary of state over an international crisis where perhaps thousands are dying is preceded by an ad showing how to fight bad breath and followed by a soap opera. Perhaps these political-commercial-electronic juxtapositions are in some way one of the significant parallels of our own age. Such parallels certainly seem unique in rhetorical history and must tell us something about ourselves. What do you think they tell us about modern society? Do they in any way help shape the way we perceive our world?

Exercises

1. John Donne and Dylan Thomas often appear to be playing with words, sounds, and ideas, but there is much control over such seeming verbal recklessness. Notice, for instance, how Thomas playfully freshens many a tired cliché such as "bosom friend." Choose some modern dichotomy that you would be most interested in writing about as a subject. Now purely as an exercise, try writing several paragraphs in Donne's style, being spontaneous with words and ideas and metaphors. Forget entirely for the moment about conventional punctuation and grammar, and let structural repetitions and the relation and extension of metaphor references guide and determine what you write. Be loose and let your words and ideas play with one another. (Check with the brief style diagram on pp. 43–44 for some of the technical alternatives of this style.) Then later, use your critical faculties to pick out your best effects and organize them into a paragraph with structural repetition related to some pattern of metaphors. Perhaps you will begin to see in your writing some metaphorical relations that you may have made intuitively while you seemed to yourself to be just playing. With a little time and effort anyone can keep editing until he comes up with a paragraph containing linguistic fireworks. It will take a little practice before you can incorporate brilliant effects as more than just decorations by making them serve the larger structures and meaning you are trying to express. In other words, it will be easier for you to learn to be verbally brilliant than to make brilliance the vehicle of meaning.

2. Now write a paragraph on the same subject you chose for exercise 1, but this time use your own habitual writing style

instead of Donne's (you may find it easier to write in your own style first before writing in Donne's). Next, write a brief discussion comparing and contrasting your habitual writing structures with Donne's. Assuming that both your own style and Donne's are equally valid, though different, combinations of linguistic structures that lend themselves to different perceptions of the same subject, what would you say is the difference between the way you and a writer like Donne perceive the chosen subject? Do you think you and Donne perceive the world in general differently as a result of your different structural habits? In precisely what ways?

"Up Against the Wall"

from NATIVE SON

Richard Wright

BIGGER took out his pack and gave Gus a cigarette; he lit his and held the match for Gus. They leaned their backs against the red-brick wall of a building, smoking, their cigarettes slanting white across their black chins. To the east Bigger saw the sun burning a dazzling yellow. In the sky above him a few big white clouds drifted. He puffed silently, relaxed, his mind pleasantly vacant of purpose. Every slight movement in the street evoked a casual curiosity in him. Automatically, his eyes followed each car as it whirred over the smooth black asphalt. A woman came by and he watched the gentle sway of her body until she disappeared into a doorway. He sighed, scratched his chin and mumbled,

"Kinda warm today."

"Yeah," Gus said.

"You get more heat from this sun than from them old radiators at home."

"Yeah; them old white landlords sure don't give much heat."

"And they always knocking at your door for money."

"I'll be glad when summer comes."

"Me too," Bigger said.

He stretched his arms above his head and yawned; his

From *Native Son* (New York: Harper & Brothers, 1940), pp. 13–19.

eyes moistened. The sharp precision of the world of steel and stone dissolved into blurred waves. He blinked and the world grew hard again, mechanical, distinct. A weaving motion in the sky made him turn his eyes upward; he saw a slender streak of billowing white blooming against the deep blue. A plane was writing high up in the air.

"Look!" Bigger said.

"What?"

"That plane writing up there," Bigger said, pointing.

"Oh!"

They squinted at a tiny ribbon of unfolding vapor that spelled out the word: U S E. . . . The plane was so far away that at times the strong glare of the sun blanked it from sight.

"You can hardly see it," Gus said.

"Looks like a little bird," Bigger breathed with childlike wonder.

"Them white boys sure can fly," Gus said.

"Yeah," Bigger said, wistfully. "They get a chance to do everything."

Noiselessly, the tiny plane looped and veered, vanishing and appearing, leaving behind it a long trail of white plumage, like coils of fluffy paste being squeezed from a tube; a plume-coil that grew and swelled and slowly began to fade into the air at the edges. The plane wrote another word: S P E E D. . . .

"How high you reckon he is?" Bigger asked.

"I don't know. Maybe a hundred miles; maybe a thousand."

"I could fly one of them things if I had a chance," Bigger mumbled reflectively, as though talking to himself.

Gus pulled down the corners of his lips, stepped out from the wall, squared his shoulders, doffed his cap, bowed low and spoke with mock deference:

"Yessuh."

"You go to hell," Bigger said, smiling.

"Yessuh," Gus said again.

"I *could* fly a plane if I had a chance," Bigger said.

"If you wasn't black and if you had some money and if they'd let you go to that aviation school, you *could* fly a plane," Gus said.

For a moment Bigger contemplated all the "ifs" that Gus had mentioned. Then both boys broke into hard laughter, looking at each other through squinted eyes. When their laughter subsided, Bigger said in a voice that was half-question and half-statement:

"It's funny how the white folks treat us, ain't it?"

"It better be funny," Gus said.

"Maybe they right in not wanting us to fly," Bigger said. " 'Cause if I took a plane up I'd take a couple of bombs along and drop 'em as sure as hell. . . ."

They laughed again, still looking upward. The plane sailed and dipped and spread another word against the sky: G A S O L I N E. . . .

"Use Speed Gasoline," Bigger mused, rolling the words slowly from his lips. "God, I'd like to fly up there in that sky."

"God'll let you fly when He gives you your wings up in heaven," Gus said.

They laughed again, reclining against the wall, smoking, the lids of their eyes drooped softly against the sun. Cars whizzed past on rubber tires. Bigger's face was metallically black in the strong sunlight. There was in his eyes a pensive, brooding amusement, as of a man who had been long confronted and tantalized by a riddle whose answer seemed always just on the verge of escaping him, but prodding him irresistibly on to seek its solution. The silence irked Bigger; he was anxious to do something to evade looking so squarely at this problem.

"Let's play 'white,' " Bigger said, referring to a game of play-acting in which he and his friends imitated the ways and manners of white folks.

"I don't feel like it," Gus said.

"General!" Bigger pronounced in a sonorous tone, looking at Gus expectantly.

"Aw, hell! I don't want to play," Gus whined.

"You'll be court-martialed," Bigger said, snapping out his words with military precision.

"Nigger, you nuts!" Gus laughed.

"General!" Bigger tried again, determinedly.

Gus looked wearily at Bigger, then straightened, saluted and answered:

"Yessuh."

"Send your men over the river at dawn and attack the enemy's left flank," Bigger ordered.

"Yessuh."

"Send the Fifth, Sixth, and Seventh Regiments," Bigger said, frowning. "And attack with tanks, gas, planes, and infantry."

"Yessuh!" Gus said again, saluting and clicking his heels.

For a moment they were silent, facing each other, their shoulders thrown back, their lips compressed to hold down the mounting impulse to laugh. Then they guffawed, partly at themselves and partly at the vast white world that sprawled and towered in the sun before them.

"Say, what's a 'left flank'?" Gus asked.

"I don't know," Bigger said. "I heard it in the movies."

They laughed again. After a bit they relaxed and leaned against the wall, smoking. Bigger saw Gus cup his left hand to his ear, as though holding a telephone receiver; and cup his right hand to his mouth, as though talking into a transmitter.

"Hello," Gus said.

"Hello," Bigger said. "Who's this?"

"This is Mr. J. P. Morgan speaking," Gus said.

"Yessuh, Mr. Morgan," Bigger said; his eyes filled with mock adulation and respect.

"I want you to sell twenty thousand shares of U.S. Steel in the market this morning," Gus said.

"At what price, suh?" Bigger asked.

"Aw, just dump 'em at any price," Gus said with casual irritation. "We're holding too much."

"Yessuh," Bigger said.

"And call me at my club at two this afternoon and tell me if the President telephoned," Gus said.

"Yessuh, Mr. Morgan," Bigger said.

Both of them made gestures signifying that they were hanging up telephone receivers; then they bent double, laughing.

"I bet that's *just* the way they talk," Gus said.

"I wouldn't be surprised," Bigger said.

They were silent again. Presently, Bigger cupped his hand to his mouth and spoke through an imaginary telephone transmitter.

"Hello."

"Hello," Gus answered. "Who's this?"

"This is the President of the United States speaking," Bigger said.

"Oh, yessuh, Mr. President," Gus said.

"I'm calling a cabinet meeting this afternoon at four o'clock and you, as Secretary of State, *must* be there."

"Well, now, Mr. President," Gus said, "I'm pretty busy. They raising sand over there in Germany and I got to send 'em a note. . . ."

"But this is important," Bigger said.

"What you going to take up at this cabinet meeting?" Gus asked.

"Well, you see, the niggers is raising sand all over the country," Bigger said, struggling to keep back his laughter. "We've got to do something with these black folks. . . ."

"Oh, if it's about the niggers, I'll be right there, Mr. President," Gus said.

They hung up imaginary receivers and leaned against the wall and laughed. A street car rattled by. Bigger sighed and swore.

"Goddammit!"

"What's the matter?"

"They don't let us do *nothing.*"

"Who?"

"The *white* folks."

"You talk like you just now finding that out," Gus said.

"Naw. But I just can't get used to it," Bigger said. "I swear to God I can't. I know I oughtn't think about it, but I can't help it. Every time I think about it I feel like somebody's poking a red-hot iron down my throat. Goddammit, look! We live here and they live there. We black and they white. They got things and we ain't. They do things and we can't. It's

just like living in jail. Half the time I feel like I'm on the outside of the world peeping in through a knot-hole in the
fence. . . ."

"Aw, ain't no use feeling that way about it. It don't help
none," Gus said.

"You know one thing?" Bigger said.

"What?"

"Sometimes I feel like something awful's going to happen
to me," Bigger spoke with a tinge of bitter pride in his voice.

"What you mean?" Gus asked, looking at him quickly.
There was fear in Gus's eyes.

"I don't know. I just feel that way. Every time I get to
thinking about me being black and they being white, me being here and they being there, I feel like something awful's
going to happen to me. . . ."

"Aw, for Chrissakes! There ain't nothing you can do about
it. How come you want to worry yourself? You black and they
make the laws. . . ."

"Why they make us live in one corner of the city? Why
don't they let us fly planes and run ships? . . ."

Gus hunched Bigger with his elbow and mumbled good-
naturedly, "Aw, nigger, quit thinking about it. You'll go nuts."

The plane was gone from the sky and the white plumes of
floating smoke were thinly spread, vanishing. Because he was
restless and had time on his hands, Bigger yawned again and
hoisted his arms high above his head.

"Nothing ever happens," he complained.

"What you want to happen?"

"Anything," Bigger said with a wide sweep of his dingy
palm, a sweep that included all the possible activities of the
world.

Then their eyes were riveted; a slate-colored pigeon
swooped down to the middle of the steel car tracks and began
strutting to and fro with ruffled feathers, its fat neck bobbing
with regal pride. A street car rumbled forward and the pigeon
rose swiftly through the air on wings stretched so taut and
sheer that Bigger could see the gold of the sun through their
translucent tips. He tilted his head and watched the slate-

colored bird flap and wheel out of sight over the edge of a high roof.

"Now, if I could only do that," Bigger said.

Gus laughed.

"Nigger, you nuts."

"I reckon we the only things in this city that can't go where we want to go and do what we want to do."

"Don't think about it," Gus said.

"I can't help it."

"That's why you feeling like something awful's going to happen to you," Gus said. "You think too much."

"What in hell can a man do?" Bigger asked, turning to Gus.

"Get drunk and sleep it off."

"I can't. I'm broke."

Bigger crushed his cigarette and took out another one and offered the package to Gus. They continued smoking. A huge truck swept past, lifting scraps of white paper into the sunshine; the bits settled down slowly.

"Gus?"

"Hunh?"

"You know where the white folks live?"

"Yeah," Gus said, pointing eastward. "Over across the 'line'; over there on Cottage Grove Avenue."

"Naw; they don't," Bigger said.

"What you mean?" Gus asked, puzzled. "Then, where do they live?"

Bigger doubled his fist and struck his solar plexus.

"Right down here in my stomach," he said.

Gus looked at Bigger searchingly, then away, as though ashamed.

"Yeah; I know what you mean," he whispered.

"Every time I think of 'em, I *feel* 'em," Bigger said.

"Yeah; and in your chest and throat, too," Gus said.

"It's like fire."

"And sometimes you can't hardly breathe. . . ."

Bigger's eyes were wide and placid, gazing into space.

"That's when I feel like something awful's going to happen

to me. . . ." Bigger paused, narrowed his eyes. "Naw; it ain't like something going to happen to me. It's . . . It's like I was going to do something I can't help. . . ."

"Yeah!" Gus said with uneasy eagerness. His eyes were full of a look compounded of fear and admiration for Bigger. "Yeah; I know what you mean. It's like you going to fall and don't know where you going to land. . . ."

Gus's voice trailed off. The sun slid behind a big white cloud and the street was plunged in cool shadow; quickly the sun edged forth again and it was bright and warm once more. A long sleek black car, its fenders glinting like glass in the sun, shot past them at high speed and turned a corner a few blocks away. Bigger pursed his lips and sang:

"Zoooooooooom!"

"They got everything," Gus said.

"They own the world," Bigger said.

"Aw, what the hell," Gus said. "Let's go in the poolroom."

5

How Form and Content Work Together in a Psychological Style

THE first sentence of this passage might almost have been written by Hemingway; but as we continue to read we can see that Wright's style, though it shares some characteristics with Hemingway's—the use of simple and compound sentences and an informal vocabulary and diction—is quite different in many ways. For example, Wright allows his narrator something that an objective stylist would probably not allow—a privileged look inside the mind and feelings of a character. Bigger, we are told, was "relaxed, his mind pleasantly vacant of purpose." Other nonobjective characteristics include Wright's use of adverbs and colorful adjectives, such as "the sun burning a dazzling yellow."

Color is so often used to modify things and people that Wright seems to be painting the scene in bold primary contrasts—red (walls), white (clouds and cigarettes), black (chins and asphalt), yellow (sun), blue (sky). Nor does Wright's use of color end with the description of the scene. Things are mentioned by the characters as interchangeable with the color of the people who are associated with them. This is a figure of speech called *metonymy,* where something is referred to not by its name, but by the name or quality of something often associated with it. For example, if we were to hear this familiar kind of news report, "The White House informed us late this afternoon that the next move is now up to Capitol Hill," we could be fairly sure that houses and hills are as mute and inert as ever, but that the president seems to be having some trouble with Congress. "You get more heat from this sun than from them old radiators at home," says Bigger. Gus answers by repeating the same idea with one substitution: "Yeah; them old white land-lords sure don't give much heat." The old radiators are seen as interchangeable with the old white landlords. And this is not the only time when a machine is interchanged with the *white* people associated with it. As Gus and Bigger stare up at the airplane, Gus observes "them white boys sure can fly." Again, the machine is automatically linked to the white color of the people asso-ciated with it. When this was written there were almost no black pilots in the United States.

Of course, we are used to black and white being em-ployed as symbols suggesting more than simple color denota-tion, though we must remember that readers in 1940 (when *Native Son* was published) were not as familiar with this symbolic convention as we are today. It may be slightly more difficult for us to see how Wright is using the sun and radiator and plane as symbols linked to the black-and-white symbol pattern.

Consider the possibility that the sun is a symbol—a kind of verbal reference whose subject is not stated or obvious in the literal context. (The symbol, as a figure of speech, is defined more fully in the next chapter, pp. 87–106.) If the sun is a reference in search of a subject, what subject does it suggest? Perhaps Wright intends the sun to be an am-biguous symbol, suggesting more than one subject. First of all, the sun is one of man's oldest symbols, one which has been woven for centuries into almost every religion and often been made a principal object of worship. In the more recent religions, if not worshiped for itself, it is at least venerated as "the eye of the Lord" or "the gift of the Lord." There has grown up around this almost universal symbol a wealth of connotations, some of which can hardly be put into words; but there might be fairly general agreement that from the times of the earliest agrarian communities where its central importance is obvious, the sun has been a symbol of life and growth and power that freely grants its benefits to all people equally and for which there is a general primary need.

Wright has his characters contrast the warmth they receive from the sun ("the gift of the Lord") with the lack of heat they receive from their land*lord*'s radiators. Wright is suggesting that warmth is a basic human need supplied freely to all, regardless of color, by nature through the sun. However, "them old white landlords" and their radiators deny to some the warmth that all humans need. The old white landlords' radiators are artificial mechanical surrogates for the power and warmth of the natural sun, which shines democratically on all alike. The way man's mechanical extensions of nature are kept turned off to some of mankind is, Wright suggests by contrasting the mechanical with the natural symbol, an unnatural perversion.

Perhaps this symbolic pattern of contrast with which Wright seems to be revealing unnatural perversion in our mechanical society is not a pattern at all, but only a coincidence that he did not intend. The danger that we are being more active as readers than the writer intended us to be and have made up a pattern in our own minds that was never in the writer's mind is always present when we try to understand just what a writer means symbolically; but that danger is considerably reduced if the writer repeats the same kind of symbolic pattern in another context. And Wright does, as we shall see, repeat the pattern that we have tentatively identified. Consider now Wright's use of the airplane and the bird as a possible symbolic pattern, like the radiator and the sun.

In the same way that the sun symbolized every man's natural need for warmth, the flight of a bird in the following paragraphs serves as a natural and almost universal symbol for what Wright suggests is another basic human need—freedom. And while the radiator is a mechanical surrogate for the fulfillment of nature, the airplane is man's mechanical extension of natural flight that "slate-colored" (i.e., black) birds as well as all others can freely enjoy. Just as Wright has suggested that the white landlords have perverted natural fulfillment of human needs by their discriminatory control of mechanisms such as radiators, so too these white "lords of the land" have denied fulfillment of other basic human needs, symbolized by a discriminatory control of other mechanisms such as airplanes.

Wright makes more of the symbolic contrast between bird and airplane than he made of the contrast between sun and radiator. "Looks like a little bird," Bigger says of the airplane; then Wright has the narrator change this simile to metaphor by describing the airplane's "white plumage." A few pages later, Wright introduces a bird with black plumage, a "slate-colored pigeon," who is able to escape the crushing mechanical rush of a streetcar by flying away from it.

Nature has endowed the black bird with beauty, independence, and freedom, attributes that a discriminatory, artificial society has not allowed black people to enjoy. Wright has his narrator describe the pigeon's "regal pride" and the grace of its ascent as it "rose swiftly through the air on wings stretched so taut and sheer that Bigger could see the gold of the sun through their translucent tips." Notice that Wright here relates his sun symbol to his bird symbol. In nature, the sun shines generously on the free and beautiful black bird. Wright then has Bigger make the analogy explicit that has already been suggested symbolically—namely, the difference between the beauty and freedom of black in nature, and the way black is discriminated against in modern society. "Now, if I could only do that," Bigger says as he watches the bird fly free. "I reckon we the only things in this city that can't go where we want to go and do what we want to do." It is the same contrast that Wright was beginning to suggest several pages earlier when Bigger wished out loud that he could learn to fly an airplane, the mechanical surrogate symbol for the independence and freedom symbolized by the flight of birds in nature: "I could fly one of them things if I had a chance." Wright has Bigger express half-aloud and to himself this longing for the excitement and power of free flight, qualified by "if I had a chance."

But Wright then has Gus, who has overheard Bigger's daydream, deny with savage mockery the softly spoken aspira-

tion for freedom. He first taunts Bigger for having overstepped
his position in society and having dared express hope:

> Gus pulled down the corners of his lips, stepped out from
> the wall, squared his shoulders, doffed his cap, bowed low
> and spoke with mock deference:
> "Yessuh."

He suggests how completely hypothetical Bigger's hope is
by tripling and making concrete the "if" qualification that
Bigger expressed vaguely as "a chance." Hard, deterministic
forces are working against that chance: "If you wasn't black
and if you had some money and if they'd let you go to that
aviation school, you *could* fly a plane." As if this were not
denial enough, notice that Wright has let Bigger answer Gus's
question about the height of the plane with the unreality and
even impossibility of "Maybe a hundred miles; maybe a thousand." With this answer Wright establishes Bigger's idealiza-
tion of the symbol. At the same time such a lack of real
knowledge about airplanes suggests that he has been deprived
of even rudimentary scientific knowledge, which points to
lack of education as another form of determinism along with
poverty and race prejudice, all working against the realization
of Bigger's psychological need.

We have seen enough skill and care in Wright's use of
repeated symbols (each of which ambiguously contains both
private and public, psychological and sociological implications)
to make us aware that possibly the whole narrative may be
organized to convey a penetrating relation between the psychology of the characters and modern society and its institutions. Wright, like so many other writers in the 1930s, read
and experimented in his own way with the theories of Sigmund Freud. Let us tentatively hypothesize that in this passage
Wright may be transforming some psychological mechanisms
into usable writing techniques to convey meaning beyond the
limitations of more conventional writing structures. Our
study of a few symbols makes it obvious that Wright wishes
us to see that there is much more at stake for Bigger and
Gus than the manifest content of their conversation about

not getting enough heat out of radiators and not piloting airplanes.

Maybe Wright has organized the entire narrative so that it is possible to consider the simple dialogue and the sometimes almost absurd-seeming laughter and game playing in a way that will reward the cooperative reader with a more profound psychological insight into the narrative. If such is the case, then the extra burden that Wright is accepting for adding a psychological dimension to the motivations of his characters requires extra effort from those who wish to study his style. If we wish to understand how he is composing well enough to use some of his techniques in our own writing, we must try to understand just how and why Wright is using psychological structures to organize his narrative in more than a conventional, logical pattern.

According to Freud, man is powerfully motivated by non-rational, unconscious desires and needs; but such drives are often in conflict with the structure of the external world. An individual's psychology can be disturbed by his conflict with reality and his inability to gratify his unconscious desires directly. Such desires may be repressed. Repression occurs when unconscious impulses or desires are forbidden access to conscious life. The psychic energy behind such desires, turned aside from a direct path by repression, may be dammed up by the conscious mind; yet the same amount of energy will persist, though it may now be distorted down strange channels disguised from the conscious mind. If the repression is intense enough, then the frustrated psychic energy will spill over into abnormal, possibly dangerous behavior. In the orthodox Freudian scheme these repressed desires are almost always sexual. But Wright seems to be adapting Freud's structures to his own writing purposes. And at this point in the narrative, Wright is illustrating nonsexual desires that are not simply Bigger's personal neurotic fantasies but are related to the political and economic institutions of external society.

In the dream state or in fantasy and play, according to Freud, a human psyche can temporarily renounce the reality that dominates the external world and enact a more or less disguised (symbolic) fulfillment of an unconscious desire. Because the psychic energy behind the desire can cause pain to the consciousness when expressed directly, a repressed desire disguises itself from the conscious, rational mind. In psychoanalysis a careful examination of symbolic dreams may be used to discover the nature of the repressed wish that is expressed only in a disguised, nonlogical manner, in ambiguous symbols, and in absurd fantasy situations. (In the next chapter, pp. 92–94, dream symbolism is discussed more fully.)

A writer who assumes the validity of Freud's structuralization of human psychic life can, when he intends to give a complete picture of the mental life of a character, set up symbolic or behavioral clues to his character's unconscious desires. He or she can do this by introducing certain kinds of distortion of verbal and active behavior that are symptoms of such repression. Since the unconscious is not rational and logical, and since behavior is being distorted, the writer cannot give us a sense of the psychic life of a character or speaker without expecting the reader, if he is given sufficient clues, to *participate* in trying to understand psychological symbols and narrative sequences that may not be logically related in any conventionally obvious way. For instance, it may not be *conventionally* understandable why a man who has been denied the opportunity of piloting an airplane will, like Bigger, say in retaliation, "if I took a plane up I'd take a couple of bombs along and drop 'em as sure as hell. . . ." But we can understand such verbal behavior on a nonlogical, symbolic level, where the powerful psychic energy of a man's drive for freedom has, because of repression, been displaced to the act of flying an airplane, which we can recognize as a symbol of the freedom he is being denied in many brutal ways.

With such psychological structures in mind let us see if and how Wright may have used them to organize the sequence of his narrative. Why, for instance, in a serious narrative does Wright introduce the nonlogical absurdities of game playing? To answer this let us briefly consider the symbolism again, this time in the light of psychology. We have seen that Wright uses the radiator and particularly the airplane to show us how much painful emotion Bigger has attached to an object because of what it symbolizes to him unconsciously. Wright invites readers to understand that both Bigger and, even more, Gus have repressed a basic human need for freedom and independent life, and that Bigger's unconscious mind has transferred its powerful psychic energy to a disguised surrogate—the wish to fly an airplane—for the original, strong desire for freedom. A reader can recognize the psychological needs that Bigger does not yet understand consciously. Wright has his narrator, by exercising the privilege of seeing into Bigger's mind, say:

> The silence irked Bigger; he was anxious to do something to evade looking so squarely at this problem.
> "Let's play 'white,' Bigger said. . . .

Evidently Wright wishes us to understand that Bigger's anxiety is painful enough for him to have to turn from direct confrontation of the problem to more indirect game playing.

Wright has his more successfully repressed character, Gus, refuse to pursue the problem. Gus turns away from even playfully disguised wish fulfillment of such painfully frustrated needs. Wright suggests a difference in character between the two that we can understand in psychological terms. As we will see at the end of the passage, Gus has the same needs and feels the same frustration of those needs as Bigger, but throughout the narrative Wright has characterized Gus primarily by showing his different psychic adjustment to the repressiveness of modern society. Wright has him accept the unfair structure of society as a given fact and has him attempt—with ironic laughter, put-downs, or refusals to pursue the issue—to save himself and Bigger from the pain of facing more directly what he considers an insoluble problem.

But Bigger finally forces Gus to play three games in succession, punctuated with irrational laughter. First they play "General," then "J. P. Morgan," then "Mr. President." Why does Wright have them play these particular games? First, each represents a position in society of almost unlimited freedom, power, and control. The general has military power and controls the mechanical force of tanks and planes and guns; J. P. Morgan is a symbol of wealth and, in the game, arbitrarily throws around his economic power by irresponsibly selling "U.S. Steel." This arbitrary act can be seen once again as symbolically linking the white world with manipulative power. As the games continue, the president, again the symbol of highest power in the white world, is about to turn his attention from Hitler and the Nazis to unleash all America's white power against the blacks who have, Bigger pretends, dared to "[raise] sand all over the country." The three games serve more than one function. Each satirizes the white power structure and at the same time seems to represent a kind of "disguised" wish fulfillment, realizing in fantasy Bigger's and Gus's repressed desires for freedom and power. These young men must act out like children the free and independent power roles from which they are excluded as men.

Bigger and Gus have apparently played such games before, maybe for wish fulfillment. But Wright does not seem to be using these games in the conventional Freudian way—as hedonistic fantasies that will allow his characters to temporarily daydream the fulfillment of desires that are frustrated in the real world, which is what Freud in his early *Interpretation of Dreams* (1900) sees as the function of games. Just before he introduces the game-playing sequence, Wright has his narrator describe Bigger's motivation this way:

> There was in his eyes a pensive, brooding amusement, as of a man who had been long confronted and tantalized by a riddle whose answer seemed always just on the verge of escaping him, but prodding him irresistibly on to seek its solution.

Wright has Gus refuse to play the games with Bigger, perhaps to suggest that a reader must not interpret such games merely as pleasurable daydreams used to escape from reality. These games are more like the "compulsive repetitions" that Freud speaks of in his later work on dreams, in which a person may confront in games or fantasies the same painful problem again and again in slightly different contexts while he tries to bring the threatening experience under control by conscious understanding. Bigger's game playing does not seem so much a withdrawal into illusory gratification as a repeated process of imaginative confrontation with the frustrating structure of society.

The organization of Wright's narrative, then, is not a conventional, logical sequence. It is a pattern of recurrent confrontation (at first oblique and ambiguous, but getting progressively more explicit) that Wright has organized for Bigger to press and Gus to avoid; and after each such confrontation Bigger seems a little closer to being conscious of the problem. But becoming more conscious of the problem is a very painful process.

> "I know I oughtn't think about it, but I can't help it. Every time I think about it I feel like somebody's poking a red-hot iron down my throat."

For purposes of artistic economy Wright has, of course, speeded up and compressed into a few pages a psychological process that might in reality take months or even years to accomplish. Wright is in a way having Bigger act as his own psychoanalyst, sketching in a dozen pages how he proceeds by compulsive repetition to bring his unconscious, symbolically expressed wishes to consciousness, to accept them as valid, and to begin to be aware of the external social causes of his repression and frustration. Bigger's painful discovery lies in his becoming consciously aware of the struggle between his most basic psychic drives and the hard, repressive structures of mechanized society that continue to frustrate those drives, thereby denying his human rights. The impossible situation is an irresistible psychic force meeting an immobile body politic. In a simple antithesis stated in parallel structure his frustration is finally made painfully but clearly conscious: "We live here and they live there. We black and they white. They got things and we ain't. They do things and we can't." These antitheses, though not nearly as elaborate as Donne's, gain force because their simplicity and honest dignity climaxes a symbolic sequence of profound psychological and social inquiry that Wright has organized for his readers to see and feel through symbols and the repeated psychic behavior of the characters.

Wright now begins to reveal that the psychic energy behind Bigger's repressed needs, which cannot be fulfilled in any normal way, is threatening to determine some very dangerous behavior. At first Wright has Bigger think the painful energy is going to be destructive to himself: "Sometimes I feel like something awful's going to happen to me." And again, a little later: "I feel like something awful's going to happen to me. . . ." But after the "slate-colored pigeon" incident makes it clearer to Bigger (and to the reader) that black has a natural right to life and beauty and freedom, Wright changes the direction of the destructive psychic energy from self-hatred and self-destructiveness to a more externally directed, if no less dangerous, feeling: "Naw; it ain't like something going to happen to me. It's . . . It's like I was going to do something I can't help. . . ."

Throughout the narrative Wright has used laughter as a gestural symbol of frustration. The irrational laughter of Gus and Bigger is more like convulsive behavior—the baring of teeth in bitter temporary release from the pain of facing a brutally impossible situation. The only way Gus has of dealing with his psychic drives in conflict with the frustrating denial of a white society is to advise Bigger ironically, "It better be funny." Wright closes the scene with Bigger and Gus no longer laughing but awfully aware of the dangerous and powerful energy that psychic frustration is about to unleash; yet they have nothing to do, no money even to get drunk, and no place to go except a poolroom. That Bigger will do something dangerous now seems understandable and psychologically determined because of the insight Wright has managed to give his readers through the symbols and organization of this seemingly simple narrative.

Because we have concentrated on Wright's psychological structures in the narrative, it might be easy to regard the subject matter of this narrative as entirely psychological and forget the clearly visualized material detail that the characters consciously perceive, beneath which Wright has structured the unconscious struggle going on inside them. Wright has particularized a visually realistic and linguistically colloquial narrative designed to evoke, as we have seen, a general symbolic suggestiveness. In realistic detail Wright shows us the airplane overhead and trucks that "swept past, lifting scraps of white paper into the sunshine," a woman's "gentle sway" disappearing into a doorway, and cars that "whizzed past" or "whirred over the smooth black asphalt," along with street cars and pigeons and a commercial that advertises in bold smoke across the clear blue sky, "Use Speed Gasoline." Even this commercial is not just a realistic detail, but understandable in symbolic terms related to other symbols we have seen Wright use. Speed is one of the attributes of power, and gasoline one of its sources in an industrial world; but Bigger and Gus ironically cannot use them at all because they are not free to do so. The power of the modern industrial world is not for their use; it will not be used to fulfill any of the black man's needs. Gus and Bigger are only passive hostages, who are being insulted by mechanized commercials from overhead, cut off by "the line" from the rest of the city, flown over, and run through by speeding cars and crushing steel trains. This section of the city, though portrayed realistically by Wright, nevertheless also is made to seem symbolic of a state of affairs much more general than these particular two men leaning up against their particular wall. It seems symbolic of the repression of black people all over the country by a mechanical white power.

Indeed, there is some evidence that Wright was attempting to symbolize something even larger—the plight of modern man—in the character and struggle of Bigger. Here is what Wright himself thought of Bigger as a symbol:

> More than anything else, as a writer, I was fascinated by the similarity of the emotional tensions of Bigger in America and Bigger in Nazi Germany and Bigger in old Russia. All Bigger Thomases, white and black, felt tense, afraid, nervous, hysterical, and restless . . . certain modern experiences were creating types of personalities whose existence ignored racial and national lines of demarcation . . . these personalities carried with them a more universal drama-element than anything

I'd ever encountered before; [and] these personalities were
mainly consequent upon men and women living in a world
whose fundamental assumptions could no longer be taken for
granted. . . .*

The typical psychoanalyst of Wright's day tended to see
the structures of society as a given reality to which the individual should be helped to "adjust" if he was "maladjusted."
The causes and remedies of abnormal psychological behavior
were looked for within the psyche of the individual and most
often located in the internal repression of some form of sexual
desire rather than possibly in the external repressiveness of
social and economic institutions that unnecessarily frustrate the
fulfillment of basic human, needs. Though Wright may be
using psychoanalytic mechanisms as organizing structures in
his writing, we have seen that his aim is not to show Bigger
as a conventional neurotic case history, tortured and repressed
by his own guilt and fears, a man who ought to learn to
adjust to the structures of external "reality." On the contrary,
Wright is indicting the structures of white mechanized society as a perversion of the natural goal of modern society,
which is to use science to extend without prejudice the fulfillment of all men's basic needs, both material and psychic.
In a more democratic technological society radiators would
be produced to extend the warmth that the sun supplies in
nature, and in general the society would extend to all humans increased fulfillment of the basic psychic needs for
freedom and survival. Wright's narrative suggests that a modern white society, whether it is conscious of this or not, is using
mechanical productivity not to extend the possibility of greater
fulfillment of the basic psychic needs of more people but, in
fact, to extend its repressive power to deny the psychic needs
of black people.

Wright had, then, as early as 1940, brought together the
two important philosophies his contemporaries, for the most
part, regarded as antithetical. Karl Marx's ideas of economic

---

* Quoted by Saunders Redding, "The Negro Writer and American Literature," in *Anger and Beyond: The Negro Writer in the United States,* ed.
Herbert Hill (New York: Harper and Row, 1966), p. 17.

determinism include the basic assumption that if you change the structures and institutions of society so that all men own the means of production, then you can better fulfill all men's needs and thus change their minds and behavior. Since Freud, on the contrary, believed that man's real problems were not in the structures of the external social system but in the structures of his own mind which he must reconcile with himself, Freud considered Marx's ideas superficial. There were few philosophers in 1940 who thought Marxian and Freudian ideas could be reconciled, but Wright managed to combine Marx and Freud so effectively in symbolic organizations that he could create moving literature from that fusion.

But if Wright's psychology proves not Bigger's neuroticism, but society's repressiveness, why not plainly indict society with a simple realistic narrative organized with conventional cause-and-effect structures? Why should Wright go to the trouble of using ambiguous symbols and organizing with absurdities of sequence that have to be understood on a psychological level? Maybe because Wright's techniques of characterization demand of a reader much more psychological involvement than is conventionally expected in a narrative. To understand the characters a reader must participate in their psychic life by trying to discover the unconscious pattern Wright has included in their verbal and physical behavior. Wright's burden as a writer is to express a minority point of view to a majority audience which has so far remained almost totally insensitive to and aloof from the minority's suffering. Without involving that audience in some way, how do you force it to see that the problem is not with the minority, but with the majority, whose apathy is responsible for allowing the repression of human needs to continue?

Wright maintains a consistent tone and attitude toward both his readers and his subject. This attitude might be called almost paradoxically "concerned neutrality" or "impartial care." He cares about Gus and Bigger and what a white society has done to them, but he is concerned that both black and white readers understand and feel what has happened. He is as impartial in making clear to white readers (obviously the majority) their total responsibility for causing the black man's pain as he is impartial in avoiding any self-gratification in sentimentality toward Bigger and Gus. Nor does he express any hostility toward white readers who had repressed Wright himself, much as Bigger is being repressed. It was a considerable accomplishment both as a writer and as a man for Wright so patiently to have worked out the writing techniques that could reveal the minority psyche both to that minority itself and to the majority that is responsible for its injuries but does not seem to care enough to end the injustice.

Here is Wright's style, expressed as a writing program or model in the form of a brief diagram. (When we refer to "Wright's style" we mean his method of composition only in the specific sample we analyzed.)

Writing Program III

BRIEF DIAGRAM OF WRIGHT'S STYLE

Syntax:

Establish a difference between the narrator (organize his syntax according to the conventions of the majority) and the characters (organize their syntax according to the conventions of some specific minority). (For example, Wright has his characters use predominantly simple or compound sentences, comparatively few sentences with dependent clauses, and generally colloquial grammar, whereas the narrator uses a more formal standard grammar and includes a higher proportion of complex sentences.)

Words:

Establish a difference between the vocabulary of the narrator, speaking in the manner of the majority, and the characters, speaking as members of some specific minority. (For example, Wright has his characters use a more colloquial vocabulary than he allows his narrator.)

Figures of Speech:

Use symbols that ambiguously contain both psychological and social implications to encourage the participation of readers in the psychic as well as social problems of some minority.

Organization:

Organize several symbols into larger patterns that relate the psychic to the social problems of a minority.

Use psychological structures rather than conventional logical structures (such as cause and effect) to organize the writing. (For example, Wright organizes seemingly absurd games and nonlogical symbolic sequences that tend to involve readers in the emotional or psychic struggles of the characters more than conventional structures might.)

Organize in a general sequence from oblique symbolic suggestiveness to more explicit statement.

Subject Matter:

Provide a particularized, visually detailed minority environment upon which you construct some larger symbolic significance. Use scene and action of narrative to make manifest latent human needs and emotions.

Attitudes or Ways of Thinking and Perceiving:

With concern, yet without sentimentality, reveal a minority point of view to an insensitive and unconcerned majority audience, using writing techniques that tend to encourage the participation and involvement of that unconcerned majority audience.

When using the narrative form, have the characters reveal their own situations dramatically with a minimum of commentary; allow the narrator to exercise the privilege of seeing into a character's mind only when it is necessary to encourage the reader to participate in or understand the psychological situation of the character.

Exercises

1. We have seen that Wright often is able, without direct commentary, to use dramatic situations with symbolic objects or gestures to suggest psychological states. For example, he suggests the close companionship between Bigger and Gus by having them smoke cigarettes together silently. Try in a sentence to suggest some psychological state of mind by words or described gestures.

2. Next, try organizing a paragraph in order to suggest a psychological experience such as alienation, wish for freedom, narrow-mindedness, narcissism, or a deteriorating relationship by composing some dramatic situation in which you use a process or game symbolically to convey this psychological experience without naming it. Test your paragraph on a friend to see if you have managed to convey psychological meaning without commentary.

3. Compose a short dialogue in which the characters talk about a clearly visualized person or object that becomes a symbol as the dialogue develops.

6

Using Symbols and
Controlling Point of View

Symbolism

EVEN though we all habitually respond to symbols in our everyday lives, in order to use Wright's style we will have to learn to control symbols so that they convey the meanings and have the effects on a reader that we intend. We will also have to consider how to organize conventional symbols into original patterns, and even how to create new symbols.

To make a metaphor (as we saw in Chapter 4) you state its reference and either state or make obvious its subject. But to make a symbol you state only its reference and leave the job of assigning subjects to the reader. When the poet William Butler Yeats wrote that men have lost something "who are not in love with Helen," he was using the word Helen (short for Helen of Troy?) as a reference that might suggest a number of possible subjects, some or all of which Yeats may have wished the reader to have in mind to complete his symbol (e.g., Helen [of Troy] might suggest beauty; or she might suggest an impossible but irresistible earthly quest for perfection; or perhaps a consuming, but dangerous or destructive love, as it proved for Paris, his family, and his country.)

A symbol can be thought of as a kind of open metaphor suggested by the writer with only a reference whose subject must be supplied by a participating reader, guided only by the context you supply. For example:

METAPHOR: My love [subject] is a *rose* [reference] in bloom.
SYMBOL: My *rose* [reference] blooms.

What is the subject of *rose* in the second quotation? Is it love, or maybe life? Or is the rose meant literally, in which case it is no symbol at all. To have any clear idea of what the symbol *rose* might mean here the writer would have to extend the sentence to offer a more provocative context to motivate us to participate in assigning some nonliteral meaning to that

Margaret Bourke-White, *The American Way* (1937).

word. The writer's *control of context* is the only way of communicating the meaning of his symbols to a reader. The simile "queer as a clockwork orange" is an old cockney saying that has an understandable meaning. But the title of Anthony Burgess's novel *A Clockwork Orange* is a symbol that carries very little, if any, meaning until we consider the title in the context of the novel or movie, which is concerned with the definition of man as a mere mechanism to be manipulated (a clockwork) or an organic being (orange) or both.

It is easy to see how context controls the meaning of visual symbols in the photograph, p. 88. What objects become symbols in this photograph? Are these objects always symbols? What did the photographer do to control your perception of symbolic meaning? The car commercial is powerfully symbolic because of the context in which the photographer framed it. Can you do the same kind of framing *with words* in order to give point to the same symbols in a short paragraph? Try it.

Here are several of William Blake's one-sentence proverbs from his *Marriage of Heaven and Hell*. What symbols does Blake use, and what might they mean?

> Drive your cart and your plow over the bones of the dead.
> The cut worm forgives the plow.
> He whose face gives no light, shall never become a star.
> No bird soars too high, if he soars with his own wings.
> The cistern contains: the fountain overflows.
> The eagle never lost so much time as when he submitted to learn from the crow.
> The tygers of wrath are wiser than the horses of instruction.
> To create a little flower is the labour of ages.

Practice making words into symbols by using one of the words below as an obvious reference that will, in a single-sentence context in which you frame it, encourage a reader to fuse that reference with subject (or subjects) outside the literal context of your sentence:

red	frost	bones	city	blood	plow
wing	dust, ashes	moon	mountain	egg	dump

light	day	wall	star	tree	road
snake	flower	fountain	ship	water, rain	machine, auto
green	hair	door	chain	stairway	shadow
fire	grass	garden	bed	eye	sandals, bare feet

You can learn to control your reader's participation in your symbols by testing your sentence on a friend and carefully adjusting your reference with respect to your sentence context until it will tend to suggest to a reader the subject that you intend. The subject, if any, that a reader will think of when he sees your symbol is not always as inevitable as a writer might wish. When you use a symbol to invite a reader to participate in assigning his own meaning, you may be more effective in involving him, but it will also be much more difficult to control the kind and quality of association that the reader will make. When a writer wants to control very carefully a fusion of reference and subject in his reader's mind he is probably safer using a metaphor or simile.

It is not much harder to organize symbols into patterns and control them than simply to use one symbol. Here is an example of a pattern of symbols from F. Scott Fitzgerald's *The Great Gatsby:*

> About half way between West Egg and New York the motor road hastily joins the railroad and runs beside it for a quarter of a mile, so as to shrink away from a certain desolate area of land. This is a valley of ashes—a fantastic farm where ashes grow like wheat into ridges and hills and grotesque gardens; where ashes take the forms of houses and chimneys and rising smoke and, finally, with a transcendent effort, of men who move dimly and already crumbling through the powdery air. Occasionally a line of gray cars crawls along an invisible track, gives out a ghastly creak, and comes to rest, and immediately the ash-gray men swarm up with leaden spades and stir up an impenetrable cloud, which screens their obscure operations from your sight.
>
> But above the gray land and the spasms of bleak dust which drift endlessly over it, you perceive, after a moment, the eyes of Doctor T. J. Eckleburg. The eyes of Doctor T. J.

Eckleburg are blue and gigantic—their retinas are one yard high. They look out of no face, but, instead, from a pair of enormous yellow spectacles which pass over a non-existent nose. Evidently some wild wag of an oculist set them there to fatten his practice in the borough of Queens, and then sank down himself into eternal blindness, or forgot them and moved away. But his eyes, dimmed a little by many paintless days under sun and rain, brood on over the solemn dumping ground.*

Can you pick out some of the symbols used here and explain their relationship to one another?

Can you organize two or three of the words in the list above (pp. 89–90) into your own pattern of symbols? Try to make up relationships between them, or even possible brief stories or scenes. For instance, it is easy to see how the color green, used as a symbol of growth and life and youth, could be organized as a contrast to frost, which might in the context of this contrast be used to suggest old age or death. Or you could create a much more unusual and ambiguous, but perhaps harder-to-control symbol pattern, if you juxtaposed these symbols in a phrase like "green frost," within a context that would suggest to the reader that these words were both symbols having contradictory subjects and yoked into a kind of symbolic paradox. Can you see any relationship on a symbolic level between dust and water, for example?

After you have organized two or more traditional symbols into some pattern in a short paragraph, you might freshen your symbols by rewriting the sentences to shift the context or add a nontraditional symbol that you think could enliven the pattern. For instance, it is easy to see how garden-tree-apple could be organized into perhaps too traditional a symbolic pattern, one that might be saved from conventionality by the addition of some nontraditional symbols or maybe a change of context from the Garden of Eden, Tree of Knowledge, Forbidden Fruit of the Biblical Genesis. Notice how Blake freshens this traditional symbol cluster by a shift in

* F. Scott Fitzgerald, *The Great Gatsby* (New York: Charles Scribner and Son, 1925), p. 23.

context, and how quite a different meaning emerges from the
following poem:

A Poison Tree

I was angry with my friend:
I told my wrath, my wrath did end.
I was angry with my foe:
I told it not, my wrath did grow.

And I waterd it in fears,
Night & morning with my tears;
And I sunnéd it with smiles,
And with soft deceitful wiles.

And it grew both day and night,
Till it bore an apple bright.
And my foe beheld it shine,
And he knew that it was mine,

And into my garden stole,
When the night had veild the pole;
In the morning glad I see
My foe outstretchd beneath the tree.

In the previous chapter we discussed very briefly some of
Freud's psychological structures that Wright adapted as writing
structures, and now we will discuss more specifically Freud's
study of dream symbols. As we focus on the symbolic structure of dreams keep in mind that Wright and other authors
often use these structures in writing narratives. Indeed, Freud
himself considered dreams and stories to be similar in the sense
that they were, he assumed, both disguised forms of wish
fulfillment.

Freud found that the structure of dreams was by no means
logical or conventional. He attempted to discover the principles or mechanisms that accounted for their peculiar symbolic structure so that he and other psychoanalysts could interpret them and perhaps gain an understanding of the
unconscious psychic life revealed in them. He found that a
dream is an extreme condensation of our unconscious thoughts.
The mechanism of *condensation* favors the use of symbols so

that every element of the dream is a shorthand reference to an extraordinary richness of unconscious thought. (Wright was obviously using sun and radiator and bird and airplane as shorthand references for much more complex but almost inexpressible thoughts going on in Bigger's mind and emotions.)

Freud found that unconscious or latent thoughts are *manifested visually* in the dream. Words, ideas, and feelings generally occur in the dream as visual "things." The dream uses symbols in which highly visual material references suggest rich and often very complex thoughts and feelings. The tendency toward condensation in these symbols favors *multiple determination* or *ambiguity* of reference that serves to suggest more than one unconscious thought or need at the same time. (Consider how rich in suggestiveness are the simple visual symbols that Wright uses, such as the slate-colored pigeon, which becomes a junction for a complex of feelings and conceptions that perhaps could not be expressed as well in any other way.)

Freud theorized that in the dream state the unconscious thoughts or latent wishes with psychic energy behind them seek a fulfillment that they are denied by the conscious mind that represses them when it is awake. The conscious mind evidently imposes some censorship on unconscious thoughts even when lulled in the dream state. In order for the unconscious to disguise its thoughts from such censorship, which seeks even in sleep to repress unconscious needs, the mechanism of *displacement* seems often to come into play in distortion (or displacement) of dream symbols. The dream is distorted enough so that the unconscious thoughts are not recognizable by the conscious censor. Perhaps an unconscious need so demanding that it has great psychic energy will be represented in the dream by a reference that may at first seem to be of little significance. The patterning of symbols may appear distorted and quite unconventional, for the organization of symbols in a dream is not structured logically or according to conventional literary narrative organizations. What we might think of as a cause-and-effect relation the dream might express by simply juxtaposing two symbols. Or perhaps the same juxtaposition might suggest (in our conventional logical terms) a comparison/contrast or a disjunctive either/or relation. (Notice that Wright's juxtaposed patterns of white and black, sun and radiator, bird and airplane, though not presented in any conventional logical order, nevertheless suggest to the reader such complex organizations as comparison and contrast of a democratic natural world with a postindustrial exclusive society, and consideration of the cause and effect of repressive social structures on the human psyche.)

According to Freud, when unconscious thoughts disguised in displaced symbols sneak past the repressive censor and express themselves, the censor may recognize them too late, and even then may attempt to reconceal the expression of unconscious needs which might give pain to the conscious mind if they are faced directly. This attempt at reconcealment after the unconscious has expressed itself Freud calls *secondary elaboration*. It is a defensive mechanism, taking the form of seemingly inconsistent or irrational behavior that covers up or denies importance to the content of the symbolic expression. We recognize it in such a comment as, "Well, it's only a dream after all." Perhaps Wright in part intended as his own adaptation of Freud's mechanism of *secondary elaboration* Gus's and Bigger's irrational laughter and Gus's statement such as, "You talk like you just now finding that out," all of which tends to deny the importance of the unconscious thoughts and needs that Bigger is persistently bringing close to full consciousness in symbols, games, and statements.

Freud's work has encouraged not only symbol using, but symbol hunting in literature, because if Freud is right then it is likely that any writer, like any dreamer, may unconsciously be using symbols that a reader, acting as a psychoanalyst, may perceive. Of course, there is a difference between these highly private idiosyncratic symbols, which the writer's unconscious is sneaking past his conscious mind in cryptic or distorted guise, and the traditional symbols shared generally within a community or culture and used by writers for so many years that their enrichment of the literature and the life of a culture operates something like a complex feedback system.

Some modern symbolism is intentionally so ambiguous that even if a reader's interpretation is opposite to what the writer had consciously in mind, he would not be bothered at all. There is a strong tendency in our modern consumer-oriented culture to elevate and encourage reading as a creative act above the act of writing. Writing without a linear plot or time/space sequence, with the use of ambiguous symbolism if it is well enough executed to maintain interest, encourages audience participation that is highly subjective, in which each reader is allowed to enjoy the illusion of creating his own work of art in his own mind.

Though the creative role of the reader of modern writing is expected to be much greater than it ever was before in literary history, and though the average student today is much more creatively trained as a reader than as a writer, nevertheless a modern writer's responsibility for some control of his reader's participation by means of the symbols he uses is still necessary in most kinds of writing.

No writer could, and few would, wish to control their symbols the way a traffic cop controls his offenders if they do not know and respond to the red-light symbol as meaning "stop" and the green light as "go." Almost all symbols that writers use are ambiguous in the sense that they suggest more than one possible subject. But a writer can become aware of the range of possible subjects that some particular symbol he intends to use is likely to evoke in a reader, given the context in which he frames it. Control of the symbol is usually a matter of adjusting the context in which you frame your reference in such a way that not all, but only a certain range, of the many possible subjects will be suggested to your reader.

Consider the possible symbolic significance of some of the everyday objects and occurrences that touch our lives in so many ways that their associations cannot but be ambiguous: for example, your desk, room, books, bed, desk lamp, window, car or motorcycle, dining hall, parents, dorm counselor, roommate, teacher, rain or snow, Saturday night, Sunday morning, etc. Now try to write a paragraph using one or more symbolic references (like the above) until you think that your reader's participation in associating subjects with your references has been made fairly predictable by the context. Test your writing control by actually trying your paragraph out on a few friends to see if their reading response is generally what you intended it to be.

Point of View

The particular balance that Wright is able to maintain among his narrator, reader, and subject does not simply happen by chance. In order to achieve such a balance in your own writing you will need to know a number of alternative ways to relate your narrator, reader, and subject and how to maintain or shift such relations.

Whether he is aware of it or not, every writer betrays some *attitude toward his reader* (even if it is one of unconcern) and some *attitude toward his subject* (and toward his characters and narrator, if he is writing in narrative form). We do not address all readers and write on all subjects with the same attitude. A letter to one's fiancé and one to the dean of admissions hardly call for precisely the same attitudes (unless you are engaged to the dean). Most effective writers, consciously or unconsciously, choose their other stylistic techniques to be consistent with their characteristic attitudes so that their whole style functions together in some integrated way.

I am speaking of a writer's attitudes toward his reader (often called *tone*) and toward his subject as separate attitudes. This distinction is useful since a writer may at the same time establish one relation with his reader and quite another with the subject. He might, for example, choose to show respect for his readers while taking a sarcastic attitude toward his subject. But it would be too simple to suppose that there is an absolute separation between a writer's attitudes toward his subject and toward his reader. Surely the kind of attitude a writer takes toward a particular subject will have some effect on the way a reader will interpret the writer's attitude toward him. And just as surely the kind of relationship that the writer sets up between himself and his readers will have some effect on the way the reader will perceive the subject and the writer's attitude toward it.

The effective writer, then, must learn to control what seems to be a subtle, interdependent relation among the author or narrator, the reader, and the subject, a relation that every writer in every piece of writing creates, whether he is aware of it or not.

But how is it possible to control this relation? How have other writers done it? First, in order to control his attitude toward the reader, a writer may choose to characterize his narrator rather than give the reader the impression that he, the writer, is speaking directly to the reader. The implication that the author is speaking directly and without artifice to the reader is, of course, as much a fiction and as difficult for the writer to effect as a highly characterized narrator who is clearly different from the author. What we know is always somewhat different from what we write, if only because to write we must translate our thought and feeling, conscious and unconscious, verbal or nonverbal, into symbols, and our translations are further restricted by the structural limitations of syntax and the very small range of rhetorical organizations that any one of us can know, much less use all at once. Some form of narrator or implied author is always created, even when, as in an essay, the author appears to be saying exactly what he thinks and feels.

One of the most basic choices open to a writer at all times, then, is whether to leave his implied author or narrator relatively *uncharacterized* or to *characterize* him to a greater or lesser degree. Some writers attempt to characterize themselves so idiosyncratically that part of the reader's job is to try to understand the *point of view* and possible limitations of the character of the implied author or narrator. It is probable that increasing a reader's interest in the character of the implied author or narrator, or placing an emphasis on the relation that the narrator is establishing with the reader may diminish the reader's interest in the subject. Consequently, the more important the writer thinks it is to keep the reader's mind exclusively on subject matter, the less likely he may be to interest the reader too much in his narrator's character. However, in some modern literature, the peculiarity of the narrator's distorted or limited view may, in fact, be the principal drama in which the writer is interested. In fact, the writer may deny the existence or importance of any objective reality or the idea of external subject matter or incident beyond a particular person's subjective view of it.

Consider the difference between a *characterized* narrator and a relatively *uncharacterized* one in these two paragraphs on the subject of a student rebellion. A relatively *uncharacterized* implied author is the narrator of the following account:

> Yesterday the president of the university called in eighty-two state troopers to disperse thirty-three students. Luckily no one was hurt except one boy who was knocked down by a rock thrown from a crowd of students jeering at the rebels. Some sympathetic students helped him to get away while the troopers calmly arrested the other thirty-two rebels. President Hunker was either misinformed about the number and purpose of the student rebels, who seemed only to be peacefully demonstrating, or perhaps he knew that they posed little, if any, real threat but decided to take advantage of a safe and easy way to get a national reputation for being capable of "firmness." I believe it was only last semester that Mr. Hunker had been forced to back down (in the face of a more serious rebellion), and the compromise he then offered the students earned him the epithet of "enlightened" in the *Campus News,* which the trustees tended to interpret as "soft on Communist conspirators."

A *characterized* implied author is the narrator of the second account:

> "How to write nice and real polite about some kind of political animal who squats in the president's chair?" I ask myself. Like sitting in the *Campus News* office scratching beard, hunching my bod over the typewriter, dangling Indian beads like magic over the keys to conjure up the news—and here it come: remember the teacher back in high school who blew up out of sight over some minute infraction of the rules

on the first day he met a class? Well he was always careful to pick some real harmless little kid who'd take it—right? And then we were all supposed to think, "Cheese, if he got that mean because that little kid slouched in his seat instead of sitting up straight, what hell he'd raise if anyone did anything *really* wrong." That is what we were *supposed* to think. But all it ever told me is that he was so up-tight scared of losing authority that he was willing to blow morality and brutalize a harmless kid to make an example. Well, that's just what our president did to thirty-three students yesterday.

How does this second description of the demonstration differ from the first? The second, or characterized, narrator is here allowed to define himself in several ways from which the reader can draw inferences about his character. The writer tells us various external things about his implied author: that he is evidently a reporter on the college newspaper, that he wears a string of beads and a beard. His rambling, colloquial sentence structure and his collegiate mixture of formal and very informal syntax and diction (e.g., *"blew up out of sight* over some *minute infraction* of the rules") help further to characterize him for the reader. The implied author's *reflexive* self-consciousness about his role as a writer who feels so strongly against the president's handling of the campus rebellion that he finds it difficult to write politely on the subject makes this implied author-narrator very different and more highly characterized than the seemingly unself-conscious or *unreflexive* implied author-narrator of the first example. Notice that both examples employ a *first-person narrator*. Evidently, whether the narrator uses *first* or *third person* makes less difference in narration than the way and degree to which the narrator is characterized and/or reflexive. Try writing a one-paragraph narrative on some campus incident where your narrator is uncharacterized and unreflexive; then write another paragraph on the same incident, this time characterizing your narrator and making him reflexive. How does this change your narrative?

Remember that Wright, in the passage we studied, does not make his narrator self-conscious about writing down his thoughts or addressing the audience. In fact, Wright gives his narrator little noticeable character. We are not told anything about his clothes, his looks, or his occupation, and little is betrayed about his feelings. His syntax and diction are not colloquial like Gus's and Bigger's, but they are not unduly formal either. Wright has decided not to use a noticeably idiosyncratic character as a narrator, but a relatively un-characterized observer, whose voice a majority of readers can accept without bias, who throws our full attention on Bigger, Gus, and their concerns, and who carries out unobtrusively the duties that Wright assigns him as narrator.

But there are other differences besides characterized and uncharacterized, reflexive and unreflexive, narration between the first and second accounts of the student demonstration. In the first account the narrator handles the subject as a summary or essaylike commentary, whereas in the second, although the narrator uses some commentary or telling, he actually shows us in a dramatic scene that requires a reader to draw more of his own conclusions. The difference between *showing* and *telling* (that is, presenting dramatically or com-menting and explaining [see Chapter 2]) is an important distinc-tion in all writing; most writing makes some combination of the two types of narration.

Often Wright, like Hemingway, presents a dramatic scene without explaining or commenting on what is being said and why; but unlike Hemingway, he evidently thinks in a few cases that it is important for the narrator to comment on or to explain the narrative. At times, too, Wright allows his nar-rator to be *privileged* (i.e., have some special knowledge be-yond the limitation of an ordinary external observer), lets him look into Bigger's mind and emotions and inform us of his moods or motivations beyond what Bigger himself says. Writers can grant their narrators various kinds of *privileges* or impose *limitations*. Wright grants his narrator the privilege of occasionally seeing inside Bigger's psyche. But Wright does not, for example, allow his narrator the temporal privilege of vision into the future or past, or the spatial privilege of telescopic or omniscient physical vision.

Many modern writers have been more concerned about imposing obvious limitations on their narrators than about granting them the extraordinary privileges of some nineteenth-century narrators. In the twentieth century we are beginning to realize more of the vastness and complexity of the universe; knowledge is expanding, change is accelerating, and many of our old assumptions have been shaken. Perhaps these modern writers are more impressed by man's limitations than they are certain enough of the "big picture" to want to create omnisciently privileged narrators who can tell us what it all means—past, present, and future. The two passages that follow on the subject of President Hunker's motives illustrate the contrast between a limited, participating, "shower" (rather than commentator) and a privileged nonparticipant who "tells" and "explains" for the most part and only occasionally "presents" dramatically for the reader to draw his own conclusions.

First, the limited presenter:

> We were standing there locked-armed and shivering. "Wonder what Hunker's going to do about us? Whatever it is I hope he gets it over before I freeze to death." Then someone yelled, "Hey, look at those beautiful riot troops. Wow! We made it. Look at all of them big devils still coming. Hunker's so up tight he's called out the whole damn state militia. Hey we really made it." I felt a quick, dull pain behind my left ear, and then I was on my knees. I could feel and hear but I couldn't see at all. Something grazed my shoulder and I reached out to grab the pig's leg so he couldn't kick me again. I could hear and feel several hundreds of them yelling and stomping all around me. I heard them yelling and cracking skulls until they got all of us and then everything got quiet and I rolled up in a ball with my arms over my face and head and just waited till the pigs dragged me away.

As far as point of view on Hunker's motivation is concerned, this excited participant is more limited than an ordinary, external observer. Even the riot description is limited to a small part of the action; after the narrator is hit his description is further limited only to what he thinks he hears and feels.

Now, here is the privileged nonparticipant, who, though she claims privileged information (beyond that of an ordinary observer) on President Hunker's motives, is quite limited in other ways:

> My husband is president of the university, so I should know something about this situation. Vernon never meant them any harm, of that I'm quite sure. He's just so afraid that they're going to try to hurt that beautiful new computer. And you know, sometimes I think he's absolutely right. I really think those filthy hippies would stop at nothing sacred. But Vernon is even more petrified of them. I always tell him that savage as they are, there just aren't enough of them to cause real trouble. But he keeps saying, "Look what Castro did with twelve little Cuban Communists," which is all he had when he first started out, if you remember. I'm sure all those hippies yelling such disrespectful and just unmentionable things at him must have seemed two or three times as dangerous to Vernon as Castro and those awful Communist guerrillas. Perhaps he did summon more than enough law officers. Still he did stop all the trouble rather quickly, you must admit.

Is this last account of the demonstration different from the other three with respect to its attitudes toward the reader and the subject? In what ways?

Another possible variation in the relation among narrator, reader, and subject that the writer determines is whether or not to have the narrator be a *participant* or only a *passive observer* in the events he is narrating. Notice that the student rebel in the third example is both a narrator and a participant in the rebellion, a role that gives his account immediacy, though not necessarily more reliability than any of the other accounts.

A writer may make his narrator either *reliable* or *unreliable*, even though he gives no privileges beyond ordinary observation; but if a writer creates a narrator limited in any way, then that narrator becomes unreliable to the degree of his limitation. Even when a writer does not limit his narrator's vision in some way, he may choose to make him unreliable in one of many possible other ways. He may, for instance, make his narrator paranoid, so that the narrator's interpretation of people around him may be extremely undependable. Now, when the writer makes his narrator unreliable he may choose if, when, and how he will let the reader know that the narrator cannot be trusted. He could, for instance, let us know in an initial scene in a psychiatrist's office that a narrator was a paranoid schizophrenic so that the reader's relation to the narrator would from the first be qualified. But a writer might also find it useful for some purposes to let the reader trust the narrator and only later correct the reader's estimate of his reliability. This might be accomplished by introducing another narrator to go over the same subject matter, supplying some very different facts that would change the reader's assumption of the reliability of the earlier narrator. In fact, some writers may wish to entertain us with several completely different points of view on the same subject or incident, narrated, for example, as is often the case in William Faulkner's novels, by several members of the same family. In such a case one narrator might serve to qualify a reader's estimate of the reliability of another narrator. For instance, Faulkner's *The Sound and the Fury* begins with a narrator, Benjie, who is mentally retarded; we know something is wrong but not quite what until other narrators take over.

Perhaps a writer might use three different narrators, each of whom had actually participated in some shameful incident, and then add a fourth narrator (who had not taken any part in the event but who had presumably observed it in an impartial manner) in order to correct earlier accounts and create questions in the reader's mind concerning the reasons for and particular nature of the distortions of the first three narrators. If we were to read all together the four passages on Hunker's motivation in quelling the student rebellion, we might have three unreliable narrators who have had doubt cast on their accounts by the privileged account of the president's wife. If I were to suggest to you, however, that the president's wife was telling the story to a fellow inmate at a mental institution to which she had been committed by her husband three years before, we would be back where we started as far as the president's motivation in calling out eighty-two state troopers was concerned.

Let us consider the possibility that a writer using several narrators' descriptions of this same event might never attempt to corroborate one narrator's view or even suggest that there was any objectively correct version of the subject or incident. The writer might wish rather to impress us with the ultimate subjectivity of all events and knowledge than to lead us to accept any singly objective standard of truth or reality.

You might now try writing several paragraphs about an incident on your own campus using several different kinds of narrators to see what alternative relations you can establish between your narrator, reader, and subject and just how you might be able to use each kind of relation to convey different information or produce different effects. You might even test your narrator's relations on a reader by trying out your paragraphs on a friend and actually finding out how a reader does respond.

For the sake of simplicity, all the possible variations in relations among the narrator or implied author, the reader, and the subject (including whether the narrator is characterized or uncharacterized, reflexive or unreflexive, reliable or unreliable, "showing" or "telling," privileged or limited, participating or passively observing) can be summed up in the metaphor *points of view.* *

In the next chapter we will continue to learn more about point of view in writing when we study how Jonathan Swift, in *A Modest Proposal,* produced irony by setting his reader's point of view at odds with his narrator's point of view. In other words, we will be studying an example of the use of an unreliable narrator and just when, how, and why Swift makes the reader aware of his narrator's unreliability.

It may seem to you that this general discussion of symbolism and point of view is applicable only to narratives such as Wright's; but quite often, expository essays use many of the techniques we have just been discussing.

*For a complete discussion of point of view consult the classic work on this subject, *The Rhetoric of Fiction* by Wayne C. Booth, 1961.

Exercises

1. Using a subject of your choice, compose in Richard Wright's style a narrative or an essay including a narrative section. Use some pattern of symbols and perhaps some games or fantasies to suggest (at first obliquely, then more and more clearly, and finally overtly) some latent needs or desires that you consider important psychologically and socially. Your audience will be both the particular minority you choose and the unconcerned and so far insensitive majority reader, whom you will be trying to involve emotionally as well as intellectually in that problem. Be sure to maintain a balance between concern for the minority-problem subject matter and concern for the general reader who does not yet, for whatever reason, understand or feel concern about your subject. (Refer to the brief diagram in Chapter 5, pp. 84–85, for a quick résumé of the most important features of Wright's style.)

   If you wish to write about the black minority as Wright did, you will have to remember that *Native Son* was written in 1939 and that some of Wright's symbols and assumptions as well as his type of dialogue may have to be reconsidered in order to fit the modern context.

   Maybe it will be less difficult for you to use another kind of minority from which to draw your subject matter. After all, each of us is a member of some minority; if not a racial or ethnic minority perhaps a regional or social or economic minority. Maybe each of us is even unique enough to represent a "minority of one," if only we could understand ourselves well enough. Other examples of possible minority points of view might include:

   a. children or adolescents in an adult world;
   b. a few students trying to get an education in a knowledge-factory university;
   c. an atheist (or a religious person) in a typical church or temple or mosque;
   d. a country person in a city (or vice versa);
   e. a person ill-at-ease in an unfamiliar place, such as a prison;

    f. a straight person in a counterculture group (or vice versa);
    g. a pacifist in the military;
    h. a women's liberationist living with a male chauvinist;
    i. an immigrant in the United States.

"A Modest Proposal

for

Preventing the Children of Poor People in Ireland
from Being a Burden to Their Parents or Country,
and for Making Them Beneficial to the Public"

Jonathan Swift

IT is a melancholy object to those who walk through this
great town, or travel in the country, when they see the streets,
the roads and cabin-doors crowded with beggars of the female
sex, followed by three, four, or six children, all in rags, and
importuning every passenger for an alms. These mothers, instead of being able to work for their honest livelihood, are
forced to employ all their time in strolling, to beg sustenance
for their helpless infants, who, as they grow up, either turn
thieves for want of work, or leave their dear native country
to fight for the Pretender in Spain, or sell themselves to the
Barbadoes.

I think it is agreed by all parties that this prodigious number of children, in the arms, or on the backs, or at the heels
of their mothers, and frequently of their fathers, is in the
present deplorable state of the kingdom a very great addi-
tional grievance; and therefore whoever could find out a fair,
cheap, and easy method of making these children sound and
useful members of the commonwealth would deserve so well
of the public as to have his statue set up for a preserver of
the nation.

From Louis A. Landa, ed., *Jonathan Swift: Gulliver's Travels and Other
Writings* (Boston: Houghton Mifflin, 1960), pp. 439–446.

But my intention is very far from being confined to provide only for the children of professed beggars; it is of a much greater extent, and shall take in the whole number of infants at a certain age who are born of parents in effect as little able to support them as those who demand our charity in the streets.

As to my own part, having turned my thoughts for many years upon this important subject, and maturely weighed the several schemes of other projectors, I have always found them grossly mistaken in their computation. It is true a child just dropped from its dam may be supported by her milk for a solar year with little other nourishment, at most not above the value of two shillings, which the mother may certainly get, or the value in scraps, by her lawful occupation of begging, and it is exactly at one year old that I propose to provide for them, in such a manner as, instead of being a charge upon their parents, or the parish, or wanting food and raiment for the rest of their lives, they shall, on the contrary, contribute to the feeding and partly to the clothing of many thousands.

There is likewise another great advantage in my scheme, that it will prevent those voluntary abortions, and that horrid practice of women murdering their bastard children, alas, too frequent among us, sacrificing the poor innocent babes, I doubt, more to avoid the expense than the shame, which would move tears and pity in the most savage and inhuman breast.

The number of souls in Ireland being usually reckoned one million and a half, of these I calculate there may be about two hundred thousand couples whose wives are breeders, from which number I subtract thirty thousand couples who are able to maintain their own children, although I apprehend there cannot be so many under the present distresses of the kingdom, but this being granted, there will remain an hundred and seventy thousand breeders. I again subtract fifty thousand for those women who miscarry, or whose children die by accident or disease within the year. There only remain an hundred and twenty thousand children of poor parents annually born: the question therefore is, how this number shall be reared, and provided for, which, as I have already said, under the present situation of affairs is utterly impossible by all the methods hitherto proposed, for we can neither employ them in handicraft or agriculture; we neither build houses (I mean in the country), nor cultivate land: they can very seldom pick up a livelihood by stealing until they arrive at six years old, except where they are of towardly parts, although I confess they learn the rudiments much earlier, during which time they can however be properly looked upon only as probationers, as I have been informed by a principal gentleman in the County of Cavan, who protested to me that he never knew above one or two instances under the age of six, even in a part of the kingdom so renowned for the quickest proficiency in that art.

I am assured by our merchants that a boy or a girl before twelve years old, is no saleable commodity, and even when they come to this age, they will not yield above three pounds, or three pounds and half-a-crown at most on the Exchange, which cannot turn to account either to the parents or the kingdom, the charge of nutriment and rags having been at least four times that value.

I shall now therefore humbly propose my own thoughts, which I hope will not be liable to the least objection.

I have been assured by a very knowing American of my acquaintance in London, that a young healthy child well nursed is at a year old a most delicious, nourishing and wholesome food, whether stewed, roasted, baked, or boiled, and I make no doubt that it will equally serve in a fricassee, or a ragout.

I do therefore humbly offer it to public consideration, that of the hundred and twenty thousand children already computed, twenty thousand may be reserved for breed, whereof only one fourth part to be males, which is more than we allow to sheep, black-cattle, or swine, and my reason is that these children are seldom the fruits of marriage, a circumstance not much regarded by our savages, therefore one male will be sufficient to serve four females. That the remaining hundred thousand may at a year old be offered in sale to the persons of quality, and fortune, through the kingdom, always advising the mother to let them suck plentifully in the last month, so as to render them plump, and fat for a good table. A child will make two dishes at an entertainment for friends, and when the family dines alone, the fore or hind quarter will make a reasonable dish, and seasoned with a little pepper or salt will be very good boiled on the fourth day, especially in winter.

I have reckoned upon a medium, that a child just born will weigh twelve pounds, and in a solar year if tolerably nursed increaseth to twenty-eight pounds.

I grant this food will be somewhat dear, and therefore very proper for landlords, who, as they have already devoured most of the parents, seem to have the best title to the children.

Infant's flesh will be in season throughout the year, but more plentiful in March, and a little before and after, for we are told by a grave author, an eminent French physician, that fish being a prolific diet, there are more children born in Roman Catholic countries about nine months after Lent than at any other season; therefore reckoning a year after Lent, the markets will be more glutted than usual, because the number of Popish infants is at least three to one in this kingdom, and therefore it will have one other collateral advantage by lessening the number of Papists among us.

I have already computed the charge of nursing a beggar's child (in which list I reckon all cottagers, labourers, and four-fifths of the farmers) to be about two shillings *per annum,* rags included, and I believe no gentleman would repine to give ten shillings for the carcass of a good fat child, which, as I have said, will make four dishes of excellent nutritive meat, when he hath only some particular friend or his own family to dine with him. Thus the Squire will learn to be a good landlord and grow popular among his tenants, the mother will have eight shillings net profit, and be fit for work until she produces another child.

Those who are more thrifty (as I must confess the times require) may flay the carcass; the skin of which artificially dressed, will make admirable gloves for ladies, and summer boots for fine gentlemen.

As to our city of Dublin, shambles * may be appointed for this purpose, in the most convenient parts of it, and butchers we may be assured will not be wanting, although I rather recommend buying the children alive, and dressing them hot from the knife, as we do roasting pigs.

A very worthy person, a true lover of his country, and whose virtues I highly esteem, was lately pleased, in discoursing on this matter to offer a refinement upon my scheme. He said that many gentlemen of this kingdom, having of late destroyed their deer, he conceived that the want of venison might be well supplied by the bodies of young lads and maidens, not exceeding fourteen years of age, nor under twelve, so great a number of both sexes in every county being now ready to starve, for want of work and service: and these to be disposed of by their parents if alive, or otherwise by their nearest relations. But with due deference to so excellent a friend, and so deserving a patriot, I cannot be altogether in his sentiments. For as to the males, my American acquaintance assured me from frequent experience that their flesh was generally tough and lean, like that of our schoolboys, by continual exercise, and their taste disagreeable, and to fatten them would not answer the charge. Then as to the females, it would, I think with humble submission, be a loss to the public, because they soon would become breeders themselves: and besides, it is not improbable that some scrupulous people might be apt to censure such a practice (although indeed very unjustly) as a little bordering upon cruelty, which I confess, hath always been with me the strongest objection against any project, howsoever well intended.

But in order to justify my friend, he confessed that this expedient was put into his head by the famous Psalmanazar,** a native of the island Formosa, who came from thence to

* Slaughterhouses.
** A contemporary impostor who published a fictitious account of Formosa in 1704.

London, above twenty years ago, and in conversation told my friend that in his country when any young person happened to be put to death, the executioner sold the carcass to persons of quality, as a prime dainty, and that, in his time, the body of a plump girl of fifteen, who was crucified for an attempt to poison the emperor, was sold to his Imperial Majesty's Prime Minister of State, and other great Mandarins of the Court, in joints from the gibbet, at four hundred crowns. Neither indeed can I deny that if the same use were made of several plump young girls in this town who, without one single groat to their fortunes, cannot stir abroad without a chair, and appear at the playhouse and assemblies in foreign fineries, which they never will pay for, the kingdom would not be the worse.

Some persons of a desponding spirit are in great concern about that vast number of poor people, who are aged, diseased, or maimed, and I have been desired to employ my thoughts what course may be taken to ease the nation of so grievous an encumbrance. But I am not in the least pain upon that matter, because it is very well known that they are every day dying, and rotting, by cold, and famine, and filth, and vermin, as fast as can be reasonably expected. And as to the younger labourers they are now in almost as hopeful a condition. They cannot get work, and consequently pine away from want of nourishment, to a degree that if at any time they are accidentally hired to common labour, they have not strength to perform it; and thus the country and themselves are in a fair way of being soon delivered from the evils to come.

I have too long digressed, and therefore shall return to my subject. I think the advantages by the proposal which I have made are obvious and many, as well as of the highest importance.

For first, as I have already observed, it would greatly lessen the number of Papists, with whom we are yearly over-run, being the principal breeders of the nation, as well as our most dangerous enemies, and who stay at home on purpose with a design to deliver the kingdom to the Pretender, hoping to take their advantage by the absence of so many good

Protestants, who have chosen rather to leave their country than stay at home and pay tithes against their conscience to an idolatrous Episcopal curate.

Secondly, the poorer tenants will have something valuable of their own, which by law may be made liable to distress, and help to pay their landlord's rent, their corn and cattle being already seized, and money a thing unknown.

Thirdly, whereas the maintenance of an hundred thousand children, from two years old, and upwards, cannot be computed at less than ten shillings a piece *per annum,* the nation's stock will be thereby increased fifty thousand pounds *per annum,* besides the profit of a new dish, introduced to the tables of all gentlemen of fortune in the kingdom, who have any refinement in taste, and the money will circulate among ourselves, the goods being entirely of our own growth and manufacture.

Fourthly, the constant breeders, besides the gain of eight shillings sterling *per annum,* by the sale of their children, will be rid of the charge of maintaining them after the first year.

Fifthly, this food would likewise bring great custom to taverns, where the vintners will certainly be so prudent as to procure the best receipts for dressing it to perfection, and consequently have their houses frequented by all the fine gentlemen, who justly value themselves upon their knowledge in good eating; and a skilful cook, who understands how to oblige his guests, will contrive to make it as expensive as they please.

Sixthly, this would be a great inducement to marriage, which all wise nations have either encouraged by rewards, or enforced by laws and penalties. It would increase the care and tenderness of mothers towards their children, when they were sure of a settlement for life, to the poor babes, provided in some sort by the public to their annual profit instead of expense. We should soon see an honest emulation among the married women, which of them could bring the fattest child to the market. Men would become as fond of their wives, during the time of their pregnancy, as they are now of their mares in foal, their cows in calf, or sows when they are ready to farrow, nor offer to beat or kick them (as it is too frequent a practice) for fear of a miscarriage.

Many other advantages might be enumerated. For instance, the addition of some thousand carcasses in our exportation of barrelled beef; the propagation of swine's flesh, and improvement in the art of making good bacon, so much wanted among us by the great destruction of pigs, too frequent at our tables, are no way comparable in taste or magnificence to a well-grown, fat yearling child, which roasted whole will make a considerable figure at a Lord Mayor's feast, or any other public entertainment. But this and many others I omit, being studious of brevity.

Supposing that one thousand families in this city would be constant customers for infants flesh, besides others who might have it at merry meetings, particularly weddings and christenings; I compute that Dublin would take off annually about twenty thousand carcasses, and the rest of the kingdom (where probably they will be sold somewhat cheaper) the remaining eighty thousand.

I can think of no one objection that will possibly be raised against this proposal, unless it should be urged that the number of people will be thereby much lessened in the kingdom. This I freely own, and it was indeed one principal design in offering it to the world. I desire the reader will observe, that I calculate my remedy *for this one individual Kingdom of* Ireland, *and for no other that ever was, is, or, I think, ever can be upon earth.* Therefore let no man talk to me of other expedients: *Of taxing our absentees at five shillings a pound: Of using neither clothes, nor household furniture, except what is of our own growth and manufacture: Of utterly rejecting the materials and instruments that promote foreign luxury: Of curing the expensiveness of pride, vanity, idleness, and gaming in our women: Of introducing a vein of parsimony, prudence, and temperance: Of learning to love our country, wherein we differ even from* Laplanders, *and the inhabitants* of Topinamboo: *Of quitting our animosities and factions, nor act any longer like the* Jews, *who were murdering one another at the very moment their city was taken: Of being a little cautious not to sell our country and consciences for nothing: Of teaching landlords to have at least one degree of mercy towards their tenants.* Lastly, *of putting a spirit of honesty, industry, and skill into our shopkeepers, who, if a resolution could now be taken to buy only our native goods, would immediately unite to cheat and exact upon us in the price, the measure and the goodness, nor could ever yet be brought to make one fair proposal of just dealing, though often and earnestly invited to it.*

Therefore I repeat, let no man talk to me of these and the like expedients, till he hath at least a glimpse of hope that there will ever be some hearty and sincere attempt to put them in practice.

But as to myself, having been wearied out for many years with offering vain, idle, visionary thoughts, and at length utterly despairing of success, I fortunately fell upon this proposal, which as it is wholly new, so it hath something solid and real, of no expense and little trouble, full in our own power, and whereby we can incur no danger in disobliging England. For this kind of commodity will not bear exportation, the flesh being of too tender a consistence to admit a long continuance in salt, *although perhaps I could name a country which would be glad to eat up our whole nation without it.*

After all I am not so violently bent upon my own opinion as to reject any offer, proposed by wise men, which shall be found equally innocent, cheap, easy and effectual. But before some thing of that kind shall be advanced in contradiction to my scheme, and offering a better, I desire the author, or authors, will be pleased maturely to consider two points. First, as things now stand, how they will be able to find food and raiment for a hundred thousand useless mouths and backs? And secondly, there being a round million of creatures in human figure, throughout this kingdom, whose whole subsistence put into a common stock would leave them in debt two millions of pounds sterling; adding those who are beggars by profession, to the bulk of farmers, cottagers, and labourers with their wives and children, who are beggars in effect; I desire those politicians who dislike my overture, and may perhaps be so bold to attempt an answer, that they will first ask the parents of these mortals whether they would not at this day think it a great happiness to have been sold for food at a year old, in the manner I prescribe, and thereby have avoided such a perpetual scene of misfortunes as they have since gone through, by the oppression of landlords, the impossibility of paying rent without money or trade, the want of common sustenance, with neither house nor clothes to cover them from the inclemencies of weather, and the most inevitable prospect of entailing the like, or greater miseries upon their breed for ever.

I profess in the sincerity of my heart that I have not the least personal interest in endeavouring to promote this necessary work, having no other motive than the *public good of my country, by advancing our trade, providing for infants, relieving the poor, and giving some pleasure to the rich.* I have no children by which I can propose to get a single penny; the youngest being nine years old, and my wife past child-bearing.

7

How Form and Content
Work Together
in an Ironic Style

WHEN we studied Hemingway's style we practiced "showing" rather than "telling"—that is, we practiced arranging and writing in order unobtrusively or covertly to mold a reader's response without having to rely on more conventional overt evaluation or commentary. Being able to show a reader how to feel rather than to tell him is a necessary first step toward writing effective irony, for what you must do to write irony is tell a reader one thing and at the same time show him covertly that you mean something quite different. But what are some of the techniques and ways of writing that will be effective enough to cue a reader that you do not mean what you, or your narrator, are saying? To find and explain some of these will be the object of the following analysis of Swift's rhetoric. Irony is useful in all kinds of writing, but without some skill and care in its cultivation it can grow into a brier patch of misunderstanding and confusion for your reader.

Swift's *Modest Proposal* offers a shocking solution—cannibalism—to the poverty of Ireland's masses. How could a writer advocate the wholesale murder and eating of babies as a solution to a social problem? If we can discover through stylistic analysis exactly *what* Swift is doing, perhaps we will be able to see *why* he is doing it. We might begin by considering the style of Swift's opening sentence, a sentence of a very different kind from any we have met so far, but fairly typical of *A Modest Proposal*. Here is Swift's sentence in a diagrammatic form:

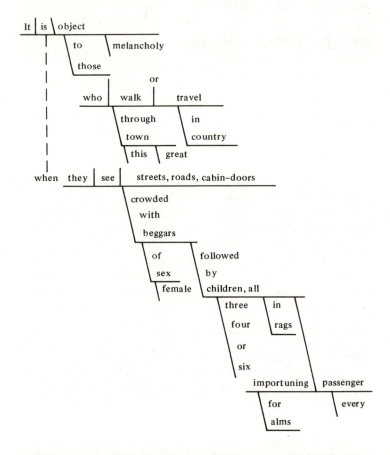

It is easy to see that the short main clause is modified by long subordinate clauses, each new branch heavy with modifiers. But the relation between the syntax of this sentence and the rest of its rhetoric needs more careful study.

Where do the abstract and general words occur in the

sentence? The word "object," an abstract noun, appears in the main clause. The more concrete and specific nouns fall in the subordinate clauses: "streets," "roads," "cabin-doors," "beggars," "three, four, or six children," "all in rags." Swift's more active and colorful verb forms, too, like "importuning," "followed," "walk," "see," "travel," are found in the subordinate part of the sentence; a form of "to be" is used in his main clause. Not only is the stronger, more arresting vocabulary located in the subordinate clauses, but the only emphatic rhetorical figures in the sentence appear there too.

What figures does Swift use? He compounds words in the phrase "the streets, the roads and cabin-doors." Another triplet occurs in the subordinate end of the sentence in his mention of "three, four, or six children." Compounding is a figure often used for emphasis: the first triplet emphasizes the present extent of the poverty in town and country, while the second emphasizes the large number of people affected both in the present and in the future. It is important to see that although we readers feel this poverty is sad and shocking, Swift's narrator uses no words that denote the feelings of the poor. He reserves, on the contrary, an emotionally detached adjective like "melancholy" to express the feelings of those who, like the narrator, must observe the poor, those "objects."

Why would Swift play his rhetoric against his narrator's point of view and sentence structure—use an arresting vocabulary and emphatic figures in the subordinate part of his sentence and keep his main clause colorless and unemphatic? The way the narrator casts his sentence seems to suggest that he considers a pitiful close-up of suffering mothers and children subordinate to the detached views and "melancholy" feelings of well-to-do observers like himself. However, in opposition to the narrator's point of view and sentence construction, Swift loads the subordinate clauses with a vivid vocabulary and emphatic compounding that take away from the narrator the command of the reader's attention and the control of his feelings. Swift has created a narrator whom he doesn't seem to agree with—and evidently does not want readers to agree with either.

In the first sentence, and in other sentences of the *Proposal*,*
the main clause reflects the point of view of the proposer,
who is trying to share with his audience a detached, long-
distance view of poverty. The subordinate clauses contain
rhetorically emphasized pity-producing realities of poverty. The
contrast alienates us, perhaps unconsciously at first, from a
narrator who can subordinate the concrete and compounded
plight of the poor to the abstract concerns of gentlemen like
himself. Swift's style operates effectively on two levels: on the
level of the proposer and his intended audience; and on
the level Swift has directed us, rhetorically, to see in a much
less detached way that reveals and condemns the proposer's
callous and selfish feelings. As readers, we are forced to share
this second point of view and not the point of view of the
narrator.

We can call the narrator's point of view the *overt* or
apparent point of view; the opposed point of view, which the
reader shares with Swift, we might call the *covert* or concealed
point of view. From the beginning of *A Modest Proposal*,
Swift disengages us from the overt narrator by providing,
through his rhetorical techniques, a covert set of values upon
which the reader can base his judgment of the values shared
by the overt narrator and people like him. In Swift's very
first sentence the direction of sympathy and interest of the
audience part company with the narrator, never again to merge.

If we now assume, temporarily at least, that the sentences we have examined are not simply false leads or un-
typical of Swift's style in *A Modest Proposal*, we can then
hypothesize that the style of these sentences might be considered a microcosm of the style of the whole *Proposal;* that
throughout the work Swift may be going to build simultaneously
a consistent overt-narrative point of view and an effectively
controlled but covert criticism of the overt point of view. Since
it will probably be easier for us to see what obvious techniques
Swift uses to set up and control his overt point of view, let
us first consider this more conventional part of Swift's rhetoric.

---

* For example, see the first two sentences of paragraph 2, p. 112.

Later we can turn to the more unusual, concealed techniques Swift uses to set up a covert point of view that discredits the proposer and offers an alternative, at every turn, to his proposal.

Rhetoric of the Overt Point of View

If you look closely at some of the sentences that the proposer uses you will notice that sometimes they are interrupted by parenthesis, and sometimes by a gratuitous detail inserted or an idea added:

> I have already computed the charge of nursing a beggar's child (in which list I reckon all cottagers, labourers, and four-fifths of the farmers) to be about two shillings *per annum,* rags included.

And Swift includes a large number of sentences in which the normal appearance of subject, verb, and complement is delayed so that the sense is not clear until the end:

> As to my own part, having turned my thoughts for many years upon this important subject, and maturely weighed the several schemes of other projectors, I have always found them grossly mistaken in their computation.

This kind of delayed-sense sentence is sometimes called a *periodic sentence.*

Not just the first one, but most of the sentences Swift constructs for the narrator or proposer are long and carefully contrived complex or compound-complex. The sentence structures that are excluded from the narrator's style (such as simple or compound, with loose subject-verb-object order) usually seem casual and colloquial, apparently the result of little conscious control or contriving. If we were to tape record an ordinary conversation and then diagram all its sentences, we would probably find that whole or fragmented simple and compound sentences, in a subject-verb-complement order, predominate. The sentences that Swift constructs for the narrator or proposer, on the contrary, take time, care, and usually a pencil and piece of scratch paper to execute well.

Swift could be using sentence structure and grammar to characterize his proposer as an extremely diligent, painstaking planner, one who offers his considered thoughts to a supposedly serious audience. This bit of characterization would be consistent with a number of direct pronouncements that Swift puts into the mouth of the proposer, such as when he has him twice assert that he has "maturely" weighed his subject for many years, or when he has him say such things as "I have reckoned upon a medium," "I have already computed the charge," "I calculate." These phrases suggest the care and cautious consideration he has given his proposal; so, too, does a figure of speech on which the proposer relies heavily. This figure is called *litotes,* a roundabout way of affirming something by negating its opposite. The proposer uses it in such phrases as "neither indeed can I deny, that . . . ," "it is not improbable that . . . ," "I believe no gentleman would repine to give ten shillings for the carcass . . ." Instead of making a positive statement, Swift has the proposer carefully deny the negative, a habit that again suggests the proposer's cautious, circumspect character.

When we look at the vocabulary Swift has given the proposer, we see that it is very sober, precise, and businesslike, and thus conforms to what we have already learned of the proposer's character. The narrator is almost ridiculously careful to specify in his calculations the "solar year" (one revolution of the earth around the sun), which makes a negligible difference of about twenty minutes from what was in Swift's time known as the "astral year" (the older, less scientific way of measuring the year as one revolution of the sun relative to the fixed stars). He remembers to include small, painful details, such as the cost of raising the average one-year-old at two shillings, "rags included," and the exact market price of a twelve-year-old: "three pounds, or three pounds and half-a-crown at most on the Exchange."

The proposer frequently makes use of words that seem more appropriate to the subject of animal husbandry than to that of economic reform: "It is true a child just dropped from its dam may be supported by her milk for a solar year. . . ." Apparently the proposer is using the language of animal husbandry not merely as a metaphor, but as a basic assumption. It is just a step for him to go from seeing the Irish poor as animals to seeing them as meat. The assumption seems to persist until, by the end of the *Proposal,* he regards as illusory even their resemblance to human beings when he calls them "creatures in human figure." Along with the vocabulary of agricultural economics the proposer uses the jargon of social arithmetic:

> Whereas the maintenance of an hundred thousand children, from two years old, and upwards, cannot be computed at less than ten shillings a piece *per annum,* the nation's stock will be thereby increased fifty thousand pounds *per annum,*

and

> Supposing that one thousand families in this city would be constant customers for infants flesh, besides others who might have it at merry meetings . . . I compute that Dublin would take off annually about twenty thousand carcasses, and the rest of the kingdom (where probably they will be sold somewhat cheaper) the remaining eighty thousand.

He has turned people into animals, then meat, and from meat, logically, into tonnage worth a price per pound. The narrator's specialized vocabularies help define him as a wide-ranging social scientist, at home in business, political economy, agricultural economics, statistics—as scrupulously careful and seemingly expert a social planner as anyone would want.

The organization of the *Proposal* shows a similar careful contriving of parts to fit an obviously premeditated formal pattern. These divisions (their names are given in parentheses) correspond dutifully to the conventional five-part organization taught in the classical-rhetoric textbooks of Swift's day. Paragraphs 1 to 7 (*exordium*) state the nature of the problem and the intention or purpose of the present proposal. Paragraphs 8 through 16 (*narratio*), beginning "I shall now therefore humbly propose my own thoughts," contain the statement of the proposal itself. A formal digression that considers and rejects one possible refinement on the proposal follows in paragraphs 17 through 19; it ends with the first sentence of paragraph 20 ("I have too long digressed, and therefore shall return to my subject"). Paragraphs 20 through 28 (*confirmatio*), beginning with the second sentence of paragraph 20 ("I think the advantages by the proposal which I have made are obvious and many"), followed by each subsequent paragraph beginning "first," "secondly," "thirdly," etc., enumerate these advantages in order to prove the worth of the proposal. Paragraphs 29 and 30 (*refutatio*), beginning "I can think of no one objection that will possibly be raised against this proposal, unless it be urged that . . . ," attempt to refute possible objections to the proposal. The final three paragraphs (*peroratio*) summarize the strongest arguments and disclaim any "personal interest in endeavouring to promote this necessary work. . . ."

The noticeably careful and mechanical manner in which the divisions of *A Modest Proposal* correspond to the conventional organization taught in the classical-rhetoric textbooks may be one technical means Swift uses to characterize the proposer: the five-part structure makes him seem conventional, formal, precisely contriving. We do not usually think of organization as a means an author might use to characterize a narrator. Yet notice how the fact that the proposal is organized in this formal way, rather than in a looser, more casual way, contributes to and complements the pattern of cautious premeditation that we have seen in the proposer's character through his sentence structure and his vocabulary.

Why would Swift want to create the impression that the proposer is consistently careful and controlled? We are stymied here if we assume that style must always mirror content. It is true that in a number of the styles that we have studied (e.g., Donne's) it does. But you will begin now to see how much more complex the relation between style and subject can be. Let us consider the possibility that Swift means the proposer's rational stylistic traits to form a contrast with his outrageous proposal.

By playing the proposer's careful control against his scheme's barbarian perversity, Swift may be able to prevent his readers from simply laughing at the ridiculousness of the proposal; instead, they will have to consider just what perverted values and assumptions would allow such a diligent, thoughtful, and conventional man to propose so perverse a plan.

When we dismiss a Hitler, for example, as a madman, we do not have to try to understand the warped assumptions and values that led to his acts. Swift makes it difficult for us to discount his proposer as a lunatic, or even to explain him away as a sadist who enjoys cruelty for its own sake; in fact, he carefully introduces evidence that the proposer is not a particularly vicious individual. Cruelty, he tells us, is his "strongest objection against any project, howsoever well intended." Swift even pointedly shows us how very sympathetic the proposer feels toward babies murdered by their unwed mothers (an expedient forced upon them by extreme poverty), when he calls attention to

> that horrid practice of women murdering their bastard children, alas, too frequent among us, sacrificing the poor innocent babes, I doubt, more to avoid the expense than the shame, which would move tears and pity in the most savage and inhuman breast.

Swift gives the proposer other opportunities to show us his ethical character—his *ethos*. The proposer frequently attempts to ingratiate himself by his humility and modesty: "I shall now therefore humbly propose my own thoughts." But then Swift has him add, "which I hope will not be liable to the least objection." Any image of humility he might have projected is erased by our surprise at his ludicrous pride. He tries to impress us favorably by letting us know of his international friendships with important men of affairs, like "a very knowing American of my acquaintance in London." Again, any favorable impression we might have formed is dispelled when this important friend turns out to be some sort of cannibal connoisseur, a man who has eaten children of various ages so often that his palate has become a reliable judge of human flesh:

> For as to the males, my American acquaintance assured me
> from frequent experience that their flesh was generally tough
> and lean, like that of our schoolboys, by continual exercise,
> and their taste disagreeable. . . ."

Then he boasts of his acquaintance with a "principal gentleman
in the County of Cavan": but we learn that this man is an
expert on petty thievery. Another friend, "a very worthy person,
a true lover of his country, and whose virtues I highly esteem,"
turns out to have been duped by the infamous Psalmanazar
hoax, and to have conceived a monstrous plan for substituting
teen-agers for venison. In each case, any good opinion the
narrator might hope that we would form of him for knowing
such an important person is counteracted by what we learn of
this acquaintance.

The proposer uses several other means to impress the audience favorably. For instance, he insinuates his middle-class
patriotism when he calls Dublin "this great city," like a Fourth
of July politician. He repeats the word "our" ("our charity,"
"our savages," "our merchants") to suggest to his readers an
identity of point of view. His plan even aids the common cause
of Protestantism, for

> it would greatly lessen the number of Papists, with whom
> we are yearly over-run, being the principal breeders of the
> nation, as well as our most dangerous enemies. . . ."

This backfires, of course, not because he has misjudged the
hatred of the Irish Protestant for the Catholic, but because he
has misjudged the revulsion that perhaps even an Irish Protestant would feel at hearing such a motivation openly avowed.

The proposer tries also to present himself as an upholder,
even a reformer, of morality in Ireland:

> Sixthly, this would be a great inducement to marriage, which
> all wise nations have either encouraged by rewards, or en-
> forced by laws and penalties.

and

> Men would become as fond of their wives, during the time
> of their pregnancy, as they are now of their mares in foal,

their cows in calf, or sows when they are ready to farrow, nor offer to beat or kick them (as it is too frequent a practice) for fear of a miscarriage.

In each of the above examples, morality is supposed to be amended by the institution of a ghastly moral perversion. His moral zeal backfires because he has no idea of the adverse effects of his moral inversion on the emotions of his readers. Finally, he presents himself as someone who is going to increase the general well-being and even pleasure of the Irish. Infants' flesh, he suggests, will be just the thing to serve at merry meetings, particularly at "weddings and christenings" (both these rituals [or sacraments] are, of course, intimately connected with the babies that will be eaten to celebrate them).

Since the proposer generally takes such great care to establish his rectitude and insinuate his expert credentials, what are we to make of such gross errors as his supposedly learned reference to Rabelais as a "grave author"? Anyone who has read Rabelais finds him wildly humorous; the proposer is evidently a man who takes literally one of the world's great satirists. Most of Swift's contemporaries would remember the Psalmanazar affair as a famous hoax—he did not come from Formosa, and fabricated the stories that he told. Yet the proposer—again taking a joke literally—quotes Psalmanazar on the details of cannibalism in Formosa. Swift gives the proposer these moments of weak-mindedness when he unwittingly throws away his credentials as an authority. The two examples I have given may not be as readily grasped by a modern student as by one of Swift's contemporaries, but no American should be able to accept the following statement at face value:

> I have been assured by a very knowing American of my acquaintance in London, that a young healthy child well nursed is at a year old a most delicious, nourishing and wholesome food, whether stewed, roasted, baked, or boiled. . . ."

The bludgeon effect of the sheer inhumanity of the proposal itself tends to blind us to other, more subtle covert means of criticizing the proposer. Think, for instance, of the lack of compassion implied by the playful and artificial alliteration of "*f*amine," "*f*ilth," and "*v*ermin," used by the proposer to characterize the direst suffering of the poor. And what are we to make of the poetic emphasis alliteration gives his picture of a fifteen-year-old girl who was first crucified, then sold to the court as meat in "*j*oints from the *g*ibbet"? The proposer seems not to realize that by playfully alliterating and embroidering horrors he increases the reader's horror of him and his proposal. If the proposer is not in control of our feelings, who is? This might be a good time to return to our initial hypothesis, based on a rhetorical study of the first sentence. Swift is manipulating two points of view, that of the overt proposer and that of a covert author. If the proposer does not control our feelings, then evidently the covert point of view does.

Rhetoric of the Covert Point of View

Dialogue is the most conventional method of handling two different points of view; to sustain two antithetical points of view in a monologue requires the creation of an unconventional, emotion-producing rhetoric. The covert point of view will have to manipulate feelings that the overt proposer has engendered by accident and let go by default.

Four distinct varieties of *verbal irony*—of saying one thing and meaning another—result from a similar clash of overt and covert points of view. The first of these four types, *the cliché image*, depends on the use of a cliché by the proposer, which is designed to come to life for the reader as an uncomfortable sense impression, turning him against the proposer. Consider what happens to the word "figure" in the phrase, "a well-grown, fat yearling child, which roasted whole will make a considerable *figure* at a Lord Mayor's feast." The proposer's use of the cliché "make [we would say 'cut'] a considerable figure" when the "figure" is not a guest but the entrée, brings the overtly colorless word "figure" to felt life as an image in the covert point of view, as the reader visualizes a crisp and burnt figure of a little child, "roasted whole," with perhaps an apple in its mouth. The audience is forced to feel the image rather than accept the proposer's cliché as a colorless idiom.

A second kind of verbal irony, the *covert pun,* results from the proposer's use of a word in the overtly material sense that has, covertly, a moral or spiritual meaning. In this group we find his use of "poor people," with "poor" meaning "indigent" to the proposer, and "pitiable" to the covert point of view. And in the phrase "instead of being a charge upon their parents or the parish," "charge" means overtly "expense," covertly suggests "moral responsibility."

Besides the use of clichés that come to life and words with material denotation and moral connotation, Swift counters the overt point of view by a third ironic device, a *covert metaphor* —the use of words that have literal meaning to the proposer but that flower covertly into metaphor. In "*butchers* will not be wanting," for instance, "butchers" stands overtly for the occupation, covertly for a murderous propensity.

A fourth ironic verbal strategy, the *obviously perverse implicit definition,* involves the proposer's use of words whose meanings are warped out of all recognition by the contexts in which they appear. What, for instance, do the words "gentleman" and "good" mean in the following sentence: "I believe no gentleman would repine to give ten shillings for the carcass of a good fat child"? To the proposer a "gentleman" is evidently not-ungenerous cannibal, and a "good" child is a dead, but tasty one. What does "thrifty" signify in this passage: "Those who are more thrifty . . . may flay the carcass" (i.e., cut off the child's skin to use for leather)? What kinds of "persons of quality" buy the carcasses of young people to serve at home to the family? And what do such words as "good table," "wholesome food," "modest," "sentiments," "practical," and many others mean in the contexts in which they appear, some repeatedly, in *A Modest Proposal?* The covert point of view criticizes the proposer's language whenever Swift puts into the context of cannibalism words that ordinarily connote decent, middle-class values.

Why would Swift thus criticize his proposer's vocabulary? Could he be suggesting that the meanings of the proposer's words have been twisted to fit false values and assumptions? Swift once compared a room whose wood-paneled walls had been warped crooked with time to the warping of society's institutions and values from their original aims and purposes. On the walls hung pictures, at crooked angles to conform to the crooked paneling, which was analogous to society's attempt to disguise its growing corruption by warping its words to fit the decayed social values and institutions. Only by reviving the original meaning of words did Swift think it was possible for society to see how far it had strayed from its original purpose and how much in need of reform (i.e., return to original purpose) were its decaying values and institutions. The proposer hangs his words to match his values, but with the covert point of view Swift reveals the warp in the proposer's definitions of important words and hence shows the reader the shocking social perversions being institutionalized when, for example, a "thrifty gentleman" has come to mean an *un*gentle man who is willing, literally as well as figuratively, to "skin" the poor.

Swift uses a different kind of covert technique in the following sentence to discredit the proposer and give the reader a positive counterproposal:

> Therefore let no man talk to me of other expedients: *Of taxing our absentees at five shillings a pound: Of using neither clothes, nor household furniture, except what is of our own growth and manufacture: Of utterly rejecting the materials and instruments that promote foreign luxury: Of curing the expensiveness of pride, vanity, idleness, and gaming in our women: Of introducing a vein of parsimony, prudence and temperance: Of learning to love our country, wherein we differ even from* Laplanders, *and the inhabitants of* Topinamboo: *Of quitting our animosities and factions, nor act any longer like the* Jews, *who were murdering one another at the very moment their city was taken: Of being a little cautious not to sell our country and consciences for nothing: Of teaching landlords to have at least one degree of mercy towards their tenants.*

This sentence contains the sort of irony that, by the very pretense of passing over a certain matter, presents it in great detail. This particular technique of irony is called *paralipsis*. Notice that Swift emphasizes the points of the counterproposal by casting them in parallel grammatical construction, creating a sentence that is unique in this essay because of its use of this rhetorical device. Each phrase also has an unqualified directness absent elsewhere in *A Modest Proposal*. Swift further attracts the Irish reader's attention to this sentence by repeating the word "our" in nearly every phrase, thereby fixing the reader with his personal share of responsibility and guilt. Notice that most of Swift's proposals in this sentence are *moral* expedients rather than material ones—including a further emphasis on the need for improved relations between landlord and tenant, people and their country.

Less obvious, but even more controlling than any of the means of generating irony we have discussed so far is Swift's use of a covert organization for the entire *Proposal*. Overtly, the proposer organizes in an unimaginative fashion, dutifully following the textbook models. Covertly, Swift is using a far more imaginative organization to guide the audience to his system of positive values. One particular word group occurs in almost every paragraph of the *Proposal*: "mother" ("father," "parent")/"child" ("infant," "babe"). On the surface this is not at all surprising, since the narrator is talking about mothers selling their children as meat; but we might have expected a smart proposer either to have avoided or to have found some more colorless substitutes for these emotion-laden words that seem to stand almost universally for a relationship of care, love, and mutual trust. By having the proposer mention frequently the parent-child relationship, Swift establishes in the reader's mind a revulsion against the narrator's complete unconcern with this basic natural bond. Other reiterated word groups include "landlord"/"tenant," "kingdom" ("country")/"people." In some sentences the landlord-tenant relation is juxtaposed with the mother-child relationship, for both landlord and mother will profit from the sale of babies:

> Thus the Squire will learn to be a good landlord and grow
> popular among his tenants, the mother will have eight shillings
> net profit, and be fit for work until she produces another child.

Why does Swift repeat these word groups and even weave
them together? Maybe our revulsion at the perversion of the
parent-child relationship is meant to be expanded to a revulsion
at other, analogously perverted, basic legal and political relations. The natural bonds between a landlord and his tenant
and between a kingdom and its citizens are very similar to
those between parents and their children: each is, ideally, a
relation of mutual trust and responsibility. The landlord and the
monarch, like the parent, are charged with providing for the
tenant, citizen, or child. Swift employs the moral outrage he has
evoked at the abuse of parent-child relations to fuel our revulsion
at the perversion of legal and political relations. These abstract
bonds could not in their own right have called up such a strong
gut reaction because they are not so intimately ingrained in common human experience. Without the analogy Swift could at
best have produced merely a negative intellectual attitude in his
readers toward such abstract concerns. Swift is using the covert
point of view to predict and control his reader's emotional
responses.

At one point Swift makes explicit the analogy between the
parent-child and the landlord-tenant perversions—just in case
some readers might not recognize the analogy without a noticeable nudge from the covert point of view:

> I grant this food will be somewhat dear, and therefore very
> proper for landlords, who, as they have already devoured
> most of the parents, seem to have the best title to the children.

This clause not only affirms the landlord-parent analogy, but it
is the first place in *A Modest Proposal* where the proposer uses
devouring people as a metaphor. Usually the proposer is quite
literal-minded, but in this instance Swift allows the covert
point of view control of part of a sentence to indicate that taking economic advantage is a kind of cannibalism. This rising
to the surface of the usually covert point of view, which is not at
all like that of the overt narrator, is another of Swift's techniques

that builds opposition to his proposer. Later, with another unusual clause in which the covert point of view again rises to the surface, Swift links devouring, as in the landlord-tenant passage, to the relations between England and Ireland. The proposer says of his proposal that it

> can incur no danger in disobliging England. For this kind of commodity will not bear exportation, the flesh being of too tender a consistence to admit a long continuance in salt, although perhaps I could name a country which would be glad to eat up our whole nation without it.

In relating the perversions of parent-child to landlord-tenant, kingdom-people, and England-Ireland, we see the covert point of view organizing its opposing case, deep in basic human emotions, by analogy. At the same time, the overt point of view has been organizing his proposal dutifully by dividing it into the five-part structure conventional in the classical-rhetoric books of Swift's time; this classical organization of the *Proposal* certainly does not have a profound emotional effect on a reader.

Unless we grasp the analogical organization, which must have had the most profound emotional effect on Swift's own contemporaries who shared the basic assumptions underlying the analogy, it is easy to overlook the fact that *A Modest Proposal* from beginning to end represents a persuasion of the deepest emotional kind toward a heartfelt restitution of legal, political, and human rights to the impoverished people of Ireland. His analogical organization may be Swift's most powerful and pervasive covert means of rallying his readers around a set of human emotional values opposed to those of the overt proposer.

We have seen how Swift has managed to separate his overt and covert points of view in every available stylistic way. We might ask, finally whether the proposer and the author are even talking about the same subject. The proposer is suggesting cannibalism as a solution to the economic conditions of Ireland. Swift clearly does not agree with this solution. Does Swift, however, even define the problem as an economic one? On the basis of the appeals Swift is making to his audience for common sense, common feeling, and common humanity, we might conclude that Swift is proposing moral regeneration rather than economic reform to counter the perversions of political, social, and economic institutions that have caused human misery in Ireland. The proposer's attitude is reasonable if we accept his assumption that the Irish poor are animals; the covert point of view seems emotionally irresistible if we accept its assumption that the Irish poor are suffering humanity.

Swift's unique achievement as a writer seems to be his inventive control of covert writing structures. With these he could shape his reader's moral feelings and emotions to condemn an overt point of view and embrace a different point of view never openly expressed.

Here is the Swift style model we have just constructed, expressed as a writing program in the form of a brief diagram. (When we refer to "Swift's style" we mean his method of composition only in the specific example we analyzed.)

Writing Program IV

BRIEF DIAGRAM OF SWIFT'S STYLE

Overt Point of View	Covert Point of View

Syntax:

Have the narrator characteristically use long, carefully contrived complex and compound-complex sentences, parenthetical remarks, interruptions, and frequent periodic sentences.	Often construct sentences so that they seem to contain two points of view working in opposition. (For example, express the narrator's point of view in the main clause, and, using such techniques as those detailed on p. 119, build a covert point of view in the subordinate clauses that involves the reader's emotions more than does the narrator's point of view.)

Overt Point of View	Covert Point of View

Words:

Have the narrator use a number of abstract words conventional to some formal or specialized vocabulary. (Swift, for example, used the polysyllabic vocabulary of social arithmetic.) Reserve any affective words to describe the feelings of the narrator and those who share his point of view rather than let the narrator use affective words to express feelings about his subject.

Use a few concrete words that arrest a reader's attention away from the abstract interests of the narrator and toward ideas and emotions that tend to favor the covert point of view. (For example, by allowing his narrator to describe the plight of the poor in concrete terms, Swift helps his reader feel and sympathize with the suffering of fellow human beings rather than be content with the cold, abstract expediencies concerning them. (See pp. 119–120 for detailed examples of Swift's use of this covert technique.)

Figures of Speech:

Let the narrator employ rhetorical figures that serve to emphasize, such as compounding, triplets, litotes, polysyndeton, paralipsis, alliteration. (These figures may also serve the covert point of view.) Use these arresting figures of speech to emphasize ideas and feelings against the overt point of view, and perhaps tuck them away in subordinate parts of the sentence that the narrator does not consider important but of only casual or incidental interest.

Produce metaphors for the narrator that relate his subject to an obviously unfair or inappropriate reference area. (For example, Swift produces metaphors for his narrator that use domestic animal husbandry and commerce as a reference area with human beings as the subject.)

Use covert figures that convey meanings the narrator does not intend. For example, words with overt material meaning but covert moral meaning, clichés that come covertly to life, common nouns that flower covertly into metaphor. (See pp. 128–129 for specific examples of Swift's use of such covert techniques.)

Overt Point of View	Covert Point of View

Organization:

Have your narrator use some very obvious conventional or mechanical organization. (For example, Swift uses a conventional—for his day—five-part rhetorical structure that was roughly equivalent to a mechanical use of our conventional tripartite "beginning - middle - end") or "introduction-body-conclusion" structure.

Include some emotionally arresting implicit organization. (For example, Swift suggests an analogy between the landlord-tenant relation and the elemental emotion-producing parent-child relationship.)

Subject Matter:

Create a narrator to argue an efficient, but inhuman, proposed solution to some grave social problem. (For example, Swift uses cannibalism as an efficient solution to the economic poverty of Ireland.)

Turn the narrator's monologue into a dialogue in your reader's mind by using the covert means mentioned below to suggest a counterargument based on common feeling and common decency as a better solution to the social problem.

Attitudes or Ways of Thinking and Perceiving:

Have your narrator assume that economic or political expediency are the audience's central values. Allow the narrator little or no realization of the reader's emotional response to the proposal.

Assume that a shared generosity, fairness, and morality are the reader's central values. Be acutely aware of and use at all opportunities the reader's probable emotional responses against the overt proposal and for the covert proposal.

Exercises

If you were to construct a sentence about a modern American subject like the following, where grammatical construction and point of view compete with an arresting vocabulary of specific and concrete words and an emphatic rhetoric, you could achieve a two-faced effect similar to that of Swift's first sentence in *A Modest Proposal:*

It is indeed a distressing experience for a tourist who travels to New York on the railroad, to see all those crowded uptown tenements with curtainless windows where, in doorways, streets, and alleys, idly sit hundreds of dirty, half-dressed, and hollow-eyed children.

Because it plays point of view against rhetoric, this sentence is a good one only if you want your reader to rebel against the person speaking. If, however, you intend your reader to accept the point of view of the narrator, the sentence is poorly written. All the emphatic compounding, all the specific, concrete, and arresting language, causes a reader to feel annoyed or uncomfortable with the cool detachment of a narrator whose values, reflected in his sentence structure and point of view, seem upside down. The reader's heart is not in the same part of the sentence as the narrator's. Had you really wanted the reader to accept the narrator's point of view, it would have been more effective to have used the arts of rhetoric on the side of the narrator rather than against him. In the following sentence, for example, the emphatic figures and arresting language are made to occur in the main clause, consistent with the narrator's point of view, while the abstract language is placed in the subordinate clauses:

My wife and I have devoted forty hard years and grown old, and worn, and tired in efforts that we hoped would raise the standard of living of those who lack the basic requirements of subsistence.

When we write about controversial, complex, and emotional subjects, where the narrator's point of view is not necessarily the only one or the most obvious one, we might be careful to weigh in a little verbal emphasis on the side of our point of view.

1. Write two sentences on some social injustice about which you

feel strongly. In the first sentence use Swift's pattern of a main clause concerned with the detached feelings or abstract concerns of the narrator or people like him and a subordinate clause (or clauses) filled with figuratively emphasized concrete detail that will move a reader but is, evidently, unfelt by the narrator. Now reverse the rhetorical emphasis and concrete detail to the narrator's concerns in the main clause and use only abstract and general, nonemphatic language in the subordinate clauses to describe the object of his concern. What is the effect of the shift of rhetoric in your second sentence?

2. Define irony by describing the process by which you as a writer can now produce it.

3. Write a paragraph-length satire (i.e., sustained irony) in which your narrator's monologue is undercut by a covert point of view. Try using some of Swift's covert techniques to control a response in your readers that will negate what your narrator says and the things he stands for. Test the effectiveness of your irony on a friend to see if it works.

8

Writing Modern Satire

As you prepare to write your own proposal on a modern subject, using Swift's structural program of an overt and an antithetical covert point of view, you should be aware that *an understanding of the moral, social, or political assumptions of modern readers, as well as how to control these, is part of the rhetorical problem that you as a writer must solve*. Needless to say, the excellence of your finished proposal will not depend on any particular political or social position you might choose to take, but rather on how intelligently you solve, considering your chosen subject and audience, the writing problems raised.

If we wish to use Swift's general stylistic program, we obviously cannot follow it slavishly because, unless an audience believes or assumes something unconsciously in the same way as Swift's audience, we cannot rely on it as Swift did to provide the basis of our covert argument. For instance, when Swift wrote, "The number of souls in Ireland being usually reckoned one million and a half, of these I calculate there may be about two hundred thousand couples whose wives are breeders," and we know that his contemporaries believed that the human world, symbolized by the soul, was completely separate from the animal world that did not share man's spiritual inheritance, then we know that he is putting into juxtaposition irreconcilable definitions of man, only one of which is correct to his audience. Since Darwin, however, it has become commonplace to consider that man may have a soul but is also an animal. When we find these two views juxtaposed today, no irony is necessarily intended.

Swift tuned his rhetoric, just as you must do, to the specific predictable emotional and intellectual responses of his own contemporary audience. If these responses are basic enough, distortion—even over hundreds of years—is minimal. The relation between parent and child, for example, remains much as it was thought to be in Swift's day—one of mutual trust and responsibility. But even so seemingly elemental and universal a bond as that of parent and child cannot be counted on to move some modern audiences. Since Freud, it may seem that a lack of mutual love and trust within families is not so *unnatural* or inhuman as an eighteenth-century audience might have considered it. In fact, the "generation gap" is likely to become even deeper as technology advances and social and moral changes accelerate and cut off the generation that is still learning from the older generations that learned different "truths." I am not suggesting that any changes between the milieu of Swift's audience and ours are necessarily good or bad, but any such changes represent the possibility of a rhetorical problem for a modern satirist, who may not be able to count on a late twentieth-century audience's shared assumptions about even so basic a human bond.

The relation between landlord and tenant, which again Swift's contemporaries thought of ideally as one of mutual trust and responsibility, has radically changed. Even in Swift's day, obviously, the landlord-tenant relation was declining from the more feudal but never ideal one of the lord of the land caring for and guarding his tenant, who, at least in theory, worked for him in a bond of mutual trust. One has only to think of slum landlords (including venerable educational institutions) and their poor tenants in our cities to begin to doubt the possibility of care and mutual trust that early eighteenth-century readers might consider *natural* to this relation. On the contrary, their *natural* relation seems to modern people (who have learned something from the theory of evolution about a much less beneficent *nature*) more a Darwinian predation of eco-

What emotions is the artist counting on his audience to supply in order to make this lithograph into effective social satire?

nomic carnivores on economic herbivores. Apparently even our definitions of *nature* and *natural* have changed. Possibly modern writers will have to find some new assumptions on which to build a covert point of view.

It may be only slightly less difficult for us to see a country's relation to its citizens as one of mutual trust and responsibility. That the relation between mother countries (like England) and the smaller countries under their protection and control (like

Ireland) should be, by nature, the same as that between parent and child seems hard to believe when we consider the ruthless modern relations that exist among the large, powerful countries and small, helpless ones. A belief that all such bonds were ordained by nature was more congenial to Swift's contemporaries, who were brought up to assume that all laws were sanctioned by analogy with a "benevolent and true" nature. Perhaps it will surprise you to know that Swift's contemporary society could have generally believed in the relation of all levels of life and realms of knowledge and activity (the family, economics, social justice, politics, morality) to one another as well as to natural law that was "self-evident" to men of "right reason." Because of their assumptions, Swift's readers would probably have grasped his covert parent-child/landlord-tenant/country-citizen analogy in the *Modest Proposal* more surely and quickly than we do and could have been counted on to react more strongly against the proposer's perversions of the natural responsibility of landlords and governments. If today's audience possibly would not respond to the same analogy Swift's audience responded to, what could you use today instead? What values and attitudes of a modern audience are so deeply rooted that they can be called from us almost unconsciously? This is a writing problem well worth considering.

Another part of Swift's covert positive proposal suggests to his readers that the meanings of words have deteriorated. Although the perversions of some words that the proposer abuses —such as "fair," "modest," and "dear"—may strike modern readers much as they must have struck Swift's contemporary audience, the misuse of certain other words by the proposer is not today as shocking and immoral as Swift must have covertly intended. Even though the word "gentleman," for instance, may not indicate to most modern people much more than gender on a rest-room door, it implied in Swift's day an important moral, social, and political entity with privileges and responsibilities. His audience would have responded with amusement but with shock as well to the corruption of the word by the proposer. Swift focuses his audience's concern on the changes in meaning of such words as "gentleman," "kingdom," "land-

lord," and "thrift" not to show them, as many a modern rela-
tivist might, the inevitability of linguistic change, but rather to
show them how to take the first step in amending their ways—
by restoring words, and then institutions, to their "right" and
"naturtal" meanings. For Swift, words stood for permanent ideal
forms. Shifts of meaning in a world of shifting contexts did not
seem as inevitable then as they do now to most of us. To Swift
and his audience, changes in meaning implied degeneration
from the truth of a better past and, therefore, seemed actually
immoral.

You may be wondering why most of Swift's covert proposals for ameliorating the lot of the Irish poor imply primarily
a return to traditional values and the stricter morality of the
past. We can learn something about our own age as well as
Swift's when we recognize that Swift does not recommend or
rely on material-aid programs such as slum clearance, full employment, or universal education to end poverty—something
we might expect of a modern writer. Swift is in no sense a
liberal believer in the betterment of human life through material progress. He is a conservative moralist who believes that
we have strayed far from the "natural" and "reasonable" institutions envisaged by our forebears. The success of his positive program depends on his developing in his readers a
sickened emotional recoil from the warped definitions and institutions that have usurped the former "true" definitions and
institutions. Few of us today are so conservative as to try to
solve present social problems by believing that the large majority of people, through a sudden change of heart, will return to
the moral solutions of the past, thus effecting a reform. Most
students, whatever modern audience they choose to address,
might find it hard to rely on a strong unconscious belief in a
better past of moral rectitude, where a gentlemanly aristocracy,
like wise parents, cared for a happy peasantry, who knew their
place in the beneficent scheme of nature.

Nor can we, as modern writers, rely, as Swift's contemporaries did, on a strong belief in common-sense moral solutions
to difficult economic and social problems, which are aggravated
in the modern world by complex technological change. It is

one thing to trust a simple morality of person-to-person. But considering the necessary, though uncomfortable, expansion of bureaucracies and corporate institutions since Swift's time, can we seriously count on a bureaucracy to have a warm heart and simple, trustworthy moral sense? In our country we apparently had to have legal definitions of civil rights by the Supreme Court, and the federal power to insure extensions of civil-rights legislation and enforcement, to begin to engage the moral sense of the nation. We all know that the last generation's moral sense alone was not enough to make them see and act on what was morally plain since Swift's time and before —that all people are human, and that no humans should be treated as subhuman.

Perhaps a whole new type of covert organization would have to be worked out for a modern Swiftian proposal to be as effective with its audience as Swift's was with his contemporaries. On the other hand, some modern writers may believe that there is still a great deal to be said for a return to the morality of the past, in spite of the slavery and imperialism and wars that others will see as part of that morality.

It is important to consider briefly the problems that rhetorical comparison and contrast uncover, for you will soon be asked to think and write your way toward your own modern solutions of such problems. Contemporary social concern, far from being extrinsic to English studies, is, especially in this instance, quite a necessary part of your writing study. You will need to determine how to set up antithetical points of view about a controversial issue and also understand the feelings, values, and assumptions of some specific audience well enough to control its attitudes by covert means.

We have, in the previous chapter, shown Swift generating irony in the *Modest Proposal* by designing a rhetoric that implicitly counters his narrator's explicit proposal. Since critical writing that contains an extended use of irony is called satire, *A Modest Proposal* is a satire—though not all satires are of the double-point-of-view type, featuring a narrator's ruthless proposal together with a positive point of view unobtrusively built into his monologue by means of a clever rhetoric.

Why would a writer ever want to set up and control two points of view? Certainly to do so is much harder than simply to control a single point of view. Yet controlling an overt as well as a covert point of view is a very compact way of shaping an audience's reaction to a large set of attitudes and assumptions, or even a whole philosophy. A number of attitudes and assumptions, instead of having to be argued against individually and (therefore) inefficiently, can be compactly molded into the tone and character of the overt narrator. If the reader's sympathies can then be turned against the narrator it can discredit all his attitudes and assumptions with one blow. What could have been, in Swift's *Modest Proposal,* a disparate group of abstract propositions (i.e., "Economics is more important than people"; "Any means to reduce the threat of Catholicism is justified"; "Ireland exists for the benefit of England") is by this means brought to life and allowed to motivate logically a shocking proposal, so that the potential for mischief of such ideas stands revealed. The covert point of view makes implicit such counterpropositions as "Men should restore to their rightful condition the natural bonds of trust and responsibility linking landlord and tenant, kingdom and citizen"; "Economic and social policies should accord with common sense, humanity, and morality"; "Catholic and Protestant should not hate one another to their mutual destruction"; and "The well-to-do should not regard the poor as objects or animals to be used, but as souls to be nurtured." But if each of these propositions were argued explicitly it would take a huge tome. The personification and then destruction of the overt point of view provide an effective, compact, and lively way to argue against hundreds of large and small, stated and implied attitudes and assumptions.

In light of what we have just discussed, notice that Swift's overt proposer is characterized more as a type than as an individual. The "round" or individual character is not best for every purpose, and a writer aiming to satirize a whole society's way of thinking rather than any individual man's might well create a type rather than an individual. Certainly Swift excludes all detail of the narrator's physical appearance, education, taste, residence, profession, and dress, and avoids giving him any personal motivation. It seems that Swift does not wish us to experience a revulsion against the single individual, but against a far too typical set of values and assumptions.

Writing this kind of proposal demands even more than the rhetorical skills we discussed in the last chapter—it demands a consideration of our audience's emotional response to the proposal. However, some kinds of satire written today, and even some other satires of Swift, are different in kind from that of *A Modest Proposal*. Often, less time is spent controlling and guiding a possibly naïve reader toward enlightenment, while much more effort goes into "putting on" the stupid or naïve reader, who takes the overt point of view at face value. Today, many writers have become convinced, for aesthetic reasons, that their best writing is accomplished when they are intuitive and spontaneous. They wish to write subjectively, and are much less interested in mastering the discipline of controlling and guiding the response of an audience that Swift's satire demands. This is not to say that modern satire is inferior to Swiftian satire; but it is very different. Swift's aesthetic aim in *A Modest Proposal* was not only to entertain but to instruct—his art is more didactic than ours. If an average reader is not already an insider when he starts to read some modern satires, he may not be promoted from innocence even when he is finished. This difference in the form and intent of satire is an interesting question to pursue. It may be caused partly by social change and the appearance of mass culture and mass education. The naïve audience in modern satire is often mass-educated, mass-cultured, middle-class—by definition, the largest number of readers. In Swift's day, the writer and his audience were a much smaller group but, on the whole, more uniformly educated, so that Swift could count on most of the audience to share his own values, although they may have fallen away from these values and may have needed considerable prodding to return. Modern satire often entertains an elite audience. The fun depends on making this relatively small "in" group laugh at the larger American middle-class Mr. and Mrs. Straight.

Some modern satire, then, presupposes two audiences: a

large audience of outsiders who accepts the overt point of view, and a small, inside audience who enjoys the "put-on." Certainly this "putting on" of a naïve audience is part of Swift's entertainment as well. But to think that this is Swift's primary purpose in *A Modest Proposal* is to miss his art and, consequently, to lose sight of one of our own major modern conditions as well—the lack of trust in any general enduring values and the fragmentation of truth. Indeed, it is for us a social, and even a political, problem as well as a rhetorical one. And at this point, a knowledge of Swift's style and a concern for contemporary interests and problems may come together as you begin to think practically of writing your own satire with modern relevance as a goal.

Now begin to consider seriously the possibility of actually writing a modern Swiftian satire of your own. You might even consider, by way of analogy, the use of a rhetorical program very similar to Swift's, but with different subject matter and in a different medium—the film *Blow-Up* (Michelangelo Antonioni, 1966).

We have found Swift controlling simultaneously two different point of view in a monologue. The overt point of view is set up and controlled by conventional rhetorical devices; the covert point of view has to be controlled in more unusual ways. Those who have not seen *Blow-Up* can imagine how a movie director might, in a film, create an overt point of view—say that of a busy fashion photographer. The director might control this point of view by following the photographer around for a day in his life. He might have him, while photographing the passing scene, by chance photograph an act of murder, which he discovers when he develops the roll of film. The director can now use all the devices for creating and sustaining suspense that we expect in conventional detective plots. How, at the same time, without introducing a new plot or "hero," could the director control a very different, even antithetical, point of view? Among the techniques he could use to establish a covert point of view might be: (1) shifting the movie camera independently of the "hero's" still (static) camera point of view in such a way that the director and not the fashion photographer would decide what to give life to or emphasize; (2) limiting the photographer to black and white while the movie camera photographs in lush color; (3) frustrating the conventional suspense and detection plot (even frustrating the "hero's" love life), so that the audience would retreat from the frustrated point of view; (4) making the point of view appear stupidly literal-minded or limited; (5) creating an illusion in which the film director and audience, but not the fashion-photographer "hero" (until the end), could participate; (6) allowing the movie camera—the covert point of view itself—to be revealed, clearly reflected in the shiny hood of the hero's car (this is like Swift's covert voice occasionally rising to the surface in "landlords . . . as they have already devoured most of the parents, seem to have the best title to the children"); (7) in the last scene, eliminating completely the overt point of view by making the fashion photographer vanish before our eyes.

Suppose that our movie director has given his overt point of view certain attitudes and assumptions about art. Let us suppose in particular that the director characterizes the fashion-photographer "hero" as a man who assumes that the purpose of art is to reflect the "real" world without distortion, that his camera provides such a mirror of reality, and that if he blew up a photograph he would discover more and more detail about reality—even, for instance, about a murder that was occurring as he took the picture. Characterization might suggest that the serious work of the fashion photographer away from his job was taking starkly realistic black-and-white photographs. He might also be shown to be so unimaginative that, for a studio prop, he buys a large wooden propeller because to the literal mind "a prop is a prop." We might also have a scene in which his inability to understand nonrepresentational art is shown. Then, by covert means, using the same rhetorical program as Swift's but with visual technique as well, the director could take the point of view away from the fashion photographer and discredit his most basic assumption—namely, that art mirrors reality. He might even include what appears to be the complete (except for the "hero") assembled cast of characters, but in different roles, at the beginning and end of the film, suggesting again that this movie's art is not reality but imaginative illusion. Finally, when the director has, through covert direction, wrested control from the limited photographer's overt point of view, the clever audience might feel a peculiar satisfaction in seeing this too-limited overt point of view literally diminished and "blown out" by the director, who has proved artistically that art is not reality, but illusion or imagination. The rhetorical program of *Blow-Up* is surprisingly similar to that used in Swift's *Modest Proposal,* even though the subject matter, medium, and some of the techniques are different.

Exercises

1. Write a satire on a modern subject, using as many of Swift's covert strategies as you can. (You may wish to refer to the style diagram on pp. 134–136.) Avoid parody. Use the general principles of Swift's style, but not verbal echoes or eighteenth-century mannerisms. You must decide whether you wish your narrator to be an individual or a type. Remember that if you characterize the narrator too much you may blunt the didactic or social purpose of your satire. Pick a subject that you consider relevant and use as powerful an emotional appeal to your audience as you can. It may be easier to develop strong emotional appeals to move a fairly restricted audience (such as youth, or some particular minority), but see if you can develop emotional appeals that will reach as large an audience as possible. Emotional appeals that move large majorities will more often then not be found on the conservative rather than progressive side of a social issue simply because only traditional or conventional values and assumptions can have had time to take deep enough root to affect a mass of people when presented only implicitly. In other words, unless you choose a relatively small audience to appeal to you may find it easier to develop a covert point of view that is basically conservative.

For example, it will be easier (unless you address an audience of computer programmers) to satirize the uncritical, progressive belief in an expanded use of computers for all purposes than it will be to satirize the equally unthinking conservative fear of anything radically new and complex. And it may be easier (except to a restricted audience of college students or women's liberationists) to satirize those who question the traditional image of women as primarily mothers and homemakers. But even though it is harder, it can be done. For instance, what would happen if you were to create a narrator with a pompous male-chauvinist's voice and attitudes proposing the replacement of women with time-sharing sex machines, or with test-tube incubators? Can you think of any progressive causes that rest on conservative values? For example, although espousing ecology today has a progressive thrust it is certainly broadly based on traditional attitudes that could easily be presented so as to appeal to the hearts of a mass audience.

General Exercises in Combining or Cross-structuring Elements of Older Styles to Create Experimental Styles

1. Make up a master sheet of all the elements (syntactical, verbal, figurative, organizational) included or excluded in the four styles we have so far analyzed and discussed, plus any other rhetorical elements you can think of.

2. Now practice cross-structuring some of these elements into new combinations:

	INCLUDE	OR	EXCLUDE
Syntax:			
Words:			
Figures of Speech:			
Organization:			

What kind of subject matter do you suppose your new stylistic combination will work with best? What sort of attitudes do you think it will convey best?

3. When you think you have put together a new style that has some significance, try writing a paragraph or two in that style. Now try writing in that style on various kinds of subjects. What kind of subject matter does the style fit best? Can you adapt or adjust it to fit that kind of subject matter even better by including or excluding other elements or modifying the elements already present? Does the new style tend to achieve any particular aesthetic aims or imply any unique attitudes or ways of thinking about or perceiving the world? Can you modify or add to the style to accentuate this tendency?

4. Keep testing the style by writing in it until you are satisfied that all the elements function together the way you want them to. Then make up a more complete diagram of the style:

	INCLUDE	OR	EXCLUDE
Syntax:			
Words:			
Figures of Speech:			
Organization:			
Attitudes or Ways of Thinking and Perceiving:			
Subject Matter:			

5. Discuss the new style's significance. What are the advantages and disadvantages peculiar to it?

6. Using the new style, compose a brief narrative or essay.

Part II

WRITING AND THINKING WITH DEFINITIONS

*I*N *much of your college work, words will be subjected to a lot more questioning and probing and discussion than you may have been used to. Take the word* definition *for example. You have probably not thought much about what this word means because you may feel that, for all practical purposes, a definition is the meaning of a word found in a desk dictionary, and defining is essentially the act of adding new words to your basic vocabulary. These next four chapters on definition will not, however, be concerned with vocabulary building, but with discovering new things about the words you already use by inquiring with various kinds of definition.*

In the chapters on style, instead of recommending the good style, *several equally good alternatives were offered, each having different advantages and disadvantages. In these chapters about definition several diverse ways of inquiring into the meaning of a word or term will be explained: Aristotelian, metaphorical, operational, contextual, stipulative, lexical, divisional. Our first objective will be to learn these alternative structures both as ways of inquiring and as ways of organizing writing.*

Like a style, each defining process presupposes certain assumptions, even though we may be unconscious of this when we use it. Our second objective in using defining structures is to be aware of what we are assuming about words and their relation (or lack of relation) to different concepts of reality. Each new defining process works differently and results in a different kind of knowledge about a word's meaning. You will see why some words will be easier to define one way and harder to define another way.

Knowledge in every field rests on the quicksand of terms that need careful definition. Many anthropologists have tried and are still trying to define one of their basic terms—culture— just as sociologists are trying to define subculture, *psychologists*

social behavior, *and biologists* species. Evolution *does not mean
today what it meant to Darwin's contemporaries. And* gravitation *does not mean to modern physicists what it meant to
Newton. In English, the definition of such basic terms as* tragedy
or poetry *is crucial. For example, is the only difference between*
poetry *and* prose *the presence or absence of a margin on the
right-hand side of the page? Definition and continual redefinition are particularly important at present when profound
changes in our environment and accelerating knowledge make it
increasingly difficult to suppose that the meaning of our words
can be found frozen in a desk dictionary.*

*As we explore the advantages and disadvantages of each
defining structure you will be encouraged to combine one kind
of definition with another until you can make up your own
structures. These new combinations should free you to fit definitions more flexibly to the specific aims of your writing. We
will study each of these definitions not only as a way of prying
into meaning, but as a writing form or paradigm immediately
available when you need to organize a definition of sentence-,
paragraph-, or essay-length. A definition can serve as the organizing structure for an essay, even though until now you may
not have thought of using a definition to structure anything
larger than a simple sentence. In the following chapters we will
consider each defining structure capable of organizing both
small and large units of writing. For example, the following
essay by Dorothy Lee inquires into the meaning of the concept*
reality. *You will see that she uses several, if not all, of the defining structures (for example, divisional, contextual, metaphorical) that we will be studying specifically in Chapters 10,
11 and 12.*

"Codifications of Reality"

Dorothy Lee

... THAT a word is not the reality, not the thing which it represents, has long been a commonplace to all of us. The thing
which I hold in my hand as I write, *is* not a pencil; I *call* it a
pencil. And it remains the same whether I call it *pencil, molyvi,
Bleistift,* or *siwiqoq.* These words are different sound-complexes
applied to the same reality; but is the difference merely one of
sound-complex? Do they refer to the same *perceived* reality?
Pencil originally meant little tail; it delimited and named the
reality according to form. *Molyvi* means lead and refers to
the writing element. *Bleistift* refers both to the form and to the
writing element. *Siwiqoq* means painting-stick and refers to
observed function and form. Each culture has phrased the reality differently. To say that *pencil,* for example, applies primarily to form is no idle etymologic statement. When we use this
word metaphorically, we refer neither to writing element nor to
function, but to form alone; we speak of a pencil of light, or a
styptic pencil.

When I used the four words for this object, we all knew
what reality was referred to; we knew the meaning of the word.
We could visualize the object in my hand, and the words all
delimited it in the same way; for example, none of them im-

From *Psychosomatic Medicine,* May, 1950, No. 12. Reprinted by permission.

plied that it was a continuation of my fist. But the student of ethnography often has to deal with words which punctuate reality into different phrasings from the ones with which he is familiar. Let us take, for instance, the words for "brother" and "sister." We go to the islands of Ontong Java to study the kinship system. We ask our informant what he calls his sister and he says *ave;* he calls his brother *kainga.* So we equate *ave* with "sister" and *kainga* with "brother." By way of checking our information we ask the sister what she calls her brother; it turns out that for her, *ave* is "brother," not "sister" as we were led to expect; and that it is her sister whom she calls *kainga.*

The same reality, the same actual kinship is present there as with us; but we have chosen a different aspect for naming. We are prepared to account for this; we say that both cultures name according to what we would call a certain type of blood relationship; but whereas we make reference to absolute sex, they refer to relative sex. Further inquiry, however, discloses that in this, also, we are wrong. Because in our own culture we name relatives according to formal definition and biologic relationship, we have thought that this formulation represents reality; and we have tried to understand the Ontong Javanese relationship terms according to these distinctions which, we believe, are given in nature. But the Ontong Javanese classifies relatives according to a different aspect of reality, differently punctuated. And because of this, he applies *kainga* as well to a wife's sister and a husband's brother; to a man's brother's wife and a woman's sister's husband, as well as to a number of other individuals.

Neither sex nor blood relationship, then, can be basic to this term. The Ontong Javanese name according to their everyday behavior and experience, not according to formal definition. A man shares the ordinary details of his living with his brothers and their wives for a large part of the year; he sleeps in the same large room, he eats with them, he jokes and works around the house with them; the rest of the year he spends with his wife's sisters and their husbands, in the same easy companionship. All these individuals are *kainga* to one another. The *ave,* on the other hand, names a behavior of great strain and propriety; it is based originally upon the relative sex of siblings, yes, but it does not signify biologic fact alone. It names a social relationship, a behavior, an emotional tone. *Ave* can never spend their adult life together, except on rare and temporary occasions. They can never be under the same roof alone together, cannot chat at ease together, cannot refer even distantly to sex in the presence of each other, not even to one's sweetheart or spouse; more than that, everyone else must be circumspect when the *ave* of someone of the group is present. The *ave* relationship also carries special obligations toward a female *ave* and her children. *Kainga* means a relationship of ease, full of shared living, of informality, gaiety; *ave* names one of formality, prohibition, strain.

These two cultures, theirs and our own, have phrased and formulated social reality in completely different ways, and have given their formulation different names. The word is merely the name of this specific cultural phrasing. From this one instance we might formulate the hypothesis—a very tentative one —that among the Ontong Javanese names describe emotive experiences, not observed forms or functions. But we cannot accept this as fact, unless further investigation shows it to be implicit in the rest of their patterned behavior, in their vocabulary and the morphology of their language, in their ritual and their other organized activity. . . .

I have discussed at length the diversity of codification of reality in general, because it is the foundation of the specific study which I am about to present. I shall speak of the formulation of experienced reality among the Trobriand Islanders in comparison to our own; I shall speak of the nature of expectancy, of motivation, of satisfaction, as based upon a reality which is differently apprehended and experienced in two different societies; which is, in fact, for each, a different reality. The Trobriand Islanders were studied by the late Bronislaw Malinowski, who has given us the rich and circumstantial material about them which has made this study possible. I have given a detailed presentation of some implications of their language elsewhere; but since it was in their language that I first noticed the absence of lineality, which led me to this study, I shall give here a summary of the implications of the language.

A Trobriand word refers to a self-contained concept. What we consider an attribute of a predicate, is to the Trobriander an ingredient. Where I would say, for example, "A good gardener," or "The gardener is good," the Trobriand word would include both "gardener" and "goodness"; if the gardener loses the goodness, he has lost a defining ingredient, he is something else, and he is named by means of a completely different word. A taytu (a species of yam) contains a certain degree of ripeness, bigness, roundedness, etc.; without one of these defining ingredients, it is something else, perhaps a *bwanawa* or a *yowana*. There are no adjectives in the language; the rare words dealing with qualities are substantivized. The term *to be* does not occur; it is used neither attributively nor existentially, since existence itself is contained; it is an ingredient of being.

Events and objects are self-contained points in another respect; there is a series of beings, but no becoming. There is no temporal connection between objects. The taytu always remains itself; it does not *become* over-ripe; over-ripeness is an ingredient of another, a different being. At some point, the taytu *turns into a yowana,* which contains over-ripeness. And the yowana, over-ripe as it is, does not put forth shoots, does not *become* a sprouting yowana. When sprouts appear, it ceases to be itself; in its place appears a *silasata.* Neither is there a temporal connection made—or, according to our own premises, perceived—between events; in fact, temporality is meaningless. There are no tenses, no linguistic distinction between past or present. There is no arrangement of activities or events into means and ends, no causal or teleologic relationships. What we consider a causal relationship in a sequence of connected events, is to the Trobriander an ingredient of a patterned whole. He names this ingredient *u'ula.*

There is no automatic relating of any kind in the language. Except for the rarely used verbal it-differents and it-sames, there are no terms of comparison whatever. And we find in an analysis of behavior that the standard for behavior and of evaluation is non-comparative.

These implications of the linguistic material suggest to my mind an absence of axiomatic lineal connection between events or objects in the Trobriand apprehension of reality, and this implication, as I shall attempt to show below, is reinforced in their definition of activity. In our own culture, the line is so basic, that we take it for granted, as given in reality. We see it in visible nature, between material points, and we see it between metaphorical points such as days or acts. It underlies not only our thinking, but also our aesthetic apprehension of the given; it is basic to the emotional climax which has so much value for us, and, in fact, to the meaning of life itself. In our thinking about personality and character, we have taken for granted the presence of the line.

In our academic work, we are constantly acting in terms of an implied line. When we speak of *ap*plying an *at*tribute, for example, we visualize the process as lineal, coming from the outside. If I make a picture of an apple on the board, and want to show that one side is green and the other red I connect these attributes with the pictured apple by means of lines, as a matter of course; how else would I do it? When I organize my data, I *draw* conclusions *from* them. I *trace* a relationship between my facts. I describe a pattern as a *web* of relationships. Look at a lecturer who makes use of gestures; he is constantly making lineal connections in the air. And a teacher with chalk in hand will be drawing lines on the board whether he be a psychologist, a historian, or a paleontologist. . . .

Our psychologists picture motivation as external, connected with the act through a line, or, more recently, entering the organism through a lineal channel and emerging transformed, again lineally, as response. I have seen lineal pictures of nervous impulses and heartbeats, and with them I have seen pictured lineally a second of time. These were photographs, you will say, of existing fact, of reality; a proof that the line is present in reality. But I am not convinced, perhaps due to my ignorance of mechanics, that we have not created our recording instruments in such a way that they have to picture time and motion, light and sound, heartbeats and nerve impulses lineally, on the unquestioned assumption of the line as axiomatic. The line is omnipresent and inescapable, and so we are incapable of questioning the reality of its presence.

When we see a *line* of trees, or a *circle* of stones, we assume the presence of a connecting line which is not actually visible. And we assume it metaphorically when we follow a *line* of thought, a *course* of action or the *direction* of an argument; when we *bridge* a gap in the conversation, or speak of the *span* of life or of teaching a *course,* or lament our *interrupted career*. We make children's embroidery cards and puzzle cards on this assumption; our performance tests and even our tests for sanity often assume that the line is present in nature and, at most, to be discovered or given visual existence.

But is the line present in reality? Malinowski, writing for members of our culture and using idiom which would be comprehensible to them, described the Trobriand village as follows: "Concentrically with the circular row of yam houses there runs a ring of dwelling huts." He saw, or at any rate, he represented the village as two circles. But in the texts which he recorded, we find that the Trobrianders at no time mention circles or rings or even rows when they refer to their villages. Any word which they use to refer to a village, such as *a* or *this,* is prefixed by the substantival element *kway* which means *bump* or *aggregate of bumps*. This is the element which they use when they refer to a pimple or a bulky rash; or to canoes loaded with yams. In their terms, a village is an aggregate of bumps; are they blind to the circles? Or did Malinowski create the circles himself, out of his cultural axiom? . . .

But the Trobrianders do not describe their activity lineally; they do no dynamic relating of acts; they do not use even so innocuous a connective as *and*. Here is part of a description of the planting of coconut: "Thou-approach-there coconut thou-bring-here-we-plant-coconut thou-go thou-plant our coconut. This-here it-emerge sprout. We-push-away this we-push-away this-other coconut-husk-fiber together sprout it-sit together root." We who are accustomed to seek lineal continuity, cannot help supplying it as we read this; but the continuity is not given in the Trobriand text; and all Trobriand speech, according to Malinowski, is "jerky," given in points, not in connecting lines.

The only connective I know of in Trobriand is the *pela* which I mentioned above; a kind of preposition which also means "to jump."

I am not maintaining here that the Trobrianders cannot see continuity; rather that lineal connection is not automatically made by them, as a matter of course. At Malinowski's persistent questioning, for example, they did attempt to explain their activities in terms of cause or motivation, by stating possible "results" of uncooperative action. But Malinowski found their answers confused, self-contradictory, inconsistent; their preferred answer was, "It was ordained of old"—pointing to an ingredient value of the act instead of giving an explanation based on lineal connection.

And when they were not trying to find answers to leading questions, the Trobrianders made no such connection in their speech. They assumed, for example, that the validity of a magical spell lay, not in its results, not in proof, but in its very being; in the appropriateness of its inheritance, in its place within the patterned activity, in its being performed by the appropriate person, in its realization of its mythical basis. To seek validity through proof was foreign to their thinking, yet they attempted to do so at the ethnographer's request. . . .

The fact remains that Trobrianders embark on, what is certainly for us, a series of acts which "must require" planning and purposiveness. They engage in acts of gift-giving and gift-receiving which we can certainly see as an exchange of gifts if we want to. When we plot their journeys, we find that they do go from point to point, they do navigate a course, whether they say so or not. Do they merely refrain from giving linguistic expression to something which they actually recognize in nature? On the nonlinguistic level, do they act on an assumption of a lineality which is given no place in their linguistic formulation?

I believe that, where valued activity is concerned, the Trobrianders do not act on an assumption of lineality at any level. There is organization or rather coherence in their acts because Trobriand activity is patterned activity. One act within this pattern brings into existence a pre-ordained cluster of acts. . . .

But all Trobriand activity does not contain value; and when it does not, it assumes lineality, and is utterly despicable. For example, the pattern of sexual intercourse includes the giving of a gift from the boy to the girl; but if a boy gives a gift so as to win the girl's favor, he is despised. Again, the kula pattern includes the eventual reception of a gift from the original recipient; the pattern is such that it keeps the acts physically and temporally completely disparate. In spite of this, however, some men are accused of giving gifts as an inducement to their kula partner to give them a specially good kula gift. Such men are labeled with the vile phrase: he barters. But this means that, unvalued and despised, lineal behavior does exist. In fact, there are villages in the interior whose inhabitants live mainly by bartering manufactured articles for yams. The inhabitants of Omarakana, about whom Malinowski's work and this study are mainly concerned, will barter with them, but consider them pariahs.

This is to say that it is probable that the Trobrianders experience reality in nonlineal pattern because this is the valued reality; and that they are capable of experiencing lineally, when value is absent or destroyed. It is not to say, however, that this in itself means that lineality is given, is present in nature, and that pattern is not. Our own insistence on the line, such as lineal causality, for example, is also often based on unquestioned belief or value. To return to the subject of procreation, the husband in our culture, who has long hoped, and tried in vain, to beget children, will nevertheless maintain that intercourse causes conception; perhaps with the same stubbornness and embarrassment which the Trobrianders exhibited when maintaining the opposite.

The line in our culture not only connects, but it moves. And as we think of a line as moving from point to point, connecting one to the other, so we conceive of roads as *running from* locality *to* locality. A Trobriander does not speak of roads either as connecting two points, or as *running from* point *to* point. His paths are self-contained, named as independent units; they

are not *to* and *from,* they are *at.* And he himself is *at;* he has
no equivalent for our *to* or *from.* There is, for instance, the
myth of Tudava, who goes—in our view—from village to
village and from island to island planting and offering yams.
The Trobriand text puts it this way: "Kitava it-shine village already (i.e. completed) he-is-over. 'I-sail I-go Iwa'; Iwa he-
anchor he-go ashore . . . He-sail Digumenu . . . They-drive
(him off) . . . he-go Kwaywata." Point after point is enumerated, but his sailing from and to is given as a discrete event. In
our view, he is actually following a southeasterly course, more
or less; but this is not given as course or line, and no directions
are even mentioned. In fact, in the several texts referring to
journeyings in the Archipelago, no words occur for the cardinal
directions. In sailing, the "following" winds are named according to where they are *at,* the place where they strike the canoe,
such as wind-striking-the-outrigger-beam; not according to
where they *come from.* Otherwise, we find names for the south-
west wind (youyo), and the northwest wind (bombatu), but
these are merely substantival names which have nothing to do
with direction; names for kinds of wind. . . .

When we in our culture deal with events or experiences of
the self, we use the line as guide for various reasons, two of
which I shall take up here. First, we feel we must arrange
events chronologically in a lineal order; how else could our historians discover the causes of a war or a revolution or a defeat?
Among the Trobrianders, what corresponds to our history is
an aggregate of anecdotes, that is, unconnected points, told
without respect to chronological sequence, or development, or
causal relationship; with no grammatical distinction made between words referring to past events, or to present or contemplated ones. And in telling an anecdote, they take no care
that a temporal sequence should be followed. For instance,
they said to Malinowski, "they-eat-taro, they-spew-taro, they-
disgusted-taro"; but if time, as we believe, is a moving line,
then the revulsion came first in time, the vomiting was the
result, coming afterward. Again, they say, "This-here . . . ripes

. . . falls-down truly gives-birth . . . sits seed in belly-his"; but certainly the seed is there first, and the birth follows in time, if time is lineal.

Secondly, we arrange events and objects in a sequence which is climactic, in size and intensity, in emotional meaning, or according to some other principle. We often arrange events from earlier to later, not because we are interested in historical causation, but because the present is the climax of our history. But when the Trobriander relates happenings, there is no developmental arrangement, no building up of emotional tone. His stories have no plot, no lineal development, no climax. And when he repeats his garden spell, his list is neither climactic, nor anticlimactic; it sounds merely untidy to us:

> The belly of my garden lifts
> The belly of my garden rises
> The belly of my garden reclines
> The belly of my garden is-a-bushhen's-nest-in-lifting
> The belly of my garden is-an-anthill
> The belly of my garden lifts-bends
> The belly of my garden is-an-ironwood-tree-in-lifting
> The belly of my garden lies-down
> The belly of my garden burgeons.

When the Trobrianders set out on their great ceremonial kula expedition, they follow a pre-established order. First comes the canoe of the Tolab wage, an obscure subclan. Next come the canoes of the great chiefs. But this is not climactic; after the great chiefs come the commoners. The order derives meaning not from lineal sequence, but from correspondence with a present, experienced, meaningful pattern, which is the recreation of realization of the mythical pattern; that which has been ordained of old and is forever. Its meaning does not lie in an item-to-item relationship, but in fitness, in the repetition of an established unit.

An ordering of this sort gives members of our society a certain esthetic dysphoria except when, through deliberate training, we learn to go beyond our cultural expectation; or, when we are too young to have taken on the phrasings of our culture. When we manipulate objects naively, we arrange them on some climactic lineal principle. Think of a college commencement, with the faculty arranged in order of rank or length of tenure or other mark of importance; with the students arranged according to increasing physical height, from shortest to tallest, actually the one absolutely irrelevant principle as regards the completion of their college education, which is the occasion for the celebration. Even when the sophisticated avoid this principle, they are not unconscious of it; they are deliberately avoiding something which is there.

And our arrangement of history, when we ourselves are personally involved, is mainly climactic. My great grandmother sewed by candle light, my grandmother used a kerosene lamp, my mother did her studying by gaslight, I did it by a naked electric ceiling light, and my children have diffused fluorescent lighting. This is progress; this is the meaningful sequence. To the Trobriander, climax in history is abominable, a denial of all good, since it would imply not only the presence of change, but also that change increases the good; but to him value lies in sameness, in repeated pattern, in the incorporation of all time within the same point. What is good in life is exact identity with all past Trobriand experience, and all mythical experience.

There is no boundary between past Trobriand existence and the present; he can indicate that an action is completed, but this does not mean that the action is past; it may be completed and present or timeless. Where we would say "Many years ago" and use the past tense, the Trobriander will say, "In my father's childhood" and use non-temporal verbs; he places the event situationally, not temporally. Past, present, and future are presented linguistically as the same, are present in his existence; and sameness with what we call the past and with myth, represents value to the Trobriander. Where we see a developmental line, the Trobriander sees a point, at most a swelling in value. Where we find pleasure and satisfaction in moving away from the point, in change as variety or progress, the Trobriander finds it in the repetition of the known, in maintaining the point; that is, in what we call monotony.

Esthetic validity, dignity, and value come to the Trobriander not through arrangement into a climactic line, but rather in the undisturbed incorporation of the events within their original, nonlineal order. The only history which has meaning for him is that which evokes the value of the point, or which, in the repetition, swells the value of the point. For example, every occasion in which a kula object participates becomes an ingredient of its being and swells its value; all these occasions are enumerated with great satisfaction, but the lineal course of the traveling kula object is not important. . . .

None of the Trobriand activities is fitted into a climactic line. There is no job, no labor, no drudgery which finds its reward outside the act. All work contains its own satisfaction. We cannot speak of S——R here, as all action contains its own immanent "stimulus." The present is not a means to future satisfaction, but good in itself, as the future is also good in itself; neither better nor worse, neither climactic nor anticlimactic, in fact, not lineally connected nor removed.

It follows that the present is not evaluated in terms of its place within a course of action leading upward to a worthy end. In our culture, we can rarely evaluate the present in itself. I tell you that Sally is selling notions at Woolworth's, but this in itself means nothing. It acquires some meaning when I add that she has recently graduated from Vassar. However, I go on to tell you that she has been assistant editor of *Vogue,* next a nursemaid, a charwoman, a public school teacher. But this is a mere jumble; it makes no sense and has no meaning, because the series leads to nothing. You cannot relate one job to another, and you are unable to see them discretely simply as part of her being. However, I now add that she is gathering material for a book on the working mother. Now all this falls in line, it makes sense in terms of a career. Now her job is good and it makes her happy, because it is part of a planned climactic line leading to more pay, increased recognition, higher rank. There was a story in a magazine about the college girl who fell in love with the milkman one summer; the reader felt tense until it was discovered that this was just a summer job, that it was only a means for the continuation of the man's education in the Columbia Law School. Our evaluation of happiness and unhappiness is bound with this motion along an envisioned line leading to a desired end. In the fulfillment of this course or career—not in the fulfillment of the self as point—do we find value. Our conception of freedom rests on the principle of non-interference with this moving line, non-interruption of the intended course of action.

It is difficult to tell whether climax is given in experience at all, or whether it is always imposed on the given. At a time when progress and evolution were assumed to be implicit in nature, our musicians and writers gave us climactic works. Nowadays, our more reflective art does not present experience climactically. Then, is emotion itself climactic? Climax, for us, evokes "thrill" or "drama." But we have cultures, like the Tikopia, where life is lived, to our perception, on an even emotive plane without thrill or climax. Experiences which "we know to be" climactic, are described without climax by them. For example, they, as well as the Trobrianders, described intercourse as an aggregate of pleasurable experiences. But Malinowski is disturbed by this; he cannot place the erotic kiss in Trobriand experience, since it has no climactic function.

In our culture, childbearing is climactic. Pregnancy is represented by the usual obstetrician as an uncomfortable means to a dramatic end. For most women, all intensity of natural physical experience is nowadays removed from the actual birth itself; but the approach of birth nevertheless is a period of mounting tension, and drama is supplied by the intensive social recognition of the event, the dramatic accumulation of gifts, flowers, telegrams. A pregnancy is not formally announced since, if it does not eventuate in birth, it has failed to achieve its end; and failure to reach the climax brings shame. In its later stages it may be marked with a shower; but the shower looks forward to the birth, it does not celebrate the pregnancy itself. Among the Trobrianders, pregnancy has meaning in itself as a state of being. At a first pregnancy, there is a long ceremonial involving "preparatory" work on the part of many people, which merely celebrates the pregnancy. It does not anchor the baby, it does not *have as its purpose* a more comfortable time during the pregnancy, it does not *lead* to an easier birth or a healthy baby. It makes the woman's skin white, and makes her be at her most beautiful; yet this *leads* to nothing, since she must not attract men, not even her own husband.

Are we then right in accepting without question the presence of a line in reality? Are we in a position to say with assurance that the Trobrianders are wrong and we are right? Much of our present-day thinking, and much of our evaluation, are based on the premise of the line and of the line as good. Students have been refused admittance to college because the autobiographic sketch accompanying their application showed absence of the line; they lacked purposefulness and ability to plan; they were inadequate as to character as well as intellectually. Our conception of personality formation, our stress on the significance of success and failure and of frustration in general, is based on the axiomatically postulated line. Yet can there be blocking without presupposed lineal motion or effort? If I walk along a path because I like the country, or if it is not important to get to a particular point at a particular time, then the insuperable puddle from the morning's shower is not frustrating; I throw stones into it and watch the ripples, and then choose another path. If the undertaking is of value in itself, a point good in itself, and not because it leads to something, then failure has no symbolic meaning; it merely results in no cake for supper, or less money in the family budget; it is not personally destructive. But failure is devastating in our culture, because it is not failure of the undertaking alone; it is the moving, becoming, lineally conceived self which has failed.

Ethnographers have occasionally remarked that the people whom they studied showed no annoyance when interrupted. Is this an indication of mild temper, or might it be the case that they were not interrupted at all, as there was no expectation of lineal continuity? Such questions are new in anthropology and most ethnographers therefore never thought of recording material which would answer them. However, we do have enough material to make us question the line as basic to all experience; whether it is actually present in given reality or not, it is not always present in experienced reality. We cannot even take it for granted as existing among those members of our society who are not completely or naively steeped in their culture, such as many of our artists, for example. And we should be very careful, in studying other cultures, to avoid the unexamined assumption that their actions are based on the predication of a lineal reality.

9

How Form and Content
Work Together
in a Defining Style

DOROTHY LEE sets up a comparison and contrast of linguistic and cultural contexts, placing a definition or example from our Western language parallel to or into antithesis with a definition or example from a non-Western language: "we arrange events and objects in a sequence which is climactic. . . . But when the Trobriander relates happenings, there is no developmental arrangement. . . ." Yet to say that she organizes by comparison and contrast, though obvious, is too general to be of much use in understanding Lee's behavior as a writer. For insight into that behavior, let us examine it more closely.

Lee begins with the commonplace distinction between word and reality and offers a concrete example consisting of several definitions of "words" that refer to the "thing" she holds in her hand and calls *pencil*. In a pair of questions—"Is the difference merely one of sound complex? Do they refer to the same *perceived* reality?"—Lee is suggesting that her readers begin to inquire beyond their common sense into the possibility that man's relation to external reality is not a direct visual one, but rather an indirect one filtered through words. She is defining reality by *dividing* it into two concepts: first, a reality separate from language; and second, perceived reality conditioned by language. The first reality exists objectively and is apparently external to man; the second, perceived reality (a limited experience of external reality heavily dependent on linguistic habits), is the only kind that we can know.

Let us consider Lee's next definition of a pair of words that, unlike *pencil,* refer to abstract concepts we cannot "visualize" in any direct common-sense way and that punctuate reality into different "phrasings" from the ones with which we are familiar. Notice that here again we are going to start with very simple, seemingly common words—"brother"/"kainga" and "sister"/ "ave"—but Lee transports the reader faraway from his own comfortable Western context (where most people he meets seem to agree that their different languages nevertheless represent the same reality).

She makes the shift from one cultural context to another more dramatic by changing from expository to narrative mode, asking us as readers to assume the point of view of anthropologists motivated to "go to the islands of Ontong Java to study the kinship system." Thus she calls a native, whom we are to imagine ourselves interviewing, "our informant." Lee's subject matter here cannot be intuitively grasped without a culture shock or some cognitive dissonance. It requires an effort of imagination on the reader's part, since we are being asked to question common-sense assumptions conditioned by our own culture that most people throughout their lives regard as obvious, unquestionable facts.

As soon as we are satisfied that we understand the Ontong definitions of brother and sister in terms of our own sense of the reality to which these words refer—"we equate *ave* with 'sister' and *kainga* with 'brother' "—then a further question to verify our common sense turns out to demolish our assurance: "By way of checking our information we ask the sister what she calls her brother; it turns out that for her, *ave* is 'brother,' not 'sister' as we were led to expect; and that it is her sister whom she calls *kainga.*" Lee now leads us as anthropologists proceeding to formulate a hypothesis: "We are prepared to account for this; we say that both cultures name according to what we would call a certain type of blood relationship; but whereas we make reference to absolute sex, they refer to relative sex." Lee guides us sequentially from our foregone commonsense conclusions about a supposedly obvious reality behind such simple words: "Further inquiry, however, discloses that in this, also, we are wrong." Finally, we must accept the conclusion that our words "brother" and "sister" do not represent the same perception of reality as the Javenese words "kainga" and "ave," for within a Javanese cultural context the use of these words "does not signify biologic fact alone," as ours does, but rather "names a social relationship, a behavior, an emotional tone."

Our difficulty in understanding the Ontong Javanese definitions of words is that we unquestioningly assume that our own definitions represent *reality* rather than only a particular perception of reality conditioned by our linguistic habits and cultural context.

Lee's organization of definitions here is somewhat like that of programmed instruction, which instead of presenting a difficult subject all at once so that readers either understand or fail to understand it, divides that subject carefully into an incremental sequence of difficulty. Each increment is so small and easy a step forward that the reader seldom makes mistakes and consequently can master with great confidence the most difficult concepts.

The more suspicious a writer is about the relation of conventional words and ideas to the new concepts she wishes to express, the more likely she might be led stylistically to use new metaphors that will adapt language as a vehicle for new insight. And this is exactly what we find in this essay. Let us consider, for example, these synonyms: "phrasing" reality, "punctuating" reality, "formulating" reality, "codifying" reality. When we look closely at these metaphors for man's relation to reality we may at first think them eccentric, since their reference is to the general area of linguistics rather than the conventional reference to sight or vision when speaking of perception (such as "to *see* reality," "to experience reality from a point of *view* or angle of *vision*," "to have in*sight*"). Lee consistently avoids using such metaphors for perception that have reference to sight or vision. Our common sense and metaphorical habits tell us that we can simply "see" what is real and what isn't. Why doesn't Lee say in her title, "Lineal and Nonlineal *Views* of Reality" rather than the unconventional "*Codifications* of Reality"? The word *view* is much easier and more familiar. But Lee's reason for using her new linguistic metaphors is that our perceptual relation with reality is not determined by what we can see, as though we were a simple camera, but rather by what and how our language conditions us to perceive. She is reversing our conventional assumption that our sense perceptions *cause* us to use certain language and is suggesting instead that it is our language that causes us to have certain sense perceptions.

Lee is not only careful in her own use of words, she often leads us to examine the relations between the words people use and the cultural context in which the words derive their meaning. This is called *contextual definition*. The following is Lee's definition of what failure means in the social context of the Trobriand Islands compared and contrasted with its meaning in Western culture:

> If the undertaking is of value in itself, a point good in itself, and not because it leads to something, then failure has no symbolic meaning; it merely results in no cake for supper, or less money in the family budget; it is not personally destructive. But failure is devastating in our culture, because it is not failure of the undertaking alone; it is the moving, becoming, lineally conceived self which has failed.

Fear of failure and love of its opposite, success, are valued in our society as primary motivators for all worthwhile activity, and our children are instilled very early with this form of fear and love. What some might proudly call "*our*" culture" as Lee shows us, is actually a marvelously subtle form of linguistically determined hang up. But her point in this contextual definition is not that the Trobriand Islanders' nonlineal culture is right and that we are wrong, but that we are habitually limited to

If the Trobriand Islanders had settled Manhattan, do you think it would have looked like this?

perceiving experience as lineal whether it is so or not, and this cultural context shapes the meaning of all our concepts. She is urging interest in and respect for cultural diversity as much more than a mere notion of tolerance—it is a necessary condition for inquiring honestly with the tools of definition to discover our cultural identity and limitations.

In addition to defining words by examining their nuances within a particular context, Lee defines words by bringing to life their dead metaphorical core. For instance, in the following *metaphorical definition* she makes herself aware of the reference areas of moribund metaphors that we, in Western culture (in contrast to the Trobriand Islanders), use without considering their implicit meaning:

> When we see a *line* of trees, or a *circle* of stones, we assume the presence of a connecting line which is not actually visible. And we assume it metaphorically when we follow a *line* of thought, a *course* of action or the *direction* of an argument; when we *bridge* a gap in the conversation, or speak of the *span* of life or of teaching a *course,* or lament our *interrupted career.*

Notice that Lee always uses definition as a tool for probing culture, never as a sterile exercise that ends with a foregone conclusion repeated from a dictionary. She not only defines many separate words and concepts throughout the essay, she uses definition as an important overall organizing structure, since the whole essay can be seen as a kind of extended definition of the concept of reality. Defining, then, is the central organizing structure in the essay in both a large and a detailed sense.

Lee evidently intends to do much more than simply show the uniqueness of the Trobriand Islanders' culture. Part of her purpose seems to be to lead us from a smug, narrow-minded closed culture to a more open and free one, employing various kinds of definitions as tools of inquiry to discover alternative perceptions that are not likely in our own culture. Unless we can get outside ourselves by studying other cultures we may not be able to understand, criticize, and extend our own cultural alternatives.

Printed below is a Trobriand Island writing program. If you were to write in this style, how do you think it would change your perceptions for the moment? Of course, you cannot become a Trobriand Islander, but you may become more aware of the coercive force of conventional speech and writing structures on our ways of thinking.

BRIEF DIAGRAM OF TROBRIAND ISLANDERS' STYLE

Subject Matter:

Use some recurrent social activity that you experience periodically.

Attitude or Ways of Thinking and Perceiving:

Avoid betraying any linear aim or goal (notice that the very words *aim* and *goal* are linear metaphors), but only "cluster" a description of some social activity in terms of what it has been, is, and always will be.

Syntax:

Avoid all adjectives and avoid adverbs of temporal relation like *after, before,* or *when.* Avoid all directional prepositions, such as *to, from, up, down,* etc. Avoid all distinctions of tense. Regardless of whether something happened in the past or will happen in the future, express all action as if it were occurring in the timeless present. Do not connect acts in any linear fashion with words like *because, since, then, therefore*—do not even use the connective *and.*

Words:

Avoid all terms of comparison. Use few words dealing with qualities; but when you do, make sure they are treated as substantives— i.e., *prettiness* or *happiness* rather than *pretty* or *happy.* Avoid all forms of the verb *to be.* Avoid the verb *to become,* since this would imply linear movement; things simply are what they always will be (e.g., a little green apple and a big red apple are separate entities rather than an unripe apple "becoming" a ripe apple).

Figures of Speech:

Avoid all metaphors that would betray any linearity (e.g., *"line* of thought," "to *draw* conclusions *from,"* "this step *leads to,"* "course of action").

Organization:

Avoid any "plot" or linear development such as spatial or temporal sequence. Avoid "logical" structures or linear organizations such as cause and effect. Organize only with ritualized or traditional social forms or behavior patterns, or object clusters.

Exercises

1. Notice how very different this non-Western style is from any of the ones we have studied so far in this text—all which are quite different from one another but generally share some kind of *linear* development and the same general linguistic structures because they are all written in English. The differences in perceived reality between these different styles are evident even though they may not be as dramatically polarized as Lee's English Trobriander. Remember that Lee went to a completely different culture and language group in order to show us how different perceived reality can be. Each style we have examined so far, by its patterns of inclusion and exclusion of certain words, definitions, and structures, implies on the part of its author a particular way of perceiving reality. And as you may have already felt, whenever you tried to follow a style program, each tends to impose on those who practice it a tendency *while using it* to perceive reality in a somewhat different way from what is habitual to them—more like the perceived reality of the original author of that style. A language or style is both an asset and a limitation—it tends to allow us to see steadily but not whole.

   We can talk about lineal or nonlineal cultures and still not have felt that difference until we actually experience nonlineal language habits. If you want now to experience for a moment a little of how it feels to think like a nonlineal Trobriand Islander, try writing on some modern subject following this set of linguistic habits.

   Below, for example, a modern American courtship is written

about in a more nonlineal style than that to which we are
accustomed:

> Woman bear man.
> Man bare teeth,
> bit woman-back.
> Woman-say, man,
> you been long back
> borne. Backbone
> broken, woman be
> broken-down. Back
> off, man, be bit.
>
> —ROBIN ELLINGTON

2. There is English language being used around you every day
that betrays on the part of the user a perceived reality that may
be very different from your own perceived reality. Suppose we
were anthropologists in the future presented with the following example of "beat/hip" language of the mid-sixties:

> The fuzz are searching our pad . . . like we listen to something
> cool and they move around us doing their thing. The fuzz ask
> one chick I really dig what is her bag and she answers, out of
> sight! . . . like she makes her bread putting on straights . . . like
> selling Campbell soup cans and Yale keyholes.

Certain linguistic habits are discernible even in this small sample.
How could we relate the pattern of linguistic habits we find here
to ways of thinking and perceiving that most probably underlie
such habits? Since many of the words used here are metaphors
or figures of speech, maybe we could start with the type of
metaphorical definition that we saw Dorothy Lee use.

The use of the word "fuzz" is an example of the figure of
speech called *metonymy*, where the proper (usual) name for
something is exchanged for the name of a characteristic or
quality associated with that thing. (This figure of speech was
discussed earlier, p. 70.) The wooly police uniforms (especially
the overcoats) worn in winter looked and felt fuzzy so that this
one characteristic, fuzz, is made to stand for the whole institution of police.

Exchanging the word "bread" for money because the purchase
of the "staff of life" (bread) is associated with the spending of
money is another example of the figure of metonymy, as is also
the word "bag."

The slang use of the word "pad" is an example of another figure of speech, called *synecdoche,* where the name of a part is made to stand for the usual name of the whole, or vice versa. A pad or pallet to sleep on is part of a house, apartment, or hotel, and is here used to refer to the whole apartment or perhaps apartment house.

So far all this is what Lee might call "idle etymologic statement," but not if we use, as she did, our definition to inquire further into how such language usage is related to habitual ways of thinking or perceiving. Note in each case how metonymy and synecdoche in this sample of writing have been used as ways to reduce a technologically complex and varied world to simple, generalized three- or four-letter words. All the technological complexity of police forces with their radios and vehicles and laboratories and computer files have been simplified to just "fuzz;" all the complexity of a money economy is reduced to its simplest terms, "bread"; and the complexity of occupations in a sophisticated technological society from plumbers to research executives are reduced to the "bag" (or briefcase) that they all carry and the "thing" they do. And a hotel or apartment, with its complex wiring circuitry, electrical appliances, heaters, air-conditioning units, and perhaps elevators, is reduced to its most basic common denominator, a "pad."

Some of the ways of thinking and perceiving that lie behind this kind of writing (whether or not the writer is conscious of the effect of his figures) are apparently an egalitarian wish to make a world of many status discriminations seem universal and equal, and a related aim of reducing to its simplest, most basic terms the complex, technological modern world.

Let us now look at a few more figures used in the writing sample, such as *synesthesia* (expressing something perceived through one sense in terms of another kind of sensation). Here, senses are mixed in the word "cool," where one of the five senses (touch) is being used to describe the auditory experience of listening. We also can see *metaphor* relating the geometric concept, "straight," to the unimaginative, narrow career and money-status lineality of the middle class. Synesthesia and metaphor as used here imply a wish to put the totality of experience back together, to relate separated parts of an overspecialized fragmented world. (The frequent use of the word "like" as an all-purpose coordinating conjunction to relate sentence fragments describing separate happenings may be part of this same criterion.)

As a result of metaphorical definition used as a tool of inquiry, we are now somewhat closer to understanding some of the perceptions that may underlie this kind of beat/hip word-use. Such mental habits, whether or not the writer is aware of them, imply criticism of the overspecialization that tends to split and fragment modern experience of the world, the inequality and status discrimination that tend to separate people from one another, and the technological complexity that tends to separate man from basic needs and values. In addition, the beat/hip word-use attempts to recommend a more basic, some might say "primitive," human existence.

Choose some person or group or culture whose linguistic behavior or style seems uncommon to you. Were any of the words they use once metaphors with live reference areas that now are dead? If so, you may be able to gain insight into word meanings and the group's assumptions by exhuming and examining the reference areas. Now, employing the tools of metaphorical and contextual definition that Dorothy Lee uses to pry into the differences in how word users seem to be perceiving reality, write an essay inquiring into the group's peculiar verbal behavior, comparing and contrasting it with the peculiar way in which you habitually talk and perceive reality.

3. Maybe in her constant use of linguistic contrast that tends to polarize two cultures into absolutely lineal and nonlineal categories, Lee is being coerced by her own linguistic habit of antithesis, which may be distorting her perception of some similarities between the cultures. Lee apparently ignores the possibility that there are still some traditional ritual patterns in our culture, that much of our own behavior is without any lineal goals. For example, do we send flowers at funerals because of some goal orientation or rather because it is patterned behavior that was "foreordained of old"? Perhaps many of our own thoughts loiter in directionless Trobriandesque clusters, pleasurable but aimless; and perhaps, too, the Trobrianders are at times more purposeful in their behavior than Lee suggests, even though they do not share our form of scientific temporal/spatial goal orientation. But even though she may be pushing it a trifle hard, surely Lee is showing us a large dif-

ference in perceived reality between the two cultures. Do you think your own behavior is lineal, nonlineal, or both? Discuss this in a brief essay.

10

Aristotelian, Metaphorical, and Operational Defining

Aristotelian Definition

X *is a kind of* A, *but differs from all other* As *with respect to the following characteristics:*

THERE are two steps in this definition. First, we must decide within what category the word to be defined best fits. Second, we must differentiate our word from other words conventionally associated within the same category.

If we were to define *viola,* for instance, we could fit it into many categories, such as material entity, or string stretcher, or musical instrument, or art object. It would be unnecessarily inefficient to pick material entity as our category since it is so broad that we would have a huge task to discriminate it from all other material entities. This is why it usually makes sense to use the most specific category to which the word to be defined can be said to belong rather than starting with a very broad general category. Whether we use art object or musical instrument as our category would probably depend on our general aims in writing. If we were writing on the art and craft of viola making in seventeenth-century Italy, we might be most concerned with the viola as an art object. But if we were writing an essay on the instrumental make-up of a modern symphony orchestra, it might be most productive to assign the viola to the category of musical instrument. Let us imagine the latter case and proceed to the second step in defining *viola*—differentiating it from other musical instruments. We could begin this step by saying that a viola, unlike brass instruments, is made of wood; to differentiate it from woodwinds, we could say it is a string instrument; to differentiate it from a guitar or harp or piano, we could say that it has only four strings and is usually bowed rather than plucked to produce a sound; and to differentiate it from a violin or cello, we could say that it is larger than a violin but considerably smaller than a cello and is, like the violin, played tucked under the chin. To further differentiate a viola from a violin we might explain that whereas a violin's strings are tuned from lowest to highest pitch, G, D, A, E (D is one note above middle C), the viola is tuned from lowest to highest pitch, C, G, D, A, which also differentiates the viola from the cello, whose strings are tuned an octave lower than the viola's. This might complete our differentiation of the viola from all other members of the category of musical instrument.

Sometimes an Aristotelian definition is called an inclusion/exclusion definition because in it we are including the word to be defined within some relevant category and then trying to exclude (or discriminate it from) other members of that category. Comparison and contrast along with example and illustration can be usefully employed in this process of discrimination.

When we use an Aristotelian definition or any other defining paradigm, whether we are conscious of it or not, we are assuming something about the nature of words, the nature of human intellectual behavior, and the nature of reality. For the way we go about organizing our language helps to determine our thinking just as surely as our thinking often determines the way we organize. When we ask ourselves, What is the smallest *category* to which a word *belongs?* we are assuming reality to be a rational, orderly sort of system where separate classes and hierarchies not only exist, but fit together in some right pattern and stay immutably the same. We may also be assuming that we can know this reality surely and clearly. And using the Aristotelian definition can lead easily to the questionable assumption that what we are doing is not defining a verbal symbol by relating it to other verbal symbols (and therefore only indirectly defining "the thing itself" by building a symbolic model that more or less fits reality), but that we are defining a "real thing" by relating it directly to the rest of reality.

The picture of reality that the typical Aristotelian definition presupposes is often too rigidly simple in hierarchical categories of classification to bear much resemblance to the ever-changing and complexly interrelated picture of reality that our modern study of the universe seems to suggest. On the other hand, an Aristotelian definition can be used (though too often it is not) with great care and precision to find very complex and subtle distinctions between the word to be defined and anything similar. The ability to make more and more careful distinctions can be a real advantage of this form of definition. But remember that no matter how analytical your distinctions in an Aristotelian structure, the direction of the definition is rigidly fixed by the class in which you decide to place the word at the very start. It is useful to test and question several different categories in order to make the best choice of category to which you might assign the word to be defined.

One of Aristotle's aims in defining was to generate assertions that could become parts of logical arguments (e.g., man is mortal; Socrates is a man; therefore, Socrates is mortal). It is easy to see, then, why he would want to keep metaphors and other colorful figures of speech out of a definitive assertion that was to be used in his logic—he was afraid they might lead to obscurity or ambiguity of inference. And it is also understandable why he ruled against allowing a word or cognate of the word to be defined into the definition—this would create a tautology that might invalidate any logical inferences he might wish to draw when he fit the definition into a logical structure and tried to deduce from it. Aristotle specifically warned against these two "errors" (tautology and metaphors) that he thought pernicious in defining, and people still too often accept Aristotle's dicta without question.

Today we do not necessarily use definition for the same purpose as Aristotle did, and so we do not need to legislate absolutely against repeating the word to be defined in some definitions. When Shakespeare has Polonius say "to define true madness, what is it but to be nothing else but mad," Shakespeare is using a blatant tautology to an Elizabethan audience that has been taught according to Aristotle's law against tautology in definition. Shakespeare, counting on adverse audience response, seems to be doing this in order to characterize the chief councilor of Denmark as something less than a clear-headed thinker.

But there are now uses of apparent tautology in defining which the reader is not expected to condemn: "Rose is a rose is a rose." And here is a stanza from the poem "Plain Speaking," by Louis MacNeice, who partially structured it by using a series of intentionally tautological definitions. In them the reader is being invited to contemplate the ultimate wisdom of definitions that insist on the concrete reality of "the thing itself" rather than engaging in an abstract analysis that may only lead farther away from the simple truth of concrete experience:

> In the beginning and in the end the only decent
> Definition is tautology: man is man,
> Woman woman, and tree tree, and world world,
> Slippery, self-contained; catch as catch can.*

MacNeice's apparent tautological definition is being used as a technique to shock the reader from a consideration of words as only *arbitrary* symbols back to an earlier philosophical position that has been abandoned by most modern thinkers influenced by linguistic study but that has recently been revived by some modern poets and literary critics—i.e., that words are not merely arbitrary "punctuations of reality," but that they and things have a real and natural relation. You may disagree with the philosophical wisdom of the poet, but it is hard to deny the effectiveness of such definition in communicating his mistrust of abstract intellectualizing.

In the following example of an Aristotelian definition used

* From *The Collected Poems of Louis MacNeice* (New York: Oxford University Press, 1967), p. 187.

to structure an entire essay, B. F. Skinner begins with an introductory first paragraph, establishing the importance of the concept of science, which he is about to define. In the second paragraph he begins in Aristotelian fashion to fit science into a category. Science, he says, is a kind of "intellectual process." He then uses the rest of this paragraph to defend his choice of category by explaining what a mistake it would be to try to fit science into some other category that might restrict it "to any particular subject matter" or to a kind of instrumentation or technology, even though scientists do use instruments. Nor does he think science should be restricted to a measuring or calculating category, even though scientists certainly use measurement in their work. In paragraphs 3 through 8, under the rubric of "Some Important Characteristics of Science," Skinner completes the second step of an Aristotelian definition by showing how we can differentiate the "unique intellectual process" of science from all other types of "intellectual processes" by explaining in detail its several most distinguishing characteristics.

A Science of Behavior *

B. F. Skinner

The immediate tangible results of science make it easier to appraise than philosophy, poetry, art, or theology. As George Sarton has pointed out, science is unique in showing a cumulative progress. Newton explained his tremendous achievements by saying that he stood on the shoulders of giants. All scientists, whether giants or not, enable those who follow them to begin a little further along. This is not necessarily true elsewhere. Our contemporary writers, artists, and philosophers are not appreciably more effective than those of the golden age of Greece, yet the average high-school student understands much more of nature than the greatest of Greek scientists. A comparison of the effectiveness of Greek and modern science is scarcely worth making.

It is clear, then, that science "has something." It is a unique

* From B. F. Skinner, *Science and Human Behavior* (New York: Macmillan, 1953), pp. 11–14.

intellectual process which yields remarkable results. The danger is that its astonishing accomplishments may conceal its true nature. This is especially important when we extend the methods of science to a new field. The basic characteristics of science are not restricted to any particular subject matter. When we study physics, chemistry, or biology, we study organized accumulations of information. These are not science itself but the products of science. We may not be able to use much of this material when we enter new territory. Nor should we allow ourselves to become enamored of instruments of research. We tend to think of the scientist in his observatory or laboratory, with his telescopes, microscopes, and cyclotrons. Instruments give us a dramatic picture of science in action. But although science could not have gone very far without the devices which improve our contact with the surrounding world, and although any advanced science would be helpless without them, they are not science itself. We should not be disturbed if familiar instruments are lacking in a new field. Nor is science to be identified with precise measurement or mathematical calculation. It is better to be exact than inexact, and much of modern science would be impossible without quantitative observations and without the mathematical tools needed to convert its reports into more general statements; but we may measure or be mathematical without being scientific at all, just as we may be scientific in an elementary way without these aids.

Some Important Characteristics of Science

Science is first of all a set of attitudes. It is a disposition to deal with the facts rather than with what someone has said about them. Rejection of authority was the theme of the revival of learning, when men dedicated themselves to the study of "nature, not books." Science rejects even its own authorities when they interfere with the observation of nature.

Science is a willingness to accept facts even when they are opposed to wishes. Thoughtful men have perhaps always known that we are likely to see things as we want to see them instead of as they are, but thanks to Sigmund Freud we are today much more clearly aware of "wishful thinking." The opposite of wishful thinking is intellectual honesty—an extremely important possession of the successful scientist. Scientists are by nature no more honest than other men but, as Bridgman has pointed out, the practice of science puts an exceptionally high premium on honesty. It is characteristic of science that any lack of honesty quickly brings disaster. Consider, for example, a scientist who conducts research to test a theory for which he is already well known. The result may confirm his theory, contradict it, or leave it in doubt. In spite of any inclination to the contrary, he must report a contradiction just as readily as a confirmation. If he does not, someone else will—in a matter of weeks or months or at most a few years—and this will be more damaging to his prestige than if he himself had reported it. Where right and wrong are not so easily or so quickly established, there is no similar pressure. In the long run, the issue is not so much one of personal prestige as of effective procedure. Scientists have simply found that being honest—with oneself as much as with others—is essential to progress. Experiments do not always come out as one expects, but the facts must stand and the expectations fall. The subject matter, not the scientist, knows best. The same practical consequences have created the scientific atmosphere in which statements are constantly submitted to check, where nothing is put above a precise description of the facts, and where facts are accepted no matter how distasteful their momentary consequences.

Scientists have also discovered the value of remaining without an answer until a satisfactory one can be found. This is a difficult lesson. It takes considerable training to avoid premature conclusions, to refrain from making statements on insufficient evidence, and to avoid explanations which are pure invention. Yet the history of science has demonstrated again and again the advantage of these practices.

Science is, of course, more than a set of attitudes. It is a search for order, for uniformities, for lawful relations among the events in nature. It begins, as we all begin, by observing single episodes, but it quickly passes on to the general rule, to scientific law. Something very much like the order expressed in a scientific law appears in our behavior at an early age. We learn the rough geometry of the space in which we move. We learn the "laws of motion" as we move about, or push and pull objects, or throw and catch them. If we could not find some uniformity in the world, our conduct would remain haphazard and ineffective. Science sharpens and supplements this experience by demonstrating more and more relations among events and by demonstrating them more and more precisely. As Ernst Mach showed in tracing the history of the science of mechanics, the earliest laws of science were probably the rules used by craftsmen and artisans in training apprentices. The rules saved time because the experienced craftsman could teach an apprentice a variety of details in a single formula. By learning a rule the apprentice could deal with particular cases as they arose.

In a later stage science advances from the collection of rules or laws to larger systematic arrangements. Not only does it make statements about the world, it makes statements about statements. It sets up a "model" of its subject matter, which helps to generate new rules very much as the rules themselves generate new practices in dealing with single cases. A science may not reach this stage for some time.

The scientific "system," like the law, is designed to enable us to handle a subject matter more efficiently. What we call the Scientific conception of a thing is not passive knowledge. Science is not concerned with contemplation. When we have discovered the laws which govern a part of the world about us, and when we have organized these laws into a system, we are then ready to deal effectively with that part of the world. By predicting the occurrence of an event we are able to prepare for it. By arranging conditions in ways specified by the laws of a system, we not only predict, we control: we "cause" an event to occur or to assume certain characteristics.

Exercises

1. Define *science* in a sentence, using the Aristotelian writing paradigm as a tool of inquiry as well as a method of organizing a compound sentence.

2. Now expand your one-sentence definition of *science* into a short paragraph of several sentences, using the Aristotelian definition as an organizing structure for the whole paragraph. Instead of using your one-sentence definition as a topic sentence, try

generating whole new sentences from constituents like phrases and clauses in the original one-sentence definition.

3. Write a one-paragraph, then a one-sentence, abstract of Skinner's essay. You can do this fairly easily once you understand how his whole essay is an Aristotelian definition of *science*.

4. Write a short essay defining a word such as *democracy*. Use the Aristotelian paradigm not only to *inquire into the meaning* of the word (for example, what is the next largest class to which *democracy* belongs? Is it a philosophy? a form of government? an ideal? an economic as well as political system? a way of life? or a ————?), but to *organize* your whole essay, as Skinner did perhaps unconsciously.

Metaphorical Definition

X *can be defined metaphorically by relating it to the following reference area:* . . .

Metaphors tend to make definitions more memorable, and so many influential definitions that we have all become familiar with are metaphorical—from that of the ruler as the "head" of the state and the ruled as the "body" politic to Karl Marx's definition of religion as the "opiate of the people." More recently, Carl Sandburg defined slang as "language which takes off its coat, spits on its hands, and goes to work." Sandburg's lively imagery would be hard to use in a logical syllogism, yet it defines his meaning forcefully and memorably. To prohibit the use of metaphors in all definition is to misunderstand the nature of language, which is almost always metaphorical even when, for example, the metaphor may have been in use for so long that we forget it is a metaphor. Were you aware, for instance, that even words like the conjunctions *moreover* and *therefore* were originally metaphors? Would anyone want to legislate against all *live* metaphors in definition but accept all *dead* ones? Of course, some metaphorical definitions do tend to be ambiguous, subjective, or difficult to test, but a definition containing fresh metaphors can be just as effective for some

purposes as one containing abstract language full of dead metaphors can be for other purposes.

Often people define their concepts metaphorically without
being aware that they are doing so. We saw how Dorothy Lee
takes advantage of this habitual use of words that originated
as metaphors, whose reference area tends to reveal a group's
basic assumptions even though they themselves may not be conscious of it. Lee uses, then, another form of metaphorical defining whose syntax would go something like this: *Since* X
*originated as a metaphor (or other figure of speech), it can be
defined by explaining the way of thinking or perceiving implied by the choice of reference area of the metaphor (or
figure).* You will find a fuller discussion, with examples, of this
kind of metaphorical defining in the previous chapter, pp.
172–179. But we did not at that time discuss the more active
form of metaphorical defining—that of coining fresh metaphors
to define words or concepts.

Here is a prose passage in which the writer has effectively
used metaphorical definition:

> This American government,—what is it but a tradition, though
> a recent one, endeavoring to transmit itself unimpaired to
> posterity, but each instant losing some of its integrity? It has
> not the vitality and force of a single living man; for a single
> man can bend it to his will. It is a sort of wooden gun to
> the people themselves. But it is not the less necessary for
> this; for the people must have some complicated machinery
> or other, and hear its din, to satisfy that idea of government
> which they have.
> —HENRY DAVID THOREAU, from *Civil Disobedience*

In the following poem a seventeenth-century poet, Andrew
Marvell, defines love metaphorically as a kind of geometric
line relation that differs from all other geometric relations by
being perfectly parallel so that the separate lines could never
touch (in a seventeenth-century Euclidian universe, at least,
if not in our Einsteinian world where parallel lines *can* meet).
In other words, the poet is using an Aristotelian definition combined with a metaphorical one by making a metaphor of the

category to which he refers love—love is a kind of geometric relation, etc.:

The Definition of Love

My Love is of a birth as rare
As 'tis, for object, strange and high;
It was begotten by Despair
Upon Impossibility.

Magnanimous Despair alone
Could show me so divine a thing,
Where feeble Hope could ne'er have flown
But vainly flapped its tinsel wing.

And yet I quickly might arrive
Where my extended soul is fixed:
But Fate does iron wedges drive,
And always crowds itself betwixt.

For Fate with jealous eye does see
Two perfect loves, nor lets them close;
Their union would her ruin be,
And her tyrannic power depose.

And therefore her decrees of steel
Us at the distant poles have placed
(Though Love's whole world on us doth wheel),
Not by themselves to be embraced,

Unless the giddy heaven fall,
And earth some new convulsion tear,
And, us to join, the world should all
Be cramped into a planisphere.*

As lines, so loves oblique may well
Themselves in every angle greet;
But ours, so truly parallel,
Though infinite, can never meet.

Therefore the love which us doth bind,
But Fate so enviously debars,
Is the conjunction of the mind,
And opposition of the stars.

—ANDREW MARVELL

* A two-dimensional representation of the globe.

Exercises

1. Can you, as Marvell did, combine the Aristotelian and metaphorical definitions to write a paragraph defining a word like *alienation,* or *freedom?* (Robert Frost once defined *freedom* as "going easy in your harness," but why not coin your own metaphor?)

2. In one sentence define a word like *thinking* by coining a bold, fresh metaphor. (If you are unsure how to produce metaphors, see the discussion of metaphor making on pp. 50–53.)

3. Now extend your metaphor and write a short paragraph more fully defining this same word.

4. Can you find and discuss a probable way óf thinking or perceiving implicit in the use of the following words and phrases that originated as metaphors or figures of speech: *soul food, soul brother, soul* (as in "she has soul")?

5. Look up the words *culture* and *psychosis* in an etymological dictionary. What ways of thinking and perceiving are reflected in the origin of each of these words? Are these implicit ways of thinking and perceiving a past chapter in cultural evolution, or are they still ingrained in our society as well as fossilized in our language?

Operational Definition

> X *can be defined by describing a process by which you can measure it, such as the following: . . .*

How can a word be "measured" or given mathematical symbolic meaning in addition to verbal meaning? In this writing paradigm the definition of a word is a description of the way you could go about measuring the "thing it represents." Charles Fourier, the nineteenth-century philosopher, had his cane marked off in standard units so that as he walked he could pause to reduce anything that interested him to a quantitative measurement. You do not need to be a walking operational definition to find this defining structure useful. For instance, although it is almost impossible to define the word *power* by an Aristotelian definition because it is so hard to find any larger category to fit the word into, the definition of *power* can nevertheless be given operationally, by describing the following process of measuring a unit of "horsepower": the amount of power it takes to do 33,000 foot-pounds of work in one minute of time. We are accustomed to using an operational definition for *hot* or *cold* because thermometers are so handy, and we all recognize either Fahrenheit or centigrade methods of measurement. We are also so used to defining *time* operationally that without a wrist watch or, at least, without being able to gauge the position of the sun we may feel that we have "lost all sense of *time*."

Regrettably, some people using operational definitions have been prone to fall into the following traps: they often measure only that which can be most easily or obviously measured, and then dismiss or ignore the possible importance of those qualities that are not readily quantifiable, and all too often act as though the nonquantifiable were, in fact, nonexistent. When we use operational definition we are assuming that the meaning of our words can and should be both accurately measurable and capable of objective verification by any one able to repeat the simple process by which we measured originally. Obviously, in the sciences such accurate and objective meaning is extremely useful. But it would be difficult to convince people that the meaning of many common words such as *love* or *mother* would profit greatly by being objectively numerical. As a matter of fact, a recent, very serious study by a pair of physiologists, Johnson and Masters, *Human Sexual Response,* attempts an operational definition of *sexual response* by describing the process by which the authors took careful measurements of acceleration of respiration, blood pressure, body temperature, etc., of many subjects during experimentally controlled sexual intercourse. Their work has proved quite valuable to science but controversial to the public—which might prefer an Aristotelian definition of *making love* (e.g., "an emotion that differs from all other emotions . . . ," etc.) to an operational one.

It may seem to us that nothing could be more obvious than the difference in meaning between the words *life* and *death,* and yet two of the most explosive social, legal, and moral issues of our day are due to the difficulty of defining these two words. The first issue is brought about by the recent surgical possibility of organ transplants, in which organs must be taken from a donor in a matter of a few minutes after he is declared legally "dead." The second issue concerns abortion and the definition of *life*.

The old definition of *death* (when the heart stops beating and the lungs stop breathing, the patient can be declared dead) would make it impossible ever to get any heart-transplant donors legally, since a donated heart cannot be allowed to stop beating until just before it is taken from the donor. With new resuscitation techniques it has become possible to keep the heart beating and otherwise to continue "life" long after the patient's brain has deteriorated beyond any hope of recovery and, indeed, even after it has stopped functioning at all. But even if the brain has "died," can the "live" heart be allowed to stop or be removed or, as medical authorities are now beginning to wonder, could some doctor because of the ambiguity in the definition of *death* be accused of malpractice or even, possibly, murder? These developments are forcing medical authorities to redefine *death operationally* by precise criteria and measurement in order to eliminate subjective value judgments from the determination of "death." Since brain cells, unlike other living tissue, cannot repair themselves, brain damage is irreversible and permanent. Brain functioning can be *measured* by the wave patterns revealed by an electroencephalogram, and a flat wave pattern for a given length of time has been suggested as the most accurate, measurable means of confirming death, even though the heart and other organs can be kept functioning by artificial means. Even if the patient could be kept functioning, he would be less like a human than like a vegetable. Is such a form of functioning life or death? According to the new operational definition, if accepted as legal as now seems likely, such vegetable functioning is considered death.

The definition of *life* is just as ambiguous as that of *death* and even more socially and morally critical. Not only do attempts to legalize or prohibit abortions depend on definitions of whether the fetus is or is not "alive," but they often depend on an operational definition by measurement of the age of the fetus or its exhibition or measurable "life signs." An accurate operational definition of whether or when a fertilized ovum or fetus can be considered to have legal life is likely to become still more critical in the future. The new possibilities of determining biochemically in an early stage of pregnancy whether or not a fetus is abnormal in some way, together with the increased possibilities of abnormal fetuses due to modern man's burgeoning industrial pollution, radioactive waste, and use of drugs and chemical additives, all of which could increase the rate of human mutations, may soon force us to decide whether or not we are willing to use our new knowledge of biology to modify or terminate the "life" of an ovum or fetus—all of which will require new legal definition.

It is likely that scientific innovations and the legal problems they may raise are going to force society at an increasing rate to redefine many of our most important concepts *operationally*. Some of these concepts (racial segregation, pollution, for example, or freedom to determine family size) that have for centuries remained ambiguous may, when they are operationally defined, produce explosive social and religious confrontations.

Until after the late philosopher of science, Percy Bridgman, made popular the term *operational definition* in 1938 to explain Einstein's procedure in defining the concept of *simultaneity* by describing simple, measurable operations, it did not often occur to researchers outside the sciences to define their terms measurably. But in the past three decades operational definitions have been used more and more often in research of all kinds. At this moment, operational defining is particularly difficult and crucial in the so-called "soft" sciences. Almost every article on sociology, psychology, anthropology, economics, or political science will grapple with an important problem of operational defining, where dictionaries are of no help at all and the writer is on his own. When quantification in a field is at an early stage, the writer may find it difficult to design some operational measurement that will define a concept. For instance, if a psychologist wants to talk about hunger he might have to design and describe some experiment where rats are deprived of food for different periods of time to see how length of deprivation in hours varies with respect to the strength of electrical charge per second that the rats are willing to withstand in order to obtain food.

But today, it is not very surprising to find even poetic styles and traditions being defined operationally, as Josephine Miles demonstrates in *Eras and Modes in English Poetry,* a study of literary history. In her book Miles explains how periods or traditions in poetry have, in the past, been defined by division according to centuries. Is this definition of poetic traditions by century simply an arbitrary convention? she asks. Will some operational measuring of differences in poetry with respect to time define the same or possibly very different poetic periods?

Miles begins her operational definition by considering "whether a closer technical look at poetic practice might not discover some descriptive principle of period sequence." * She defines three *modes* of poetry determined by measurement of the largest percentage of one of three types of sentence structures: phrasal types (adjectival mode); clausal types (predicative mode); and phrasal/clausal types (balanced mode). She counts and shows the results of her measurement of the number of each type of sentence in samples of poetry written from 1500 to 1900 to find which type or mode of sentence structure is used the most at what times in history. And this enables her at last to define operationally a number of distinct poetic *eras* in a graph plotted from her measurement

* Josephine Miles, *Eras and Modes in English Poetry* (Berkeley: University of California Press, 1957), p. 2.

of dominant sentence types with respect to time over a period
of four centuries:

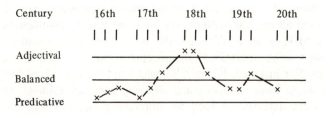

Operational definition represents a sort of turning our backs
on the apparent complexity of reality in order to reapproach it
from a simpler, more measurable angle, which, in the long run,
may provide us with new insight into an even more complex
reality that was not perceivable to us before we started defining.
Josephine Miles's relatively simple operational definition of
poetic periods and styles, or "eras and modes," provides many
new insights and certainly generated much new research in her
field.

Exercises

1. Can you think of a way of operationally defining a word or
   concept not usually thought of in operational terms, such as
   democracy? For example, to qualify as a democracy, what
   percentage of citizens, men or women or both, must be franchised? At what age? What percentage of the franchised votes are
   needed to elect? How many *alternative* candidates for the same
   office should there be in each democratic election? Can you have
   a democratic election with only one candidate running, or even
   with several running who still present only one alternative because
   they all share the same stance on the issues? Now define your
   concept in a brief essay by describing the process by which you
   think it could be measured.

2. Try to set up and conduct a quantifiable experiment that could generate the data necessary to operationally define *reading comprehension* or *writing competence*.

3. Can you cross-structure the Aristotelian and operational paradigms into a new kind of definition? For example, first find the next larger class to which the word belongs, and then differentiate it from all other members of that class by using some process of measurement as the basis for discrimination. (For instance, in defining *Stradivarius violin*, it could be differentiated from a cheap factory-made violin in terms of the *measurable* difference in the number of harmonics when a note on one or the other is played.) Try to combine the Aristotelian and operational paradigms to define some words or concept such as the following: *pollution, overpopulation, industrial monopoly, recession, human brain.*

4. A measurable concept, called intelligence quotient (IQ), is a form of operational definition much used and abused. What does IQ measure? Are any useful cognitive skills not measured? Consider the assumptions underlying this particular definition and its possible limitations. What do you think IQ means to the researchers, institutions, and agencies who use it to discriminate among people? Now write several paragraphs discussing the advantages and disadvantages of defining social concepts operationally.

11

Contextual and Stipulative Defining

In context 1, X means A; but in context 2, X may mean B; while in context 3, X means neither A nor B, but something more like C; ...

IT would be a mistake to assume that the sole function of verbal symbols is to communicate ideas. Many words, depending on context, convey meanings—connotations—well beyond the restricted sense of what they name, designate, or refer to. They may express emotional attitudes, evoke some passion, or perhaps attempt to provoke action or express emotional attitudes. A little prayer that was first printed in the *New England Primer* in the year 1781 is still familiar to us:

> Now I lay me down to sleep
> I pray the Lord my soul to keep.
> If I should die before I wake,
> I pray the Lord my soul to take.

All the words are very simple, and they *denote* today what they did in 1781—that is, none of the words has changed appreciably in signification, so there should be no difference in the meaning of the little prayer. Today it is a sentimental ritual that neither the child nor the parent takes very seriously. But this represents a great difference in the prayer's meaning because of a shift in social and historical context. In America, from 1781 until the beginning of this century, the mortality rate among infants was so high that it seems almost unbelievable to us today. Only about half of the babies born could ever live to be more than a few years old, and many a parent awoke to a still cradle. In 1781 the line "If I should die before I wake" bore a deadly serious meaning for both the parent and the child praying.

It was also the context that changed the meaning of *transplanted heart* from a horror film on television, where a heart transplant from a fresh corpse into another body was being accomplished by Dr. Frankenstein, to an excited account in the late news of a heart transplant from a fresh corpse into the body of another man by Dr. Christiaan Barnard. The denotative meaning of "heart transplant" was the same in both instances, but the Frankenstein film, because of its Gothic underground laboratory and sinister context, carried an emotional meaning fraught with horror, while a few minutes later the shaken TV viewer was again contemplating "heart transplant" but in the context of modern medical science, this time presumably experiencing a glow and warmth of pride in the latest accomplishment of modern humanity.

But there are other functions of meaning, aside from emotional ones, that can change in a different context. Sometimes the denotative meaning changes too. When we draw a line and then draw a circle above it, the result would probably have only geometric meaning for us. But if we introduce a line on each side of our diagram to form a rectangle around it, we will be adding the convention of the frame to our original diagram that will change the context and also quite possibly the meaning of the original line and circle. (See figures on p. 204.) The circle above the line can now be defined as the sun, rising above the horizon. Why do I assume the sun is rising rather than setting? If we add within the simple context of the frame some conventional activity, such as a man in soiled clothes unhitching a pair of tired-looking horses or maybe cows heading toward the barn and a maid milking, that normally occurs in late afternoon, we might, because of these slight changes in context, decide that the circle above the horizon means a setting rather than a

---

Describe the symbols above. Do they mean anything?

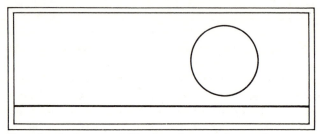

Now what do they mean? Why does the rectangle around
the symbols make a difference?

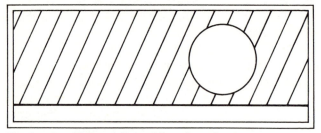

How has the addition of diagonal lines changed
the symbols' meaning? Why?

rising sun. But we are still defining the circle as the sun. If we
were to draw some light parallel lines to shade the area within
the frame, except for the circle, we might change the meaning
of the circle from sun to moon. The meaning of a symbol,
either pictorial or verbal, depends to some extent on the context in which you frame it.

We have so far been using *context* in two senses: the *immediate frame* (such as the picture we have just discussed) or

the *external world frame* (for example, the sociohistorical changes that have shifted the meaning of the 1781 prayer). In writing, the immediate frame is often called the *verbal context*. Notice how the word *sophisticated* shifts in meaning when framed in different verbal contexts:

> Our 2002 computer contains an even more *sophisticated* circuitry.
> Before he can be elected he'll first have to prove acceptable to the *sophisticated* urban voter.
> Dirty books and movies rated X are a little too *sophisticated* for my taste.

The verbal context is always an important determinant of word sense, and, in fact, some highly specialized or technical words outside the theoretical postulates of which they are a part have little or no meaning (look up *phlogiston* in a dictionary) or have radically changed meanings. In Aristotelian physics *gravity* is an essence built into some objects as part of their nature; *gravity* means an attractive force that operates between bodies as a result of their mass in Newtonian physics; in Einstein's general theory of relativity *gravity,* now usually called *gravitation,* means a dynamic field that is a manifestation of matter from which it cannot be separated.

Choose a word such as *beauty, force, program, mass, good, juvenile, space,* and illustrate several different meanings by changing its verbal context. Note that apart from some context these words have only possible or potential meanings.

The basic assumption in using a contextual definition is that the meaning of a word is not essentially unalterable or universal, but is relative to some specific frame of reference. This assumption probably fits all words, though some seem to slither about more freely than others. The act of defining such chameleon words can often profitably include a consideration of at least the more usual contexts in which the word appears. For example, consider the meaning of the word *love* in the context of a soap opera, a religious service, or a brothel. Yet carried to extremes, this assumption behind contextual defining would render human culture and communication systems impossible. For if most words did not retain some conventional meaning from context to context, speakers or writers would have to devise a whole new linguistic system every time they changed their frame of reference. Some stable, conventional word meaning is the glue necessary to hold language together—though too much glue may make it sticky or rigid.

Many words, even when their general meaning remains fairly stable, change their *specific* meaning from context to context. Take the term *deus ex machina,* "a god from a machine." When we look it up in a dictionary we learn that this Aristotelian Greek term is expressed in Latin, which means the Romans must have adopted it and passed it on to us since we find it in modern English dictionaries. Even though the phrase has a history of over two thousand years, it seems to indicate the same denotative meaning over the entire period: "In classical tragedy a god from outside the immediate plot who is suddenly introduced into that plot by the writer to effect an unexpected solution to some difficulty confronting the characters." Yet the term must have been used in so many different contexts during this time that a dictionary definition could not possibly consider all of them. For example, when the term *deus ex machina* is used in the context of discussing a modern Western movie instead of classical tragedy, referring not to a Greek hero's difficulty being solved by the introduction of a god to help him, but to a wagon train surrounded by hostile Indians and out of ammunition that is saved at the last minute by the sudden appearance of a cavalry regiment that was just happening by, it would, in this context, mean specifically the U.S. Cavalry.

Modern comics extol the fortuitous outside help of supermen who, in the nick of time, solve apparently insoluble problems for the characters. In the context of the comics, then, *deus ex machina* might be used to refer to a figure like Mighty Mouse or Batman. In a nineteenth-century romantic context a benevolent mother nature frequently rescues characters or saves them unexpectedly. In the context of many a sentimental novel or popular song, the term *deus ex machina* might refer to the power of love that often fortuitously seems to save an impossible marriage as well as rescue almost any other unpleasant situation. In still another context, *deus ex machina* might refer to any fortuitous instrument, such as a yellow submarine that rescues the Beatles and presumably all humanity from the menacing Blue Meanies. In the context of the modern nonfictional world, men often can be said to depend on *deus ex machina* solutions to real problems. The "god from the machine" seems to be modern technology, which we rely on to save us at the last moment, as though life were like a bad play to be resolved improbably in our favor to save us from our progressive air pollution, urban disintegration, nuclear proliferation, and overpopulation, which, we often seem to think, we need not take steps to remedy for ourselves. It might be interesting to consider the possible meanings of *deus ex machina* in other modern contexts. Who or what are the modern "gods" that seem to be relied on to rescue people from their difficulties? Will enough money solve *any* problems? You might learn a lot about our unconscious beliefs and myths if you were to inquire further.

Exercises

1. Define the difference context makes in your interpretation of the detail and the whole of *The Peaceable Kingdom,* p. 208.

2. Have you noticed how different groups in our society disagree on the meaning (sometimes denotative as well as connotative) of important words like *patriotism, police, middle class, science, sex, permissiveness, militant, revolution,* and *women's liberation?* What are the different meanings these words have, depending on the social context in which they are used? Can you think of any other words that shift meanings when employed in different contexts?

3. Use the contextual paradigm to inquire into the meanings of a word like *ecosystem* or *radical,* and then use this contextual

Edward Hicks, *The Peaceable Kingdom* (1844).

paradigm to structure a short essay of several paragraphs. Now compact your definition into a paragraph, organized with the contextual paradigm. Finally, make your contextual definition concise and economical enough to structure a sentence of several clauses.

4. Try to define a phrase or word such as *simultaneity, time,* or *map making* by cross-structuring the contextual definition with the operational definition.

5. Try defining *inside surface* or *outside surface* in the context of a Möbius strip. What does your difficulty here suggest about the relationship between conventional concepts and modern science? Is the acceleration of science likely to increase the need for redefinition?

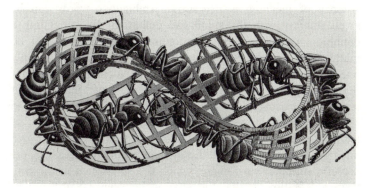

M. C. Escher, *Möbius Belt II* (1970).

6. Define *pollution* with respect to several different ecosystems. Are certain substances always polluting, or do the substances we consider pollutants depend on the ecological context in which we find them? We would not call oxygen a pollutant today because we are animals who need it to survive. However, in the context of the world before the evolution of animals, oxygen gas given off by vegetation was a form of pollution that must have begun to accumulate since animals were not yet available to consume it.

7. Can you define the contextual relations between people, objects, and distances in the lithograph on p. 153?

Stipulative Definition

From now on, whenever I use the word X *I shall always mean* A, *which should not be confused with* X's *other possible meanings,* B *or* C *or* D, . . .

We have seen how many words vary in meaning as we use them, and yet to communicate in writing some stability or consistency of meaning is necessary. Ambiguous words can be given stability with the stipulative definition. By stipulating a definition we are implying a promise to our readers that no matter what context we frame a word in we will stick to only one meaning of that term without equivocation. Sometimes that promise is hard to keep no matter how careful we might try to be, because meaning is often slippery and it is easy to equivocate unintentionally. We must assume the presence of ambiguity in a word in order to feel the need to stipulate one unequivocal meaning for it. Another assumption implicit in the use of a stipulative paradigm, which is also implicit in the contextual definition, is that the relation between a word and its meaning or the thing it indicates is not natural or fixed or absolute in any way, but is simply conventional.

Unlike other kinds of definitions, stipulation implies a concern for the future meaning of a word rather than the past or present meanings. Thus we can stipulate any one of the past or current meanings or even assign a new meaning to a word. When stipulating one of several current meanings to clarify ambiguous words like *love* or *beauty,* it is often desirable to annul in a reader's mind all the other possible meanings. Choosing and sticking to a successful stipulative definition may well necessitate a writer's private use of other forms of definition (the contextual, for example), in order to become aware of all current connotations as well as denotations and to assess the occasions for unconscious straying either on our own part or on the part of our readers.

A writer should certainly be aware that readers commonly allow irrelevant emotional connotations that a word may have had in previous contexts to influence their present perceptions of that word. Advertising copy writers know that it makes a difference whether, when they mean underarm deodorant, they call it "safeguard" spray or "antisweat" spray. Politicians, too, know that "a rose by any other name" would probably not smell as sweet to most people, and that taxpayers will more enthusiastically support a "safeguard system" than an "antiballistic missile system" even if they have much the same meaning and cost about the same.

The economist Thorstein Veblen was careful to stipulate a very precise meaning for his term *conspicuous waste,* a term that denotes a kind of consumption whose purpose is not to produce something necessary or useful to society:

> The use of the term "waste" is in one respect an unfortunate one. As used in the speech of everyday life the word carries an undertone of deprecation. It is here used for want of a better term that will adequately describe the same range of motives and of phenomena, and it is not to be taken in an odious sense, as implying an illegitimate expenditure of human products or of human life. . . . The use of the word "waste" as a technical term, therefore, implies no deprecation of the motives or of the ends sought by the consumer under this canon of conspicuous waste.*

When Veblen continues to use this "technical" term throughout his book in concrete contexts that are designed to disgust us with vulgar and self-indulgent displays of our society's squandered resources, it is almost impossible to think of "conspicuous waste" without feeling some deprecating or odious connotations that he has specifically denied intending in his

* Thorstein Veblen, "Conspicuous Consumption," in *The Theory of the Leisure Class.*

stipulation. This tension between context and stipulation that Veblen creates for ironic purposes is a possibility of which we ought to be aware lest it happen to us unintentionally. We know that context is a powerful determinant of some words' meanings, and to avoid confusing a reader or generating unintentional irony when using a stipulative definition we must constantly be careful to keep harmony between our stipulated term and the contexts in which we frame it.

It is fairly easy to stipulate for a word one of the current meanings with which your audience is already familiar. But what happens when you stipulate a brave new meaning for a comfortable old word your audience has for years related to some quite different meaning or meanings? For example, the women's liberation movement has stipulated a new meaning for *chauvinist*, and radical writers of the late sixties stipulated a new meaning for *violence* so that it would refer to societal repressiveness in all its forms. To fly in the face of your readers' habits will force those readers to question their common sense; and perhaps this is just what you want. But to make a person question his own common sense is to come dangerously close to provoking his hostility as a reaction to momentary fear of insecurity. When a writer decides to chance this questioning of the conventional, he'd better have something important to teach the reader and let him know it pretty fast.

If you want to stipulate some unfamiliar meaning, it is often easier to get your audience to accept your idea if you make up a new word for it instead of trying to stretch an older word to cover the new meaning. At least you will not chance arousing hostility but only the indifference of an aesthetic snub if your new word is both unfamiliar and infelicitous. But if a new word or phrase stipulation catches on, time and familiarity have a way of anesthetizing any aesthetic sense. Even English professors have begun dearly to love such words as *objective correlative* or *archetypal patterns* or *transformational grammar* that seemed shocking barbarisms when new. The reason we never find "jargon" in Standard English is because when specialized words become generally useful enough to be accepted, dictionaries and English teachers no longer call them "jargon."

The trouble with stipulating a new word is that if your reader remembers it until the end of your essay you're lucky; if he continues to remember it or uses it later you have been paid a very high compliment indeed. For instance, several years ago someone cleverly stipulated the short stem *cept* for any idea that was part of a larger concept, but it has never caught on. Do you think *psychedelic* or *swinger,* new word stipulations that became so popular several years ago, will last and find a permanent place in Standard English?

Though we might suppose the primary purpose of a stipulative definition is to make the meaning of a word less ambiguous and more specific, this is not always the case. Sometimes it can be very useful to know how to stipulate a general rather than a specific meaning for a word. Administrators, like college deans or politicians, and leaders of large disparate groups of people often need to stipulate general rather than specific definitions so that they can communicate economically and broadly without alienating individuals or minorities of their public. A dean of students, for example, who decided to stipulate an exhaustive specific rather than short general meaning of *student freedom* would probably not last long, for he would seem to be restricting that freedom by defining its precise limits, and thus would invite students to try to extend these limits. Precision and specificity are not always to be desired in writing. It is sometimes very useful to be able to say *few* or *many* rather than attempt to state exact numbers for every situation. Constitutions and codes of law that stipulate minutely specific definitions rather than broad general ones would not only be lengthy and intricate but would probably soon break down because of the impossibility of reinterpreting precisely worded laws to apply them in new cases and inevitably changing social contexts. Though ambiguous general definitions have their uses, such definitions are often the tool of the dangerous demagogue as well as the honest politician.

The following stipulative definition of *the state,* from Adolf Hitler's *Mein Kampf,* is the ultimate example of perversion of the power of defining. Hitler is defining the state or nation as a society with the same "blood," rather than a society that inhabits the same geographic area or shares a common linguistic or legal tradition. This racist definition, although it was an insanely ambiguous stipulation, was accepted by many and helped determine the misery and death of millions of people all over Europe in the late 1930s and early 1940s. Although we may find it almost incredible that any society could ever have entertained such a definition, it is even more shaking to be aware that similar forms of racist definition of our own state and institutions, perhaps often accepted unconsciously, constitute a severe problem in our country and in our own time.

> Since Nationality or rather race does not happen to lie in language but in the blood, we would only be justified in speaking of a Germanization if by such a process we succeeded in transforming the blood of the subjected people. But this is impossible. Unless a blood mixture brings about a change, which, however, means the lowering of the level of the higher race. The final result of such a process would consequently be the destruction of precisely those qualities which had formerly made the conquering people capable of victory. Especially the cultural force would vanish through a mating with the lesser race, even if the resulting mongrels spoke the language of the earlier, higher race a thousand times over.*

For very different reasons Stokely Carmichael in the following excerpt considers definition the indispensable tool to dig under and expose the roots of racism:

Black Power **

I want to start off with definitions by using a quote from one of my favorite books, which is *Alice in Wonderland,* by Lewis Carroll. In the book there's a debate between Humpty Dumpty

* Adolf Hitler, *Mein Kampf,* trans. Ralph Mannheim (Boston: Houghton Mifflin, 1971), pp. 284–289. Reprinted by permission of Houghton Mifflin Company.
** From *To Free a Generation: The Dialectics of Liberation,* ed. David Cooper (New York: Collier Books, 1968). Reprinted by permission of the Institute of Phenomenological Studies.

and Alice around the question of definitions. It goes like this:

"When I use a word," Humpty Dumpty said, in a rather scornful tone, "it means just what I choose it to mean. Neither more nor less."

"The question is," said Alice, "whether you can make words mean so many different things."

"The question is," said Humpty Dumpty, "who is to be master. That is all."

Now I think that Lewis Carroll is correct. Those who can define are the masters. And white western society has been able to define, and that's why she has been the master. And we want to follow up with a lot of those examples, because I think that the white youth of my generation in the West today does not understand his own subconscious racism, because he accepts the writings of the West, which has destroyed, distorted and lied about history, so that he starts off with a basic assumption of superiority which is not even recognizable.

Frederick Douglass, the great black leader of the 1800s, said that when a slave stops obeying a master, then and only then does he seek his liberation. Camus said the same thing 100 years later on the first page of *The Rebel* when he said that when a slave stops accepting definitions imposed upon him by his master, then and only then does he begin to move and create a life for himself. That's very important, because what the people of the Third World are going to have to do today is to stop accepting the definitions imposed on them by the West. Let's give some examples.

The first one is that the history books tell you that nothing happens until a white man comes along. If you ask any white person who discovered America, they'll tell you "Christopher Columbus". And if you ask them who discovered China, they'll tell you "Marco Polo". And if you ask them, as I used to be told in the West Indies, I was not discovered until Sir Walter Raleigh needed pitch lake for his ship, and he came along and found me and said "Whup—I have discovered you." And my history began.

But let us examine the racism in that statement. Let us examine it very closely. Columbus did not discover America. Columbus may be the first recorded white man to have set foot in America. That is all. There were people there before Columbus. Unfortunately, those people were not white—unfortunately for the white West, fortunately for us, they weren't white. But what happens is that white western society never recognizes the existence of non-white people, either consciously or subconsciously. So that all around the world, the peoples of the Third World never did anything until some white man came along—and that's why China's non-existent, because Mao won't let no white folk in there. Yeah. And pretty soon Hong Kong is going to be non-existent because they're going to kick them out.

So that the situation you have is that history has been written—but indeed it has been so distorted. One of the biggest lies, I think, that western society could have told was to name itself Western Civilization. And now all through history we were studying Western Civilization, and that meant that all else was uncivilized. And white kids who read that today never recognize that they're being told that they are superior to everybody else because they have produced civilization. At best, that's a misnomer, at worst, and more correctly, it's a damn lie. Yes. Western Civilization has been anything but civilized. It has been most barbaric, as a matter of fact. We are told that Western Civilization begins with the Greeks, and the epitome of that is Alexander the Great. The only thing that I can remember about Alexander the Great was that at age twenty-six he wept because there were no other people to kill, murder and plunder. And that is the epitome of Western Civilization. And if you're not satisfied with that, you could always take the Roman Empire. Their favorite pastime was watching men kill each other or lions eating up men. They were a civilized people. The fact is that their civilization, as they called it, stemmed from the fact that they oppressed other peoples. And that the oppression of other people allowed them a certain luxury, at the expense of those other people. That has been interpreted as "civilization" for the West, and that is precisely what it has done. The only difference is that after the Roman Empire, when the British Empire—on which the sun never used to set, but today it sets, sometimes it don't even rise—began to exploit non-white people, what they did was they let colour be the sole choice of the people they would exploit.

Now that's very important because as we go along you can see one of the best examples you can see today. You see, because you've been able to lie about terms, you've been able to call people like Cecil Rhodes a philanthropist, when in fact he was a murderer, a rapist, a plunderer and a thief. But you call Cecil Rhodes a philanthropist because what he did was that after he stole our diamonds and our gold, he gave us some crumbs so that we can go to school and become just like you. And that was called philanthropy. But we are renaming it: the place is no longer called Rhodesia, it is called Zimbabwe, that's its proper name. And Cecil Rhodes is no longer a philanthropist, he's known to be a thief—you can keep your Rhodes Scholars, we don't want the money that came from the sweat of our people.

Now let us move on to present times. I'm always appalled when some white person tells me that "progress is being made". I always ask him "progress for whom? And from whom?" Progress for white people might be made, because I would say that since World War II they have learned a little about how to get along with people of colour. But I don't think there's been progress for the black people, there's not been progress for the people of colour around the Third World. And progress will not be measured for us by white people. We will have to tell you when progress is being made. You cannot tell us when progress is being made, because progress for us means getting you off our backs, and that's the only progress that we can see.

Now then, we want to talk about cultural integrity versus cultural imposition, because that stems from definitions. Because the white West felt somehow that it was better than everybody else—I remember when I was a young man in the West Indies, I had to read Rudyard Kipling's *The White Man's Burden*. I thought the best thing the white man could do for me was to leave me alone, but Rudyard Kipling told them to come and save me because I was half savage, half child. It was very white of him. What has happened is that the West has used force to impose its culture on the Third World wherever it has been. If a few settlers left England to go to Zimbabwe, there was no reason for them to rename that country after themselves, Rhodesia, and then force everybody to speak their language, English. If they had respect for the cultures of other people, they would have spoken the language of those people and adopted their religions. But what in fact happened was because the West was so powerful—that's the word nobody wants to talk about, power. It was only power that made people bow their heads to the West, you know. They didn't bow it because they liked Jesus Christ, or because they liked white folks. No, Machiavelli said a long time ago that "people obey masters for one of two reasons. Either they love them, or they fear them." I often ask myself whether or not the West believes the Third World really loves them and that's why they've obeyed them. But it's clear that they feared them. The West with its guns and its power and its might came into Africa, Asia, Latin America and the USA and raped it. And while they raped it they used beautiful terms. They told the Indians "We're civilizing you, and we're taming the West. And if you won't be civilized, we'll kill you." So they committed genocide and stole the land, and put the Indians on reservations, and they said that they had civilized the country.

They weren't satisfied with that. They came to Africa and stole Africans and brought them to the USA, and we were being brought there to be "civilized", because we were cannibals and we ate each other, and they were going to give us a better life, which was, of course, slavery.

Exercises

1. Why doesn't Stokely Carmichael simply look up the definition of words like *discovered, philanthropist,* or *civilized* in a dictionary? What is the purpose of his inquiry into the meaning of such words?

2. Discuss Hitler's stipulative definition of *the state.* Do you agree that a state is a community of blood? Stipulate your own definition of a *democratic state* (or *country*) in a brief essay. This may necessitate arguing against some of the other current meanings of *democracy* and *state* (or *country*).

3. Most arguments are not disputes over substantive issues as the disputants often seem to think, but semantic misunderstandings that can best be clarified by one of the debaters stipulating the precise sense in which he is using key terms. "If a tree falls in the forest with no one around to hear it, does it make a

noise?" If you want to waste time and effort, try arguing about this without stipulating a precise definition for *noise*. Is *noise* disturbing vibrations impinging on the human eardrum, or is it irregular wave motion of molecules? The following assertions cannot be argued about intelligently until their terms have been unequivocably defined:

a. Our schools are too permissive.
b. Welfare cheats the rich and ruins the poor.
c. Sexism and racism in America were responsible for the ruthless conduct of our war in Indochina.
d. Draft dodging is never a patriotic act.
e. The joke he told was humorous in spite of the fact that nobody in the audience understood it.
f. I'm no radical, but what this country needs is a revolution.
g. Teaching machines may impart skills, but not education.
h. Romanticism was a more creative movement than classicism.

Show that each of these assertions contains equivocal terms by stipulating at least two different definitions for each key term that would make you *agree* with the assertion according to your first definition and *disagree* with it according to the second.

4. Concrete words like *table, desk, chair, book* tend to be relatively stable in meaning compared to the kind of abstract words often used in college-level writing such as the following:

liberal	culture	art
intuitive	instinct	literature
romantic	evolution	music
meaningful	adaptation	religion
primitive	ecology	community
progress	superstition	sympathy

Write a sentence for each of these words, stipulating one of the possible meanings. Pick one of these short stipulative definitions and expand it into a paragraph. Now develop your paragraph into a stipulative definition of several paragraphs.

12

Lexical and Divisional Defining

Lexical Definition

> *At historical time* T, X *meant* A; *at time* T′, X *could mean either* A *or* B, *etc.; presently at time* T″, X *no longer means* A, *but can mean* B *or* C *or* D, *etc., and these word changes may provide the following insight into human society and mind: . . .*

In the last chapter we spoke of the need in a stipulative definition to be aware of a word's current and past meanings to avoid confusion between the sense you are stipulating and any number of other possible meanings. We are now going to discuss a type of definition that will help give us this kind of awareness. The *lexical* (or historical) definition is a more or less accurate and complete record of a word's meanings up to and including its current meanings. I said "more or less accurate and complete" since in even a few years a word like *brainwash,* for example, has been used by so many different groups and in so many different contexts that it would be practically impossible to record all the alterations of meaning it has undergone.

But aside from having too much information, one obvious problem in writing an accurate history of a word's meaning is that up until very recently only a fairly small group of people, most of whom were at the very top level of society, could write. What some particular word meant to an elite few whose books were by chance preserved may not at all have been the meaning used by the man in the street. Lexicographers are caught between two difficulties. On the one hand, they have too much information about modern usage to record it all and hence, in the interest of economy and clarity, must make more or less biased decisions to ignore some usages and call attention to others. On the other hand the scant records of earlier times introduce the bias of class and chance because, whether or not it was truly representative of common usage, the lexicographer must record whatever little was preserved after centuries of wars and fire and flood.

A lexical definition is based on a series of assertions about how a word was or is actually used and thus, unlike some other kinds of definitions, presents valid or invalid statements capable of verification. For the correctness of a lexical definition is not tested by the truth of the word's meaning, but rather by the recorded facts of human behavior. Is it true that the Old English word *dreor* (our *dreary*) meant blood? This depends entirely on recorded evidence for how English writers actually used the word in the eighth to the thirteenth centuries.

Using a lexical definition can be a fairly scholarly endeavor unless, of course, as an aid to our research we use a dictionary that defines words historically, such as the multivolume *Oxford English Dictionary on Historical Principles* (called *OED* for short). Since it contains entries for about half the words in the English language and records their usage for the last thousand years, the *OED* can be very useful to you in lexical defining, as long as you remember that even this dictionary has limitations of the kind we have already specified for all lexical definitions. Since they are necessarily so incomplete, most small desk dictionaries, even though they may appear to be using lexical definitions, are really *stipulating* the socially approved meanings of words rather than accurately recording the range of past and current meanings. In such dictionaries past usage, when it appears, may be indicated by referring to it as "archaic," while the most contemporary usage is often termed "colloquial," and only the conventional usage of conservative written English recommended as standard.

What are the possible assumptions underlying a lexical definition? An early assumption about language (Swift shared it—see p. 130) was that words all have "true" original meaning any deviation from which supposedly removed us further from the "real" sense of the word. Consequently, looking up the etymological or historical part of a lexical definition was assumed to be important for fixing or legislating the original or past meaning of a word and keeping it from change. But we now more commonly assume that alterations in the meanings of our words are natural and inevitable. And we know that etymology, or what a word originally meant, is not a reliable guide to its meaning at present. Why, then, should we have any interest today in the earlier meanings of words? Remember that Dorothy Lee (p. 157) disparaged "idle etymologic statement," referring to the mere collection of arcane knowledge about word origins when it is put to no use in understanding human culture or cognitive behavior. But we can, as she did, actually use such lexical knowledge as a tool to gain insight into human social and cognitive behavior.

For instance, it makes no difference to our current meaning of *bonfire* to learn that it originally meant *"bone* fire." Yet the early reference of bonfire to funeral pyres and burning heretics at the stake or other fiery human executions or sacrifices and their relation to victory celebrations or festivals, the occasions for which bonfires are still lighted today (for example, after a winning football game), could tell us something interesting about the process of human ideas and society over the past 1,000 years.

The vicissitudes of environment and society and changes in ideas, institutions, and technology profoundly affect word usage and thus meaning. Sometimes a word meaning mutates or becomes obsolete because of geographical dislocation of a community using the word, such as happens in migration, foreign invasions, and now daily as a result of our growing world-wide communication system. For example, when the English first landed in America, their word *corn* had a very general meaning, like our words *grain* and *cereal;* but it was not long before *corn* narrowed in meaning to refer to Indian maize, a unique feature of the New World. What do you suppose were the effects of the Norman conquest on the vocabulary of the English language? What will be the effects of mass communications? At times word sense was altered because of a social, technological, or philosophical revolution. For instance, consider the changes in meaning given to words like *repression, unconscious, ego, complex, psyche* after Sigmund Freud's writings became well known. Word meanings vary, too, as a result of the way one class or age group of society uses a word as distinct from other social groups. Word meanings tend to become *elevated* or *degraded,* depending on class association. Both *knight* and *knave* are respectively elevated and degraded forms of the same Old English word meaning boy, a close relative of the modern German word for boy, *Knabe,* which has retained its original neutral connotation. Is our word *boy* neutral or becoming degraded in connotation? Why? *Vulgar* was earlier neutral in meaning and without pejorative connotations, referring to the everyday customs of common people. Can you imagine why it became degraded? In addition to alterations of sense as a result of social tension, words quite often tend to drift in either a more *generalized* or more *specialized* direction from their former meanings. For example, *liquor* formerly meant any liquid, but today is used in a more specialized way, while a word like *adamant,* which formerly meant diamond, has now a generalized sense of hard or intransigent, an obvious quality of diamonds.

Examining the way words have gained altered meanings can also give us a special kind of insight into the way the human brain functions. For instance, look up the word *jack* and its cognates in the *OED.* You will find *Jack* was a generic name for servant. The usefulness of *Jack,* the servant, must have been *metaphorically transferred* to an implement, a *jack,* that helped make a tough job easier. We find the word often *combined* to form more specialized meanings, such as a *boot jack* and *hydraulic jack.* And we find "jack" *shifting grammatical function* in the sentence from noun to other parts of speech, such as the verb *to jack*. Try to classify some other ways in which *jack* has mutated in use and meaning, such as *hijacking* and, more recently, *skyjacking*.

Now look up the word *cast* to see if some of the same kinds of word mutations have occurred. Do you think your classification reveals something about human cognitive processes? We don't have to believe that such mental processes are *innate* in human nature, as some maintain; we can, instead, accept Jean Piaget's hypothesis that mental processes are "constructed" as the human infant matures in relation to his environment. Yet whatever their source, some human brain structures seem to help alter words in fairly predictable ways.

Consider the following essay in which Raymond Williams assumes that a change, occurring around 1800, in the meaning of several important words was indicative of some larger change in social thinking, perhaps correlated with the political and industrial revolutions near the end of the eighteenth century. Notice that by *combining* lexical and contextual defining into a more useful form of organization for his purposes, Williams is able to inquire into and contrast social contexts before and after 1800.

Key Words *

In the last decades of the eighteenth century, and in the first half of the nineteenth century, a number of words, which are now of capital importance, came for the first time into common English use, or, where they had already been generally used in the language, acquired new and important meanings. There is in fact a general pattern of change in these words, and this can be used as a special kind of map by which it is possible to look again at those wider changes in life and thought to which the changes in language evidently refer.

Five words are the key points from which this map can be

* From Raymond Williams, Preface, in *Culture and Society, 1780–1950* (New York: Columbia University Press, 1958), pp. xiii–xvii.

drawn. They are *industry, democracy, class, art* and *culture.* The importance of these words, in our modern structure of meaning, is obvious. The changes in their use, at this critical period, bear witness to a general change in our characteristic ways of thinking about our common life: about our social, political and economic institutions; about the purposes which these institutions are designed to embody; and about the relations to these institutions and purposes of our activities in learning, education and the arts.

The first important word is *industry,* and the period in which its use changes is the period which we now call the Industrial Revolution. *Industry,* before this period, was a name for a particular human attribute, which could be paraphrased as "skill, assiduity, perseverance, diligence." This use of *industry* of course survives. But, in the last decades of the eighteenth century, *industry* came also to mean something else; it became a collective word for our manufacturing and productive institutions, and for their general activities. Adam Smith, in *The Wealth of Nations* (1776), is one of the first writers to use the word in this way, and from his time the development of this use is assured. *Industry,* with a capital letter, is thought of as a thing in itself—an institution, a body of activities—rather than simply a human attribute. *Industrious,* which describes persons, is joined, in the nineteenth century, by *industrial,* which describes the institutions. The rapid growth in importance of these institutions is seen as creating a new system, which in the 1830s is first called *Industrialism.* In part, this is the acknowledgement of a series of very important technical changes, and of their transforming effect on methods of production. It is also, however, an acknowledgement of the effect of these changes on society as a whole, which is similarly transformed. The phrase *Industrial Revolution* amply confirms this, for the phrase, first used by French writers in the 1820s, and gradually adopted, in the course of the century, by English writers, is modelled explicitly on an analogy with the French Revolution of 1789. As that had transformed France, so this has transformed England; the means of change are different, but the change is comparable in kind: it has produced, by a pattern of change, a new society.

The second important word is *democracy,* which had been known, from the Greek, as a term for "government by the

people," but which only came into common English use at the
time of the American and French Revolutions. Weekley, in
Words Ancient and Modern, writes:

> It was not until the French Revolution that *democracy* ceased
> to be a mere literary word, and became part of the political
> vocabulary.

In this he is substantially right. Certainly, it is in reference to
America and France that the examples begin to multiply, at
the end of the eighteenth century, and it is worth noting that
the great majority of these examples show the word being used
unfavorably: in close relation with the hated *Jacobinism,* or
with the familiar *mob-rule.* England may have been (the word
has so many modern definitions) a democracy since Magna
Carta, or since the Commonwealth, or since 1688, but it certainly did not call itself one. *Democrats,* at the end of the
eighteenth and the beginning of the nineteenth centuries, were
seen, commonly, as dangerous and subversive mob agitators.
Just as *industry* and its derived words record what we now call
the Industrial Revolution, so *democracy* and *democrat,* in their
entry into ordinary speech, record the effects, in England, of the
American and French Revolutions, and a crucial phase of the
struggle, at home, for what we would now call democratic
representation.

Industry, to indicate an institution, begins in about 1776;
democracy, as a practical word, can be dated from about the
same time. The third word, *class,* can be dated, in its most important modern sense, from about 1772. Before this, the
ordinary use of *class,* in English, was to refer to a division or
group in schools and colleges: "the usual Classes in Logick
and Philosophy." It is only at the end of the eighteenth century
that the modern structure of *class,* in its social sense, begins to
be built up. First comes lower *classes,* to join *lower orders,*
which appears earlier in the eighteenth century. Then, in the
1790s, we get *higher classes; middle classes* and *middling classes*
follow at once; *working classes* in about 1815; *upper classes* in
the 1820s. *Class prejudice, class legislation, class consciousness,
class conflict* and *class war* follow in the course of the nineteenth
century. The *upper middle classes* are first heard of in the
1890s; the *lower middle class* in our own century.

It is obvious, of course, that this spectacular history of the new use of *class* does not indicate the *beginning* of social divisions in England. But it indicates, quite clearly, a change in the character of these divisions, and it records, equally, a change in attitudes towards them. *Class* is a more indefinite word than *rank,* and this was probably one of the reasons for its introduction. The structure then built on it is in nineteenth-century terms: in terms, that is to say, of the changed social structure, and the changed social feelings, of an England which was passing through the Industrial Revolution, and which was at a crucial phase in the development of political democracy.

The fourth word, *art,* is remarkably similar, in its pattern of change, to *industry.* From its original sense of a human attribute, a "skill," it had come, by the period with which we are concerned, to be a kind of institution, a set body of activities of a certain kind. An *art* had formerly been any human skill; but *Art,* now, signified a particular group of skills, the "imaginative" or "creative" arts. *Artist* had meant a skilled person, as had *artisan;* but *artist* now referred to these selected skills alone. Further, and most significantly, *Art* came to stand for a special kind of truth, "imaginative truth," and *artist* for a special kind of person, as the words *artistic* and *artistical,* to describe human beings, new in the 1840s, show. A new name, *aesthetics,* was found to describe the judgment of art, and this, in its turn, produced a name for a special kind of person— *aesthete. The arts*—literature, music, painting, sculpture, theatre —were grouped together, in this new phrase, as having something essentially in common which distinguished them from other human skills. The same separation as had grown up between *artist* and *artisan* grew up between *artist* and *craftsman. Genius,* from meaning "a characteristic disposition," came to mean "exalted ability," and a distinction was made between it and *talent.* As *art* had produced *artist* in the new sense, and *aesthetics aesthete,* so this produced *a genius,* to indicate a special kind of person. These changes, which belong in time to the period of the other changes discussed, form a record of a remarkable change in ideas of the nature and purpose of art, and of its relations to other human activities and to society as a whole.

The fifth word, *culture,* similarly changes, in the same critical period. Before this period, it had meant, primarily, the "tending of a natural growth," and then, by analogy, a process of human training. But this latter use, which had usually been a culture *of* something, was changed, in the nineteenth century, to *culture* as such, a thing in itself. It came to mean, first, "a general state or habit of the mind," having close relations with the idea of human perfection. Second, it came to mean "the general state of intellectual development, in a society as a whole." Third, it came to mean "the general body of the arts." Fourth, later in the century, it came to mean "a whole way of life, material, intellectual and spiritual." It came also, as we know, to be a word which often provoked either hostility or embarrassment.

The development of *culture* is perhaps the most striking among all the words named. It might be said, indeed, that the questions now concentrated in the meanings of the word *culture* are questions directly raised by the great historical changes which the changes in *industry, democracy* and *class,* in their own way, represent, and to which the changes in *art* are a closely related response. The development of the word *culture* is a record of a number of important and continuing reactions to these changes in our social, economic and political life, and may be seen, in itself, as a special kind of map by means of which the nature of the changes can be explored.

I have stated, briefly, the fact of the changes in these important words. As a background to them I must also draw attention to a number of other words which are either new, or acquired new meanings, in this decisive period. Among the new words, for example, there are *ideology, intellectual, rationalism, scientist, humanitarian, utilitarian, romanticism, atomistic; bureaucracy, capitalism, collectivism, commercialism, communism, doctrinaire, equalitarian, liberalism, masses, mediaeval* and *mediaevalism, operative* (noun), *primitivism, proletariat* (a new word for "mob"), *socialism, unemployment; cranks, highbrow, isms* and *pretentious.* Among words which then acquired their now normal modern meanings are *business* (= trade), *common* (= vulgar), *earnest* (derisive), *Education* and *educational, getting-on, handmade, idealist* (= visionary), *Progress, rank-and-file* (other than military), *reformer* and *reformism, revolutionary* and *revolutionize, salary* (as opposed to "wages"), *Science* (= natural and physical sciences), *speculator* (financial), *solidarity, strike* and *suburban* (as a description of attitudes). The field which these changes cover is again a field of general change, introducing many elements which we now point to as distinctively modern in situation and feeling.

In his last paragraph, Williams mentions a number of words that also changed radically in meaning or were first used around 1800. Choose several of these words that you find interesting and look up each in the *OED*. Do you find any relation between the new meanings that occur for each word and the social and intellectual context just before and after 1800? You may want to refresh your memory of that social and intellectual milieu by consulting an encyclopedia or general English history. Can you now write a short speculative history of ideas for the 1800 period using a *combination* of the *lexical and contextual* definitions such as Williams used as an organizing structure? Your operating assumption, like Williams's, must be that a shift in the meanings of several important words at some particular time is likely to reflect a more general change in the history of human ideas. (You will find that you do not really need to know much about the history of the 1800 period to hypothesize a change in social structures or attitudes from the record of word changes.)

Exercises

1. Forgetting or ignoring a term's earlier meaning sometimes is the occasion for inventiveness when a speaker or writer adapts the term to a new sense. For example, "the silent majority" was a popular euphemism for "the dead" in the nineteenth century, but resurrected unwittingly by conservative politicians in the late 1960s and early 1970s to mean that an outspoken opposition to war was merely a noisy minority, while the truly patriotic majority maintained a decorous repose on such issues. Look up in the *OED* the earlier meanings of the words printed in italics in each of the following popular old sayings still used today:

a. Feed a cold and *starve* a fever (originally "starve *of* fever"—you'll see why when you look it up).
b. It's the exception that *proves* the rule.

Is our modern sense of these maxims consistent with the intended meaning of the earlier English advice? What does the difference suggest about society, past and present?

2. In the past 1,000 years and more that the English language has been in use, some words have changed considerably in meaning. For example:

doom	lust	guy	deer	enthusiasm
humor	shirt	shambles	meat	disease
project	silly	moral	smug	picture
boycott	faculty	cunning	virtue	bull's-eye
nice	mistress	mob	harlot	ordeal

Look up each of these words in the *OED*. Is social class dynamics the only kind of change that has determined shifts in the sense of these words? List and classify the different kinds of changes that have occurred in this sample of words. Can you suggest some hypothesis to explain the evolution of word meanings in general? Does your hypothesis offer any insight into the functioning of the human mind or the evolution of culture?

Pick out one or more of these words for which you perceive interesting differences in the way the words were used then and now. Write from your research *and imagination* a short essay comparing social ideas or institutions in the past and present.

3. Here are a few words that have been coined or changed in meaning much too recently to have been recorded in the *OED*.

hippie	radical liberal	male chauvinist
brainwash	to waste	social engineering
conservatism	socialism	cool
welfare	third world	model
sexism	conditioning	psychedelic

Suppose you were asked to make an entry in a new edition of the *OED*. Write as complete a lexical definition as you can of one of the above words that has more than one current meaning, and in some cases has meanings that are no longer used even though the word is relatively new. What insight did researching your lexical definition give you into contemporary society?

Divisional Definition

There are two syntactical paradigms that might be helpful in defining by division:

> *There are* n *kinds of* X.
> X *is composed of* n *parts.*

The first will cue you into a definition by *external* division, and the second into a definition by *internal* division. For instance, in defining *college* we might first divide it *externally* into two kinds, public and private; maybe we could change our basis of division and differentiate between two-year and four-year colleges; or maybe, changing our basis of division again, we might say that there are several kinds of colleges, such as liberal-arts colleges, agricultural colleges, engineering colleges, etc.

In defining *college* by *internal* division, we could show how colleges are partitioned into a number of conventional departments, such as the department of English, the department of physics, and the departments of mathematics, history, or biology, etc. So far we have been acting as though the definition of *college* is a foregone conclusion that we are simply restating. But, though these department divisions are the traditional way to divide colleges, many academic communities are beginning to rethink the conventional definition of college by considering new bases of division, more consistent with our changing needs and assumptions about the meaning of education. Could education be improved and made more interesting if several traditional departments, such as those of English, art, music, mathematics, languages, and linguistics, were combined into a new division of "symbolic communication," for example? Would there be any advantage in such a division? Or could English be combined with psychology, history, political science, sociology, and anthropology, where perhaps a number of interdisciplinary courses could be taught by a team of teachers with different kinds of knowledge working together? After all, the study of literary writing is really the study of one kind of human behavior and might profit by a knowledge of other kinds of human behavior related to it.

Can you think of some new basis for dividing *college* that might redefine it for the better? Redividing *college* is a challenge, though it is probably easier for you than for your teachers since they have become habituated to the conventional divisions and may have a hard time even understanding why anyone would want to redefine categories that to them seem quite natural. Too often, the presumption behind continuing to use a conventional division is not that it represents simply one way of defining a word or concept, but that the habitual division is an immutable and true attribute of the "thing" for which, it is assumed, the word stands.

In using the internal-division paradigm, we assume that whatever we are trying to define is not a simple, indivisible whole, but some complex or combination that can be successfully analyzed into parts or characteristics. But you should realize that this assumption has its limitations. Not only are some substances very difficult to analyze (as every chemist knows), but other things, especially living things, are so complexly and subtly organized that to divide part from part is to risk losing the functional relations that make up the organism. As a matter of fact, some people would flatly deny that you can separate an "organic *whole*" into *parts*. This idea of the indivisibility of organic wholes has been metaphorically applied to many other things besides organisms. Musical compositions, paintings, poetry have all been said to be "organic wholes" and, therefore, if divisible at all, extremely difficult to dissect without losing the patient on the operating table. The difficulty in internal division of a complexly functioning organization or organism is to maintain respect for the integrity of the whole and the mutual interaction of each part you divide it into.

Some words, such as *calcium chloride* or *automobile,* that denote inorganic compounds or machinery composed of parts seem to lend themselves to definition by division, whereas other words that denote more complex organizations, such as *mob,* are not as easy. Consider how you could divide *mob* in order to help explain its meaning to someone. First, let's consider defining it internally. Surely, anyone who has seen a mob knows that it is something more than the enumeration of the individual people of which it is composed. Separately, Joe Jones and Charley Smith and Pam Green, etc., may be fairly reasonable and law-abiding people; but brought together into a mob they no longer continue to operate as an aggregate of individuals. They become some new entity that is obviously something more than and different from the arithmetical sum of its parts. However, we might be able to shed light on some kinds of mob behavior by investigating its division into a few leaders who give sanction and confidence to a larger group of blind followers, whose growing fanaticism, in turn, feeds back confidence to the leaders.

Or we could divide *mob* externally by inquiring into the possible kinds of mobs: those banded together for an ideal we might call "ideological mobs"; those banded together out of starvation or physical desperation we could call "physiological mobs." Or, dividing on another basis, we might speak of "armed" and "unarmed" mobs. But maybe *mob* is better divided into three kinds rather than two. But which three? The division might be statistical: "those involving one hundred or fewer people," "those composed of from one hundred to one thousand people," and "those comprised of over one thousand people." There are many bases for division, which include temporal, spatial, cause and effect, statistical, and patterns of attributes or characteristics (such as emotional, intellectual, physical). You must decide which is the most significant division relative to your specific purpose in defining.

Contour farming is one way of dividing arable soil. What are some other ways of defining land by dividing it?

Here is one of Shakespeare's many definitions by division (*Hamlet*, II, ii). You may not immediately be able to perceive any consistent basis of division, although it would have been clear to a Renaissance reader that Shakespeare was thinking of man as a microcosm, whose many parts were analogous to various parts of the whole universe, since man was thought to be part of earth's "dust" or clay from which he was originally formed in the Garden of Eden. Man contained animal attributes too, and, at the same time, his highest intellectual faculties made him analogous to heavenly beings like angels. Yet it is traditionally said of man, despite his more noble but temporary attributes, "Dust thou art, and to dust thou shalt return":

What a piece of work is a man! How noble in reason! How infinite in faculties! In form and moving how express and

admirable! In action how like an angel! In apprehension how
like a god! The beauty of the world! The paragon of animals!
And yet, to me, what is this quintessence of dust?

Exercises

1. Write a divisional definition of *context* in a one- or two-page
   paper. Express your essay in one paragraph. Now abstract the
   paragraph definition to a single sentence.

2. The Zuñi Indian language divides the color spectrum differently
   than we. For example, they have no words to describe the
   range of colors from yellow to red that we call *orange;* they
   apparently do not perceive the same division of color that we
   see. In some other languages there is only one word used to
   describe both blue and green. Would people brought up without
   the divisions of blue and green to which our language has
   accustomed us perceive the grass and sky as simply different
   shades of the same color? Does our available vocabulary tend
   to determine our perception of divisions? In a brief essay, define
   a term such as one of the following—*life style, literature, art,
   music, social elite, the world, human need, play, education.*
   Combine divisional with stipulative definition by stipulating a new
   word, or words, to make a division possible that perhaps has
   not been perceived before.

3. Combine divisional with operational definition to organize an
   essay defining a term such as one of the following: *democracy,
   war, success, the good life, learning, pollution.* For example, we
   could divide *democracy* into two kinds, "apparent" and "real."
   Real democracy might be operationally defined as a state
   governed by representatives elected by secret ballot by a minimum of 90 per cent of the total population, who must have lived
   more than five years within its territorial borders, who are over
   the age of eighteen, and who are registered to vote in elections
   held at intervals of not more than four years; and for each

office, there must be a choice of candidates representing at least two different political philosophies or goals. *Apparent democracy* is one that claims to be a democracy and satisfies some, but not all, of the operational criteria for real democracy.

General Exercises in Combining Definitions

By cross-structuring one basic defining paradigm with another into a new and more complex structure, we can create many more types of definition, and adapt an organization to accomplish almost any specific defining purpose.

1. Choose a key term in another course you are studying this semester (for example, *adaptation* in biology, *language* in linguistics, *culture* in anthropology, *class* in sociology, *primitive* in art history, or *poetry* in English), or pick any of the words below, and try to construct various definitions of your word using *each* of the defining structures previously explained: Aristotelian, metaphorical, operational, contextual, stipulative, lexical, divisional.

subculture	determinism	relevance	human nature
communication	intellectual	the elite	species
behavior	primitive art	education	instinct
progress	objectivity	sexism	traditional art
compassion	sensitivity	racism	alienation
education	identity crisis	freedom	ecosystem

2. Write a short essay, carefully (but not mechanically) organized with the best combination of two or three of the several definitions you constructed for exercise 1, and then, in a paragraph or two, explain why you think this particular combination defines the term best.

3. Compress the definition essay you wrote for exercise 2 into a paragraph of not more than 150 words. Now rewrite the definition even more concisely with not more than fifty words expressed in a sentence or two.

4. In order to explain the meaning of a word, the definer constructs a verbal model. This linguistic model may or may not

fit "reality," but it is certainly a man-made structure and not "reality" itself. Definitions are never "real" even though they may seem to be and we may intend them to be so. This does not mean that all definitions are meaningless or simply vehicles for communication. It seems that some definitions are better, or at least more useful, models than others. And if we keep testing and adjusting our definition we may be able to modify it until it better reflects what we *perceive* to be reality. But we have been using the word *reality* as though we all understand what that is. Define *reality,* using any combination of defining paradigms.

5. The defining paradigms we have studied can be combined to inquire into the meaning of a program, process, problem, discipline, or institution such as the following:

automation	population	community
corporate	problem	game theory
enterprise	pollution	penology
the family	welfare reform	system of checks and
urban ghetto	communism	balances
ethics	two-party system	general-systems theory
imperialism	racism	aesthetics
colonization	sexism	ecology

With the aid of some combination of the basic forms of definition, organize an essay defining one of the above. Then summarize your definition in a single sentence.

Part III

WRITING AND THINKING WITH ASSUMPTIONS

*I*N the following reading selection we will see how E. H. Carr builds his study of history on the premise that historians in different ages are unconsciously governed by the dominant assumptions or beliefs of their cultural milieus. But it is not only in writing history that certain assumptions tend to determine what we think and write. In fact, any writing without some assumptions is quite inconceivable. Unless we had some set of assumptions and criteria we would be forced to view our environment passively and indiscriminately, without relevance or relation: here now blue—here now green—here now gray movement—here now pain.*

Common sense suggests that our conventional assumptions provide the truth about reality. It is easy and comforting to act as though these assumptions are somehow written into the universe. Indeed, it is only fairly recently that philosophers and scientists have begun to investigate the difference between the way our brains structure reality and reality as it may exist apart from what we assume about it.

There are several reasons for tentatively accepting the premise that our conventional assumptions do not represent ultimate truth, but are only more or less accurate approximations or "models" of reality. For example, questioning and transcending conventional assumptions could enable us to adjust our social, economic, and political models rapidly enough to avoid such crises as the ecological one that now endangers our own survival as well as that of other organic species. In the past, the kind of overwhelming cultural, economic, and political changes that we must face increasingly often today came about only through bloody revolution, foreign invasion, or natural catastrophe. Because people in the past thought of their assumptions as universal truths rather than more or less useful models of reality, their reaction time was usually too slow to allow their society to adjust peacefully to significantly changing ideas or environment.

But in rejecting the static absolutism of the past we need not become apathetic relativists who think one opinion is as good as another—as though we had no assumptions or that they did not matter. Being committed (at least temporarily) to some set of assumptions is essential to clear thinking and writing. Having a definite set of criteria and assumptions makes our minds much more active and efficient within a certain band or channel, just as using a squelch on a radio keeps only the dominant signal strong by blocking out weaker alternative signals. However, the disadvantage of habitually using certain assumptions and excluding others is that we may become so narrow that we will find it difficult to perceive the world in other possible ways. Some assumptions at the present time make more sense than others, though our cultural milieu is bound to change and may likely make our present set of assumptions obsolete. But there is no reason we cannot change our assumptions, provided we can become aware of them. Without awareness of assumptions we remain mechanical members of our society, dangerously oblivious to the abstractions that govern us and without the ability to question them or to seek alternative new assumptions. The first requisite of intellectual freedom is to discover the assumptions that restrict our thinking and writing.

Learning to find assumptions in the following four chapters will make it possible for us to communicate and argue effectively with audiences whose beliefs we can recognize as being different from our own. It will also allow us to organize assertions or opinions on different subjects by finding and relating the assumptions that underlie the opinions. Finally, awareness of assumptions can make it possible for us to avoid our own conventional assumptions—those clichés of thought that keep writing from being fresh and original.

"The Historian and His Facts"

Edward H. Carr

WHAT is history? Lest anyone think the question meaningless or superfluous, I will take as my text two passages relating respectively to the first and second incarnations of *The Cambridge Modern History*. Here is Acton in his report of October 1896 to the Syndics of the Cambridge University Press on the work which he had undertaken to edit:

> It is a unique opportunity of recording, in the way most useful to the greatest number, the fullness of the knowledge which the nineteenth century is about to bequeath. . . . By the judicious division of labour we should be able to do it, and to bring home to every man the last document, and the ripest conclusions of international research.
>
> Ultimate history we cannot have in this generation; but we can dispose of conventional history, and show the point we have reached on the road from one to the other, now that all information is within reach, and every problem has become capable of solution.[1]

And almost exactly sixty years later Professor Sir George Clark, in his general introduction to the second *Cambridge Modern History,* commented on this belief of Acton and his

From *What Is History?* (New York: Knopf, 1961), ch. I.
[1] *The Cambridge Modern History: Its Origin, Authorship and Production* (Cambridge University Press; 1907), pp. 10–12.

collaborators that it would one day be possible to produce "ultimate history," and went on:

> Historians of a later generation do not look forward to any such prospect. They expect their work to be superseded again and again. They consider that knowledge of the past has come down through one or more human minds, has been "processed" by them, and therefore cannot consist of elemental and impersonal atoms which nothing can alter. . . . The exploration seems to be endless, and some impatient scholars take refuge in scepticism, or at least in the doctrine that, since all historical judgments involve persons and points of view, one is as good as another and there is no "objective" historical truth.[2]

Where the pundits contradict each other so flagrantly the field is open to enquiry. I hope that I am sufficiently up-to-date to recognize that anything written in the 1890's must be nonsense. But I am not yet advanced enough to be committed to the view that anything written in the 1950's necessarily makes sense. Indeed, it may already have occurred to you that this enquiry is liable to stray into something even broader than the nature of history. The clash between Acton and Sir George Clark is a reflection of the change in our total outlook on society over the interval between these two pronouncements. Acton speaks out of the positive belief, the clear-eyed self-confidence of the later Victorian age; Sir George Clark echoes the bewilderment and distracted scepticism of the beat generation. When we attempt to answer the question, What is history?, our answer, consciously or unconsciously, reflects our own position in time, and forms part of our answer to the broader question, what view we take of the society in which we live. I have no fear that my subject may, on closer inspection, seem trivial. I am afraid only that I may seem presumptuous to have broached a question so vast and so important.

The nineteenth century was a great age for facts. "What I

[2] *The New Cambridge Modern History,* I (Cambridge University Press; 1957), pp. xxiv–xxv.

want," said Mr. Gradgrind in *Hard Times,* "is Facts. . . . Facts alone are wanted in life." Nineteenth-century historians on the whole agreed with him. When Ranke in the 1830's, in legitimate protest against moralizing history, remarked that the task of the historian was "simply to show how it really was (*wie es eigentlich gewesen*)" this not very profound aphorism had an astonishing success. Three generations of German, British, and even French historians marched into battle intoning the magic words, *"Wie es eigentlich gewesen"* like an incantation —designed, like most incantations, to save them from the tiresome obligation to think for themselves. The Positivists, anxious to stake out their claim for history as a science, contributed the weight of their influence to this cult of facts. First ascertain the facts, said the positivists, then draw your conclusions from them. In Great Britain, this view of history fitted in perfectly with the empiricist tradition which was the dominant strain in British philosophy from Locke to Bertrand Russell. The empirical theory of knowledge presupposes a complete separation between subject and object. Facts, like sense-impressions, impinge on the observer from outside, and are independent of his consciousness. The process of reception is passive: having received the data, he then acts on them. *The Shorter Oxford English Dictionary,* a useful but tendentious work of the empirical school, clearly marks the separateness of the two processes by defining a fact as "a datum of experience as distinct from conclusions." This is what may be called the common-sense view of history. History consists of a corpus of ascertained facts. The facts are available to the historian in documents, inscriptions, and so on, like fish on the fishmonger's slab. The historian collects them, takes them home, and cooks and serves them in whatever style appeals to him. Acton, whose culinary tastes were austere, wanted them served plain. In his letter of instructions to contributors to the first *Cambridge Modern History* he announced the requirement "that our Waterloo must be one that satisfies French and English, German and Dutch alike; that nobody can tell, without examining the list of authors where the Bishop of Oxford laid down the pen, and whether Fairbairn or Gasquet,

Liebermann or Harrison took it up." [3] Even Sir George Clark, critical as he was of Acton's attitude, himself contrasted the "hard core of facts" in history with the "surrounding pulp of disputable interpretation" [4]—forgetting perhaps that the pulpy part of the fruit is more rewarding than the hard core. First get your facts straight, then plunge at your peril into the shifting sands of interpretation—that is the ultimate wisdom of the empirical, common-sense school of history. It recalls the favourite dictum of the great liberal journalist C. P. Scott: "Facts are sacred, opinion is free."

Now this clearly will not do. I shall not embark on a philosophical discussion of the nature of our knowledge of the past. Let us assume for present purposes that the fact that Caesar crossed the Rubicon and the fact that there is a table in the middle of the room are facts of the same or of a comparable order, that both these facts enter our consciousness in the same or in a comparable manner, and that both have the same objective character in relation to the person who knows them. But, even on this bold and not very plausible assumption, our argument at once runs into the difficulty that not all facts about the past are historical facts, or are treated as such by the historian. What is the criterion which distinguishes the facts of history from other facts about the past?

What is a historical fact? This is a crucial question into which we must look a little more closely. According to the common-sense view, there are certain basic facts which are the same for all historians and which form, so to speak, the backbone of history—the fact, for example, that the Battle of Hastings was fought in 1066. But this view calls for two observations. In the first place, it is not with facts like these that the historian is primarily concerned. It is no doubt important to know that the great battle was fought in 1066 and not in 1065 or 1067, and that it was fought at Hastings and not at Eastbourne or Brighton. The historian must not get

[3] Acton: *Lectures on Modern History* (London: Macmillan & Co.; 1906), p. 318.
[4] Quoted in *The Listener* (June 19, 1952), p. 992.

these things wrong. But when points of this kind are raised, I am reminded of Housman's remark that "accuracy is a duty, not a virtue." [5] To praise a historian for his accuracy is like praising an architect for using well-seasoned timber or properly mixed concrete in his building. It is a necessary condition of his work, but not his essential function. It is precisely for matters of this kind that the historian is entitled to rely on what have been called the "auxiliary sciences" of history— archaeology, epigraphy, numismatics, chronology, and so forth. The historian is not required to have the special skills which enable the expert to determine the origin and period of a fragment of pottery or marble, to decipher an obscure inscription, or to make the elaborate astronomical calculations necessary to establish a precise date. These so-called basic facts which are the same for all historians commonly belong to the category of the raw materials of the historian rather than of history itself. The second observation is that the necessity to establish these basic facts rests not on any quality in the facts themselves, but on an *a priori* decision of the historian. In spite of C. P. Scott's motto, every journalist knows today that the most effective way to influence opinion is by the selection and arrangement of the appropriate facts. It used to be said that facts speak for themselves. This is, of course, untrue. The facts speak only when the historian calls on them: it is he who decides to which facts to give the floor, and in what order or context. It was, I think, one of Pirandello's characters who said that a fact is like a sack—it won't stand up till you've put something in it. The only reason why we are interested to know that the battle was fought at Hastings in 1066 is that historians regard it as a major historical event. It is the historian who has decided for his own reasons that Caesar's crossing of that petty stream, the Rubicon, is a fact of history, whereas the crossing of the Rubicon by millions of other people before or since interests nobody at all. The fact that you arrived in this building half an hour ago on foot, or on a

[5] M. Manilius: *Astronomicon: Liber Primus,* 2nd. ed. (Cambridge University Press; 1937), p. 87.

bicycle, or in a car, is just as much a fact about the past as the fact that Caesar crossed the Rubicon. But it will probably be ignored by historians. Professor Talcott Parsons once called science "a selective system of cognitive orientations to reality." [6] It might perhaps have been put more simply. But history is, among other things, that. The historian is necessarily selective. The belief in a hard core of historical facts existing objectively and independently of the interpretation of the historian is a preposterous fallacy, but one which it is very hard to eradicate. . . .

The nineteenth-century fetishism of facts was completed and justified by a fetishism of documents. The documents were the Ark of the Covenant in the temple of facts. The reverent historian approached them with bowed head and spoke of them in awed tones. If you find it in the documents, it is so. But what, when we get down to it, do these documents—the decrees, the treaties, the rent-rolls, the blue books, the official correspondence, the private letters and diaries—tell us? No document can tell us more than what the author of the document thought—what he thought had happened, what he thought ought to happen or would happen, or perhaps only what he wanted others to think he thought, or even only what he himself thought he thought. None of this means anything until the historian has got to work on it and deciphered it. The facts, whether found in documents or not, have still to be processed by the historian before he can make any use of them: the use he makes of them is, if I may put it that way, the processing process. . . .

At this point I should like to say a few words on the question of why nineteenth-century historians were generally indifferent to the philosophy of history. The term was invented by Voltaire, and has since been used in different senses; but I shall take it to mean, if I use it at all, our answer to the question: What is history? The nineteenth century was,

[6] Talcott Parsons and Edward A. Shils: *Toward a General Theory of Action,* 3rd. ed. (Cambridge, Mass.: Harvard University Press; 1954), p. 167.

for the intellectuals of Western Europe, a comfortable period
exuding confidence and optimism. The facts were on the whole
satisfactory; and the inclination to ask and answer awkward
questions about them was correspondingly weak. Ranke piously
believed that divine providence would take care of the meaning
of history if he took care of the facts; and Burckhardt with a
more modern touch of cynicism observed that "we are not
initiated into the purposes of the eternal wisdom." Professor
Butterfield as late as 1931 noted with apparent satisfaction
that "historians have reflected little upon the nature of things
and even the nature of their own subject." [7] But my predeces-
sor in these lectures, Dr. A. L. Rowse, more justly critical,
wrote of Sir Winston Churchill's *The World Crisis*—his book
about the First World War—that, while it matched Trotsky's
History of the Russian Revolution in personality, vividness,
and vitality, it was inferior in one respect: it had "no philosophy
of history behind it." [8] British historians refused to be drawn, not
because they believed that history had no meaning, but because
they believed that its meaning was implicit and self-evident.
The liberal nineteenth-century view of history had a close
affinity with the economic doctrine of *laissez-faire*—also the
product of a serene and self-confident outlook on the world.
Let everyone get on with his particular job, and the hidden
hand would take care of the universal harmony. The facts of
history were themselves a demonstration of the supreme fact
of a beneficent and apparently infinite progress towards higher
things. This was the age of innocence, and historians walked
in the Garden of Eden, without a scrap of philosophy to cover
them, naked and unashamed before the god of history. Since
then, we have known Sin and experienced a Fall; and those
historians who today pretend to dispense with a philosophy of
history are merely trying, vainly and self-consciously, like members of a nudist colony, to recreate the Garden of Eden in their

[7] Herbert Butterfield: *The Whig Interpretation of History* (London:
George Bell & Sons; 1931), p. 67.
[8] Alfred L. Rowse: *The End of an Epoch* (London: Macmillan & Co.;
1947), pp. 282–3.

garden suburb. Today the awkward question can no longer be evaded.

During the past fifty years a good deal of serious work has been done on the question: What is history? It was from Germany, the country which was to do so much to upset the comfortable reign of nineteenth-century liberalism, that the first challenge came in the 1880's and 1890's to the doctrine of the primacy and autonomy of facts in history. The philosophers who made the challenge are now little more than names: Dilthey is the only one of them who has recently received some belated recognition in Great Britain. Before the turn of the century, prosperity and confidence were still too great in this country [i.e., England] for any attention to be paid to heretics who attacked the cult of facts. But early in the new century, the torch passed to Italy, where Croce began to propound a philosophy of history which obviously owed much to German masters. All history is "contemporary history," declared Croce,[9] meaning that history consists essentially in seeing the past through the eyes of the present and in the light of its problems, and that the main work of the historian is not to record, but to evaluate; for, if he does not evaluate, how can he know what is worth recording? In 1910 the American philosopher, Carl Becker, argued in deliberately provocative language that "the facts of history do not exist for any historian till he creates them." [10] These challenges were for the moment little noticed. It was only after 1920 that Croce began to have a considerable vogue in France and Great Britain. This was not perhaps because Croce was a subtler thinker or a better stylist than his German predecessors, but because, after the First World War, the facts seemed to smile on us less propitiously than in the years before 1914, and we were

----

[9] The context of this celebrated aphorism is as follows: "The practical requirements which underlie every historical judgment give to all history the character of 'contemporary history,' because, however remote in time events thus recounted may seem to be, the history in reality refers to present needs and present situations wherein those events vibrate" (Benedetto Croce: *History as the Story of Liberty* [London: George Allen & Unwin; 1941], p. 19).
[10] *Atlantic Monthly* (October 1928), p. 528.

therefore more accessible to a philosophy which sought to diminish their prestige. Croce was an important influence on the Oxford philosopher and historian Collingwood, the only British thinker in the present century who has made a serious contribution to the philosophy of history. He did not live to write the systematic treatise he had planned; but his published and unpublished papers on the subject were collected after his death in a volume entitled *The Idea of History,* which appeared in 1945.

The views of Collingwood can be summarized as follows. The philosophy of history is concerned neither with "the past by itself" nor with "the historian's thought about it by itself," but with "the two things in their mutual relations." (This dictum reflects the two current meanings of the word "history" —the enquiry conducted by the historian and the series of past events into which he enquires.) "The past which a historian studies is not a dead past, but a past which in some sense is still living in the present." But a past act is dead, *i.e.* meaningless to the historian, unless he can understand the thought that lay behind it. Hence "all history is the history of thought," and "history is the re-enactment in the historian's mind of the thought whose history he is studying." The reconstitution of the past in the historian's mind is dependent on empirical evidence. But it is not in itself an empirical process, and cannot consist in a mere recital of facts. On the contrary, the process of reconstitution governs the selection and interpretation of the facts: this, indeed, is what makes them historical facts. "History," says Professor Oakeshott, who on this point stands near to Collingwood, "is the historian's experience. It is 'made' by nobody save the historian: to write history is the only way of making it." [11]

This searching critique, though it may call for some serious reservations, brings to light certain neglected truths.

In the first place, the facts of history never come to us "pure," since they do not and cannot exist in a pure form:

[11] Michael Oakeshott: *Experience and Its Modes* (Cambridge University Press; 1933), p. 99.

they are always refracted through the mind of the recorder. It follows that when we take up a work of history, our first concern should be not with the facts which it contains but with the historian who wrote it. Let me take as an example the great historian in whose honour and in whose name these lectures were founded. Trevelyan, as he tells us in his autobiography, was "brought up at home on a somewhat exuberantly Whig tradition"; [12] and he would not, I hope, disclaim the title if I described him as the last and not the least of the great English liberal historians of the Whig tradition. It is not for nothing that he traces back his family tree, through the great Whig historian George Otto Trevelyan, to Macaulay, incomparably the greatest of the Whig historians. Dr. Trevelyan's finest and maturest work *England under Queen Anne* was written against that background, and will yield its full meaning and significance to the reader only when read against that background. The author, indeed, leaves the reader with no excuse for failing to do so. For if, following the technique of connoisseurs of detective novels, you read the end first, you will find on the last few pages of the third volume the best summary known to me of what is nowadays called the Whig interpretation of history; and you will see that what Trevelyan is trying to do is to investigate the origin and development of the Whig tradition, and to root it fairly and squarely in the years after the death of its founder, William III. Though this is not, perhaps, the only conceivable interpretation of the events of Queen Anne's reign, it is a valid and, in Trevelyan's hands, a fruitful interpretation. But, in order to appreciate it at its full value, you have to understand what the historian is doing. For if, as Collingwood says, the historian must re-enact in thought what has gone on in the mind of his *dramatis personae*, so the reader in his turn must re-enact what goes on in the mind of the historian. Study the historian before you begin to study the facts. This is, after all, not very abstruse. It is what is already done by the intelligent undergraduate who, when recommended to read a work by

[12] G. M. Trevelyan: *An Autobiography* (London: Longmans, Green & Company; 1949), p. 11.

that great scholar Jones of St. Jude's, goes round to a friend at St. Jude's to ask what sort of chap Jones is, and what bees he has in his bonnet. When you read a work of history, always listen out for the buzzing. If you can detect none, either you are tone deaf or your historian is a dull dog. The facts are really not at all like fish on the fishmonger's slab. They are like fish swimming about in a vast and sometimes inaccessible ocean; and what the historian catches will depend partly on chance, but mainly on what part of the ocean he chooses to fish in and what tackle he chooses to use—these two factors being, of course, determined by the kind of fish he wants to catch. By and large, the historian will get the kind of facts he wants. History means interpretation. Indeed, if, standing Sir George Clark on his head, I were to call history "a hard core of interpretation surrounded by a pulp of disputable facts," my statement would, no doubt, be one-sided and mis-leading, but no more so, I venture to think, than the original dictum.

The second point is the more familiar one of the historian's need of imaginative understanding for the minds of the people with whom he is dealing, for the thought behind their acts: I say "imaginative understanding," not "sympathy," lest sym-pathy should be supposed to imply agreement. The nineteenth century was weak in mediaeval history, because it was too much repelled by the superstitious beliefs of the Middle Ages and by the barbarities which they inspired, to have any imag-inative understanding of mediaeval people. Or take Burck-hardt's censorious remark about the Thirty Years' War: "It is scandalous for a creed, no matter whether it is Catholic or Protestant, to place its salvation above the integrity of the nation." [13] It was extremely difficult for a nineteenth-century liberal historian, brought up to believe that it is right and praiseworthy to kill in defence of one's country, but wicked and wrong-headed to kill in defence of one's religion, to enter into the state of mind of those who fought the Thirty Years' War. This difficulty is particularly acute in the field in which

[13] Jacob Burckhardt: *Judgments on History and Historians* (London: S. J. Reginald Saunders & Company; 1958), p. 179.

I am now working. Much of what has been written in English-speaking countries in the last ten years about the Soviet Union, and in the Soviet Union about the English-speaking countries, has been vitiated by this inability to achieve even the most elementary measure of imaginative understanding of what goes on in the mind of the other party, so that the words and actions of the other are always made to appear malign, senseless, or hypocritical. History cannot be written unless the historian can achieve some kind of contact with the mind of those about whom he is writing.

The third point is that we can view the past, and achieve our understanding of the past, only through the eyes of the present. The historian is of his own age, and is bound to it by the conditions of human existence. The very words which he uses—words like democracy, empire, war, revolution—have current connotations from which he cannot divorce them. Ancient historians have taken to using words like *polis* and *plebs* in the original, just in order to show that they have not fallen into this trap. This does not help them. They, too, live in the present, and cannot cheat themselves into the past by using unfamiliar or obsolete words, any more than they would become better Greek or Roman historians if they delivered their lectures in a *chlamys* or a *toga*. The names by which successive French historians have described the Parisian crowds which played so prominent a role in the French revolution—*les sans-culottes, le peuple, la canaille, les bras-nus*—are all, for those who know the rules of the game, manifestos of a political affiliation and of a particular interpretation. Yet the historian is obliged to choose: the use of language forbids him to be neutral. Nor is it a matter of words alone. Over the past hundred years the changed balance of power in Europe has reversed the attitude of British historians to Frederick the Great. The changed balance of power within the Christian churches between Catholicism and Protestantism has profoundly altered their attitude to such figures as Loyola, Luther, and Cromwell. It requires only a superficial knowledge of the work of French historians of the last forty years on the French revolution to recognize how deeply it has been affected by the

Russian revolution of 1917. The historian belongs not to the past but to the present. Professor Trevor-Roper tells us that the historian "ought to love the past." [14] This is a dubious injunction. To love the past may easily be an expression of the nostalgic romanticism of old men and old societies, a symptom of loss of faith and interest in the present or future.[15] *Cliché* for *cliché,* I should prefer the one about freeing oneself from "the dead hand of the past." The function of the historian is neither to love the past nor to emancipate himself from the past, but to master and understand it as the key to the understanding of the present.

If, however, these are some of the insights of what I may call the Collingwood view of history, it is time to consider some of the dangers. The emphasis on the role of the historian in the making of history tends, if pressed to its logical conclusion, to rule out any objective history at all: history is what the historian makes. Collingwood seems indeed, at one moment, in an unpublished note quoted by his editor, to have reached this conclusion:

> St. Augustine looked at history from the point of view of the early Christian; Tillemont, from that of a seventeenth-century Frenchman; Gibbon, from that of an eighteenth-century Englishman; Mommsen, from that of a nineteenth-century German. There is no point in asking which was the right point of view. Each was the only one possible for the man who adopted it.[16]

This amounts to total scepticism, like Froude's remark that history is "a child's box of letters with which we can spell any word we please." [17] Collingwood, in his reaction against "scissors-and-paste history," against the view of history as a

[14] Introduction to Burckhardt: *Judgments on History and Historians,* p. 17.
[15] Compare Nietzsche's view of history: "To old age belongs the old man's business of looking back and casting up his accounts, of seeking consolation in the memories of the past, in historical culture" (*Thoughts Out of Season* [London: Macmillan & Co.; 1909], II, pp. 65–6).
[16] Robin G. Collingwood: *The Idea of History* (London: Oxford University Press; 1946), p. xii.
[17] James Anthony Froude: *Short Studies on Great Subjects* (1894), I, p. 21.

mere compilation of facts, comes perilously near to treating history as something spun out of the human brain, and leads back to the conclusion referred to by Sir George Clark in the passage which I quoted earlier, that "there is no 'objective' historical truth." In place of the theory that history has no meaning, we are offered here the theory of an infinity of meanings, none any more right than any other—which comes to much the same thing. The second theory is surely as untenable as the first. It does not follow that, because a mountain appears to take on different shapes from different angles of vision, it has objectively either no shape at all or an infinity of shapes. It does not follow that, because interpretation plays a necessary part in establishing the facts of history, and because no existing interpretation is wholly objective, one interpretation is as good as another, and the facts of history are in principle not amenable to objective interpretation. I shall have to consider at a later stage what exactly is meant by objectivity in history.

But a still greater danger lurks in the Collingwood hypothesis. If the historian necessarily looks at his period of history through the eyes of his own time, and studies the problems of the past as a key to those of the present, will he not fall into a purely pragmatic view of the facts, and maintain that the criterion of a right interpretation is its suitability to some present purpose? On this hypothesis, the facts of history are nothing, interpretation is everything. Nietzsche had already enunciated the principle: "The falseness of an opinion is not for us any objection to it. . . . The question is how far it is life-furthering, life-preserving, species-preserving, perhaps species-creating." [18] The American pragmatists, moved, less explicitly and less wholeheartedly, along the same line. Knowledge is knowledge for some purpose. The validity of the knowledge depends on the validity of the purpose. But, even where no such theory has been professed, the practice has often been no less disquieting. In my own field of study I have seen too many examples of extravagant interpretation riding roughshod over facts, not to be impressed with the reality of

[18] Froude: *Beyond Good and Evil,* Ch. i.

this danger. It is not surprising that perusal of some of the more extreme products of Soviet and anti-Soviet schools of historiography should sometimes breed a certain nostalgia for that illusory nineteenth-century haven of purely factual history.

How then, in the middle of the twentieth century, are we to define the obligation of the historian to his facts? I trust that I have spent a sufficient number of hours in recent years chasing and perusing documents, and stuffing my historical narrative with properly footnoted facts, to escape the imputation of treating facts and documents too cavalierly. The duty of the historian to respect his facts is not exhausted by the obligation to see that his facts are accurate. He must seek to bring into the picture all known or knowable facts relevant, in one sense or another, to the theme on which he is engaged and to the interpretation proposed. If he seeks to depict the Victorian Englishman as a moral and rational being, he must not forget what happened at Stalybridge Wakes in 1850. But this, in turn, does not mean that he can eliminate interpretation, which is the life-blood of history. Laymen—that is to say, non-academic friends or friends from other academic disciplines—sometimes ask me how the historian goes to work when he writes history. The commonest assumption appears to be that the historian divides his work into two sharply distinguishable phases or periods. First, he spends a long preliminary period reading his sources and filling his notebooks with facts: then, when this is over, he puts away his sources, takes out his notebooks, and writes his book from beginning to end. This is to me an unconvincing and unplausible picture. For myself, as soon as I have got going on a few of what I take to be the capital sources, the itch becomes too strong and I begin to write—not necessarily at the beginning, but somewhere, anywhere. Thereafter, reading and writing go on simultaneously. The writing is added to, subtracted from, re-shaped, cancelled, as I go on reading. The reading is guided and directed and made fruitful by the writing: the more I write, the more I know what I am looking for, the better I understand the significance and relevance of what I find. Some historians probably do all this preliminary writing in their head without using pen, paper, or typewriter, just as some people play chess in their heads without recourse to board and chess-men: this is a talent which I envy, but cannot emulate. But I am convinced that, for any historian worth the name, the two processes of what economists call "input" and "output" go on simultaneously and are, in practice, parts of a single process. If you try to separate them, or to give one priority over the other, you fall into one of two heresies. Either you write scissors-and-paste history without meaning or significance; or you write propaganda or historical fiction, and merely use facts of the past to embroider a kind of writing which has nothing to do with history.

Our examination of the relation of the historian to the facts of history finds us, therefore, in an apparently precarious situation, navigating delicately between the Scylla of an untenable theory of history as an objective compilation of facts, of the unqualified primacy of fact over interpretation, and the Charybdis of an equally untenable theory of history as the subjective product of the mind of the historian who establishes the facts of history and masters them through the process of interpretation, between a view of history having the centre of gravity in the past and the view having the centre of gravity in the present. But our situation is less precarious than it seems. We shall encounter the same dichotomy of fact and interpretation again in these lectures in other guises—the particular and the general, the empirical and the theoretical, the objective and the subjective. The predicament of the historian is a reflexion of the nature of man. Man, except perhaps in earliest infancy and in extreme old age, is not totally involved in his environment and unconditionally subject to it. On the other hand, he is never totally independent of it and its unconditional master. The relation of man to his environment is the relation of the historian to his theme. The historian is neither the humble slave, nor the tyrannical master, of his facts. The relation between the historian and his facts is one of equality, of give-and-take. As any working historian knows, if he stops to reflect what he is doing as he thinks and writes, the historian is engaged on a continuous process of moulding his facts to his interpretation and his interpretation to his facts. It is impossible to assign primacy to one over the other.

The historian starts with a provisional selection of facts and a provisional interpretation in the light of which that selection has been made—by others as well as by himself. As he works, both the interpretation and the selection and ordering of facts undergo subtle and perhaps partly unconscious changes through the reciprocal action of one or the other. And this reciprocal action also involves reciprocity between present and past, since the historian is part of the present and the facts belong to the past. The historian and the facts of history are necessary to one another. The historian without his facts is rootless and futile; the facts without their historian are dead and meaningless. My first answer therefore to the question, What is history?, is that it is a continuous process of interaction between the historian and his facts, an unending dialogue between the present and the past.

13

How Form and Content
Work Together
in an Assumptive Style

The Thesis

THIS essay by E. H. Carr demonstrates a way of organizing writing that, for convenience, we can call "assumptive style." Carr's subject is the philosophy of history writing, a broad and complex subject that he simplifies by considering only the writings of Western European and American historians dating back no further than the 1830s. He limits his subject further by picking out the most basic assumptions of only two opposed philosophies or traditions of history writing that, he indicates, separated the nineteenth and twentieth centuries.

First, Carr explains the nineteenth-century assumption that *history is a self-evident or obvious induction based on all the available objective facts relating to a specific incident:* let us call this assumption a *thesis.* Next, as an *antithesis,* Carr presents the opposed twentieth-century assumption that *history has no objective facts, but that all history, including the so-called "facts" of history, are based on each historian's subjective interpretations, which in turn are governed by assumptions implicit in the historian's cultural milieu and social or political philosophy and perhaps even in his personal psychology.* In the final portion of the essay Carr, condemning both of these extreme assumptions, offers a *synthesis* of the two. He defines history as a tension or process of interaction between fact and interpretation.

An *assumption* is a belief that governs our writing and thinking behavior; we usually do not state it, but simply take it for granted. And a *philosophy* or *tradition* could be said to be a set or system of interrelated assumptions. In the first paragraph of his essay, Carr sets up a clash between two quotations illustrative of the two opposed philosophies—one written by Acton at the end of the nineteenth century, and the other written by Clark in the middle of the twentieth century: "The clash between Acton and Sir George Clark is a reflection of the change in our total outlook on society over the interval between these two pronouncements." He makes it plain from the first that he does not completely agree with either quotation: "I hope that I am sufficiently up-to-date to recognize that anything written in the 1890's must be nonsense. But I am not yet advanced enough to be committed to the view that anything written in the 1950's necessarily makes sense." But it is not till the last sentence of the last paragraph of the essay that he offers us a third, alternative philosophy of history. Between his first and last paragraphs Carr makes two contrary philosophies of history clear by finding and stating and then questioning the basic assumptions upon which each philosophy depends.

In this first paragraph Carr has chosen to pit two contradictory quotations against one another. As you probably noticed, this habit of setting up a clash of contraries is characteristic of his writing throughout the essay. But why would a writer repeat this structure until it seems as much *a way of thinking* as an element of style? Is it possible that this linguistic structure of setting up contraries is related to a larger structure of organization we have already discussed that pits thesis against antithesis before arriving at a synthesis? This larger structure is often called *dialectic.* Carr may be able to accomplish the dialectic most dramatically and vividly by setting up a kind of artificial *dialogue* where quotations are taken out of their original contexts and pitted against each other as contraries. The effect of this technique is as though Acton and

Clark, for example, were really contradicting each other in an actual debate over which the reader is privileged to sit as arbiter.

Notice that Carr begins this first paragraph with the simple question: What is history? This question will be repeated often to remind the reader to question his own assumptions more deeply and perhaps jar him from a complacent attitude toward history writing.

Not only does Carr begin his first paragraph with a short, simple sentence, but he characteristically begins and often ends paragraphs with short, simple sentences. For example, the second paragraph begins: "The nineteenth century was a great age for facts." The third begins: "Now this clearly will not do." And the fourth begins: "What is a historical fact?" Throughout the essay Carr makes every fourth or fifth sentence simple and short. Perhaps he wishes to give the reader points of ease and clarity among otherwise long, complex, and abstract sentences.

Now let us examine in greater detail Carr's organization of assumptions into thesis, antithesis, and synthesis and consider how he introduces and verifies the assumptions that he claims constitute the nineteenth-century philosophy of history —*the thesis*. First, a number of nineteenth-century opinions are inductively introduced as though they were voiced by people on the same side in a discussion group. A Dickens character is quoted: "Facts alone are wanted in life." Carr quotes Ranke's opinion that the task of the historian is "simply to show how it really was." Then Carr personifies the philosophic movement of positivism: "First ascertain the facts, said the positivists, then draw your conclusions from them." Next speaks *The Shorter Oxford English Dictionary,* which defines a fact as "a datum of experience as distinct from conclusions." Finally Carr generalizes a common-sense view of history:

1. History consists of a corpus of ascertained facts.
2. The facts are available to the historian in documents, inscriptions, and so on, like fish on the fishmonger's slab.

3. The historian collects them, takes them home, and cooks and serves them in whatever style appeals to him.

Notice that Carr uses an extended fishmarket metaphor to express these abstract assumptions about a philosophy of history in as concrete and interesting a way as possible for the general reader. But the metaphors Carr chooses imply an adverse value judgment. Equating the primary concept of the common-sense view of history with dead fish on a slab is certainly a linguistic put-down. And, of course, Carr is aware that he is biasing his readers with pejorative metaphors.

We might at this point recall some of the theological metaphors that Carr uses, such as at first illustrating the nineteenth-century "belief" in facts by a quotation from C. P. Scott: "Facts are sacred, opinion is free." But as soon as Carr begins to criticize nineteenth-century assumptions, he also begins to refer to the elevation of facts as a "heresy" and a superstitious "cult" rather than the orthodoxy in which nineteenth-century historians thought they believed. And finally he reduces their cult to the most unseemly and perverse form of worship, a "fetish":

> The nineteenth-century fetishism of facts was completed and justified by a fetishism of documents. The documents were the Ark of the Covenant in the temple of facts. The reverent historian approached them with bowed head and spoke of them in awed tones.

Carr uses this ludicrous extended metaphor to imply an even more adverse value judgment than he is stating overtly. This very purposeful use of reductive metaphors suggests again that Carr is by no means attempting to write in an objective, value-free social-science style. In addition, Carr overtly attacks the common-sense view of history by questioning its assumption of objectivity. "What is the criterion which distinguishes the facts of history from other facts about the past?" he asks. A *criterion* is an assumption about value or relevance. The criterion taken for granted by the common-sense school of historians is that "facts, like sense-impressions, impinge on the

observer from outside, and are independent of his consciousness." Carr counters this with another possible criterion to
distinguish facts:

> that the necessity to establish these basic facts rests not on
> any quality in the facts themselves, but on an *a priori* decision
> [i.e., a prior commitment to certain assumptions] of the
> historian. . . . The facts speak only when the historian calls on
> them: it is he who decides to which facts to give the floor, and
> in what order or context.

Carr now argues for this criterion and against the common-
sense criterion for the next several paragraphs by presenting
one example or anecdote after another to persuade his reader
that history is not "value free" or "objective" study but is more
subjective, more like "a selective system of cognitive orientations to reality."

The Antithesis

Now we are ready to investigate the construction of an
antithesis of the nineteenth-century "cult of facts," the change
in relation between the historian and his facts that occurred
in the first half of the twentieth century. Carr proceeds very
much as he did in developing the thesis, but now he raises
voices against the voices he had speak for the thesis.

The author lets us hear Croce voice the opinion "All history is 'contemporary history,' " from which Carr immediately
abstracts two assumptions: "that history consists essentially in
seeing the past through the eyes of the present and in the light
of its problems, and that the main work of the historian is not
to record, but to evaluate; for, if he does not evaluate, how
can he know what is worth recording?"

Now, after this preview of assumptions to come, Carr lets
us first hear opinions expressed by representative modern historians like Becker ("the facts of history do not exist for any
historian till he creates them"), Collingwood ("all history is
the history of thought" or "history is the re-enactment in the

historian's mind of the thought whose history he is studying"), and Professor Oakeshott ("History is the historian's experience. It is 'made' by nobody save the historian: to write history is the only way of making it"). From opinions like these Carr abstracts a set of three basic assumptions and their implications, which underlie the antithetical view of history. This time he does not use reductive metaphors to cast doubt on the assumptions, but instead calls the assumptions "neglected truths," although he admits they may call for some serious reservations. Here is the first assumption and implication:

> In the first place, the facts of history never come to us "pure," since they do not and cannot exist in a pure form: they are always refracted through the mind of the recorder. It follows that when we take up a work of history, our first concern should be not with the facts which it contains but with the historian who wrote it.

Rather than give many examples of why this assumption must be wrong, Carr gives an example from Trevelyan to illustrate how correct the assumption is.

In fact, Carr uses this first assumption of the antithetical view of history to question the fish metaphor with which he made fun of the corresponding assumption of the thesis view, and extends the metaphor in a new direction when he writes:

> The facts are really not at all like fish on the fishmonger's slab. They are like fish swimming about in a vast and sometimes inaccessible ocean; and what the historian catches will depend partly on chance, but mainly on what part of the ocean he chooses to fish in and what tackle he chooses to use —these two factors being, of course, determined by the kind of fish he wants to catch.

The second assumption of the antithetical view of history that Carr abstracts from the opinions of representative modern historians above is that "History cannot be written unless the historian can achieve some kind of contact with the mind of those about whom he is writing." Again, he gives examples of how this was particularly neglected by the nineteenth century and how even today this is often still neglected, for instance in the work of Communist historians writing about the history of capitalist countries and vice versa. Carr himself, throughout his essay, is quite careful to try to understand why earlier historians assumed what they did. He goes to considerable trouble to understand these historians in the intellectual, economic, and political contexts of their age. For example, he suggests that the assumptions governing history writing in the nineteenth century may have been related to larger assumptions that also tended to govern economic and political beliefs: "The liberal nineteenth-century view of history had a close affinity with the economic doctrine of *laissez-faire*—also the product of a serene and self-confident outlook on the world."

The third assumption of the antithetical school of history is "that we can view the past, and achieve our understanding of the past, only through the eyes of the present." Carr immediately draws out an implication of this third basic assumption, that the "very words which [the historian] uses—words like democracy, empire, war, revolution—have current connotations from which he cannot divorce them."

Carr humanizes his abstract dialectic of thesis/antithesis by putting the historians of the nineteenth century into dialogue with the historians of the mid-twentieth century. He has made history concrete and immediate for his readers by marshaling quotations from both sides, as though they constituted a record of conversation between people engaged in basic controversy.

Now that he has allowed that controversy to be won completely by the voices forming the antithesis, Carr is ready to qualify the victory of the antithesis by extrapolating the following assumption and criterion, which he considers dangerous implications of the three basic assumptions on which it depends:

1. there is no "objective history at all: history is what the historian makes."
2. "the criterion of a right interpretation is its suitability to some present purpose."

To show that the first implication is not simply a possibility but that it is an assumption already beginning to govern the opinions of some modern historians, Carr quotes Collingwood ("There is no point in asking which was the right point of view. Each was the only one possible for the man who adopted it"), Froude ("history is 'a child's box of letters with which we can spell any word we please' "), and George Clark ("there is no 'objective' historical truth").

To illustrate the spread of the implicit new criterion, which Carr considers even more dangerous than the implicit assumption we have just discussed, he uses the words of Nietzsche, who had already enumerated the principle: "The falseness of an opinion is not for us any objection to it. . . . The question is how far it is life-furthering, life-preserving, species-preserving, perhaps species-creating."

At first Carr had apparently subscribed to the more moderate assumptions of the twentieth-century view of history, for he does not call them assumptions at all, but instead "neglected truths." Almost immediately, however, by extrapolating its most extreme implications and criticizing these, he establishes an interpretive or subjective antithesis to set against the objective extreme of the "cult of facts" that he had already established and criticized. In other words, Carr is purposely ignoring, in favor of his *thesis versus antithesis* organization of assumptions, moderate views of history and moderate historians and their work. Notice at this point how his dialectical organization has affected his interpretation of history writing since 1830. Consistent with his organization he has chosen generally the facts, quotations, and historians that will tend to support his extremes, and has ignored many good but more moderate quotations and historians that do not fit the dichotomy he is organizing.

It can be said of Carr's historical writing, as of *all* writing, that *organization is interpretation*. Carr has organized an objective extreme from among all the varied assumptions behind nineteenth-century history writing, and, fulfilling his organization of a dialectic process, he has abstracted from among the many alternative assumptions underlying twentieth-century history writing a polarized subjective extreme and has finally rejected both extremes as "a dichotomy of fact and interpretation." But if neither the nineteenth- nor the twentieth-century philosophies of history are acceptable, what is the modern historian to do? Obviously some compromise or synthesis must be arrived at.

The Synthesis

This process of synthesis is described by Carr in metaphors that make it sound like the precarious voyage of Odysseus. Writing modern history is like

> navigating delicately between the Scylla of an untenable theory of history as an objective compilation of facts, of the unqualified primacy of fact over interpretation, and the Charybdis of an equally untenable theory of history as the subjective product of the mind of the historian who establishes the facts of history and masters them through the process of interpretation, between a view of history having the centre of gravity in the past and the view having the centre of gravity in the present.

Car is rejecting both the nineteenth-century objective and the twentieth-century subjective criteria of relevance and replacing them with a much more ancient criterion—that man must strive to maintain a moderation or mean between extremes. This criterion is as old as Aristotle, and even older. It is a criterion that for many centuries has guided much writing of all kinds, including history writing. For the humanist, life itself could be described as a continuous process of interaction between man and his environment, an unending dialogue between the present and the past; and so Carr defines history.

Since it is commonly said that the problems faced by Odysseus reflect the universal predicament of man, Carr next begins to suggest the humanist way to synthesize extremes by accepting them as archetypal tensions or universal paradoxes between which men must perennially compromise. Because in the humanist view not only historians but all men for all time are in the process of moderating between extremes, the danger all of a sudden goes out of the predicament in which Carr had put modern history: "But our situation is less precarious than it seems." Is the process of writing history, then, no more difficult than any man's process of living? Human life is an unending dialogue between paradoxes which may never be resolved:

> We shall encounter the same dichotomy of fact and inter-
> pretation again in these lectures in other guises—the particular
> and the general, the empirical and the theoretical, the objec-
> tive and the subjective. The predicament of the historian is a
> reflexion of the nature of man. . . . [History] is a continuous
> process of interaction between the historian and his facts, an
> unending dialogue between the present and the past.

Notice that Carr's definition of history as a "dialogue" is reflected precisely in the way he has organized and interpreted the history of history writing in this essay. A dialogue is essentially a literary form, and to organize history into antithetical quotations is to present it, partly at least, as dramatic literature. Carr is at his best in presenting the dialogue between thesis and antithesis; his synthesis, it seems to me, is the weakest part of the essay. Can you think of a better synthesis?

Exercises

1. Write a brief history of an event. What were the "facts" concerning this event, and how did you decide? Of all the facts you collected, what made you select the ones you used. Did you avoid any facts? Why? Do you consider your history in any way biased? What are the sources of your bias?

2. Organize a dialectical argument of the kind Carr uses by finding the underlying assumptions of the opposing sides and relating these assumptions in order to form the structure of your essay—

for example, thesis assumptions, antithetical assumptions, synthesis. Choose your own subject or one of the following:

a. whether a peaceful world will someday be possible or whether wars are necessary
b. whether or not a future technological utopia of leisure and plenty for all can evolve
c. whether or not science and technology are a blessing or a curse to humanity
d. whether or not mass education can mean a higher quality of learning for all
e. whether or not primitive art is superior to our own

Your argument, since it deals with assumptions, will be necessarily somewhat abstract, but consider some of the techniques Carr employs to make an otherwise very abstract intellectual discussion about the philosophy of history as concrete and informal as possible. By using synonyms or metaphors as frequent replacements he keeps his key terms from seeming overworked. Some other ways of saying *criterion* appear to be "a selective system," "decided for his own reasons that," "understand the significance and relevance of," "guided and directed and made fruitful by." Some of the synonyms for *assumption* that Carr uses in order to avoid making his already abstract subject sound only more abstract with jargon or technical terms are "view," "picture," "hypothesis," "theory"; and a *set of assumptions* is sometimes called a "philosophy," "school," or "version." Another technique for alleviating the abstract intellectuality of his essay is his bold and lively use of metaphor and the witty, often almost folksy, phrases he occasionally employs to keep his prose as informal as possible: "This inquiry is liable to stray . . . ," "what bees he has in his bonnet," "always listen out for the buzzing."

14

Discovering Assumptions

AN assumption can be defined as a stated or unstated, conscious or unconscious attitude that tends to govern our writing and thinking behavior. Assumptions help to determine even the simplest acts of writing. For example, the assertion "I will write to you later" assumes that time is linear and progresses from present to future, that "you" and "I" will both still exist at a later time, that the intended reader will understand all the linguistic meaning conveyed by these queer marks on paper called written English. Obviously, changing any of these implicit beliefs (for example, substituting the assumption that one of the two correspondents was about to die) might elicit very different writing behavior.

Longer or more complex examples of writing tend to be governed by many more assumptions, perhaps so many that it would be hard to try to list them all. In the following opinion written in 1899 by the American scientist Albert A. Michelson about the kind of discoveries that could be expected in physics during the twentieth century, can we find what seem to be the most important operating assumptions:

> Our future discoveries must be looked for in the sixth place of decimals.*

* Quoted in Lloyd W. Taylor, *Physics: The Pioneer Science,* 2 vols. (New York, 1941), II, p. 1.

Michelson seems to assume that the Newtonian model of the physical universe in which he was operating at the end of the nineteenth century would never be replaced and that, therefore, physicists must only be concerned with making their measurements more accurate down to a millionth of an inch (the sixth decimal place, 0.000001). Most people before the twentieth century assumed that science gave sure knowledge of the truth about nature. This general assumption about science governs Michelson's specific assumption that Newtonian physics would not be questioned or superceded in the future.

Particularly after Einsteinian physics overturned the Newtonian model of the universe early in the twentieth century, many scientists began to question the assumption that science is the absolute truth about nature and began to favor an alternative—that science provides only a *model* of nature (an "as if"). Hence, it is not likely that a modern physicist would write an opinion like Michelson's today. For example, in *The Nature of Scientific Thought* a contemporary scientist, Marshall Walker, writes:

> The notion that scientific knowledge is *certain* is an illusion. A scientist, explicitly or implicitly, assumes the existence of a universe external to himself that is the source of his sensations. He notices certain regularities in his sensations, and infers that there are regularities in the behavior of the universe. He calls these regularities of the external universe *laws of nature* and attempts to represent them by mathematical models, which have become progressively more successful in accurate predictions. It is tempting to infer that the model is beginning to resemble the *thing out there,* but such an inference can never be verified. No prediction can be known to be certain —nature may deviate from the model without prior notice, and it is in this sense that scientific knowledge is never certain.*

Which attitude about science is closest to your own? Do you assume science has found out once and for all the truth

* Marshall Walker, *The Nature of Scientific Thought* (Englewood Cliffs, N.J.: Prentice-Hall, 1963), p. 6.

about nature, or do you believe that science is the creation of imaginative models of nature that are continually being tested and that always run the risk of being superceded? Which assumption makes science seem more interesting to you?

Human communication often breaks down because people persist in *opinion conflict* when the underlying difficulty is really a *difference in basic assumptions*. For example, consider the cause of this communication block:

> FRANK: That atheist John Wilson can't be a true conscientious objector to war, and I say he's just another draft dodger.
> JOE: John is not a draft dodger.
> FRANK: Oh, yes, he is.
> JOE: He's not.

What are the assumptions underlying Frank's original opinion? Presumably that John Wilson is an atheist, and that no atheists can be conscientious objectors. The difficulty here seems to be an assumption about what constitutes conscientious objection to war. Maybe if Frank and Joe could transcend the level of opinion and try to discuss their assumptions about conscientious objection, communication might begin again. Once we become aware of the assumptions underlying an opinion, it is then possible to entertain alternatives to those assumptions that can free us to consider, argue against, and perhaps even modify that opinion. For instance, can you think of an alternative to the belief that no atheists can be conscientious objectors? Would a change of assumptions underlying the concept of conscientious objection to war render Frank's first opinion questionable?

One or more *implications* are predictable from each opinion we write. Assumptions are prior to and determine opinions or assertions, whereas implications are the possible consequences that follow from an assertion. If this assertion is true—"the bacteria known as E choli has such a potential reproductive rate that if it were allowed to multiply unchecked for only 24 hours the resulting pile of bacteria would be almost as large as Earth itself"—then one of its implications is that we would all be overrun and perish in only a few hours if our increasing chemical pollution ever chanced to destroy the biological restraints that now stabilize the E choli population. It also implies that even slight ecological imbalance is much more hazardous than we may have imagined, and that if we abuse the environment beyond a certain point there may be little or no time left to reverse our folly.

What are the most likely implications that can be projected from each of the following statements:

1. Very soon now biologists will have made it possible for either a man or a woman to reproduce thousands of exact copies (like identical twins) of himself or herself by means of nonsexual reproduction called *cloning*.

2. When mammals, even with an abundance of food, are forced to live in close proximity, certain physical and psychological changes occur. These changes begin when the crowding progresses beyond a certain point called *tolerance distance*. Exceeding tolerance distance assures a shorter life span for the inhabitants. Their adrenal glands are overactive, cholesterol builds up to a dangerous level, mutants and stillbirths happen more frequently, and an increasing proportion of the population becomes sterile and abnormal in behavior.

Now let us investigate further how assumptions can govern writing behavior. Our goal is to become more aware of the unstated and often unconscious thought processes that underlie all writing, including our own. If you have not had much practice at abstracting assumptions from your own or other's writing, you might begin to discover them by imagining that a pattern of written opinions or assertions is somewhat analogous to a mathematical series.

For example, in a series such as:

$$1, 4, 9, 16 \ldots,$$

the assumption or principle of order governing the series seems to be that you compose it by writing down the square of the successive numbers 1, 2, 3, 4, etc. This implies that the next figure in the series would be 25. Here is another series followed by the assumption governing it and the implication of the next symbol in the series:

$$1, 1, 2, 4, 8, 16 \ldots,$$

Assumption: that you compose this series by beginning with 1 and adding the previous numbers in the series to arrive at the next figure.

Implication: that the next symbol in the series would be 32.

Can you abstract the assumption behind this series:

$$1, 6, 11, 16, 21 \ldots$$

How can we predict that the next figure in this series will be 26?

We can see that each of these series is governed by a different assumption or principle. Once we have abstracted what we think is the assumption underlying a series we can predict the next step in the series. Our prediction will be correct if we have abstracted the right assumption. We are now in a position to see how analogous is the mental process of abstracting the assumptions governing the linguistic symbols in the following example:

> Without Grant, the North might very well have lost the Civil War to Lee.
> Without Napoleon, France might never have had its moment of grandeur.
> Without General Washington, the United States might never have been born.
> Without Martin Luther, the Protestant Reformation might never have occurred.

Can you think of an assumption that could have determined this series of opinions?

The more complete the series, the more probable will be the proposed assumption that we believe governs the series. But the abstracting of assumptions is always merely a hypothesis. For instance, consider as an assumption governing the above series that *important historical movements are determined not by economic or social forces, but by the behavior of individual men,* or as Thomas Carlyle once wrote, "The history of the world is but the biography of great men." This is, of course, a very questionable assumption, but it seems fairly probable that the author of the above series of opinions was being governed by it consciously or unconsciously in his writing. What do you think the author of the series would have to say about the Vietnam war?

What makes abstracting assumptions from writing more difficult than abstracting the assumptions of mathematical series is that opinions organized in formal parallel series such as the ones above are unusual in writing. (As an exception you may remember that John Donne [Chapter 3], in his seventeenth-century style, did use many examples of parallel assertions governed by the same assumptions.)

The six opinions below do *not* form a series. Yet the statement of each of these separate opinions contains a revealing enough *context* for you to find an assumption that most probably governed its writing. Try your skill at abstracting the assumption (or assumptions) governing each of the following opinions:

1. Did you see the size of the textbook in that course? Why it's as big as a dictionary—an atlas, even. Boy, this school's getting too hard for me!

2. Some people can write and others can't and that's all there is to it.

3. I'm going into science, so how do you expect me to come up with all those deep inner meanings in a poem?

4. Teacher to student: You are a very good student—you always keep your shirt tucked in, and your hair is nice and short.

5. Principal to teacher: You are an excellent teacher—there haven't been any parent complaints, and you're always just where you're supposed to be in the lesson plan.

6. Reporter to captured thrill-slayer: What twisted you all up inside? Thrill-slayer to reporter (*with ironic smirk*): They didn't have no playgrounds in my school.

Looking directly at the abstract assumptions that govern our own thinking and writing is very difficult because, for the most part, we did not consciously choose our own assumptions from a wide range of alternatives. Our parents, friends, and teachers helped form them as well as the books we read and the films and TV shows we saw. They were inculcated slowly without our being conscious of them. As a result we cannot readily conceive alternatives to habitual assumptions that we have simply taken for granted as basic truths and have thus become locked into. In the beginning of our study of assumptions it will be much easier, because we know alternatives to them, to see how the traditional assumptions of an earlier era or foreign culture limit and govern the thinking and writing of that era or culture.

For example, let us suppose that we were asked to report the catching of a very large and unusual fish. We might feel free to write many different possible essays on the fish, since we all share a number of assumptions upon which to base fish stories. These shared assumptions in any one generation or era or subculture are not really infinite, however, as we might suppose, but tend in practice to be rather limited and limiting to a writer. This limiting influence of shared assumptions is responsible for coercing many writers into what we call "typical" or "conventional" writing.

In about 1580 a typical English writer would tell a fish story very differently than we would be likely to write one today. Suppose that the sixteenth-century writer saw a large shark drawn up on the seashore. He could describe the shark as an *unnatural* monster because he did not assume evolution, and therefore perceived the shark simply as a monstrous fish rather than as a species of carnivore that had evolved as *naturally* as any other species and fills a niche in the ecology of the sea. The sixteenth-century writer could begin to organize his writing about the fish in what would for us seem a strange way, but to an Elizabethan quite conventional—he could describe a series of unnatural or monstrous births that had taken place in his vicinity for the past year or so, such as a two-headed child born to a local family, and perhaps a monstrous calf with six legs born several years before in a nearby county. He might well proceed from this "unnatural" monster series to another series of what he could consider "unnatural" events, involving perhaps recent eruptions of plague in the neighborhood, or, perhaps, some serious drought or flood. He might next mention some recent comet or other astronomical anomaly, which he considered an "unnatural" event, or some current social upheaval or rebellion.

This structuring of his writing would probably seem disjointed, even *non sequitur,* to us because we do not share the Elizabethan assumptions about ancient customs and status quo being "natural," and any disruption, change, or innovation being essentially "unnatural" and evil.

Since natural law and order was assumed to embrace the whole universe from plants and animals and stars to human social customs and institutions, it is easy to see why a writer of that period could structure his essay with a series of freaks or disorders in nature (from the monstrous shark through the two-headed child and six-legged calf and the apparently freakish comet to the plague and recent civil disorders) and conclude from this series a universal pattern of moral retrogression and growing evil.

Another structure that the sixteenth-century man writing about the fish might typically use would be a contrast between selected instances of glory, virtue, and order in past records, and selected instances of contemporary weakness and vice to accompany the disorder he had already discovered in the present society. This structure would be conventional for him, because in the sixteenth century people widely shared an assumption that the world, rather than *progressing,* was actually *retrogressing* from a far better past—the Golden Age or the Garden of Eden. This assumption of future progress that many of us take for granted today did not have very strong support until the scientific revolution began to accelerate in the eighteenth and nineteenth centuries, making at least *material* progress obvious from generation to generation. Do you assume that the world is getting better or, antithetically, growing worse? Or can you think up a new assumption that would be a more complex synthesis of this thesis and antithesis? If the past was inevitably better than the present, then it followed that anything *new* must be presumed to be not as good as that more anciently established. Hence, instead of taking pride in being the originator of some departure from traditional wisdom, a Renaissance writer would most likely take pains to cite established authority as its ultimate source, and even believe himself that his new idea had an ancient sanction. To be *original* was not thought to be a very good thing by people who held the assumption of inevitable retrogression.

To end his essay on the shark, the sixteenth-century writer, assuming, as did many of his contemporaries that the end of the world prophesied in the Bible (and especially in the Apocalypse of John) was indeed near at hand, might point out finally that the monstrosity beached on the seashore was but one more evil portent foreshadowing the approaching end of the world. He could thus finish his essay with a threat to his readers to amend their lives before it was too late. This sort of pious exhortation, which though very common in the sixteenth century seems too preachy for modern taste, was conventionally determined by the ancient aesthetic assumption, often voiced, that good writing must serve the reader in two ways: besides being *pleasurable,* it must be made somehow *morally profitable.* Today we more often assume that good writing should dispense with gratuitous moralizing and be more purely entertaining. This assumption makes a difference in our writing.

Notice the close relations among these typical sixteenth-century assumptions we have just discussed. They seem to form a kind of interdependent system or combination. What is your combination of operating assumptions when you write? Are they as well related, as interdependent, as these?

Now let us see how a similar set of assumptions is combined by Shakespeare (also writing in the sixteenth century), in *Hamlet,* into artistic structures used to build suspense, to create mood, and (together with imagery) to convey a growing sense of decay in the court of Denmark. In the very first scene, Shakespeare calls attention to the fact that something is wrong in Denmark by staging an "unnatural" occurrence—the appearance of a ghost. Another indication of Denmark's "disordered" existence is its "unnatural" preparations for war. Shakespeare has one of his characters make explicit an analogy between the "unnatural" ghost and the preparations for war in Denmark and the alledged appearance of ghosts in the streets of Rome and the sunspots, comets, and eclipses (in Shakespeare's time, comets and eclipses were considered unnatural events because they interrupted the familiar order of things) that occurred just before Julius Caesar was murdered and the Roman Empire thrown into chaos and civil war. In the beginning of the second scene, Shakespeare has King Claudius remind the Elizabethan audience that the "unnatural" crime of incest stains the throne of Denmark. Today our very different assumptions about incest often confuse us as to Shakespeare's meaning. At the time Shakespeare wrote the play it was unlawful in England and assumed to be "unnatural incest" for a man to marry his dead brother's widow. Even in the middle of the nineteenth century, when the law prohibiting marriage with a brother's widow was finally changed, some Churchmen warned that permitting such "incest" would rot the moral fiber of England. Hence, Shakespeare has King Claudius pointedly proclaim his "incest" when he refers to his brother's widow, Gertrude, as "our sometime sister, now our Queen" and announce the moral turpitude of the whole court of Denmark when he says, "nor have we herein barr'd/Your better wisdoms, which have freely gone/With this affair along." When the ghost in Act I, scene v, tells Hamlet of the even more "unnatural" crimes of treason and fratricide, an Elizabethan audience, seeing the whole pattern of "unnatural" occurrences and disorders in the court and kingdom of Denmark that Shakespeare has carefully organized in these opening scenes, might well accept the judgment that something is "rotten" there.

Another set of earlier assumptions—Plato's—had (and still occasionally has) enormous influence on people's thinking and writing; but it is fairly easy for us to see them now as assumptions rather than truths. An assumption championed by Plato almost two and a half millennia ago that is still quite often relied on, maintains that it is the unfortunate lot of all material objects to fall short of their absolute essence or

spiritual ideal. Only in our subjective minds, say the Platonists, can we have insight into spiritual ideals such as perfect
justice, perfect truth, perfect beauty, perfect love, or perfect
oak tree, perfect man, perfect circle. No one has ever seen a
perfect circle, for example, because no material instruments,
however carefully made, could ever accomplish this; and yet
we keep trying to make more and more perfect circles. Therefore, according to Platonists, we must have some spiritual
knowledge of the essence of circularity, or else how could we,
in building better and better instruments to form a more perfect
circle, strive toward something about which we have no notion? Do you assume that justice is the behavior of judges in
interpreting the law according to the Constitution or that there
is such a thing as justice over and above what any constitution
says or judge rules? Does it make any difference which of these
assumptions a person holds?

Now if, as Plato assumed, our subjective or spiritual mind
(our soul) were the only reliable source of knowledge concerning the essence of things or concerning absolute truths about the
universe, then our body with its five senses merely perceives half-
truths or lies. Hence, Plato assumed that all of nature, including
the human body, was inferior and would only mislead us with
false knowledge if we were to study it empirically; that nature,
including our bodies, imprisons our spirit, which seeks always to
leave the inferior natural world and to escape to the spiritual
world. In fact, Plato assumed that reality was our subjective
idea of things, and that the material things themselves were
but misleading semblances that only appeared to be real. These
assumptions may seem strange to you in their ancient form,
but they were later combined with Judeo-Christian assumptions, and as a result are very much with us in, for instance,
the assumption that the material life is somehow inferior to the
spiritual life; that our bodies and natural functions are things
to be ashamed of; that the material world is full of misleading
temptation, but if we resist it we may attain a better spiritual
life after our bodies die; that man's capacity for subjective
thought—his soul—separates him from the rest of nature,
which is assumed not to possess this "soul."

In the next section of this book Paul Shepard discusses in an essay on ecology how some of these very assumptions, which he refers to as "Christian Platonism," keep modern society from being able to understand and accept an ecological viewpoint. If Plato's assumption *that spirit is real and material an empty semblance* is thought of as a thesis, can you frame its antithesis. Aristotle supplied a synthesis in his assumption that these spiritual essences, rather than existing in a world separate from material nature, as Plato taught, were inherent in natural objects, which, though more or less imperfect entities, were motivated toward realizing their spiritual potential. And this presumed natural motivation of objects was a way of explaining motion in the universe that held sway for about two thousand years. Why did heavy bodies fall? Because, imperfect as they were, they evidently possessed some spark or potential that motivated them to try to actualize their essence or natural purpose, thus falling. This essence of falling was called *gravity*. Lighter bodies arose because they possessed an essence of rising, called *levity*. Aristotle assumed that *gravity and levity were inherent in the objects themselves,* and, therefore, no external forces, such as the attraction of the earth, were necessary or even relevant to their motion. To move vertically up or down was the essence or "nature" of terrestrial bodies, while extraterrestrial objects, like planets, the moon, and stars, moved in circles because it was their essence or "nature" to do so. The assumption that *motion or behavior can be explained by finding that it is the essence or "nature" of the body so to behave* is still used today when, for instance, we assume *that there is such a thing as "human nature," which can be used to explain some of man's motivations and behavior.* What is the Aristotelian assumption behind this familiar kind of statement:

> They say the government, one of these days, it going to guarantee every citizen at least several thousand dollars a year to live on whether he works or not. Guaranteed income won't work, though; it's unnatural and goes against human nature.

Can you find another contemporary opinion based on this

Aristotelian assumption that attempts to explain a phenomenon by ascribing it to the essence, purpose, or "nature" of the thing itself?

Now let us turn from the discussion of some alternative assumptions about nature to some alternative assumptions about art. Beginning with the Romantic movement and throughout the nineteenth century it became conventional to assume that *Art, rather than attempting to imitate or mirror reality, was essentially an illusion opposed to material reality and expressing the heightened imagination of the artist.* This assumption is still widely accepted in intellectual circles today. It fit nineteenth-century art quite well, but it was applied as a criterion of the best in all art at all times—hence it would have been close to heresy to think that in one of the greatest of all narratives, the *Iliad,* Homer was attempting to imitate reality fairly accurately, almost like a geographer of a real city of Troy, which lay between the Simoïs (i.e., Dombrek) and the Scamander (i.e., Menderes) rivers. But at least one man, Heinrich Schliemann, operating on the assumptions that not all artists had worked according to the criterion that the Romantics were now using to judge art and that *art at an earlier time may often have attempted to imitate or mirror the environment with material accuracy,* used Homer's description of the geography of Troy to find, at the confluence of two rivers on a plain in modern Turkey near a town called Hissarlik, a mound that he began to excavate. He uncovered the ruins of a score of cities, one on top of another, and finally discovered the remains of the historical fortress of Troy, which existed not only in the "world" of Homer's *Iliad,* but in the real world as well.

What are your assumptions about art or literature? Do you assume that *there is one essential set of universal aesthetic principles for art of all times and cultures?* The assumption that *all art was created according to the same aesthetic principles which modern artists are working toward* implies that we can judge all art produced by all cultures at all times in terms of our own aesthetic principles. Or do you assume *that there may have been different aesthetic aims in different eras and cultures,* which implies that in order to judge the art of another era or culture we would have to be sensitive to their aesthetic assumptions as well as our own? Would it make a difference which assumption you held?

Exercises

1. Try, in a few sentences, to evaluate some museum art object of a different era or civilization, using one aesthetic assumption. Then, shifting to another aesthetic assumption, see if the shift changes in any way your thinking and writing behavior.

2. Sometimes our assumptions can keep us from being good readers of literature. For example, we will not be likely to detect irony in literature unless we can shift from the common assumption that the speaker or narrator in prose or poetry is the writer himself to the assumption that the speaker or narrator is not necessarily to be equated with the author and is often intended to be as fictional as any character in the narrative. Notice how difficult it would be to understand Swift's *A Modest Proposal* without the latter assumption being one of our alternatives. Can you think of any differences of assumptions (about literature or life) that made it difficult for you to interpret some poem, story, novel, or drama?

3. Discuss the assumptions governing each of the following opinions on literature:

   Salinger writes good stories because he talks about people like all of us, while the characters in *Oliver Twist* are fantastic, and Shakespeare's *Midsummer Night's Dream* is not as good as the comedy I saw last night on TV where the characters sounded just like my mother and dad when they're having a fight.

   How can you tell what a literary classic is when for five hundred years a medieval allegory, the *Romance of the Rose,* was considered the greatest of all masterpieces, and yet today no teacher would think of assigning it in a basic course and no student who wasn't a masochist would think of reading it?

4. Anthropologists tell us that some cannibal tribes called themselves by a name that in their language meant "the human beings" or "the people," while to the surrounding tribes to whom they were hostile they sometimes assigned a generic name meaning "man-meat." What kind of behavior would you expect of a captor who kept referring to you as "steak" or "pork chop"? It is rather easy to understand why some who assume that they are fully human can be capable of inhumanity toward certain other people whom they assume are something less than human. Cannibals are, of, course, not the only people holding these assumptions. Many people today, often unconsciously, assume that they are human but that people of other races, ethnic backgrounds, or even professions or generations are not fully human. What kind of assumptions and behavior might we predict of Western soldiers fighting in the East who refer to all Asians, friends and foes, as "Gooks"? Can you think of any assumptions that keep people you know from being more helpful and friendly to one another? What are some of the assumptions that are making it difficult for nations to work together toward a peaceful and better life on earth for everyone?

5. In some countries students are graded by rows rather than individually. All students in a row receive the same grade, which is arrived at by averaging the individual grades. Students in the same row depend on and help one another and form close interpersonal relations and compete only as a group with people in other rows.

   Discuss the assumptions that govern the above practices that are different from our own. Do our educational conventions have any assumptions behind them? What are they? For example, are there any assumptions behind the fact that our educational system considers it natural to motivate learning by assigning each student an individual competitive grade and would consider it unfair and impossible to motivate learning by averaging grades after group competition? Would a school system that accepted several different methods of grading as being equally valid and that allowed students to choose the way they wished to be graded in different classes have any advantages?

6. State an antithesis to each of the following assumptions. In each case try to think of a third assumption that would be a

synthesis of the thesis and antithesis. Which of the three assumptions do you think you share and why? (Notice that what
you are doing in this exercise is practicing one way of cross-
structuring older assumptions in order to generate new ones.)

a. Human nature never changes.
b. The purpose of prison is to punish criminals and to offer an
   unpleasant example in order to discourage any more crimes.
c. The voice of moderation is always closest to the truth.
d. An institution or corporation can be as moral as an
   individual.
e. Knowledge is objective and value free.
f. Feelings and intuition lead us back to convention and habit,
   and if we listen to them we are more likely to be conservative than innovative.
g. Human beings could live in love and harmony if only in-
   stitutionally provoked hostilities or racial tensions or something else external did not stand in the way of communication
   between people.
h. We are truly human only when we act spontaneously—
   completely without habit or convention.
i. A person is perfectly free as long as nobody is telling
   him what to do and he is behaving just the way he wants to.

7. Choose one of the following abstract assumptions and extrapolate its implications into a paragraph filled with concrete detail
   in which the assumption itself is never stated even though it
   governs what you write:

   a. Maturity is a process rather than a fixed state.
   b. Man cannot live without his illusions.
   c. In an impersonal world it is foolish for a person to take
      either fortune or misfortune personally.
   d. The burning issues of the past are not the burning issues
      of the present.
   e. Even the way we *want* to behave has been conditioned by
      society.
   f. Our schools do not succeed in encouraging creativity but
      only in drilling students in narrow cultural orientations.

8. According to Clinton Rossiter in *Conservatism in America,* the
   following are typical conservative assumptions:

Man, says the Conservative, is a composite of good and evil, a blend of ennobling excellences and degrading imperfections. He is not perfect; he is not perfectible. If educated properly, placed in a favorable environment, and held in restraint by tradition and authority, he may display innate qualities of rationality, sociability, industry, decency and love of liberty. Never, no matter how he is educated or situated or restrained, will he throw off completely his other innate qualities of irrationality, selfishness, laziness, depravity, and corruptibility. Man's nature is essentially immutable and the immutable strain is one of deep-seated wickedness. Although some Conservatives find support for their skeptical view of man in recent experiments in psychology, most continue to rely on religious teaching and the study of history. Those who are Christians, and most Conservatives are, prefer to call the motives for iniquitous and irrational behavior by its proper name: Original Sin.

The Conservative is often accused of putting too much stress on man's wickedness and irrationalty and of overlooking his many good qualities, especially his capacity for reason. The Conservative's answer is candid enough. He is well aware of man's potentialities but he must counter the optimism of the liberal and radical with certain cheerless reminders that are no less true for telling only half the truth: that evil exists independently of social or economic maladjustments; that we must search for the source of our discontents in defective human nature rather than in a defective social order; and that man, far from being malleable, is subject to cultural alteration only slowly and to a limited degree. The Conservative therefore considers it his stern duty to call attention as did John Adams, to "the general frailty and depravity of human nature."

Notice how well each of the assumptions fits the others so that in combination they form almost a self-verifying system— almost a complete way of perceiving and thinking about society. What are its implications? List concisely in a paragraph like Rossiter's what you consider to be typical *liberal* assumptions. Write a short argument against either the liberal or conservative set of assumptions.

9. Write two paragraphs about some recent or approaching political election using first one and then the other set of assumptions (conservative or liberal) from exercise 8. In another paragraph explain the change in your writing behavior.

10. Adopt Plato's assumptions for the moment and write an opinion

(not necessarily your own) on the hope for progress through technology. Now write your own opinion on this same subject. What are the assumptions that appear to govern your own opinion?

11. What are the assumptions and criteria underlying *organic gardening?* Write a brief argument for or against organic gardening.

12. Do we mold culture, or does culture shape us? Discuss the implications of both assumptions in a page or two.

13. A distinction was made in the literature of the past between a "hero" and a "heroine." What assumptions have determined this distinction? Do you agree with them? Can you offer any alternative assumptions? What are the implications of these alternative assumptions for the literature of the future?

15

Discovering Criteria

SOME assumptions, especially those that tend to determine our value judgments and our sense of what is significant or relevant, operate on a higher level of abstraction than other assumptions and can be referred to as *criteria of relevance*. In other words, although all assumptions are abstract, some—criteria—are more abstract than others and function as superassumptions.

Because they are so very abstract we are not often consciously aware of the criteria that govern much of our own and others thinking and writing. Generally speaking, the more abstract the assumption, the less likely we are to be able to argue against it, to test and question it, or to seek alternatives to it, and, therefore, the more persistently will it tend to determine thinking and writing behavior. As we will see shortly, many of the highly abstract criteria still in use today are extremely ancient, having endured unconsciously from generation to generation.

For example, E. H. Carr explained how pervasive and coercive was the nineteenth-century historians' largely unconscious criterion that *ascertaining facts is the most relevant activity of the history writer*. Of course, this criterion not only determined the writing of opinions such as "take care of the facts and the interpretation will take care of itself," but was related to a number of other assumptions that this "fact"

290 Writing and Thinking with Assumptions

school of historians shared. Like the empiricist philosophers, they held that facts are hard kernels of verifiable truth which, of course, assumes further that "truth" can indeed be objectively verified so that all historians in all periods, countries, and cultures would perceive it in the same way. As a result of this combination of criterion and related assumptions the practical effect on writing history was that specialized monographs bristling with facts to support a traditional interpretation, which seemed obvious, were to be preferred to essays expressing bold, new historical interpretations that reordered some facts, ignored others, and included new data that had not before been considered facts of history.

Discovering a criterion of relevance on which an opinion or conclusion is based is essentially the same mental process that we illustrated when discussing assumption finding in Chapter 14. For example, in the following series of statements what is the most probable criterion that could govern all of them?

> I can't see why anyone argues against capital punishment when you consider how much it costs the taxpayer every year to feed and lodge convicted murderers.

> I'm against providing low-cost housing in our city because it will only tend to attract poor families with low taxable income but lots of children to increase the enrollment of city schools, which people like me are going to have to bear the cost of. Considering the rising costs of education, I'd like a nice, quiet town of prosperous older people well past childbearing.

> War is inevitable, and anyway occasional small wars that don't last long are very good for my business. I'm under government contract to manufacture steel coffins, but if the war lasts too long then up goes the price of steel and down goes my profit margin. I think a good, brisk little war of about two and a half to three years fought somewhere on the Asian continent (since I always make a little more on long-distance shipping) might be most desirable.

We might abstract something like the following criterion, which seems to underlie each of the above opinions: *all social or moral issues are to be decided only in terms of how they touch one's personal pocketbook.* What do you think the person who expressed the opinions above might have to say about tax reform?

Can you find the criterion apparently governing the opinions expressed in the two passages below?

> "Of course she might have loved him just for a minute, when they were first married—and loved me more even then, do you see?"
> Suddenly he came out with a curious remark.
> "In any case," he said, "it was just personal."
>
> —F. SCOTT FITZGERALD, *The Great Gatsby*

> . . . look at it this way: on the one hand, we have a stupid, senseless, worthless, wicked, and decrepid old hag, who is of no use to anybody and who actually does harm to everybody, a creature who does not know herself what she is living for and who will be dead soon, anyway. You see what I mean, don't you? All right; now listen, please. On the other hand, we have a large number of young and promising people who are going to rack and ruin without anyone lifting a finger to help them—and there are thousands of them all over the place. Now, a hundred or even a thousand of them could be set on the road to success and helped at the very start of their careers on that old woman's money, which is to go to a monastery. Hundreds, perhaps thousands of lives could be saved, dozens of families could be rescued from a life of poverty, from decay and ruin, from vice and hospitals for venereal diseases—and all with her money. Kill her, take her money, and with its help devote yourself to the service of humanity and the good of all.
>
> —FYODOR DOSTOEVSKY, *Crime and Punishment*

Could you frame an argument by stating and recommending alternative criteria to those underlying the opinions in the second passage?

The world is filled with people, parties, groups, and governments who operate according to different (even opposing) criteria. Let us consider the following common example of a clash between criteria in education. Science and math students on the one hand and English or humanities students on the other typically feel that they cannot do well in both English and math, since it is supposed that each requires a different kind of brain. It is much more likely that the difference between doing well and doing poorly in both English and math is not having two brains but having the ability to recognize a difference and to be able to shift from one criterion of relevance to another. For example, a person taking a mathematics course is encouraged to solve a problem, even a complex problem, in the simplest possible way. This is the aim of a criterion called "mathematical elegance." Students are discouraged from making a problem any more complex than it must be and in a math course may even have their grades lowered for introducing any data or extraneous equation that is not absolutely necessary in the solution of the problem.

This criterion of "elegance," much used in math and science, thus aims at finding *the simplest possible interpretation of or solution to a problem.* Now a student who transfers this criterion to an English course may, when asked to write an interpretation of, for instance, "The Waste Land," by T. S. Eliot, find that his English instructor considers his "elegant" interpretation, no matter how diligently he worked on it, hopelessly simple-minded, for "The Waste Land" is full of intentional irony, paradox, and ambiguous symbols that were written to be interpreted in more than one way. In short, the criterion of relevance in writing an interpretation of a poem in an English class, far from aiming at the simplest interpretation, is often to aim at being able to perceive and discuss the maximum *complexity* and suggestive ambiguity that the writer may have intended. Have you ever been caught in a similar criteria clash?

Of course, not all writers aim, as does T. S. Eliot , to be so complex and allusive that each composition is a kind of echo chamber of Western civilization. We have seen how Hemingway, Donne, Wright, and Swift each operate according to different criteria of relevance which tend to determine diverse styles of writing. We have also seen in the analysis of Carr's essay how important different criteria of relevance are in channeling the writing behavior of diverse schools of historians. Carr emphasized only two criteria that have determined historical writing. But in addition to the criterion of fact and the criterion of interpretation (or Carr's proposed synthesis of them), several more criteria have governed or still tend to govern the writing of history. Certain schools of historians used to assume repeating cycles in history and followed the criterion that *history writing should group events into cyclical patterns* (for example, periods of peace and plenty followed by periods of war and famine). Others assumed the guidance of an invisible providential hand working out a preordained historical destiny and followed the criterion that *history should discover or organize an order, preordained pattern, or ultimate meaning in the record of events.* For example, Biblical history and most of Shakespeare's history plays are organized into what appears to be a providential pattern of events to justify the ways of God to man. Some contemporary historians, on the other hand, follow a more modern existential criterion of absurdity—that *history writing should accept and reflect the lack of meaning and order in a sequence of events*—and, consequently, write a history of frustrated purposes, full of paradoxes, ironies, and ambiguities.

Particularly in the nineteenth and early twentieth centuries, many historians believed in a basic pattern of progressive evolution in history and followed the criterion that *history should discover a pattern of progress,* while many modern historians seem to have been disillusioned with the belief in progressive evolution in history and, therefore, share with ancient historians the apocalyptic criterion that *history should discover a pattern of retrogression in successive historical events.* Patterns of the decline and fall of empires or cultures including our own are considered by these historians more relevant subjects in history writing than progressive patterns.

Most of us have been exposed to a criterion of history writing that used to be much more popular than it is today— that *history should make readers more moral or patriotic or sagacious by picking out or formulating from the welter of events certain short instructive anecdotes or fables,* such as the one about George Washington and the cherry tree that used to be repeated to grade schoolers in history class until, it was hoped, they too "could not tell a lie." Of course, there are subtler and much better forms of pedagogical history writing that use anecdotes or fables and have some practical, moral, or intellectual effect on the reader. Most early biographies, such as Plutarch's *Lives,* illustrate lessons in vice and virtue and the uses and abuses of power. And even Machiavelli's *The Prince* arranges events of history primarily to instruct students in the uses of power.

Another alternative criterion of relevance in history writing is that *history should discover the determinism of events.* The operating assumption is that all historical events have antecedent causes. But determinists differ greatly in their assumptions about what kind of deterministic forces are the most significant. Some, like Marx, assume that economic forces are the most significant determinant of all historical events, while others assume that intellectual ideas determine events or that politics and diplomacy are the most important determinants. Other historians who have studied Freud may tend to assume that the unconscious psychological motivations of humanity are the ultimate determinants of history. Of course, there are some historians who, following the determinist criterion, assume multiple causation for every event and try to discover the blend of forces (economic, intellectual, psychological, etc.) that together determine a specific event.

Writing history, as we can see, is not a simple matter, since besides the few criteria mentioned here there are many more and related assumptions modifying each of the criteria. Also, few, if any, writers hold to only one criterion, and the possible number of different combinations of criteria would obviously be very large. Consequently, it is usually the uniqueness not of any particular criterion used, but of the blend or combination of criteria that differentiates one writer from another. You might pick some historical event that interests you (the America-Indochina war, for example) and, adopting a *combination* of two of the historical criteria just discussed, write a brief history of the event. How did the criteria you chose tend to determine the way you thought and wrote?

Since criteria of relevance are on a very high level of abstraction, they are often interdisciplinary rather than confined to one field. We should not be surprised to see some of the same criteria that govern the writing of historians governing the writing aims of literary critics. The "fact" school of historical writing finds its counterpart in the school of literary historians who follow the criterion that *students of literature should discover the historical facts relevant to the production and social or intellectual context of a literary work.* More recently, some critics have decided that even the concept of the objective reality of the text must be abandoned, so that literary criticism, like history writing, would be purely a matter of interpretation. Here is Leslie Fiedler in an article on modern literary criticism:

> [Criticism] will not be primarily concerned with structure or diction or syntax, all of which assume that the work of art "really" exists on the page rather than in the reader's apprehension and responses. Not words on the page but words in the world, or, rather, words in the head, at the private juncture of a thousand contexts—social, psychological, historical, biographical, geographical—in the consciousness of the reader.

Just as history carried to its extreme by the interpretive schools had become merely the writings of historians, literature for more and more readers has lately become merely the interpretations of critics with no objective text or historical frame of reference to relate the aims of the writer to his own economic, political, intellectual, and aesthetic context. Much criticism published in learned journals today deals more with the writings of other critics on the work in question than with the work itself in its historical context. Can you, imagining yourself the literary counterpart of E. H. Carr, suggest a way to synthesize these opposed schools of literary study?

There is no one absolute criterion used to judge human behavior. If there were, interpersonal relations might be much easier as well as much more narrow-mindedly repressive. In fact, the concept of tolerance and respect for other cultures and life styles is probably not possible without knowledge of diverse criteria with which to assess the behavior of our fellow humans. Can you think of some criteria that we and our neighbors commonly use to evaluate one another? How do you decide between good or poor friends, teachers, movies? What are some alternatives to your criteria held by other people that you can respect?

As long as we remain only dimly aware of the source of our biases in the criteria that we have been programmed with unconsciously by parents, teachers, and peer groups and do not seek possible alternative criteria to extend the range of our understanding, we will only be able to communicate with the socially, culturally, or racially monolithic group which shares our narrow combination of criteria.

If human relations could be improved by learning and practicing a greater range of interpersonal criteria, it may also be possible to improve our education generally by seeking more alternatives to our present range of academic criteria of relevance. What educational criteria do you operate on? What is a good course or a good class? Do you like to get the "facts" or the "big picture," or do you consider facts and interpretation equally relevant, as does E. H. Carr? Is education something you will *be given* by your teachers or something that you must *get* for yourself? Should education teach us how to adapt ourselves to society or how to change society to adapt it to our needs? Should education be "molding a fixed character" in us and inculcating belief in some "unchanging values and universal truths," or should we be presented with many alternative values and models of reality and encouraged to make choices and define ourselves by the process of our growth and change rather than become "fixed" in any conventional set of assumptions and criteria?

Here is another rather typical classroom clash of criteria: *the aim of isolating a single narrow problem to discuss or solve* is often at odds with *the aim of attacking a broad problem or*

*problems too large or too profound to admit of any simple
discussion or solution.* But in the process of struggling with the
broad problem, a student can often generate some new directions for study and research even though no solution is possible
at the time of writing. The student who uses the second criterion
and bites off a subject much too difficult to chew and swallow
immediately may often become more interested in the paper he
is writing, and perhaps learn more, since many new directions
for continued rumination and research will present themselves,
than the student who isolates and narrows his subject or problem until it admits of complete discussion or solution. Of course,
the student who chooses the criterion of *isolating a narrow,
immediately solvable problem* will almost always get the better
grade since it is customary for teachers to use the criterion of
narrowing the problem in evaluating student compositions. This
bias in favor of the criterion of isolating narrow problems that
admit of immediate solution, while often avoiding theoretical
work on much more crucial problems that seem not to have
immediate solutions, has become general throughout our society. Applied know-how is still commonly considered more
relevant than theoretical research, in spite of the practical consequences of some theoretical breakthroughs. Obviously, both
criteria are important. The problems of pollution, and racism
and poverty, for example, have no simple immediate solutions
and yet seem worthy of study even if such study does nothing
more than generate research toward an eventual solution.

Suppose that teachers occasionally assigned broad challenging problems that the student could not hope to solve immediately or discuss completely and then evaluated the student's work according to the criterion of how much new
research and interest it generated? Would increased use of
such a criterion in assigning papers and projects encourage
some people to attack more challenging social problems after
they left school? Or do you think that the narrow-problem-
solving criterion is so ingrained in our society that the use of
this criterion in assigning and grading papers is not a cause,
but merely a symptom, of our general neglect of important

problems that do not admit of easy or immediate solution? Can you think of any large problem that should be investigated even though it might be very complex?

So far, we have been discussing *single* criteria. Now let us consider something a little more difficult. How, for example, could we abstract a *whole set* of criteria underlying some ancient Greek art (i.e., its combination of aesthetic aims) from a passage in the *Iliad* (ca. 800 B.C.), where Homer describes in detail what he considers to be a most wonderful work of art that the god Hephaestus is creating in making a shield for Achilles? First of all, the shield itself is described as consisting of "five layers of hide" encircled by a "threefold rim round the edge of shining metal." We can conclude from this description that there was no dichotomy between art and usefulness—that is, the early Greeks did not evidently share the late nineteenth- and early twentieth-century criterion that *art is to be distinguished from practical value* or, in other words, "art for art's sake." Upon this stout shield of leather and metal Hephaestus "wrought the Earth, and the sky, and the Sea, the untiring Sun and the full Moon, and all the stars that encircle the sky. . . ." This seems like a lot to compact into one shield and already hints at another possible aesthetic criterion—that *a work of art should aim at universal detailed inclusiveness* rather than at narrowing subject matter down to a single object or a "slice of life." To fill out his universe Hephaestus "fashioned two cities of mortal men." "In the first was wedding and feasting. . . . The other city had two armies besieging it round about." Notice the symmetry of a city at peace, suggesting life, and a city at war, suggesting death. This implies the possibility of an aesthetic criterion of symmetry—that *elements of a work of art should be composed in parallel or antithetical* relations with one another.

At several points Hephaestus seems to be praised according to a *criterion of "realism"*—that *art should mirror "real" life.* In praise of the realistic depiction embossed on the shield, of men at war Homer says, "they looked like living men as they struggled and fought and pulled back the dead bodies from either side." And again Homer explains in detail a scene on the

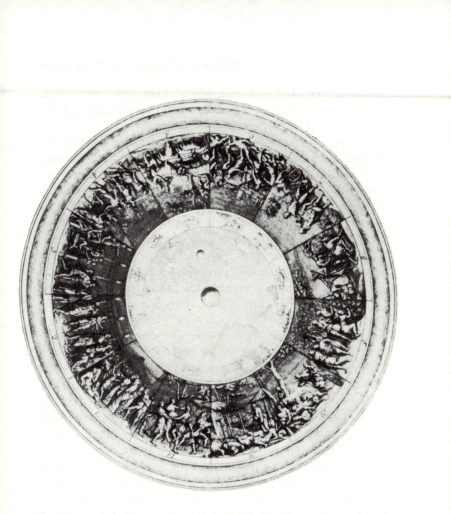

The Shield of Achilles, from the first edition of Pope's *Iliad* (1750).

shield of men plowing a field, which, if you have ever watched it, makes the earth just turned up by the plow a different shade and texture from the harder, drier surface crust: "The soil was black behind them, and looked like soil under the plow, although it was gold. That was a wonderful thing."

Besides the scene where "the plowmen were driving their teams up and down with a turn at the end," there are three more scenes which form a kind of symmetrical group of representative or symbolic agrarian activities. Plowing symbolizes spring because that is when it is done. The next activity of cutting and binding grain, where "hands were reaping with sharp sickles," is described in realistic detail and is emblematic of summer. Autumn is represented by a vineyard heavy with grapes, where "Boys and girls in merry glee carried the honey-sweet fruit in baskets of wickerwork." Winter is portrayed by a herd of cattle with "Golden herdsmen stalk[ing] beside them, four men with nine quick-footed dogs." These spring, summer, autumn, winter activities imply not only a criterion of realism, but also fulfill the criteria of symmetry and inclusiveness because they form a complete seasonal series. Finally the shield is bordered around its edge with the ocean, so that the whole shield, including all its scenes, seems a representational map of the Greek macrocosm. Perhaps one further criterion may be suggested by the fact that Homer always describes the scenes on the shield primarily as the objective activities of man rather than as subjective states of mind. This aesthetic criterion, that *the objective portrayal of action is a relevant function of art,* is very different from the modern, more subjective criterion that we are used to in much poetry today—that *relevant art aims at expressing subjective feelings rather than portraying objective action.* Can you write a short narrative governed by the same combination of aesthetic criteria that shaped the art of Achilles' shield? How might the narrative differ from the way you would ordinarily write it? What does this imply about your own combination of aesthetic criteria? Can you now state some of the aesthetic criteria that determine your own appreciation of narrative writing?

It should not surprise us to find that the same visual

aesthetic criteria implied in Homer's praise of Achilles' shield seem to be among Homer's own literary criteria as well. For example, a criterion of symmetry is apparently followed in the composition of the *Iliad* when one hero or battle is paralleled or put into antithesis with another, or when a council of the gods is balanced with a council among the Greeks. Homer seems to be using the criterion of universality when he includes all the gods as well as numerous armies from far-flung countries in the Greek-Trojan war. These inclusions make it seem an almost universal struggle—certainly a world war (considering the boundaries of the known world in 800 B.C.). Also the many similes and digressions of the *Iliad* manage to include in the poem the universal arts and activities of gods and men at peace and war.

This criterion of universality, by which *even a single event should be considered in terms of its relation to the whole universe*, implies a belief in the interrelationship of microcosm and macrocosm. Such a belief in recent years was somewhat out of fashion, for many artists were more interested in making small statements about single incidents or feelings, and generally considered larger statements pretentious or "talking big." But such a narrow slice-of-life criterion seems to be on the wane at the moment, since the aesthetic criterion of universal inclusiveness is getting a helping hand from world-wide communications systems and from ecologists who keep reminding us that what appear to be singular events are always interrelated with the whole ecosystem. For instance, the rock-culture dust jacket for one of the Rolling Stones's record albums, "Their Satanic Majesties Request," with its universal inclusion of art masterpieces from both East and West from all historical periods, its world map along the border, its cities and societies both ancient and modern together with scenes of peace and war, and even extraterrestrial bodies like the planet Saturn and the moon, is rather typical of counterculture art and interests (e.g., *The Whole Earth Catalog* was a best seller) of the late 1960s and early 1970s, and yet seems to share at least one aesthetic criterion with Achilles' shield.

Can you think of any other criteria of relevance that are

either dying out or, on the contrary, being used more often today than in the past?

We commonly evaluate according to a single criterion in restricted situations such as operating a machine efficiently or a business enterprise economically. The ravages to our ecology, already evident, suggest that maximizing for only one or two similar criteria such as productive growth or efficiency can work wonders for a short time but may prove unwise or possibly even fatal if continued over a span of time. Compassion for other humans and respect for the environment that we all share are two more criteria that could be *combined* with those of productivity and efficiency if we wish to maintain or improve the *quality* of life for our children and grandchildren. But evaluating according to a combination of criteria is difficult and new; we are so accustomed to ignoring all values except one simple, easily measurable standard. John Scharr, explains, in the following paragraph, the institutionalized set of unquestioned assumptions and criteria that acts like a social inertia to delay the acceptance of new, more complex combined criteria:

> . . . The system works not because recognizable human authority is in charge, but because its basic ends and its procedural assumptions are taken for granted and programmed into men and machines. Given the basic assumptions of growth as the main goal and efficiency as the criterion of performance, human intervention is largely limited to making incremental adjustments, fundamentally of an equilibrating kind. The system is glacially resistant to genuine innovation, for it proceeds by its own momentum, imposes its own demands, and systematically screens out information of all kinds but one. The basic law of the whole is: because we already have machines and processes and things of certain kinds, we shall get more machines and processes and things of closely related kinds, and this by the most efficient means.*

Interdependent relations almost always exist between a criterion of relevance and other assumptions that are usually

---

* John Scharr, "Legitimacy in the Modern State," in *Power and Community,* ed. Sanford Levinson and Philip Green (New York: Pantheon Books, 1970), pp. 303–304.

governed by or occasionally modify the effects of the criterion. For example, a criterion that has been much used since the beginning of recorded history and is still often used in one form or another even today to determine important value judgments is that *whatever is most natural is best.* Now obviously such a criterion depends heavily on assumptions about "nature." Some men, like Andrew Carnegie, decided on the basis of Darwin's theory of organic evolution and Herbert Spencer's writings on social evolution, that the survival of the fittest— tooth-and-claw competitiveness—even among the human species in modern society, was "natural." Then, using the criterion that whatever is most natural is best, Carnegie argued that it would be best for the human species to manipulate society to force each individual into fierce economic competition, where the fit and the unfit would be given, in a free enterprise society, the maximum chance to survive or not to survive. Other men, like the Russian Prince Kropotkin arrived at a very different assumption about nature, even after studying Darwin's theory. Kropotkin found much evidence in Darwin's writings and in his own observation to confirm him in the assumption that cooperation among members of a species was more important to the species' survival than ruthless individual competition to weed out the unfit. Using the same general criterion as Carnegie, Kropotkin (because of his different assumptions about what was natural) argued that compassionate cooperation among free individuals would provide the best human society, since to him it was most "natural."

Other assumptions about what is natural also affect the application of the criterion *whatever is most natural is best.* Some people assume that the present balance of nature or the present balance of society (some rich, some poor, some powerful institutions, some weak institutions) is the only "natural" balance, and therefore they argue for the status quo and against societal change of any kind except that which will preserve the present balance. As Alexander Pope put it, "Whatever is, is right." But other people assume that the so-called "balance of nature" and the balance in society is always changing and that, therefore, change is more "natural" than the status quo. But now one's assumption about what *kind* of change would be most "natural" comes into play. And what about the *rate* of change? Some people assume that infinitesimally slow, steady change is most like evolution, and thus most "natural." Other people argue that evolution does not usually move at the same slow, steady pace, but that profound differences occur swiftly during rapid accelerations of evolutionary change, followed by long periods of relatively little change. Drastic changes in the environment and in organic species caused by the great glaciers offer examples of evolutionary acceleration. Furthermore, some scientists hypothesize that there was a period when far higher concentrations of oxygen seem to have occurred on earth just before the time animals first appeared. In other words, before animals appeared, vegetables were polluting the earth with oxygen gas they gave off as waste product. The environment was favorable then for the rise of an organic being that consumed the waste oxygen from plants. An oxygen ratio at least several times higher than the present ratio might account for the proliferation of species of animals during that period. Many animal species may have appeared in a relatively short time due to the increased rate of mutations that is known to occur in the case of high-oxygen environments. What do you think would happen in evolution today if some mutant beast or bacteria began to thrive on sulphur dioxide or some other pollutant from our sources of energy?

Thus it has been assumed by some scientists that evolution takes place not at the same slow, steady pace but at varying rates, sometimes in short bursts, followed by slower periods of change. Such periods of accelerated evolution bear a close resemblance to revolutionary change in society; some people assume that rapidly accelerated evolution is just as "natural" as slow, steady change and have argued according to the general criterion of *what is natural is best* that, therefore, it might be best for society from time to time to undergo rapidly accelerated evolution, if not revolution.

For an example of writing governed by the criterion *whatever is natural is best* consider the following passage from Adolf Hitler's *Mein Kampf*. Hitler expects you to agree with his major criterion and with his assumptions about what nature is really like. Notice how cleverly he argues *if* you accept his criterion and assumptions:

> . . . Columbus's eggs lie around by the hundreds of thousands, but Columbuses are met with less frequently.
>
> Thus men without exception wander about in the garden of Nature; they imagine that they know practically everything and yet with few exceptions pass blindly by one of the most patent principles of Nature's rule: the inner segregation of the species of all living beings on this earth.
>
> Even the most superficial observation shows that Nature's restricted form of propagation and increase is an almost rigid basic law of all the innumerable forms of expression of her vital urge. Every animal mates only with a member of the same species. The titmouse seeks the titmouse, the finch the finch, the stork the stork, the field mouse the field mouse, the dormouse the dormouse, the wolf the she-wolf, etc.
>
> Only unusual circumstances can change this, primarily the compulsion of captivity or any other cause that makes it impossible to mate within the same species. But then Nature begins to resist this with all possible means, and her most visible protest consists either in refusing further capacity for propagation to bastards or in limiting the fertility of later offspring; in most cases, however, she takes away the power of resistance to disease or hostile attacks.
>
> This is only too natural.
>
> Any crossing of two beings not at exactly the same level produces a medium between the level of the two parents. This means: the offspring will probably stand higher than the racially lower parent, but not as high as the higher one. Consequently, it will later succumb in the struggle against the higher level. Such mating is contrary to the will of Nature for a higher breeding of all life. The precondition for this does not lie in associating superior and inferior, but in the total victory of the former. The stronger must dominate and not blend with the weaker, thus sacrificing his own greatness. Only the born weakling can view this as cruel, but he after all is only a weak and limited man; for if this law did not prevail, any conceivable higher development of organic living beings would be unthinkable. . . .

No more than Nature desires the mating of weaker with stronger individuals, even less does she desire the blending of a higher with a lower race, since, if she did, her whole work of higher breeding, over perhaps hundreds of thousands of years, might be ruined with one blow.

Historical experience offers countless proofs of this. It shows with terrifying clarity that in every mingling of Aryan blood with that of lower peoples the result was the end of the cultured people. North America, whose population consists in by far the largest part of Germanic elements who mixed but little with the lower colored peoples, shows a different humanity and culture from Central and South America, where the predominantly Latin immigrants often mixed with the aborigines on a large scale. By this one example, we can clearly and distinctly recognize the effect of racial mixture. The Germanic inhabitant of the American continent, who has remained racially pure and unmixed, rose to be master of the continent; he will remain the master as long as he does not fall a victim to defilement of the blood. . . .

Everything we admire on this earth today—science and art, technology and inventions—is only the creative product of a few peoples and originally perhaps of *one* race. On them depends the existence of this whole culture. If they perish, the beauty of this earth will sink into the grave with them.

However much the soil, for example, can influence men, the result of the influence will always be different depending on the races in question. The low fertility of a living space may spur the one race to the highest achievements; in others it will only be the cause of bitterest poverty and final undernourishment with all its consequences. The inner nature of peoples is always determining for the manner in which outward influences will be effective. What leads the one to starvation trains the other to hard work.

All great cultures of the past perished only because the originally creative race died out from blood poisoning.

The ultimate cause of such a decline was their forgetting that all culture depends on men and not conversely; hence that to preserve a certain culture the man who creates it must be preserved. This preservation is bound up with the rigid law of necessity and the right to victory of the best and stronger in this world.

> Those who want to live, let them fight, and those who do not want to fight in this world of eternal struggle do not deserve to live.

Exercises

1. Write a brief argument against Hitler's position by questioning his criterion, or assumptions, or both, and recommending alternatives.

2. See the eighteenth-century illustration of Achilles' shield on p. 299. Is this the way you perceive the shield? Draw your own sketch of the shield. How does it differ from the Neoclassic illustration? How are your assumptions and criteria different from those of the eighteenth century?

3. In the mid-eighteenth century Samuel Johnson recommended corporal punishment instead of competitive emulation in these terms:

> I would rather . . . have the rod to be the general terrour to all, to make them learn, than tell a child, if you do thus, or thus, you will be more esteemed than your brothers or sisters. The rod produces an effect which terminates in itself. A child is afraid of being whipped, and gets his task, and there's an end on't; whereas, by exciting emulation and comparisons of superiority, you lay the foundation of lasting mischief; you make brothers and sisters hate each other.
>
> —JAMES BOSWELL, *Life of Johnson*

What is Samuel Johnson's criterion of human relations? What are the implications of his statement on education? What do you suppose he would say were he alive today to witness our classrooms? Do you assume with Johnson that there are but two means of motivating learning—either beatings or competition? Can you think of any other possible motivations upon which to design another (perhaps better) education system? Write a short critique of our present system of education using Johnson's criterion, but not necessarily recommending corporal punishment.

4. Writing can only be judged and its significance verified with respect to some criterion or combination of criteria rather than some Aristotelian essence or absolute value inherent in the writing itself. This, of course, implies a certain relativity of significance, but does not mean that we cannot be sure of value. Even though we realize that our judgments are valid only with respect to a given set of criteria, we can, nevertheless, make clear and forceful evaluations. The selection of criteria below is not by any means an exhaustive list, but it may give you some idea of the possible range of alternative criteria. Practice *combining* as many of these criteria as you can until you understand and can shift among a broad range of alternatives. Try judging a sample of your own writing, using not one criterion but different combinations of criteria. In which set of criteria did your writing seem most relevant or significant? Is this the same combination of criteria you used to write in? Write a short essay according to a combination of criteria that you think most congenial to you, and list the criteria you used so that your instructor can evaluate your work according to the same combination of criteria you used to write it.

Alternative Criteria

The most significant essay might aim at:

a. solving a specific problem
b. posing a problem carefully but not necessarily solving it
c. posing or solving a problem not in isolation, but in relation to its ecosystem or total environment
d. having a practical effect on the audience (changing attitudes or motivating to action)
e. accurately mirroring "reality"
f. maintaining logical consistency
g. fitting current ideas
h. framing a hypothesis likely to generate fruitful new research
i. being provocative with the most startling implications
j. economy or "elegance" of expression
k. proposing a hypothesis from which you can make predictions capable of empirical testing

l. such careful organizing that most people following your sequence of steps would arrive at the same conclusion
m. being most economically efficient
n. being most compassionate
o. stating clear generalizations backed up with relevant concrete facts or examples
p. communicating with the largest number of people, without boring the best minds
q. making difficult thinking and writing appear easy
r. taking the most alternatives into consideration in order to arrive at a judgment
s. displaying professional knowledge of the conventions—being well informed
t. being innovative
u. revealing or relying on the enduring, perennial, universal, or archetypal nature of any subject rather than some recent or innovative idea of it
v. displaying the strongest subjective feelings about the subject
w. revealing alternatives or dichotomies and holding them in tension
x. providing a compromise or synthesis between antithetical extremes
y. investigating the antecedent deterministic causes governing en event or underlying a problem
z. satisfying some more highly specialized criteria in a specific field

16

Using Assumptions
and Criteria to Argue
and Organize

SOME people have the ability to see relations or contradictions in what may seem to others to be an apparently disparate conglomeration of facts and opinions. A lecture or assignment that one student sees as a boring irrelevancy may be fit by another into a larger context of assumptions. The latter student can consequently relate more of his knowledge and reading to the lecture or assignment. Now the difference between people who practice this ability and those who do not appears so obvious that often the ability is mistaken for an innate gift and is referred to as "insight"—the mysterious attribute of an elite few. But most, if not all, of the insight in seeing relations in apparently disparate opinions depends on the learned ability to abstract assumptions and criteria that we began to develop in the previous chapters. We can now apply this growing ability to useful purpose in perceiving relationships in our environment of heterogeneous opinions. But we will not be able to see relations if we concentrate on mere opinions rather than the assumptions that govern them. For example, can you see any relations between these two statements?

A. In your heart you know he's right.

B. Fifty million Frenchmen can't be wrong.

At the level of opinions there is seemingly no relation between the first quotation, which was a political slogan for the Gold-water campaign for the presidency of 1964, and the second, which used to be, when Paris was still considered to be the sex capitol of the world, a popular way of proving that it is love that makes the world go round, or something of that nature. However, if we move to the level of assumptions governing these opinions we may see some relation that might allow us to organize them. An obvious assumption behind the assertion "In your heart you know he's right" is that the standard of truth or morality is subjective and internal rather than something that can be decided externally or objectively (either or both truth and morality may be involved since the word *right* is ambiguous in this respect). An assumption we can abstract from the assertion "Fifty million Frenchmen can't be wrong" is the converse of the first assumption, namely that the standard for judging truth or morality is an external and objective, in this case a numerically measurable matter, which makes a subjec-tive/internal standard of morality irrelevant. It is easy to see how we could organize the two opinions as contrasting exam-ples of two diametrically opposed standards of truth or moral-ity. Which criterion do you agree with? Can you think of these two criteria as *thesis* and *antithesis* and find a *synthesis?*

Now let us try to see relations and/or contradictions among a more difficult set of opinions. The several opinions that fol-low may seem, at first, quite without the probability of any coherent relations or contradictions:

Opinion A

I am not guilty of racism because I personally have never acted to hurt a black person. If it's the whole system they're against then they talk about racism, why that's like being against the weather. The weather and the system may not always be fair but that's just the way it is. Society is something that just naturally grew that way and society, like nature, is not always fair. But tampering with the whole system won't work because men can't play God.

Opinion B

Have you ever noticed that men fighting on both sides of a

war really believe that they are killing morally, according to conscience? But obviously they cannot both be right in killing each other. Either they are both wrong or one is more right than the other. The UN or some other international organization ought to decide whether both are wrong or which one is right. Then we might be able to eliminate war.

Opinion C

All criminals are coerced for one reason or another into acting against society. Sometimes the source of coercion lies within the fractured psyche of the individual as in the case of insanity, or sometimes the coercion may be caused by the public failure to provide each citizen with the freedom of enough social alternatives. But in any case unless the pattern of coercion is somehow altered it is unlikely that criminals, no matter how much time they serve in prison, will be able to resist committing future crime.

Opinion D

The primary function of education in a democracy must be to educate all who desire it—a function that is lost sight of when teachers spend most of their time categorizing their students by means of a grading system that tends to perpetuate learning handicaps and weed out potential applicants for the benefit not of the students, but of admissions officers and personnel directors.

Opinion E

My favorite anecdote is the one about the two baby brother lice who, once upon a time, played together in a large dairy barn. One day, while playing hide-and-seek, they fell by chance into separate cracks in the barn floor and did not see each other until they were middle-aged. The first louse had fallen into a very fortunate crack behind a milk barrel that overflowed daily onto the floor and into the crack, while the second louse had fallen by mischance into a crack in the middle of the barn, which was often scrubbed with lye and kept very clean. When they finally emerged from their cracks the first louse was prosperously fat and sleek and barely recongnized his poor childhood playmate who staggered across the floor looking feeble and emaciated.

"How did you do it?" said the poor louse weakly.

And the large louse responded, "Well, you see, it was an arduous struggle for intellectual perfection and physical fitness coupled with rigorous moral discipline and grueling labor, and to be perfectly honest with you, brother, I must confess that my obvious personal charm perhaps gave me a slight initial advantage."

Opinion A seems to assume or imply:

1. that bigotry and prejudice are simply matters of the free, conscious choice of individuals rather than larger problems of unconscious social conditioning;
2. that the growth of social institutions (the system) is not determined by choice of people, but rather by the processes of "nature";
3. that we cannot expect anything "natural" to be perfectly fair;
4. that people cannot change their social institutions no matter how much they may dislike them, since only God can interfere in "nature."

Can you think of other assumptions or implications?

Opinion B seems to assume or imply:

1. that morality is a prime factor in people's behavior;
2. that there are two possible bases for morality—internal feelings and external rules;
3. that a person acting according to an objectively defined external morality would behave differently from a person acting according to a subjective internal morality;
4. that wars would be eliminated if both sides could learn to operate according to an external or international morality based on objectively defined rules.

Opinion C seems to assume or imply:

1. that people are not inherently free to choose whatever they want;
2. that determinism is not just physical restraint but uncon-

sciously may control the very things that a person wishes or feels he or she needs;

3. that freedom is not simply a private, individual matter but is to some extent determined by external conditions, such as social or physical environment;
4. that freedom is having the maximum number of alternatives in any given situation;
5. that since society can increase the alternatives open to people, it could therefore grant more freedom.

Opinion D seems to assume or imply:

1. that most students are not motivated, but discouraged or held back by the grading system;
2. that democracy implies more than equality before the law, and that democratic equality should, among other things, mean equal freedom for all to be as well educated as only the few have been in the present system;
3. that differences in intelligence or scholarly aptitude deserve no special favor in democratic education, since all will receive the best education available;
4. that all students could benefit equally from the best education if both teachers and students were free of the grading system.

Opinion E seems to assume or imply:

1. that there is an analogy between these lice and people;
2. that environmental chance determines initial advantages between similarly endowed individuals, which advantages are compounded as time goes on until it is hard to believe that such different individuals were once equal;
3. that instead of acknowledging the determinism of environmental chance, which provided an advantage, individuals, either through ignorance of determinism or hypocrisy, ascribe to themselves superior personal merit or natural gifts to account for their good fortune, while their brothers' or sisters' misery is ascribed to personal weakness;
4. that the forces which determine our lives and fortunes are

impersonal, even though we seem unable to refrain from interpreting what happens to us in personal terms.

Finding assumptions underlying opinions is only the first step in organizing. Next you must try to find relations (contradictions as well as agreements) among the assumptions we have found, and then decide how some or all of these opinions could be organized. For example, are all the opinions governed by a common assumption? In that case, they could be compared to one another. Or if each opinion contained a unique assumption about one subject (the limits of human freedom, for example), they could be contrasted. Or perhaps several opinions complement each other and at the same time contradict several other opinions, in which case you might want to organize in terms of comparison/contrast or maybe thesis/antithesis/synthesis. In the assumptions we isolated above, for instance, the issue of freedom versus determinism is central to the assumptions behind each of the opinions, as is also the issue of *the individual and his relation to society*. See if you can use these or find some other relations and/or contradictions among the assumptions to organize a brief argument in favor of one or two and against several of the opinions above.

Arming yourself with a pencil and paper while you read, write down assumptions underlying each of the following set of selections. (For example, does Ortega y Gasset in the second selection share any Aristotelian assumptions of the kind discussed in Chapter 14?)

> . . . What goes largely unexamined, often even unacknowledged (yet is institutionalized nonetheless) in our social order, is the birthright priority whereby males rule females. Through this system a most ingenious form of "interior colonization" has been achieved. It is one which tends moreover to be sturdier than any form of segregation, and more rigorous than class stratification, more uniform, certainly more enduring. However muted its present appearance may be, sexual dominion obtains nevertheless as perhaps the most pervasive ideology of our culture and provides its most fundamental concept of power.

This is so because our society, like all other historical civilizations, is a patriarchy. The fact is evident at once if one recalls that the military, industry, technology, universities, science, political office, and finance—in short, every avenue of power within the society, including the coercive force of the police, is entirely in male hands. As the essence of politics is power, such realization cannot fail to carry impact. What lingers of supernatural authority, the Deity, "His" ministry, together with the ethics and values, the philosophy and art of our culture—its very civilization—as T. S. Eliot once observed, is of male manufacture.*

—KATE MILLETT (1970)

The instant we see a woman, we seem to have before us a being whose inward humanity is characterized, in contrast to our own male humanity and that of other men, by being essentially confused. Let us waive the pejorative connotation with which this word is usually understood. Confusion is not a defect in a woman, any more than it is a defect in man not to have wings. Even less, in fact—for it makes some sense to wish that man had wings like hawks and angels, but it does not make sense to want woman to stop being "substantially" confused. This would amount to destroying the delight that woman is to man by virtue of her confused being. Man, on the contrary, is made up of clarities. Everything in him is given with clarity. You are to understand, of course, "subjective clarity," not actual, objective clarity concerning the world and his fellow human beings. Perhaps everything he thinks is sheer nonsense; but within himself he sees himself clearly. Hence in the masculine inwardness everything normally has strict and definite lines, which makes the human male a being full of rigid angles. Woman, on the other hand, lives in a perpetual twilight; she is never sure whether she loves or not, will do something or not do it, is repentant or unrepentant. In woman, there is neither midday nor midnight; she is a creature of twilight. Hence she is constitutionally secret. Not because she does not report what she feels and what befalls her, but because normally she cannot express what she feels and what befalls her. It is a secret for her too. This gives woman the softness of

* Kate Millett, *Sexual Politics* (New York, 1970), pp. 24–25.

forms which belongs to her "soul" and which for us is the typically feminine.*

—José Ortega y Gasset (1957)

The education of women should always be relative to that of men. To please, to be useful to us, to make us love and esteem them, to educate us when young, to take care of us when grown up, to advise, to console us, to render our lives easy and agreeable; these are the duties of women at all times, and what they should be taught in their infancy.

—Jean Jacques Rosseau (eighteenth century)

Women are only children of a larger growth. . . . A man of sense only trifles with them, humors and flatters them, as he does with a sprightly, forward child; but he neither consults them about, nor trusts them with serious matters.

—Lord Chesterfield (eighteenth century)

For the last five years men have been telling me the most delicious things—that I'm sexy, all woman, that perfect combination of a lady in the living room and a marvelous bitch in bed, sensual, beautiful, a modern Aphrodite, maddeningly exciting, the epitome of the Sensuous Woman. Some of the most interesting men in America have fallen in love with me. I have received marriage proposals from such diverse personalities as a concert pianist, a best-selling author, the producer of three of America's most popular television shows, a bomb expert for the CIA, a trial attorney, an apple grower, a TV and radio star, and a tax expert. . . . For, through intelligence and hard work, I have become a Sensuous Woman.

And that's what almost every man wants.
More than beauty
More that brilliance
More than great housekeeping abilities
More than a model mother to his children
He wants a Sensuous Woman
Because she makes him *know* that he is the most remarkable man that ever lived.

---

* José Ortega y Gasset, *Man and People,* trans. Willard Trask (New York : Norton, 1957), pp. 130–131.

Women who can clean, look good, and mother children are a dollar a dozen, but a woman who can make a man feel his uniqueness is worth the world to him.*

—"J" (1969)

Can you now see any relation among the assumptions you have found? Which ones agree? Which are antithetical? What do you think Kate Millett would have said about "J" 's assumptions?

Exercises

1. Organize a brief essay discussing the last five quotations. Perhaps some assumptions are older or more conventional than others, in which case you could organize your discussion of the selections chronologically and explain how assumptions have changed to fit the modern context of man/woman relations. (But, then, how do you explain the fact that "J" 's, one of the most recent selections, seems to share more assumptions with Rousseau than with Kate Millett?)

2. The process of analyzing, thinking about, and organizing these opinions is the same as that required in thinking about and organizing a good *research paper.* After you finish your brief essay discussing some of the selections, begin to research this issue of man/woman relationships, gathering more opinions to confirm or perhaps modify or qualify the organization of assumptions you have already composed in exercise 2. Now write a research paper organized on the level of *assumptions* and *implications* about man/woman relations. Avoid merely stringing out quotations on an opinion level. If you use quotations or source material, footnote these in some simple, consistent fashion that usefully informs your reader of sources but

* "J," *The Sensuous Woman* (New York, 1969), pp. 9–11.

does not burden him with unnecessary details. (You might refer to *The MLA Style Sheet* or any similar method of foot-noting.) Here is a brief bibliography on the subject that might help you begin your research:

ADAMS, ELSIE, and MARY LOUISE BRISCOE, *Up Against the Wall, Mother: A Women's Liberation Reader* (Beverly Hills, Calif., 1971).

BEARD, MARY R., *Woman as a Force in History*

BIRD, CAROLINE, *Born Female* (New York, 1970).

CADE, TONI, ed., *The Black Woman: An Anthology* (New York, 1970).

DE BEAUVOIR, SIMONE, *The Second Sex,* trans. H. M. Parshley (New York, 1953).

DE ROUGEMONT, DENIS, *Love in the Western World,* trans. Montgomery Belgion (New York, 1956).

FIGES, EVA, *Patriarchal Attitudes* (New York, 1970).

FIRESTONE, SHULAMITH, *The Dialectic of Sex: The Case for Feminist Revolution* (New York, 1970).

FLEXNER, ELEANOR, *A Century of Struggle*

FREUD, SIGMUND, "Femininity," in *New Introductory Lectures on Psychoanalysis,* Standard ed., ed. and trans. James Strachey (New York, 1965).

FRIEDAN, BETTY, *The Feminine Mystique* (New York, 1963).

MEAD, MARGARET, *Male and Female: A Study of the Sexes in a Changing World* (New York, 1967).

MILLETT, KATE, *Sexual Politics* (New York, 1970).

MITCHELL, JULIET, *Woman's Estate* (New York, 1972).

RAINWATER, LEE, RICHARD COLEMAN, and GERALD HANDEL, *Workingman's Wife: Her Personality, World and Life Style* (Dobbs Ferry, N.Y., 1959).

The Woman Question: Selections from the Writings of Karl Marx, Frederich Engels, V. I. Lenin, Joseph Stalin, rev. ed. (New York, 1970).

3. What are the assumptions and criteria stated or unstated that govern the following selection by Alvin Toffler?

In the technological systems of tomorrow—fast, fluid and self-regulating—machines will deal with the flow of physical materials; men with the flow of information and insight. Machines will increasingly perform the routine tasks: men the intellectual and creative tasks. Machines and men both, instead of being concentrated in gigantic factories and factory cities, will be scattered across the globe, linked together by amazingly sensitive, near-instantaneous communications. Human work will move out of the factory and mass office into the community and the home.

Machines will be synchronized, as some already are, to the billionth of a second; men will be de-synchronized. The factory whistle will vanish. Even the clock, "the key machine of the modern industrial age," as Lewis Mumford called it a generation ago, will lose some of its power over purely human, as distinct from purely technological, affairs. Simultaneously, the organizations needed to control technology will shift from bureaucracy to Ad-hocracy, from permanence to transcience, and from a concern with the present to a focus on the future.

In such a world, the most valued attributes of the industrial era become handicaps. The technology of tomorrow requires not millions of lightly lettered men, ready to work in unison at endlessly repetitious jobs, it requires not men who take orders in unblinking fashion, aware that the price of bread is mechanical submission to authority, but men who can make critical judgments, who can weave their way through novel environments, who are quick to spot new relationships in the rapidly changing reality. It requires men who, in C. P. Snow's compelling term, "have the future in their bones."

Finally, unless we capture control of the accelerative thrust—and there are few signs yet that we will—tomorrow's individual will have to cope with even more hectic change than we do today. For education the lesson is clear: its prime objective must be to increase the individual's "cope-ability"—the speed and economy with which he can adapt to continual change. And the faster the rate of change, the more attention must be devoted to discerning the pattern of future events.

It is no longer sufficient for Johnny to understand the past. It is not even enough for him to understand the present, for the here-and-now environment will soon vanish. Johnny must learn to anticipate the directions and rate of change. He must, to put it technically, learn to make repeated, probabilistic, increasingly longrange assumptions about the future. And so must Johnny's teachers.

To create a super-industrial education, therefore, we shall first need to generate successive, alternative images of the future—assumptions about the kinds of jobs, professions, and vocations that may be needed twenty to fifty years in the future; assumptions about the kind of family forms and human relationships that will prevail; the kinds of ethical and moral problems that will arise; the kind of technology that will surround us and the organizational structures with which we must mesh.

It is only by generating such assumptions, defining, debating,

systematizing and continually updating them, that we can deduce
the nature of the cognitive and affective skills that the people
of tomorrow will need to survive the accelerative thrust.*

Using Toffler's set of assumptions and criteria rather than your
own, write a brief critique of the present education in secondary
school or first year of college. Now write your own opinion on
the same subject. What are the assumptions and criteria that
seem to govern the opinion you expressed?

4. What are Leslie White's assumptions and criteria in the following passage?

Everyone—every individual, every generation, every group—
has, since the very earliest period of human history, been born
into a culture, a civilization, of some sort. It might be simple,
crude and meager, or it might be highly developed. But all cultures, whatever their respective degrees of development, have
technologies (tools, machines), social systems (customs, institutions), beliefs (lore, philosophy, science) and forms of art.
This means that when a baby is born into a cultural milieu, he
will be influenced by it. As a matter of fact, his culture will
determine how he will think, feel, and act. It will determine what
language he will speak, what clothes, if any, he will wear, what
gods he will believe in, how he will marry, select and prepare his
foods, treat the sick, and dispose of the dead. What else *could*
one do but react to the culture that surrounds him from birth to
death? No people makes its own culture; it inherits it ready-
made from its ancestors or borrows it from its neighbors.

It is easy enough for man to believe that he has made his
culture, each generation contributing its share, and that it is he
who controls and directs its course through the ages. Does he not
chip the arrowheads and stone-axes, build carts and dynamoes,
coin money and spend it, elect presidents and depose kings, compose symphonies and carve statues, worship gods and wage war?
But one cannot always rely upon the obvious. It was once obvious
that the earth remained stationary while the sun moved; anyone
could see that for himself. We are now approaching a point in
modern thought where we are beginning to suspect that it is not
man who controls culture but the other way around. The feat of
Copernicus in dispelling the geocentric illusion over four hundred
years ago is being duplicated in our own day by the culturologist

* Alvin Toffler, *Future Shock* (New York, 1970), pp. 356–358.

who is dissipating the anthropocentric illusion that man controls his culture.

There seems to be only one answer left and that is fairly plain—after one becomes used to it, at least. Cultures must be explained in terms of culture. As we have already noted, culture is a continuum. Each trait or organization of traits, each stage of development, grows out of an earlier cultural situation. The steam engine can be traced back to the origins of metallurgy and fire. International cartels have grown out of all the processes of exchange and distribution since the Old Stone Age and before. Our science, philosophy, religion, and art have developed out of earlier forms. Culture is a vast stream of tools, utensils, customs, beliefs that are constantly interacting with each other, creating new combinations and syntheses. New elements are added constantly to the stream; obsolete traits drop out. The culture of today is but the cross-section of this stream at the present moment, the resultant of the age-old process of interaction, selection, rejection, and accumulation that has preceded us. And the culture of tomorrow will be but the culture of today plus one more day's growth. The numerical coefficient of today's culture may be said to be 365,000,000 (i.e., a million years of days); that of tomorrow: 365,000,000 + 1. The culture of the present was determined by the past and the culture of the future will be but a continuation of the trend of the present. Thus, in a very real sense *culture makes itself.* At least, if one wishes to explain culture scientifically, he must proceed *as if* culture made itself, *as if* man had nothing to do with the determination of its course or content. Man must be there, of course, to make the existence of the culture process possible. But the nature and behavior of the process itself is self-determined. It rests upon its own principles; it is governed by its own laws.*

Using White's set of assumptions write a discussion of Toffler's selection. Would you yourself agree with the discussion you have just written? Where would you differ? Why?

5. Try combining White's and Toffler's assumptions. Does this combining suggest any possible new assumptions or implication?

6. Here is a selection by Rachel Carson. See if you can find her assumptions and criteria.

    . . . It took hundreds of millions of years to produce the life

* Leslie A. White, *The Science of Culture: A Study of Man and Civilization* (New York, 1969; first ed., 1949), pp. 336–341.

that now inhabits the earth—eons of time in which that developing and evolving and diversifying life reached a state of adjustment and balance with its surroundings. The environment,
rigorously shaping and directing the life it supported, contained
elements that were hostile as well as supporting. Certain rocks gave
out dangerous radiation; even within the light of the sun, from
which all life draws its energy, there were short-wave radiations
with power to injure. Given time—time not in years but in millennia—life adjusts, and a balance has been reached. For time
is the essential ingredient, but in the modern world there is no
time.

The rapidity of change and the speed with which new situations are created follow the impetuous and heedless pace of
man rather than the deliberate pace of nature. Radiation is no
longer merely the background radiation of rocks, the bombard-
ment of cosmic rays, the ultraviolet of the sun that have existed
before there was any life on earth; radiation is now the unnatural creation of man's tampering with the atom. The chemicals
to which life is asked to make its adjustment are no longer merely
the calcium and silica and copper and all the rest of the minerals
washed out of the rocks and carried in rivers to the sea; they are
the synthetic creations of man's inventive mind, brewed in his
laboratories, and having no counterpart in nature.

To adjust to these chemicals would require time on the
scale that is nature's; it would require not merely the years of a
man's life but the life of generations. And even this, were it by
some miracle possible, would be futile, for the new chemicals
come from our laboratories in an endless stream; almost five
hundred annually find their way into actual use in the United
States alone. The figure is staggering and its implications are not
easily grasped—500 new chemicals to which the bodies of men
and animals are required somehow to adapt each year, chemicals
totally outside the limits of biologic experience.*

What would you predict Toffler would say about Rachel Carson's essay? Explain.

7. In the passage by Edwin Boring that follows see if you can pick
out the assumptions and criteria:

   . . . Is man quite free to think as he will or are his beliefs
   but a reflection of the climate of fact and opinion that envelops
   him, and the circumstances that belong to the century, the
   country, and the family in which he lives?

* Rachel L. Carson, *The Silent Spring* (Boston, 1962), pp. 6–7.

This problem is not made easier when we realize that man's belief that he is free may itself be predetermined. The belief in freedom could be man's greatest delusion—nearly, if not quite, immutable. It is conceivable, you see, that there could be a society of talking robots, designed so that they continue to interact one with another in accordance with the principles on which they have been constructed, all of them chattering the while about their behavior in words that imply that each is free to choose whatever he does; that each, choosing freely, thus becomes responsible for his own conduct—a society of robots in which everyone asserts his own freedom for the excellent reason that he is *not* free to deny it. . . .

Sometimes the humanists raise the question, not whether behavior can be controlled but whether it should be. It is hard for me to take this question seriously. You need all the knowledge of control that you can have. Only then are you prepared to consider how it should be used.

Education and government are instituted for the purpose of human control. I prepare this paper in the hope that by it I may exercise some small degree of thought-control upon all who read it. Skinner claims to have better and surer methods for the design of behavior than have been available heretofore. You should see his pigeons, taught to earn their livings by the rewarding of their successes (not by punishment of their failures). So it is that he envisages a happy society, in which success and reward are the rule, and frustration has been reduced or eliminated by good social design. No one, of course, ever designs frustration into a machine so that it tries to make the same wheel go in opposite directions at the same moment.

One objection made to the behavioral scientists' development of human control is that their power might get into the hands of evil men. This objection seems to me to miss the point. Surely any elite that undertook to use behavioral science to enslave the world would find beneficence more efficient than maleficence. Slavery would be designed as a happy and desirable state, and, if these successful slaves still felt that they needed variety in their companionship, variety can be designed too. All you need is the specifications for *n* personalities and the desirable frequency for each of them, to get mass production going. . . .

As man alters the world in which he lives, he has to trust that he will be able to adjust it to himself or else adjust himself to it. So far the advance of civilization has consisted of these changes and adjustments, and I see no reason to fear that the behavioral determinists are starting something that will get out of hand. The attempt to control men's actions and thoughts is as old as history. You cannot have social engineering that does not conscript the individual.*

Do White and Boring share any common assumptive ground? How would they be likely to praise, criticize, or extend Toffler's ideas? Do you agree with the assumptions of White and Boring? If not, how do your assumptions differ from theirs?

8. What assumptions and criteria govern Sigmund Freud's opinions in the following passage?

> For a wide variety of reasons, it is very far from my intention to express an opinion upon the value of human civilization. I have endeavoured to guard myself against the enthusiastic prejudice which holds that our civilization is the most precious thing that we possess or could acquire and that its path will necessarily lead to heights of unimagined perfection. I can at least listen without indignation to the critic who is of the opinion that when one surveys the aims of cultural endeavour and the means it employs, one is bound to come to the conclusion that the whole effort is not worth the trouble, and that the outcome of it can only be a state of affairs which the individual will be unable to tolerate. My impartiality is made all the easier to me by my knowing very little about all these things. One thing only do I know for certain and that is that man's judgements of value follow directly his wishes for happiness—that, accordingly, they are an attempt to support his illusions with arguments. I should find it very understandable if someone were to point out the obligatory nature of the course of human civilization and were to say, for instance, that the tendencies to a restriction of sexual life or to the institution of a humanitarian ideal at the expense of natural selection were developmental trends which cannot be averted or turned aside and to which it is best for us to yield as though they were necessities of nature. I know, too, the objection that can be made against this, to the effect that in the history of mankind, trends such as these, which were considered unsurmountable, have often been thrown aside and replaced by other trends. Thus I have not the courage to rise up before my fellowmen as a prophet, and I bow to their reproach that I can offer them no consolation: for at bottom that is what they are all demanding—the wildest revolutionaries no less passionately than the most virtuous believers.

* Edward G. Boring, "When Is Human Behavior Predetermined?" *Scientific Monthly*, 84 (1957), 189–194.

The fateful question for the human species seems to me to be whether and to what extent their cultural development will succeed in mastering the disturbance of their communal life by the human instinct of aggression and self-destruction. It may be that in this respect precisely the present time deserves a special interest. Men have gained control over the forces of nature to such an extent that with their help they would have no difficulty in exterminating one another to the last man. They know this, and hence comes a large part of their current unrest, their unhappiness and their mood of anxiety.*

If Freud had just read the selections by Toffler, White, Carson, and Boring, how would he have been likely to react to them? Why would he perceive relations among them that perhaps you did not perceive before this? How do your assumptions about human freedom and determinism differ from those you have been considering in these selections.

9. Have the relations and contradictions you have so far recognized among these selections given you any new ideas or modified any of your old assumptions? Explain. Do you think we and our institutions are going to change in any way in the near future?

10. Pick one or two of the selections above and write an argument against them, using a thesis/antithesis organization somewhat like E. H. Carr's, by questioning and offering alternatives to these assumptions or showing where their implications would lead and explaining why some alternative assumptions would have implications that are better or more likely. Can you finally arrive at a synthesis of your thesis and antithesis?

* Sigmund Freud, *Civilization and Its Discontents,* Standard ed., trans. and ed. James Strachey (New York, 1962), pp. 91–92.

Part IV

A RHETORIC
OF REPERCEPTION

IN the following essay Paul Shepard states that "We are hidden from ourselves by habits of perception." What does he mean? Dorothy Lee showed how difficult it is for a person who perceives reality in a certain way, largely determined by linguistic habits and basic assumptions, to suddenly begin to reperceive reality. Shepard, as we shall see, makes clear that even within the same culture there are competing ways of perceiving reality, and that some ways of perceiving ourselves in relation to the rest of nature may lead to our extinction as a species.

But reperceptions do not occur often—perhaps not often enough for us to become aware of new problems or to take advantage of new possibilities. Science and technology are changing both the intellectual and physical environment so fast that only people who become adept at reperception can expect to make satisfactory adjustments to the many changes that are going to take place in a lifetime. Basic change in conventional assumptions and criteria and a resultant change in the perception of reality that these tend to determine are very difficult for us to make. Our educations all too frequently leave us unaware of our assumptions and criteria, which tend to become absolute values—unconscious, untested, and unquestioned.

Getting locked into a set of absolute, unquestionable assumptions and criteria, and thus into a rigid perception or point of view, may have been defensible in the past, when it was likely that any set of assumptions acceptable to one generation would be equally acceptable to several succeeding generations. For, in the past, new problems and outlooks were not being brought about by the kinds of scientific and technological accelerations that are characteristic of our age and most probably of future ages.

It has been said that the difference between our world and the world of our grandparents' childhood is greater than the difference between the latter and the world of Julius Caesar. Consider that our physical and cultural environment has been profoundly shaped by several innovations that are not much more than fifty years (or two generations) old, if that: radio, television, electric light, automobiles, airplanes, central heating and air conditioning, atomic energy, birth-control pills, films, sound recording, refrigeration, antibiotics, computers. More scientists are alive and working now than have ever lived before, assuring an even greater rate of innovation in the next generation.

Some people today may feel nostalgic about the "good old days" when the assumptions and criteria inculcated in the first two decades of life provided a platform of unquestionable "truth" that would serve them for a lifetime. But there is really no reason why humans over thirty, or of any age, must become intellectual anachronisms. Redefining our idea of maturity from absolute rigidity to a process of continuing growth in relation to changes in our culture and environment might enlarge our characters and extend our human worth and enjoyment.

But how will this be possible? What could help us is a rhetoric of reperception *with which to see reality in a fresh light and which we can use in writing and speaking to bring about reperception in others. Considering what we have already learned about assumptions and criteria of relevance in the preceding chapters (14–16), an effective rhetoric of reperception could be mastered by learning three more processes: testing and questioning of conventional ideas and assumptions* (Chapter 19); *generating new alternative ideas and assumptions by combining two or more conventional ones* (Chapter 20); *evaluating or verifying new alternatives according to some specific criterion or set of criteria* (Chapter 21).

The act of reperception, which will be discussed in Chapter 18, does not consist of a sudden brilliant insight by a person of genius. The romantic view of creativity as something mysterious and magical with which only an elite few are endowed has led most of us to accept uncreative roles in school and in life. These next five chapters assume that creativity is an intellectual process that can be encouraged and developed in each of us.

We should make it clear that we are not advocating a continuous switching of perceptions, like trying on telescopic, microscopic, or kaleidoscopic glasses for the sake of novelty. A major change in our perception of reality every few weeks or months would obviously not give us time enough to arrange our knowledge and articulate it according to the new assumptions and criteria before we had to change again. Probably a minimum of several years of operating in the same set of assumptions and criteria that determine a certain perception of reality, all of which we can call simply a cultural paradigm, *would be necessary for the individual to explore fully its possible riches and write easily and effectively within the paradigm. It is not at all impossible that we will be called on in the future to change cultural paradigms almost every decade. Obviously changes in an assumption here or a criterion there, and a corresponding minor shift of perception, will happen often; but a rate of major reperception—i.e., an interdependent set of basic assumptions, or cultural paradigm, change—of from ten to fifteen years would give us a series of relatively permanent intellectual bases from which to write and think clearly. A set of assumptions is worth retaining, however, only for as long as we can remain effective and productive in it without going stale or becoming anachronistic. A cultural paradigm is not necessarily true or absolute; it is rather a convenience to which we may knowingly commit ourselves for some years, realizing that the basic assumptions, criteria, and the particular point of view they engender all run the risk of sooner or later needing fundamental reconsideration, replacement, and reperception. Indeed, our present perceptions, which even now may seem not to fit so well the world around us, will almost surely need periodic refocusing in order for us to retain clear vision as our world accelerates from here into the future.*

"Ecology and Man—a Viewpoint"

Paul Shepard

ECOLOGY is sometimes characterized as the study of a natural "web of life." It would follow that man is somewhere in the web or that he in fact manipulates its strands, exemplifying what Thomas Huxley called "man's place in nature." But the image of a web is too meager and simple for the reality. A web is flat and finished and has the mortal frailty of the individual spider. Although elastic, it has insufficient depth. However solid to the touch of the spider, for us it fails to denote the *eikos*—the habitation—and to suggest the enduring integration of the primitive Greek domicile with its sacred hearth, bonding the earth to all aspects of society.

Ecology deals with organisms in an environment and with the processes that link organism and place. But ecology as such cannot be studied, only organisms, earth, air, and sea can be studied. It is not a discipline: there is no body of thought and technique which frames an ecology of man.[1] It must be therefore a scope or a way of seeing. Such a *perspective* on the human situation is very old and has been part of philosophy and art for thousands of years. It badly needs attention and revival.

---

[1] There is a branch of sociology called Human Ecology, but it is mostly about urban geography.

Man is in the world and his ecology is the nature of that *inness*. He is in the world as in a room, and in transience, as in the belly of a tiger or in love. What does he do there in nature? What does nature do there *in him?* What is the nature of the transaction? Biology tells us that the transaction is always circular, always a mutual feedback. Human ecology cannot be limited strictly to biological concepts, but it cannot ignore them. It cannot even transcend them. It emerges from biological reality and grows from the fact of interconnection as a general principle of life. It must take a long view of human life and nature as they form a mesh or pattern going beyond historical time and beyond the conceptual bounds of other humane studies. As a natural history of what it means to be human, ecology might proceed the same way one would define a stomach, for example, by attention to its nervous and circulatory connections as well as its entrance, exit, and muscular walls. . . .

Individual man *has* his particular integrity, to be sure. Oak trees, even mountains, have selves or integrities too (a poor word for my meaning, but it will have to do). To our knowledge, those other forms are not troubled by seeing themselves in more than one way, as man is. In one aspect the self is an arrangement of organs, feelings, and thoughts—a "me"—surrounded by a hard body boundary: skin, clothes, and insular habits. This idea needs no defense. It is conferred on us by the whole history of our civilization. Its virtue is verified by our affluence. The alternative is a self as a center of organization, constantly drawing on and influencing the surroundings, whose skin and behavior are soft zones contacting the world instead of excluding it. Both views are real and their reciprocity significant. We need them both to have a healthy social and human maturity.

The second view—that of relatedness of the self—has been given short shrift. Attitudes toward ourselves do not change easily. The conventional image of a man, like that of the heraldic lion, is iconographic; its outlines are stylized to fit the fixed curves of our vision. We are hidden from ourselves by habits of perception. Because we learn to talk at the same time we learn to think, our language, for example, encourages us to see ourselves—or a plant or animal—as an isolated sack, a thing, a contained self. Ecological thinking, on the other hand, requires a kind of vision across boundaries. The epidermis of the skin is ecologically like a pond surface or a forest soil, not a shell so much as a delicate interpenetration. It reveals the self enobled and extended rather than threatened as part of the landscape and the ecosystem, because the beauty and complexity of nature are continuous with ourselves.

And so ecology as applied to man faces the task of renewing a balanced view where now there is man-centeredness, even pathology of isolation and fear. It implies that we must find room in "our" world for all plants and animals, even for their otherness and their opposition. It further implies exploration and openness across an inner boundary—an ego boundary—and appreciative understanding of the animal in ourselves which our heritage of Platonism, Christian morbidity, duality, and mechanism have long held repellant and degrading. The older countercurrents—relics of pagan myth, the universal application of Christian compassion, philosophical naturalism, nature romanticism and pantheism—have been swept away, leaving only odd bits of wreckage. Now we find ourselves in a deteriorating environment which breeds aggressiveness and hostility toward ourselves and our world.

. . . Our historical disappointment in the nature of nature has created a cold climate for ecologists who assert once again that we are limited and obligated. Somehow they must manage in spite of the chill to reach the centers of humanism and technology, to convey there a sense of our place in a universal vascular system without depriving us of our self-esteem and confidence.

. . . If nature is not a prison and earth a shoddy way-station, we must find the faith and force to affirm its metabolism as our own—or rather, our own as part of it. To do so means nothing less than a shift in our whole frame of reference and our attitude towards life itself, a wider perception of the landscape as a creative, harmonious being where relationships of things are as real as the things. Without losing our sense of a great human destiny and without intellectual surrender, we must affirm that the world is a being, a part of our own body.[2]

Such a being may be called an ecosystem or simply a forest or landscape. Its members are engaged in a kind of choreography of materials and energy and information, the creation of order and organization. (Analogy to corporate organization here is misleading, for the distinction between social (one species) and ecological (many species) is fundamental.) The pond is an example. Its ecology includes all events: the conversion of sunlight to food and the food-chains within and around it, man drinking, bathing, fishing, plowing the slopes of the watershed, drawing a picture of it, and formulating theories about the world based on what he sees in the pond. He and all the other organisms at and in the pond act upon one another, engage the earth and atmosphere, and are linked to other ponds by a network of connections like the threads of protoplasm connecting cells in living tissues.

The elegance of such systems and delicacy of equilibrium are the outcome of a long evolution of interdependence. Even society, mind and culture are parts of that evolution. There is an essential relationship between them and the natural habitat: that is, between the emergence of higher primates and flowering plants, pollinating insects, seeds, humus, and aboreal life. It is unlikely that a manlike creature could arise by any other means than a long arboreal sojourn following and followed by a time of terrestriality. The fruit's complex construction and the mammalian brain are twin offspring of the maturing earth, impossible, even meaningless, without the deepening soil and the mutual development of savannas and their faunas in the last geological epoch. Internal complexity, as the mind of a primate, is an extension of natural complexity, measured by the variety of plants and animals and the variety of nerve cells —organic extensions of each other.

The exuberance of kinds as the setting in which a good mind could evolve (to deal with a complex world) was not only a past condition. Man did not arrive in the world as

[2] See Alan Watts, "The World is Your Body," in *The Book on the Taboo Against Knowing Who You Are*. New York: Pantheon Books, 1966.

though disembarking from a train in the city. He continues to arrive, somewhat like the birth of art, a train in Roger Fry's definition, passing through many stations, none of which is wholly left behind. This idea of natural complexity as a counterpart to human intricacy is central to an ecology of man. The creation of order, of which man is an example, is realized also in the number of species and habitats, an abundance of landscapes lush and poor. Even deserts and tundras increase the planetary opulence. Curiously, only man and possibly a few birds can appreciate this opulence, being the world's travelers. Reduction of this variegation would, by extension then, be an amputation of man. To convert all "wastes"—all deserts, estuaries, tundras, ice-fields, marshes, steppes and moors—into cultivated fields and cities would impoverish rather than enrich life esthetically as well as ecologically. By esthetically, I do not mean that weasel term connoting the pleasure of baubles. We have diverted ourselves with litterbug campaigns and greenbelts in the name of esthetics while the fabric of our very environment is unravelling. In the name of conservation, too, such things are done, so that conservation becomes ambiguous. Nature is a fundamental "resource" to be sustained for our own well-being. But it loses in the translation into usable energy and commodities. Ecology may testify as often against our uses of the world, even against conservation techniques of control and management for sustained yield, as it does for them. Although ecology may be treated as a science, its greater and overriding wisdom is universal.

That wisdom can be approached mathematically, chemically, or it can be danced or told as a myth. It has been embodied in widely scattered economically different cultures. It is manifest, for example, among pre-Classical Greeks, in Navajo religion and social orientation, in Romantic poetry of the 18th and 19th centuries, in Chinese landscape painting of the 11th century, in current Whiteheadian philosophy, in Zen Buddhism, in the world view of the cult of the Cretan Great Mother, in the ceremonials of Bushman hunters, and in the medieval Christian metaphysics of light. What is common among all of them is a deep sense of engagement with the landscape, with profound connections to surroundings and to natural processes central to all life.

It is difficult in our language even to describe that sense. English becomes imprecise or mystical—and therefore suspicious—as it struggles with "process" thought. Its noun and verb organization shapes a divided world of static doers separate from the doing. It belongs to an idiom of social hierarchy in which all nature is made to mimic man. The living world is perceived in that idiom as an upright ladder, a "great chain of being," an image which seems at first ecological but is basically rigid, linear, condescending, lacking humility and love of otherness.

We are all familiar from childhood with its classifications of everything on a scale from the lowest to the highest: inanimate matter/vegetative life/lower animals/higher animals/men/angels/gods. It ranks animals themselves in categories of increasing good: the vicious and lowly parasites, pathogens and predators/the filthy decay and scavenging organisms/indifferent wild or merely useless forms/good tame creatures/and virtuous beasts domesticated for human service. . . .

The rejection of animality is a rejection of nature as a whole. As a teacher, I see students develop in their humanities studies a proper distrust of science and technology. What concerns me is that the stigma spreads to the natural world itself. C. P. Snow's "Two Cultures," setting the sciences against the humanities, can be misunderstood as placing nature against art. The idea that the current destruction of people and environment is scientific and would be corrected by more communication with the arts neglects the hatred for this world carried by our whole culture. Yet science as it is now taught does not promote a respect for nature. Western civilization breeds no more ecology in Western science than in Western philosophy. Snow's two cultures cannot explain the antithesis that splits the world, nor is the division ideological, economic or political in the strict sense. The antidote he proposes is roughly equivalent to a liberal education, the traditional prescription for making broad and well-rounded men. Unfortunately, there is little even in the liberal education of ecology-

and-man. Nature is usually synonymous with either natural resources or scenery, the great stereotypes in the minds of middle-class, college-educated Americans.

One might suppose that the study of biology would mitigate the humanistic—largely literary—confusion between materialism and a concern for nature. But biology made the mistake at the end of the 17th century of adopting a *modus operandi* or life style from physics, in which the question why was not to be asked, only the question how. Biology succumbed to its own image as an esoteric prologue to technics and encouraged the whole society to mistrust naturalists. When scholars realized what the sciences were about it is not surprising that they threw out the babies with the bathwater: the information content and naturalistic lore with the rest of it. This is the setting in which academia and intellectual America undertook the single-minded pursuit of human uniqueness, and uncovered a great mass of pseudo distinctions such as language, tradition, culture, love, consciousness, history and awe of the supernatural. Only men were found to be capable of escape from predictability, determinism, environmental control, instincts and other mechanisms which "imprison" other life. Even biologists, such as Julian Huxley, announced that the purpose of the world was to produce man, whose social evolution excused him forever from biological evolution. Such a view incorporated three important presumptions: that nature is a power structure shaped after human political hierarchies; that man has a monopoly of immortal souls; and omnipotence will come through technology. It seems to me that all of these foster a failure of responsible behavior in what Paul Sears calls "the living landscape" except within the limits of immediate self-interest.

What ecology must communicate to the humanities—indeed, as a humanity—is that such an image of the world and the society so conceived are incomplete. There is overwhelming evidence of likeness, from molecular to mental, between men and animals. But the dispersal of this information is not necessarily a solution. The Two Culture idea that the problem is an information bottleneck is only partly true; advances in biochemistry, genetics, ethology, paleoanthropology, comparative physiology and psychobiology are not self-evidently unifying. They need a unifying principle not found in any of them, a wisdom in the sense that Walter B. Cannon used the word in his book *Wisdom of the Body*,[3] about the community of self-regulating systems within the organism. If the ecological extension of that perspective is correct, societies and ecosystems as well as cells have a physiology, and insight into it is built into organisms, including man. What was intuitively apparent last year—whether aesthetically or romantically—is a find of this year's inductive analysis. It seems apparent to me that there is an ecological instinct which probes deeper and more comprehensively than science, and which anticipates every scientific confirmation of the natural history of man.

It is not surprising, therefore, to find substantial ecological insight in art. Of course there is nothing wrong with a poem or dance which is ecologically neutral; its merit may have nothing to do with the transaction of man and nature. It is my impression, however, that students of the arts no longer feel that the subject of a work of art—what it "represents"—is without importance, as was said about 40 years ago. But there are poems and dances as there are prayers and laws attending to ecology. Some are more than mere comments on it. Such creations become part of all life. Essays on nature are an element of a functional or feedback system influencing men's reactions to their environment, messages projected by men to themselves through some act of design, the manipulation of paints or written words. They are natural objects, like bird nests. The essay is as real a part of the community—in both the one-species sociological and many-species ecological senses —as are the songs of choirs or crickets. An essay is an Orphic sound, words that make knowing possible, for it was Orpheus as Adam who named and thus made intelligible all creatures.

What is the conflict of Two Cultures if it is not between science and art or between national ideologies? The distinction rather divides science and art within themselves. An example

---

[3] New York: W. W. Norton, 1932.

within science was the controversy over the atmospheric testing of nuclear bombs and the effect of radioactive fallout
from the explosions. Opposing views were widely published and
personified when Linus Pauling, a biochemist, and Edward
Teller, a physicist, disagreed. Teller, one of the "fathers" of the
bomb, pictured the fallout as a small factor in a world-wide
struggle, the possible damage to life in tiny fractions of a per-
cent, and even noted that evolutionary progress comes from
mutations. Pauling, an expert on the hereditary material, knowing that most mutations are detrimental, argued that a large
absolute number of people might be injured, as well as other
life in the world's biosphere.

The humanness of ecology is that the dilemma of our
emerging world ecological crises (over-population, environmental pollution, etc.) is at least in part a matter of values
and ideas. It does not divide men as much by their trades as
by the complex of personality and experience shaping their
feelings towards other people and the world at large. . . . The
dangerous eruption of humanity in a deteriorating environment
does not show itself as such in the daily experience of most
people, but is felt as general tension and anxiety. We feel
the pressure of events not as direct causes but more like omens.
A kind of madness arises from the prevailing nature-con-
quering, nature-hating and self- and world-denial. Although in
many ways most Americans live comfortable, satiated lives,
there is a nameless frustration born of an increasing nullity.
The aseptic home and society are progressively cut off from
direct organic sources of health and increasingly isolated from
the means of altering the course of events. Success, where its
price is the misuse of landscapes, the deterioration of air and
water and the loss of wild things, becomes a pointless glut,
experience one-sided, time on our hands an unlocalized ache.

The unrest can be exploited to perpetuate itself. One familiar prescription for our sick society and its loss of environmental equilibrium is an increase in the intangible Good
Things: more Culture, more Security and more Escape from
pressures and tempo. The "search for identity" is not only a
social but an ecological problem having to do with a sense

of place and time in the context of all life. The pain of that search can be cleverly manipulated to keep the *status quo* by urging that what we need is only improved forms and more energetic expressions of what now occupy us: engrossment with ideological struggle and military power, with productivity and consumption as public and private goals, with commerce and urban growth, with amusements, with fixation on one's navel, with those tokens of escape or success already belabored by so many idealists and social critics so ineffectually.

To come back to those Good Things: the need for culture, security and escape are just near enough to the truth to take us in. But the real cultural deficiency is the absence of a true *cultus* with its significant ceremony, relevant mythical cosmos, and artifacts. The real failure in security is the disappearance from our personal lives of the small human group as the functional unit of society and the web of other creatures, domestic and wild, which are part of our humanity. As for escape, the idea of simple remission and avoidance fails to provide for the value of solitude, to integrate leisure and natural encounter. Instead of these, what are foisted on the puzzled and troubled soul as Culture, Security and Escape are more art museums, more psychiatry, and more automobiles.

If naturalists seem always to be *against* something it is because they feel a responsibility to share their understanding, and their opposition constitutes a defense of the natural systems to which man is committed as an organic being. Sometimes naturalists propose projects too, but the project approach is itself partly the fault, the need for projects a consequence of linear, compartmental thinking, of machine-like units to be controlled and manipulated. If the ecological crisis were merely a matter of alternative techniques, the issue would belong among the technicians and developers (where most schools and departments of conservation have put it).

Truly ecological thinking need not be incompatible with our place and time. It does have an element of humility which is foreign to our thought, which moves us to silent wonder and glad affirmation. But it offers an essential factor, like a necessary vitamin, to all our engineering and social planning, to our poetry and our understanding. There is only one ecology, not a human ecology on one hand and another for the sub-human. No one school or theory or project or agency controls it. For us it means seeing the world mosaic from the human vantage without being man-fanatic. We must use it to confront the great philosophical problems of man—transience, meaning, and limitation—without fear. Affirmation of its own organic essence will be the ultimate test of the human mind.

17

How Form and Content
Work Together
in a Reperceptive Style

OUR analysis of Shepard's essay begins by examining carefully this three-sentence microcosm of the whole essay:

> If nature is not a prison and earth a shoddy way-station, we must find the faith and force to affirm its metabolism as our own—or rather, our own as part of it. To do so means nothing less than a shift in our whole frame of reference and our attitude towards life itself, a wider perception of the landscape as a creative, harmonious being where relationships of things are as real as the things. Without losing our sense of a great human destiny and without intellectual surrender, we must affirm that the world is a being, a part of our own body.

Shepard's subject here is the relation of the individual to the world. In the conditional first clause of the first sentence he uses "prison" and "shoddy way-station" as metaphors to suggest how traditional assumptions alienate a person from his world. In these metaphors the individual is assumed to be a suffering soul, forced to inhabit a hostile or inferior region that he or she cannot really relate to. As we shall soon see in other instances besides this, it is characteristic of Shepard's writing that he uses metaphors carefully in order to question lack of relation or hostile relation as well as imply new, more satisfying alternative relations between human beings and the environment.

343

In the consequent clause of the first sentence, emphasized with alliterations, "we must *f*ind the *f*aith and *f*orce to *aff*irm its metabolism as our own—or rather, our own as part of it," a rather unconventional metaphor for the world, "its metabolism," is used to establish a very different kind of relation between the individual and the environment. This time an anatomical reference of the metaphor implies that nature is a macroorganism that is formed partly of, and within which functions, each individual as a microorganism. Notice the syntactical parallelism in this clause that serves to turn into a reversible process a static subject-object relation—"to affirm its metabolism as our own—or rather, our own as part of it." This is an unusual construction in English because we usually do not perceive the world in such a way that subjects and objects are in the *process* of acting on one another. Such a construction implies that individual *things,* like subjects and objects, may not be as important as the *processes of interrelation* between them. We express in conventional English grammar simple, one-way relations between things: subjects act on objects in one direction. But Shepard is encouraging his reader to perceive a much more complex type of reversible-reaction relation between subject and object in an interdependent environment that functions like one huge organism.

That this fundamental reperception of the world and our relation to it will be difficult to accomplish is made explicit in the second sentence: "To do so means nothing less than a shift in our whole frame of reference." Apparently, upsetting a reader's conventional linguistic expectations with extraordinary metaphors and unconventional syntax in the first sentence at the same time as he questions conventional assumptions that provide a rigid and antiecological "frame of reference" and "attitude" is a necessary prelude to the generation of a new ecological perception.

In the last of our three-sentence microcosm of Shepard's essay, let us consider how he expresses the new perception he is offering: "Without losing our sense of a great human destiny and without intellectual surrender, we must affirm that the world is a being, a part of our own body." In the independent clause we find Shepard using the same kind of macroorganic metaphor as he used in the second sentence, "a being" to describe the world. He uses an appositive—"the world is a being, a part of our own body"—to express the same kind of reversible relation between the world and the individual that we found him manipulating syntax to express in the first sentence. The dependent clause of the last sentence implies a relation between humanism and science as parallel qualifications:

Without losing our sense of a great human destiny	i.e., without disregarding humanism
and without intellectual surrender	i.e., without disregarding science

As Shepard later explains in considerable detail, C. P. Snow and others have argued that there is a dangerous dichotomy between science and humanism that has polarized into two conflicting cultures. What Shepard is suggesting in this sentence (and says overtly in other places) is that by adopting the ecological set of assumptions, which are both scientific and humane, a kind of third culture could come into existence in which the formerly polarized cultures can become fused.

The pattern of rhetoric in these three sentences is essentially the same as the rhetoric Shepard uses in the essay as a whole. This basic rhetoric of reperception seems to consist of three processes as follows:

1. testing or questioning conventional assumptions and ideas;
2. introducing a new, alternative set of assumptions;
3. evaluating and recommending the adoption of new alternatives that will facilitate a reperception of an idea or object on the part of the reader.

Of course, these three processes do not always happen in order, one after the other, but often are developed concurrently. We saw in the first sentence, for example, that Shepard employs all three processes of this basic rhetoric; that in the second sentence the necessity and difficulty of the third process is made explicit; and that finally, in the last sentence, Shepard uses both the second and third processes.

Questioning Conventions

Let us now turn from our study of these three sentences to consider the rhetoric of the essay as a whole. Throughout the essay the testing and questioning of conventional assumptions and ideas takes place. One of his principle means of testing and bringing into question what he considers dangerously simple-minded, conventional assumptions is his careful examination and exposure of misleading words and figurative language. For instance, at one point Shepard exposes to criticism the use of the familiar possessive in such habitual phrases as "our world," "our planet," "our environment: "we must find room in 'our' world for all plants and animals, even for their otherness and their opposition." Also, he often calls several assumptions into question at the same time. In his attack on the philosophy that the "purpose of the world was to produce man, whose social evolution excused him forever from biological evolution," he first lists several related assumptions upon which it depends:

> Such a view incorporated three important presumptions: that nature is a power structure shaped after human political hierarchies; that man has a monopoly of immortal souls; and omnipotence will come through technology. It seems to me that all of these foster a failure of responsible behavior in what Paul Sears calls "the living landscape" except within the limits of immediate self-interest.

He has already tested and will continue to call these three conventional assumptions into question throughout his essay.

Shepard, as we saw in our initial analysis, uses unconventional grammatical structures both to question convention and express new alternative assumptions. His syntax shifts our attention from the conventional subject-acting-on-object relationship habitual in English usage. Consider these three parallel questions: "What does he [man] do there in nature? What does nature do there *in him?* What is the nature of the transaction?" Our conventional syntax does not tend to call on its users to perceive this kind of complex reversible relation between subject and object that ecologists are now asking us to perceive.

Employing a complex series of similes and parallels expressing unusual relations, Shepard writes, "[Man] is in the world as in a room, and in transcience, as in the belly of a tiger or in love." The complexity of the interrelationships that we are forced to consider here is more than just linguistically surprising. Man's experience of love and terror in the universe is expressed both in the imagery and in the syntax.

Shepard utilizes an unusual vocabulary of relation words, including some nouns made up of a function or relational word and a *-ness* suffix, for much the same purpose as his changes in syntax. How can we discuss a world of profound interrelations when we have so few words in our language that can express them? "Man is in the world and his ecology is the nature of that *inness*," says Shepard, inventing the odd word "inness" to suggest a complexity of relations that no familiar word could convey. There are many words and phrases that Shepard employs to emphasize the importance of relationships: "relatedness," "likeness," "interconnection," "interpenetration," "interdependent," "mutual feedback," "community of self-regulating systems," "ecosystem." Shepard uses throughout the essay the linguistic device of parallelism, emphasizing relationships within the ecosystem. For example, "Biology tells us that the transaction is always circular, always a mutual feedback." His syntactical parallels link us with nature and tie together a world we too often perceive as isolated and alien from us.

Generating New Alternatives

The second process in a rhetoric of reperception is generating alternative assumptions to replace those being questioned. By cross-structuring older premises with one another, Shepard produces a new alternative to a set of conventional assumptions introduced more than a decade ago by C. P.

Snow, in a work entitled *The Two Cultures and the Scientific Revolution* (New York, 1959). Snow's assumptions are that there exists at present a world cultural crisis; that the crisis is the result of a rift between the sciences and the humanities; that a dichotomy in basic attitudes produces not one cohesive culture, but a split culture; and that these two cultures are often at odds due to ignorance of one another. First, Shepard questions Snow's dichotomy between a scientific culture and a humanistic culture and affirms their common stake in a changed ecological attitude:

> What is the conflict of Two Cultures if it is not between science and art or between national ideologies? The distinction rather divides science and art within themselves.

In order to generate a new alternative to Snow's set of assumptions, Shepard crosses two of Snow's assumptions—

1. that a dichotomy in basic attitudes produces not one cohesive culture, but a split culture;
2. that there is at present a world culture crisis

—with several common ecological and historical assumptions—

1. that we, and our society and culture, are not separate from nature, but an intricate part of the larger ecology (ecosystem);
2. that modern people-centered culture results in polluted cities and careless technology and has cut us off from our roots in the natural environment until we have become such dangerous abusers of our natural heritage that we have precipitated a world ecological crisis;
3. that our cultural attitude toward our natural dependency has not always been one of abuse or alienation, but that in earlier cultures, Western as well as Eastern, humans seem to have felt and acted as though they were related to the ecosystem and that thus an alternative cultural attitude hallowed by ancient tradition is available to us.

When Shepard cross-structures these assumptions, he produces a new set of assumptions that is different from either Snow's ideas or earlier ecological ideas:

1. that the rift that causes the present world cultural and ecological crisis is not science versus humanities, but a mistaken attitude toward the relation between the individual and the environment that not only separates us from our physical environment but alienates us from our earlier cultural tradition as well;

2. that if we could return to the traditional attitude toward a profound relation between the individual and the environment, we could begin to heal both the present world ecological and the cultural crises, which stem from our mistaken conventional assumptions and criteria.

Shepard puts the lesson of his cross-structure in these terms: "Affirmation of its own organic essence will be the ultimate test of the human mind." Shepard's cross-structures have related ecology to social, psychological, and cultural issues as well as environmental issues, which we will consider in somewhat more detail later.

While Shepard rejects the ancient concept of the "great chain of being," he finds another ancient concept—the relation between a microcosm (the individual) and a macrocosm (nature) more acceptable. He cross-structures this microcosm/macrocosm concept with modern ecological assumptions to produce the concept of microorganismic man as part of macroorganismic environment. Shepard presents them both as functioning organic systems, the complexity and interrelatedness of one mirroring the complexity and interrelatedness of the other. As a result, not only is the environment constantly referred to as a "being," but Shepard uses many human physiological metaphors to describe the natural world. He writes of the world as a "huge vascular system" and of its "metabolism" and its "network of connections like the threads of protoplasm connecting cells in living tissues." Some are so bold as to surprise us and shock us into reperceiving an organic relation between ourselves and the entire natural world that we may have known, but of which we never before realized the full implications. Consider this bold anatomical metaphor for the world: "As a natural history of what it means to be human, ecology might proceed the same way one would define a stomach."

Shepard extends the implications of the analogy between microorganism and macroorganism into a somewhat mysterious relationship. In writing of each individual's intuition of his own body he continues,

> If the ecological extension of that perspective is correct, societies and ecosystems as well as cells have a physiology, and insight into it is built into organisms, including man. What was intuitively apparent last year—whether aesthetically or romantically—is a find of this year's inductive analysis.

According to Shepard, then, ecological "truth" can be attained as well by primitive intuition as by sophisticated scientific method. In fact, he suggests that primitive insight may be a surer route to ecological knowledge than scientific method:

> It seems apparent to me that there is an ecological instinct which probes deeper and more comprehensively than science, and which anticipates every scientific confirmation of the natural history of man.
>
> It is not surprising, therefore, to find substantial ecological insight in art.

This rather surprising statement from a scientist seems to proceed from a point of view more metaphysical than ecological. It is based on an assumption of science as a pursuit of the "absolute truth" about nature which the body might intuit before the mind understood. If your assumption, like my own, is that neither science nor human intuition ever tells us the "truth" about nature but only suggests more or less likely models of nature that at best allow only a certain degree of prediction, then you may not think Shepard gains anything by shifting from scientific to metaphysical speculation at this point in his discussion. But as we will soon see, this shift into metaphysics fits a number of Shepard's writing goals throughout the essay. First, it allows him to put science and the humanities on an equal footing as far as what he calls the "ecological point of view" is concerned. Second, it allows him to find a long and impressive tradition for ecological intuition in the art and philosophy and religion of the past. Third, it will allow him to establish a relation between individual feelings of dissatisfaction and alienation among people and the modern world ecological crisis, and offer a cultural alternative that might remedy both individual malaise and ecological pollution. And finally, the shift into metaphysics is not an isolated instance, but contributes to Shepard's recommendation of the new ecological alternative as an all-encompassing *"cultus"* or culture/religion. Do you think ecology needs to be recommended in religious terms? How else might Shepard have recommended it?

Shepard does not think that a scientific criterion of prediction and verification could by itself effect reperception toward his new view of ecology. In fact, Shepard pleads against seeing ecology as a discipline or scientific field of research:

> But ecology as such cannot be studied, only organisms, earth, air, and sea can be studied. It is not a discipline: there is no body of thought and technique which frames an ecology of man. It must be therefore a scope or a way of seeing.

In defining *ecology* Shepard takes it to be "a new way of seeing" rather than a disciplined program of study, and his metaphors for ecological thinking are primarily visual: "a kind of vision," "a way of seeing," "a view," "a point of view," "a perspective." He must, consequently, find some ways other than merely imparting learned ecological information to effect this fundamental change in perception. Once he has *tested and questioned conventional antiecological assumptions,* until he has brought them into crisis and then *generated alternative assumptions*, one more step may be necessary to facilitate reperception—*the evaluation or recommendation of the new alternative assumption* as more significant than the conventional assumption. This last step may be crucial, for, as he says:

Attitudes toward ourselves do not change easily. The conventional image of a man, like that of the heraldic lion, is iconographic; its outlines are stylized to fit the fixed curves of our vision.

Evaluating and Recommending a New Alternative

Shepard recommends his new ecological point of view by employing several criteria, but the most pervasive criterion seems to be metaphysical. He often uses metaphysical, even theological, terms. For instance, he calls for a kind of higher "wisdom" to unify separate sciences into ecological thinking:

> "advances in biochemistry, genetics, ethology, paleoanthropology, comparative physiology and psychobiology are not self-evidently unifying. They need a unifying principle not found in any of them, a wisdom. . . .

Shepard writes of an ecological reperception of the world as though it were almost a religious conversion: "Truly ecological thinking . . . does have an element of humility which is foreign to our thought, which moves us to silent wonder and glad affirmation." And, finally, Shepard states that such ecological reperception will do what religions are traditionally called upon to do—give people new courage to face, in their modern forms, perennial and universal metaphysical problems: "We must use it [the new ecological viewpoint] to confront the great philosophic problems of man—transcience, meaning, and limitation—without fear."

In recommending a definition of ecology as a "way of seeing," Shepard early in his essay makes a case for its ancient traditional roots:

> Such a *perspective* on the human situation is very old and has been part of philosophy and art for thousands of years. It badly needs attention and revival.

But, according to Shepard, there is also a false, antiecological culture that, while it is in control of men's minds and though it has caused our cultural and ecological crisis, is hard to uproot because "The older countercurrents—relics of pagan myth, the universal application of Christian compassion, philosophical naturalism, nature romanticism and pantheism—have been swept away, leaving odd bits of wreckage." In reviving ancient words and myths and concepts of art and philosophy Shepard is carrying out a "revival" of the ecological culture that he has said so "badly needs attention and revival." In the very first paragraph Shepard has recommended to modern usage when speaking of ecology the concept denoted by the ancient Greek word *eikos*—"the habitation"—along with its metaphysical connotation that suggests "the enduring integration of the primitive Greek domicile with its sacred hearth, bonding the earth to all aspects of society."

Consider also Shepard's insistence on a similarly metaphysical connotation of another ancient word, *"cultus,"* whose denotation physically resembles our word *culture:* "But the real cultural deficiency is the absence of a true *cultus* with its significant ceremony, relevant mythical cosmos, and artifacts." When we remember that the revival of a true *cultus* is the solution Shepard is offering for the social/environmental problems that confront us today, it should not surprise us that he has recommended ecological thinking to his readers not only, or even primarily, in scientific terms, but also in metaphysical terms.

In addition to the metaphysical criterion that we have just discussed, Shepard uses a very basic criterion of *survival* of the species. Survival is a most powerful criterion and needs little explanation since it is made obvious whenever Shepard uses the words "environmental deterioration" or "environmental pollution." It is the conventional way for writers to recommend a change toward ecological thinking.

But Shepard is using still other criteria. One of these is a problem-solving criterion. Shepard writes that the society, psychology, and contemporary culture is "sick" and in "crisis." How can we solve the social, psychological, and cultural problems of the modern world? Shepard suggests many times that all these problems are interdependent with the environmental problem. We have seen that by extending the concept of microorganism and macroorganism Shepard can suggest that if

the macroorganism is sick the microorganism—the individual—
cannot be perfectly healthy, either physically or psychologically.
He is making just such functional links among social, psychological, cultural, and environmental phenomena, for instance,
when he writes:

> The dangerous eruption of humanity in a deteriorating environ-
> ment does not show itself as such in the daily experience of
> most people, but is felt as general tension and anxiety. We feel
> the pressure of events not as direct causes but more like
> omens. A kind of madness arises from the prevailing nature-
> conquering, nature-hating and self- and world-denial.

Such ecologically defined concepts of evil fit into Shepard's
scheme for a universal ecological metaphysics. Shepard often
relates ethical and physical concepts by linking them in dual
modifiers. In the sentence, "It [ecological thinking] reveals the
self enobled and extended rather than threatened as part of
the landscape and the ecosystem, because the beauty and
complexity of nature are continuous with ourselves," Shepard
uses two pairs of modifiers in the same sentence. The first pair,
"enobled and extended," will relate a moral judgment about
degree of nobility or virtue with a physical adjective, "extended"; and in the second pair, "beauty and complexity," we
see an aesthetic judgment about beauty linked with another
physical adjective, "complexity," that in the context of this
essay (which elevates complex ecological relations over simplified linear relations that falsify nature) is almost a value judgment
itself.

Aesthetic terms, as well as ethical ones, can be found often
in Shepard's essay, and this brings us to his use of an aesthetic
criterion in addition to the others. He writes, for example, in
musical-aesthetic terms of "perception of the landscape as a
creative, *harmonious* being." [italics added] And investing
ecology metaphorically with the aesthetics of dance, he says:
"Its members are engaged in a kind of *choreography* of materials and energy and information, the creation of order and
organization." At still another point in his essay Shepard speaks
of perceiving ecology in artistic or architectural terms: "seeing

the world mosaic." He cross-structures an ecological point of view with an "esthetic" point of view when he laments the possible extinction of certain species and landscapes:

> To convert all "wastes"—all deserts, estuaries, tundras, ice-fields, marshes, steppes and moors—into cultivated fields and cities would improverish rather than enrich life esthetically as well as ecologically. By esthetically, I do not mean that weasel term connoting the pleasure of baubles.

As Shepard is careful to point out in this qualification, he is not using an "art for art's sake" aesthetic criterion that to him would make poetry, painting, and other arts as well as the beauty of the environment trivial ivory-tower exercises. His criterion seems to be that all art is but part of an ecological aesthetic aimed at perceiving and appreciating the beauty of a myriad of complex relations within the unity of nature. This kind of ecological aesthetic criterion is universal enough to apply to poetry, painting, and the other arts because each has a definite organic function within the ecosystem:

> They are natural objects, like bird nests. The essay is as real a part of the community—in both the one-species sociological and many-species ecological senses—as are the songs of choirs or crickets. An essay is an Orphic sound, words that make knowing possible, for it was Orpheus as Adam who named and thus made intelligible all creatures.

Notice how skillfully Shepard emphasizes the relation between ecology and aesthetics by paralleling and even alliterating the words "choirs or crickets." The music humans make in singing metaphysical praises to a Creator is no less a part of nature than the music crickets make. Shepard cross-structures writing and music and metaphysics again in the last sentence of this quotation when he says, "An essay is an Orphic sound." The Orpheus myth, about a singer whose verses were so sweet that they had power over the creatures of nature and even over life and death, is next related to the Biblical myth of Adam's naming of all the animals in the Garden of Eden. It is not by accident that Shepard relates Greek and Biblical myth, for both are at the very foundation of the ancient tradition that Shepard claims has fairly recently been cut off, by a narrow, egocentric antinature philosophy, from its true ecological roots in older tradition. It is the earlier aesthetic and metaphysical tradition of both East and West which Shepard sees as essentially ecological in point of view, that he is resurrecting in this essay to make up for our present "cultural deficiency" and to solve our social, psychological, and environmental problems as well.

Exercises

1. Consider all the implications of the following quotation from Shepard's essay:

> The elegance of . . . [eco]systems and delicacy of equilibrium are the outcome of a long evolution of interdependence. Even society, mind and culture are parts of that evolution. There is an essential relationship between them and the natural habitat. . . .

For example, if we accept Shepard's assertions that we must be prepared to consider science and technology as parts—merely extensions—of nature by means of man's biological inheritance of a larger primate brain, we must also perceive as an illusion the oft-touted dichotomy between art and nature—that in fact there is not even a difference between art and nature since

> Essays on nature are an element of a functional or feedback system influencing men's reactions to their environment, messages projected by men to themselves through some act of design. . . . They are natural objects, like bird nests.

Writing behavior, if slightly more intricate, is as much a natural phenomenon as spiders weaving diverse tapestries. Apparently literature, like spider webs, could conceivably be studied as both an art and a science of organic behavior. How might you go about studying art forms scientifically as natural objects?

2. Discuss the clash between a short-range growth and profit motive criterion and the longer-range criterion of ecological survival. What are the advantages and disadvantages of each criterion? Could the two criteria be combined in some way into a third, new criterion, or is there a limit to growth and, therefore, must our economic system be halted or changed before it destroys our planet?

3. Write a short essay designed to facilitate reperception in your readers. As a subject choose some reperception you have undergone recently that you think worth sharing. Organize your essay as Shepard did his, using the three processes:

   a. testing and questioning convention;
   b. generating and introducing a new alternative;
   c. evaluating and recommending the new alternative.

18

Conventional Perceptions
and the
Process of Reperception

WHY do our perceptions remain conventional? By what process could we reperceive? When writing gets dull and predictable we are quick to single out tired phrases or clichés as the cause of the offense. But using worn words is probably only a symptom of a much more pervasive and larger problem—the difficulty of reperceiving a world that has been blunted by our habitual assumptions. Studies and experiments reveal how human perceptions both visual and intellectual are dependent upon conventional assumptions, so that as long as assumptions persist unquestioned, perceptions are not likely to freshen. Consider this discussion of one of many experiments described in an article entitled "Experiments in Perception," by W. H. Ittelson and F. P. Kilpatrick, from *Scientific American* (August, 1951):

> . . . If an observer in a dark room looks with one eye at two lines of light which are at the same distance and elevations but of different lengths, the longer line will look nearer than the shorter one. Apparently he assumes that the lines are identical and translates the difference in length into a difference in position. If the observer takes a wand with a luminous tip and tries to touch first one line and then the other, he will be unable to do so at first. After repeated practice, however, he can learn to touch the two lines quickly and accurately. At this point he no longer sees the lines as at different distances; they now

358

look, as they are, the same distance from him. He originally assumed that the two lines were the same length because
that seemed the best bet under the circumstances. After he had
tested this assumption by purposive action, he shifted to the
assumption, less probable in terms of past experiences but still
possible, that the lines were at the same distance but of
different lengths. *As his assumption changed, perception did
also.* [My italics.]

The key to reperception appears to be some purposive questioning of conventional assumptions and the availability or
generation of an alternative assumption which we then verify
according to some criterion that satisfies us.

Reperception is often considered the first step in the creative process, whereas it is more often the last. For example,
until Charles Darwin questioned the biological assumptions
of his day and gave us the new concept of natural selection,
few people would have been likely to perceive the round,
dark spots and larger semicircular pattern on each wing of
some species of butterfly as anything but remarkable coloration.

PHOTOGRAPH BY PRESCOTT SMITH (1973).

After Darwin, however, it was not so difficult to reperceive
these two spots and semicircular patterns together as mimick-
ing the eyes and head of an owl or hawk that feeds on the

smaller birds that in turn prey on that species of butterfly. When the small bird is about to attack, the butterfly opens its wings to reveal the image of its predator's predator. This could give a slight selective advantage to the most realistic mimic who might escape while its predator is temporarily confused, and so live to pass on its wing-eye genes. Over millions of years some species of butterfly would evolve very realistic images on their wings. But all this is not so obvious for us to perceive while looking at spots on a butterfly—it depends on the prior acceptance of a number of basic assumptions not available till after Darwin's theory of evolution.

Reperception seldom occurs spontaneously. Even Darwin himself could not perceive clear visual evidence of glaciers having gouged the earth in their passing until other scientists questioned his traditional geological assumption and suggested the new assumption that glaciers once covered much of the land we now inhabit. Darwin describes in his autobiography how he remained unperceptive while standing in a glacial valley full of obvious evidence:

> We spent many hours in Cwm Idwal, examining all the rocks with extreme care, as Sedgwick was anxious to find fossils in them; but neither of us saw a trace of the wonderful glacial phenomena all around us; we did not notice the plainly scored rocks, the perched boulders, the lateral and terminal moraines. Yet these phenomena are so conspicuous that, as I declared in a paper published many years afterwards in the *Philosophical Magazine,* a house burnt down by fire did not tell its story more plainly than did this valley. If it had still been filled by a glacier, the phenomena would have been less distinct than they now are.*

We usually suppose that an artist, whose vision has been trained to notice more than casual observers, would not fail to perceive what now seems obvious to us; but for centuries many artists painted horses running with both front legs stretched out and both rear legs back. It wasn't until photographs of horses revealed the way their legs are actually

* Charles Darwin, *Autobiography and Selected Letters,* ed. Francis Darwin (1892), p. 26.

positioned when running that all artists began to reperceive what now seems obvious.

Eadward Muybridge, *Horse in Motion*, Wet Plate Photo (1878). The horse, Sallie Gardner, owned by Leland Stanford, running at 1.40 gait over Palo Alto Track, San Francisco, June 19, 1878.

Medieval artists could have seen that babies' and children's anatomy is very different from mature human anatomy. The head is much larger proportionally and the length of the legs and arms are different from that of adults in proportion to the size of the hands, feet, and the rest of the body. But medieval and even early Renaissance painting and drawings reveal that artists for centuries perceived Infants with the anatomy and even the musculature of little men in the arms of Madonnas. Phillip Aries in *Centuries of Childhood* explains that childhood in the Middle Ages and Renaissance was not perceived in the same way that we perceive it, as a separate time and kind of life and development. A child once weaned was considered a little adult and treated accordingly. Children were punished for things we would now consider quite natural for them at their age to do. And decent, even kind, parents expected their children to work long hours under strict conditions that we with our different assumptions about childhood

Enthroned Madonna and Child, Byzantine school (thirteenth century). National Gallery of Art, Andrew Mellon Collection.

find barbaric and difficult to understand. But we are only beginning to learn that not just childhood is a separate time with different behavioral problems and developments, but adolescence and young adulthood too are significantly different ages than any other and with quite different problems than childhood and adulthood. Adolescence has usually been considered only a somewhat awkward and generally ignored transition between childhood and maturity rather than a separate age in itself. Why do you think we are just beginning to perceive the importance of adolescence and young adulthood?

Perceiving is not a passive act. It is a grasping after meaning according to our assumptions. But when our habitual assumptions guide us to perceive the same meaning in a series of similar events, the process of perception hardens into routine and reduces the meaning to a convention that in turn serves to corroborate and reinforce the same old assumptions. And so it goes, often for centuries.

Sometimes a new tool or instrument will make us aware of something we had not seen before so that we may finally question an earlier assumption that has misled us and find alternatives for it that facilitate reperception. The planet Uranus for almost a hundred years before Herschel discovered it had been observed and perceived as a star. In 1781 Herschel, using his new and better telescope, was able to see that Uranus appeared to have a much larger disc size than is usual with stars, and because he now began to question his earlier assumption about Uranus being a star, he noticed for the first time Uranus's motion. He accordingly chose an unfortunate alternative assumption, reperceiving Uranus as a comet and announcing his discovery. It was months later, after the supposed new comet had been tracked long enough to make evident that its observed orbit was most probably planetary, that another alternative assumption was verified and Uranus was generally reperceived as a new planet in the solar system.

For many centuries, until two or three hundred years ago, people assumed that normal human behavior was the result of an equal balance in the human body of four potent liquids called humors: black bile, yellow bile, blood, phlegm. An imbalance, consisting of an excess of one of the four humors, was assumed to cause a particular type of abnormal behavior. An excess of black bile was assumed to cause a "melancholic" or brooding psychological state; an excess of yellow bile a "choleric" or angry state; an excess of blood was thought to occasion a "sanguine" or manic personality; an excess of phlegm a "phlegmatic" or unresponsive psychological state. Humor imbalance could be caused by certain kinds of weather conditions, by eating particular foods in excess, or by some significant change in the routine of a person's thought or behavior, such as might be occasioned by a parent's decease. For example, a death in the family of a man living in 1600 might cause him to dress in black and look pale and intense, and keep to himself reading and sighing and even, perhaps, cause him to neglect his personal appearance. If he exhibited such behavior his contemporaries would likely perceive it as symptoms of the mental illness melancholia and treat it accordingly by trying to soften the effects with medicine or perhaps a trip to a foreign country for a change of weather to neutralize the supposed excess of black bile. Other causes might produce the same symptoms of melancholia, of course, such as rejection by a loved one or, possibly, thwarted ambition and a desire for revenge. It was important to diagnose the right cause if there were several possible causes, because melancholia was considered a form of insanity and could become dangerous.

Because we do not perceive certain patterns of behavior in the same way as people did in 1600, it is sometimes hard for us to understand the motivation of the characters in a play like Shakespeare's *Hamlet,* which was written for an audience who would perceive immediately that Hamlet (dressed in black) was exhibiting the symptoms of the mental illness melancholia:

> Lord Hamlet, with his doublet all unbrac'd,
> No hat upon his head, his stockings fouled,
> Ungarter'd, and down-gyved to his ankle,
> Pale as his shirt, his knees knocking each other,
> And with a look so piteous in purport

> As if he had been loosed out of hell
> To speak of horrors,—he comes before me.
> [II, i, 78–84]

Hamlet's behavior could be caused primarily by his father's sudden death, as his mother thinks ("I doubt it is no other but the main, / His father's death and our o'erhasty marriage"—II, ii, 56–57), or by Ophelia's apparent rejection of Hamlet's love. This latter cause is insisted upon by Polonius, who had ordered Ophelia not to see Hamlet and to send back his letters:

> And my young mistress thus I did bespeak:
> "Lord Hamlet is a prince out of thy star.
> This must not be;" and then I prescripts gave her,
> That she should lock herself from his resort,
> Admit no messengers, receive no tokens.
> Which done, she took the fruits of my advice;
> And he, repell'd,—a short tale to make—
> Fell into a sadness, then into a fast,
> Thence to a watch, thence into a weakness,
> Thence to a lightness, and, by this declension,
> Into the madness wherein now he raves,
> And all we mourn for.
>
> KING. Do you think 't is this?
> [II, ii, 140–151]

Shakespeare has King Claudius spend much time trying to verify this cause, and even has him hide behind an arras to hear Hamlet chat with Ophelia, until the king decides that Polonius's diagnosis of the cause is wrong. Where a modern reader might think such scenes a silly waste of time, an Elizabethan audience would understand exactly why the king shows such intense interest in Hamlet's and Ophelia's love life, because they would perceive that King Claudius was testing and eliminating Polonius's diagnosis that frustrated love for Ophelia was the primary cause of Hamlet's insanity. With frustrated love eliminated as a possible cause, the real cause would seem now very likely to be thwarted ambition, since Claudius had usurped Prince Hamlet's rightful throne. With this conclusion, Hamlet's melancholia becomes considerably more dangerous to Claudius —a plot to revenge himself and overthrow the usurper could be, as Claudius now supposes, hatching in Hamlet's diseased brain. Claudius decides to send this now dangerous madman away immediately from the Danish court on a sea voyage to a different climate:

> KING. Love! his affections do not that way tend;
>   Nor what he spake, though it lack'd form a little,
>   Was not like madness. There 's something in his soul
>   O'er which his melancholy sits on brood,
>   And I do not doubt the hatch and the disclose
>   Will be some danger; which for to prevent,
>   I have in quick determination
>   Thus set it down: he shall with speed to England
>   For the demand of our neglected tribute.
>   Haply the seas and countries different
>   With variable objects shall expel
>   This something-settled matter in his heart,
>   Whereon his brains still beating puts him thus,
>   From fashion of himself. What think you on 't?
>
>   [III, i, 170–183]

Such analyses of mental illness in earlier literature are sometimes difficult for us to perceive sympathetically today, since our very different assumptions lock us into our own peculiar perception of abnormal patterns of human behavior and their cures and dangers. Of course, our psychology may seem a century from now just as eccentric as a psychology based on the four humors now seems to us.

We have been discussing historical examples of perceptual hang ups. Perhaps it is time to become aware of an example or two of our own perceptual conservatism. Only in the past decade has the theory that all the continents were once close together and later drifted apart been taken seriously. Francis Bacon discussed such a hypothesis as long ago as 1620, soon after the first English settlement in America and after fairly good maps of the western hemisphere had been produced. These maps suggested an obvious jigsaw-puzzle fit between South America and Africa and between North America and

North Africa/Europe. But some years later Isaac Newton proposed what has since become the conventional view: that the earth, though once hot, began cooling, and long ago became rigid on the surface. The continents have remained rigid ever since, but the continued cooling contractions forced up mountain ranges along the weaker margins of continents or in soft sedimentary basins. Then in 1912 Alfred Wegener brought together a mass of evidence from different fields, including paleontology as well as geology, to propose a theory of continental drift. But

The position of the continents about 180,000,000 years ago.

most geologists refused to reperceive the impression of rigid, immovable continents with which they were brought up and that most of their conventional operating assumptions supported. It was not until April, 1963, that an article tentatively favorable to the Wegener theory appeared in *Scientific American,* written by the Canadian scientist, J. Tuzo Wilson, who states that "most geologists, with notable exceptions among those who work around the margins of the southern continents," still adhere to the immovable continent theory. Five years later, in the April, 1968, issue of *Scientific American,* an article by Patrick N. Hurley on "The Confirmation of Continental Drift" was published with a map (see p. 367) that showed how the continents were probably closely related over one hundred eighty million years ago. During the 1960s and since, geology has been an exciting battleground between some geologists (mostly younger ones) who were not educated exclusively in the older set of assumptions and other geologists who could not readily reperceive the earth, which they had so long assumed was a rigid surface with fixed continents and fixed ocean basins. The newer theory perceives the earth as somewhat plastic, with perhaps convection currents, caused by its hot interior, forcing the continents like huge plates of rock to drift slowly (a few centimeters a year on the average) over the surface of the earth, fracturing and reuniting in slowly changing patterns that push up mountain ranges and cause earthquakes. But you may be thinking, "No wonder it was so difficult and took so long to reperceive such a slow and monumental movement as continental drift." So let us next consider something we have all seen but few of us have perceived.

On clear, sunny summer days when the sun is directly overhead, look at the sidewalk or hold a piece of paper under a low-hanging tree branch and you will see, if the leaves are close enough together, perfect circles of light of different intensities shimmering back and forth across one another as the wind rustles the leaves. When the sun is not directly overhead or at right angles to sidewalk or paper you may see ovals of light instead of circles. If the leaves are far apart you may see jagged, irregular light patterns, which is what most of us expect to see and do perceive even when the patterns are perfect circles of light, tiny image reflections of the sun. During a partial solar eclipse the pattern of light on the sidewalk will take the shape of tiny crescents reflecting that portion of the sun still visible. It is the same phenomenon that you see when you punch a small hole in one end of a box and then, putting the box over your head and looking at the other end to see an apparently (no matter how irregular the hole) perfect circle of the sun, watch it change gradually to a smaller and smaller crescent while a solar eclipse is in progress. Circles or ovals of light shimmering on sidewalks under trees on any sunny day is a common enough sight for each of us to have observed it, but most of us have ignored the phenomenon even when it was in our field of vision, because no one had ever questioned our habitual assumption that the sun shining through leaves must "naturally" form irregular shapes of light. Such neat circles seem too symmetrical (and hence too "artificial") to conform

Meandering river.

to our essentially nineteenth-century aesthetic criterion of the asymmetry of nature. But nature may well be more symmetrical than we perceive. For example, consider pine needles, which form always in tufts of five in the white pine and in tufts of three in a different species. Does the aerial photograph of a river on the preceding page suggest that rivers meander haphazardly as in romantic paintings, or do they tend to follow fairly symmetrical (sine wave) curves? Why might rivers behave in this fashion? Can you think of any other examples of symmetry in nature? As a result of this discussion, some of us may soon perceive the light-circle phenomenon for the first time, since our conventional assumption about the asymmetry of nature has been brought into question and an alternative assumption has been proposed.

If an event or phenomenon is quite new to us and we have not had time to develop habitual assumptions about it, changing our initial perception of it can be accomplished without much difficulty as soon as we are provided with the assumptions and criteria upon which the new perception of the phenomenon depends. This is why it is easier for students studying geology for the first time to accept the continental-drift theory than it is for older practicing geologists, who must question contrary assumptions that have become habitual over the years. A change in perception of some new phenomenon, like a bubble-chamber photograph, can often be accomplished by simply becoming familiar with some assumptions about what we are seeing without the difficult process of questioning earlier assumptions. What looks like modern art or an unusual tangle of wispy lines and dashes to the person who first sees a bubble-chamber photograph can be reperceived by him, after he learns a few new physical concepts, as interesting line and dash records of subnuclear events.

Can you reperceive this drawing of a woman's head (on the facing page) so that you see a different woman's head? It is fairly easy to achieve reperception in a drawing like this, since outside the simple visual and motor habits we develop while looking at the picture, no conventional assumptions are

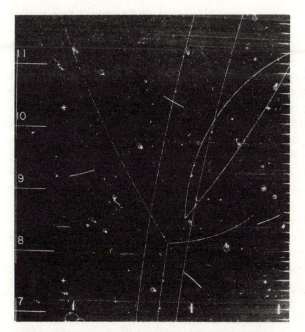

Bubble-chamber photograph. Berkeley Radiation
Laboratory

involved. We merely shift from assuming a curved line to be the profile of one woman to seeing the same line as the nose of another, or vice versa; there is no web of long-held beliefs tying us to one way of perceiving the drawing. But even when perception is anchored by habitual assumptions, reperception can be facilitated or made more likely. For instance, one of the purposes of the first eight chapters of this book was to explain the rhetorical habits and assumptions behind several alternative styles so that by temporarily adopting someone else's rhetorical routine you could quickly and almost painlessly reperceive the world in several ways from which your own habits and assumptions may have previously restricted you.

In some fields, relatively frequent reperception is induced by the very nature of the discipline being pursued. In the past four hundred years science has facilitated an incredible rate of intellectual reperception, greater than ever before in the intellectual history of man. But even in that relatively fast-moving field, T. S. Kuhn, in *The Structure of Scientific Revolutions* (1962) has given us many examples of the basic conservatism of scientific perception, and a theory to explain it. In the practice of normal science, where precise measurements and very complete and explicit descriptions are the rule, anomalies (such as experiments that should work out in a certain way and don't) stand out rather clearly. Such anomalies make it fairly obvious to scientists that some conventional assumptions about nature that they have so far trusted in can no longer be said to fit the reality of this new situation. These anomalies, if they persist, may lead to crises, then to the testing and questioning of basic operating assumptions, and finally to the proposal of some new assumption or hypothesis that may culminate in a reperception of nature. In science, then, reperception seems built into the system; but for most of us, unfortunately, the processes of first testing and questioning conventional assumptions, then generating and finally verifying new ones are not automatic. The following chapters are designed to illustrate with examples and develop with exercises these three cognitive processes that are likely to facilitate reperceptions of reality and encourage more creative thinking and writing.

Exercises

1. Do you think you perceive the world differently from your teachers or your parents or your roommate? What are the differences in "perceived reality"? Are there any differences between your basic assumptions and criteria and theirs that may account for the difference in the way you each perceive reality? How could you persuade them to perceive the same reality that you do?

2. Do you perceive differences between men and women besides the obvious physiological ones? Are there any assumptions behind your perception of differences? Do you think any of these assumptions are questionable? How do you think adopting some alternative assumptions might begin to change one's perception of the role relations between men and women, and possibly change social behavior?

3. The perception of humor depends on an audience's ability to shift rapidly from one set of assumptions to a different set. What is the shift in assumptions that accounts for the perception in each of the following jokes told by the comedian Woody Allen:

    My mother sent me to interfaith camp every summer, where I was sadistically beaten up by boys of every race, color, and creed.

    This bully was standing over me cursing foully, and threatening me with a knife, and fibbing.

    People have accused me of being cynical about love, but this is not true. As a matter of fact I think love is a beautiful thing between two people . . . [pause] . . . and between three or four it's absolutely fantastic.

4. Write a short science-fiction narrative in which you introduce a person from another world who perceives reality quite differently from us and brings into question some of our very basic assumptions, offering possible alternatives.

5. Consider this diagram of Dante's perception of the universe What assumptions do you think he would have had to hold in

order to perceive the universe in this way? Draw the scheme of the universe that you perceive. What assumptions govern your perception and how do they differ from Dante's? Does your perception also differ from that of Copernicus and Newton, both of whom changed profoundly the idea of the universe that Dante perceived?

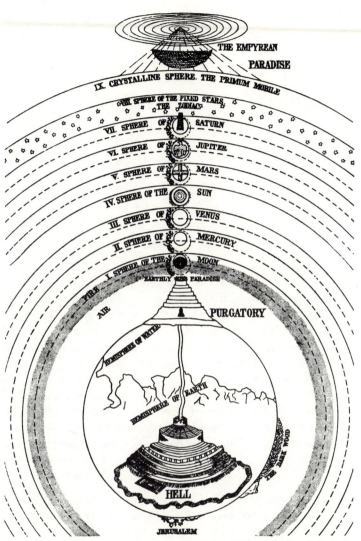

FIG. 39.—Dante's Scheme of the Universe modified from Michelangelo Caetani, Duca di Sermoneta, *La materia della Divina Commedia di Dante Alighieri*, Monte Cassino, 1855.

19

Testing and
Questioning Conventions

THE last chapter shows that our perceptions are not likely to
be fresh unless we can question and generate alternatives to
our habitual assumptions. Conventional ideas and assumptions
could never have gained wide acceptance unless they had
initially seemed "true." Hence a convention, a kind of cliché
of thought, is commonly passed on uncritically year after
year. But the historical context in which a convention was
originally verified necessarily changes; perhaps new sources of
knowledge or instruments of observation become available to
cast doubt on it; perhaps related assumptions have been questioned and replaced, leaving the convention without the obvious support it once enjoyed.

Consider the following conventional assumption:

> The Middle Ages was a repressive and intellectually stag-
> nant period, whereas the Renaissance flowered into a time of
> great creativity.

When we hear a convention like this often repeated, we tend
to consider it an obvious fact and, as a result, may find it very
hard to test or question, even when that is our purpose. But
we can begin to test and perhaps bring into question any convention if we use an approach called *transformational testing.*

There are a number of structural changes that we can make in the statement of a convention that may help us see anomalous exceptions to it, if it is weak, until possibly the whole convention is brought into crisis and we are ready to seek a new, more relevant, or more accurate alternative to it. Transformational testing must be approached in a relaxed, almost playful attitude coupled with a keen probing alertness ready to take immediate advantage of unforseen implications, weaknesses, or alternatives.

Reversal Transformation

The simplest structural transformation of a conventional assertion is a reversal. For example:

> The *Renaissance* was a repressive and intellectually stagnant period, whereas the *Middle Ages* flowered into a time of great creativity.

After any transformation has been made in the conventional assertion, the next step is to try to test the transformation, no matter how ridiculous that might at first appear; for often a vigorous transformational testing will generate new data and considerations that may at least provide reasons to be more critical and cautious in our acceptance of a conventional assumption. Could we attempt to prove that the Renaissance was in some ways a less creative period than the Middle Ages? How about architecture? If we researched great examples of architecture, such as Mont St. Michel and Chartres, we would find that architecture flourished in the Middle Ages more than in the Renaissance. When were the infamous Inquisition and witch hunts most repressive? If we look this up, we find these were most virulent *not* during the Middle Ages, but during the Renaissance. Furthermore, the printing press and universities (Oxford, Cambridge, the Sorbonne, etc.) were all innovations of the Middle Ages rather than the Renaissance. The *reversal* transformation has made us conscious of some exceptions to this conventional assumption, but we cannot suppose that these

Chartres Cathedral.

few anomalies can yet be said to seriously bring into question and crisis our acceptance of a convention that we have only begun to test. Let us proceed to somewhat more sophisticated transformations.

General-to-Specific Transformation

We could use the general-to-specific (or vice versa) transformation that would replace any general noun in the sentence with a more specific noun, and change the conventional statement to something like this:

Erasmus, Shakespeare, Cervantes, and *da Vinci* were men of great creativity, whereas *Aquinas, Dante, Chaucer,* and *Dürer* were repressive and intellectually stagnant.

Now obviously something is wrong in the second clause of the assertion. Dante and Chaucer were as creative writers as Cervantes and Shakespeare. Dürer was not a less creative artist than da Vinci. Indeed, in philosophical creativity it is hard to believe that any Renaissance philosopher, even Erasmus, could match the importance of the medieval philosopher Aquinas. As we begin to fill in more and more particular names of creative men of the Middle Ages and Renaissance we must conclude that if the Renaissance has any creative edge on the Middle Ages it is in the *quantity* of good artists and writers. In terms of *quality* alone it is hard to best writers like Dante and Chaucer. The comparison of quantity leads us into another transformation. We are now getting closer to being able to question the original assumption.

Comparative-Quantity Transformation

In the comparative-quantity transformation we can, for example, change the original universal assertion to a particular assertion as follows:

> Only *some* types of intellectual endeavor, such as painting and sculpture, displayed great creativity during the Renaissance (most philosophy, for instance, was very derivative), whereas only *some* types of endeavor, such as lyric poetry and individualized portraiture during the Middle Ages could be said to be intellectually stagnant. (However, frame stories and allegories flourished.)

We can defend this transformation by using the information gleaned from earlier transformations to adduce evidence to show that, as in most periods of history, the behavior of men in both the Middle Ages and Renaissance was characterized by a quantity of creative acts in some fields and intellectual stagnation in others. For instance, we have already seen that in philosophy and architecture on a massive scale the Middle Ages seems to have had the creative advantage.

Definitional Transformation

In the definitional transformation, instead of taking definitions for granted we can try various alternative definitions of the key words in the conventional assertion. We should first become aware of (perhaps encircle) the terms of concepts in the conventional statement upon which the sense depends:

> The *Middle Ages* was a *repressive* and *intellectually stagnant* period, whereas the *Renaissance* flowered into a time of great *creativity*.

A number of alternative definitions of each of these five key words or phrases in the conventional statement could be generated by the many defining structures (such as Aristotelian, operational, divisional) that we have already discussed (Part II). Let us consider the definition of *Renaissance,* for example. What is the genus of *Renaissance?* Is it a historical period of time, or a timeless spirit or attitude toward the world that might be shared by men of different historical periods? Could we define it operationally by an opening date, say 1350, and closing date of 1550? This might work for the Italian Renaissance, but in 1550 Sir Walter Raleigh (1552?–1618), Edmund Spenser (1552?–1599), Sir Philip Sidney (1554–1586), Francis Bacon (1561–1626), Christopher Marlowe (1564–1593), and William Shakespeare (1564–1616) of the English Renaissance were not yet born. We might have to define the word divisionally, since in fact the Italian Renaissance is almost over before what is called the Dutch Renaissance begins, followed by the French Renaissance and then the English Renaissance. In the context of art history, does the word *Renaissance* mean something different from the word *Renaissance* in the context of literary history or the history of science? Does a consideration of the many definitional alternatives that might be used for the word *Renaissance,* as well as alternative definitions for the remaining four words, help to test the essential vagueness in the convention? It begins to appear quite possible now to question a conventional assumption that at first may have seemed simply self-evident.

Implicit-Assumptions Transformation

Even assumptions contain other implicit assumptions, usually at a higher level of abstraction. First we will look for implicit assumptions underlying the conventional assumption. Then we can consider possible alternative assumptions and so bring the convention into crisis. The conventional assumption,

> The Middle Ages was a repressive and intellectually stagnant period, whereas the Renaissance flowered into a time of great creativity,

seems to contain among others the following assumptions and implications:

1. that creativity can suddenly spring from a context of stagnation, which implies the possibility in history;
2. that radical discontinuity can occur from one year to the next; and
3. that human behavior in adjacent historical periods can be diametrically opposed.

It is easy to test this set of assumptions by considering, for example, a set of alternative assumptions that forms what seems to be at least as accurate a model of the evolution of culture:

1. that human behavior has antecedent causes;
2. that the character of an age made up of the collective thought and behavior of many diverse people and generations must have some antecedent roots; and
3. that these roots can be found in the thought and behavior of earlier generations (i.e., that the seeds of the Renaissance are to be looked for in the Middle Ages).

This transformation of implicit assumptions tends to bring

into question the whole original convention implying an antithesis between the Renaissance and the Middle Ages. An antithesis is a clever linguistic technique that lends spice and wit to writing, but for that very reason antithesis is often used even when it is unwarranted by the facts of a situation or implies assumptions that are untenable.

Implicit-Criteria Transformation

The implicit-criteria-of-relevance transformation is often a useful way to test an assumption. First we must find the probable implicit criterion or criteria upon which the assumption is based. In the case of our original conventional assumption, which obviously elevates creativity ("flowered") over tradition ("stagnant period"), one implicit criterion seems to be that

> the excitement of accelerated innovation and change is to be preferred over the stability of working well within a long accepted tradition.

We can now transform the original convention by considering the possibility of alternative criteria, for example:

1. that unless a tradition is in serious crisis, changes and innovations for their own sake are often inferior to the assumptions of the original tradition; and
2. that the direction and significance of an innovative change rather than creativity for its own sake must determine whether a change is better than the tradition from which it differs.

This transformation should lead us to inquire into the direction of the creative innovation in the Middle Ages that led to the Renaissance, and perhaps compare it with the direction of creative innovation in the Renaissance which led to the Baroque and Neoclassic periods.

This criterion of judging creativity by its significance and consequences rather than simply by the fact that it is innovative should give us pause in our own efforts at testing and questioning a traditional assumption. Unless vigorous testing reveals that a conventional assumption is indeed questionable and in crisis, it may be better to hold to the convention rather than change it simply for the sake of novelty. Novelty for its own sake is rarely a constructive and progressive criterion of relevance.

We ought to consider, then, as we proceed whether our testing of the traditional assumption about the Middle Ages and the Renaissance has really rendered it questionable, or whether we should decide, for lack of evidence that might change it, simply to retain the traditional assumption as it stands. What do you think so far?

Figurative Transformation

In the figurative transformation we find, and test alternatives to, any pivotal or instrumental metaphors or other figures. In the conventional assertion

> The Middle Ages was a repressive and intellectually *stagnant* period, whereas the Renaissance *flowered* into a time of great creativity.

there seems to be an instrumental metaphor that determines a good part of the meaning, though we may not be fully aware of its influence until we test it. It is a growth and stagnation metaphor, or, more concretely, some sort of swamp flower blooming above a stagnant pool. Is the growth metaphor warranted here without acknowledging the probability that the "stagnant" Middle Ages must have started and nurtured the seed and plant so that when it "flowered" it could be called the Renaissance? In other words, could we not transform the metaphor to suggest that the Renaissance is but a later stage of a continuous organic process? Such a transformation would suggest that the Renaissance is the culmination of the Middle Ages, and might be stated in this way:

The vigorous and seminal minds of the ninth through the fourteenth centuries planted the flowers that were soon to bloom in a garden that men later separated from its roots by calling it, misleadingly, a renaissance or rebirth.

What kind of evidence could we use to test the validity of such a figurative transformation?

Before we turn to the next transformation for testing and questioning, let us realize that there is a more hidden, yet not less important, pair of instrumental metaphors buried in the conventional assertion. The terms *Middle Ages* and *Renaissance* contain metaphors that partly determine how we will conceive the relation between them. The use of the word *middle* suggests a nondescript period *between* one important period (Classical) and another (Renaissance or Modern). The term *Renaissance* means a rebirth and suggests it is the first *re*birth of civilization and culture since the earlier Classical age ended and the Middle Ages began. In the metaphors that form the words—in the very structure of the historical terminology—there is, then, a built-in prejudice against the significance of the Middle Ages and in favor of the Renaissance. Try out some alternative terms to replace *Middle Ages* and *Renaissance* and see if this transformation leads to any further questioning of the traditional assumption. Our unquestioning use of these biased terms illustrates how easy it is for convention to persist and become habitual by uncritical acceptance, until we are willing to assume the burden of testing tradition to see if it is still sound.

Diagrammatic Transformation

In using the diagrammatic transformation we might turn the convention into alternative diagrams or statistical measurements. What might they look like? What sort of diagram best represents the difference in creativity between the two periods? Can you transform the conventional assumption into other diagrams besides these that may help to question it further?

Can you imagine what research would be necessary to construct or test a graph with some numerical data?

In order to get statistics on creativity we might count the number of mechanical inventions per one hundred years or the number of art objects produced, or both. This could give us two graphs (one for the Renaissance and one for the Middle Ages) that we could then compare to verify or question the traditional assumption. We might also count and graph the number of artists or thinkers in each period, or count the number of different styles, art techniques, or variety of subject matter. Of course, since the Middle Ages was earlier than the Renaissance, and consequently less of its art and records have survived, such statistical analysis might be less

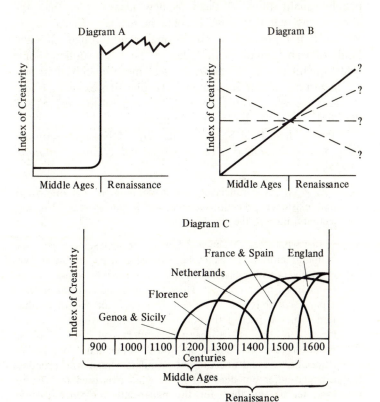

than fair to the Middle Ages. What other indices of creativity could we use to define operationally the difference between the Middle Ages and the Renaissance in a graph or diagram?

We have now subjected the conventional assumption to eight different transformations in order to test its validity. Do you now believe the convention has proved its right to persist unchanged, or do you think it questionable in part so that it should be modified, or do you consider the whole assumption in crisis and can you state an alternative assumption about the relation between the Renaissance and the Middle Ages that you think should replace the convention?

Next, let us test a somewhat more difficult set of assumptions. The assumptions of existentialism are so recent that people usually think of them as new ideas rather than the conventions that they have become in the last decade or so. We need not proceed in any formal way through all eight kinds of transformations in order to test a convention. Some transformations will reveal weaknesses more quickly than others in testing certain conventions. To question existential conventions we will use the reversal, the general-to-specific, and the implicit-assumptions transformations.

Here is Jean-Paul Sartre's statement of basic assumptions from his book enitled *Existentialism and Human Emotions* (1957):

> . . . What [existentialists] have in common is that they think that existence precedes essence, or, if you prefer, that subjectivity must be the starting point.
>
> Just what does that mean? Let us consider some object that is manufactured, for example, a book or a paper-cutter: here is an object which has been made by an artisan whose inspiration came from a concept. He referred to the concept of what a paper-cutter is and likewise to a known method of production, which is part of the concept, something which is, by and large, a routine. Thus, the paper-cutter is at once an object produced in a certain way and, on the other hand, one having a specific use; and one can not postulate a man who produces a paper-cutter but does not know what it is used for. Therefore, let us say that, for the paper-cutter, essence—that is,

the ensemble of both the production routines and the properties which enable it to be both produced and defined—precedes existence. Thus, the presence of the paper-cutter or book in front of me is determined. Therefore, we have here a technical view of the world whereby it can be said that production precedes existence. . . . What is meant here by saying that existence precedes essence? It means that, first of all, man exists, turns up, appears on the scene, and only afterwards, defines himself. If man, as the existentialist conceives him, is indefinable, it is because at first he is nothing. Only afterward will he be something, and he himself will have made what he will be. Thus, there is no human nature, since there is no God to conceive it. Not only is man what he conceives himself to be, but he is also only what he wills himself to be after this thrust toward existence.

Man is nothing else but what he makes of himself. Such is the first principle of existentialism. It is also what is called subjectivity, the name we are labeled with when charges are brought against us. But what do we mean by this, if not that man has a greater dignity than a stone or table? For we mean that man first exists, that is, that man first of all is the being who hurls himself toward a future and who is conscious of imagining himself as being in the future. Man is at the start a plan which is aware of itself, rather than a patch of moss, a piece of garbage, or a cauliflower; nothing exists prior to this plan; there is nothing in heaven; man will be what he will have planned to be.

A restatement of these basic existential assumptions might look as follows:

1. for people alone, existence precedes essence or definition; and
2. subjectivity must be the starting point.

A general-to-specific transformation might suggest the specific example of the computer which, according to this assumption, must have its assigned purpose before it is brought into existence. But we know that new uses and purposes for the existence of computers are still being discovered. No one who gave existence to the first computer could have foreseen an ultimate definition. It is common in modern technology to bring something into existence before we can even imagine a purpose for it. A laser was not given existence so that it could become a scalpel used in eye surgery. But we have learned recently that it can cut and cauterize deep in the eye without making a surface incision. In the case of the laser, the computer, and, indeed, technology generally, it can be said that existence precedes essence. This conclusion surely contradicts existentialism's assumption of man's *unique* existence before essence.

If the inventions of modern technology, such as atomic energy, do not have essence or final definition before existence but can be given better purposes than those to which they may initially have been put, then it would seem that a good case could be made for becoming less concerned with the subjective self and more concerned with objects like computers or atomic energy. For the purposes to which such objects may ultimately be put are matters directly pertinent to our own and mankind's future meaning or survival. In other words we could restate and might be able to defend a reversal of the second assumption: objectivity (rather than subjectivity) must be the starting point.

Let us test an implication of the first assumption:

except for people, essence precedes existence.

We had already begun to propose the counterassumption that *all* things exist before their essences, purposes, or definitions can be known. Even garbage may be treated and recycled to be used in a way nobody suspected when they threw it out. New drugs and new uses for these drugs are being discovered almost daily from trees and plants whose purposes were evidently not fully defined before their existence.

But now let us see what happens when we reverse the assumption that for people alone, existence precedes essence:

for people alone, essence or definition precedes *existence*.

We are born into a culture. A machine has no culture; it does not object to being assigned any new purpose whatsoever. Only we (before we are old enough to object) are taught a language that inevitably inculcates some definite set of assumptions about what a human being is, or should be, and what his or her relation is to the rest of the world. It is difficult for us to change the traditional feelings and assumptions and perceptions that culture determines for us. Subjectivity will not change cultural programming; in fact, habitually relying on one's subjective feelings and intuitions may actually reinforce rather than overcome those feelings and intuitions that one's culture has most effectively inculcated. The rest of the world has no culture. Atomic energy is apparently as content to cure cancer as blow up cities. Perhaps the differences we could make objectively in the world outside ourselves are more important than existentialists think, since they could change not merely our technology, but culture and, therefore, the meaning of being human. Maybe at this point we could propose a kind of objective global existentialism as an alternative to conventional existentialism that alienates man from the rest of the world. Global existentialists could end their isolation from the material world of nature and technology because the material world would no longer be assumed to be a static, foregone conclusion whose meaning was determined before its existence. If one is not alienated from but intimately related to the world of nature and technology, one can work ecologically toward redefining the purposes of technology and relating its wastes and products more wisely to nature, viewed as a whole system.

The cognitive process of testing and questioning a conventional assumption is not simply a negative skill but, on the contrary, if used together with the process of generating alternative assumptions, can be very productive of innovative thinking and writing. In the next chapter, we will discuss in detail how to generate alternative concepts or assumptions. But let us consider in a few exercises that follow the possibility of some innovative consequences in testing and questioning conventions.

Exercises

1. You may wish to continue to test the conventional assumption about the Middle Ages and the Renaissance by considering further each of the transformations that we started. Write a brief essay (a) upholding, questioning in part, and modifying, or (b) calling into crisis and totally replacing the conventional assumption.

2. Using the transformation that you consider most likely to reveal weaknesses in each specific case, briefly test several conventional assumptions below to see whether or not they can be brought into question or crisis. Some of the following conventions will resist or defy questioning much better than others:

   a. war has always existed and will continue to exist as long as man survives;
   b. human nature is essentially good (or evil);
   c. the Communists were responsible for the cold war;
   d. the truth will always win if all sides of an argument are presented;
   e. individual competition is the best form of motivation for all human endeavor;
   f. a relative morality means no morality at all;
   g. America is an essentially racist country;
   h. white settlers had to rid America of the menace of the savage red men;
   i. high civilization can flourish only when law and order is maintained;
   j. the pursuit of individual freedom will lead to the greatest good for the greatest number;
   k. woman's place is in the home;
   l. the best policy would be to take from those according to their abilities and give to others according to their needs;
   m. the demands of reason and feeling are necessarily opposed;
   n. the world has progressed for the past two thousand years;
   o. human nature does not change;
   p. our free enterprise system may not be perfect, but it is better than any other known system;

q. heterosexual monogamy is the only natural form of marriage;
r. for a society to function well, all people must share the same basic assumptions or beliefs;
s. science and technology lead ultimately to dehumanization and ecological crisis;
t. the more educated you are, the more likely you will be to get a job.

3. John Milton, in a passage from *Paradise Lost,* places Eve and women lower than Adam and men on the "chain of being":

> Too much of ornament, in outward show
> Elaborate, of inward less exact.
> For well I understand in the prime end
> Of Nature her the inferior, in the mind
> And inward faculties, which most excel;

For Milton "the prime end of Nature," the most important part of human nature, is "the inward faculties," the highest of which Milton evidently assumes is "the mind" or intellect. And since Milton assumes the inferiority of woman's intellect, according to his criterion of what is most significant among the inward faculties, women are considered inferior products of nature.

In the late eighteenth and the nineteenth centuries, among some of the romantic writers, woman's position was reversed. The same criterion was used: that whoever excelled in the highest of the inward faculties was best. The big difference was brought about by a profound change in the assumptions about the heirarchy of the "inward faculties." In Milton's seventeenth century and before, the intellect was considered the highest of all the faculties with imagination and feelings ranking much lower on the scale. However, the romantics changed this hierarchy by assuming that imagination and feeling were higher faculties than the intellect. Though women were still considered somehow intellectually inferior, they were generally believed to be more spontaneous in feeling and imagination. Women were elevated in the nineteenth century, then, according to the same criterion and for the same assumed closeness to feelings and lack of intellect that caused Milton to judge them inferior. They were put on a romantic pedestal without the assumption of intellectual inferiority being questioned or reconsidered. Is this resulting ambivalent attitude toward women still troubling us in the modern world?

Find a conventional contemporary quotation honoring romantic femininity but explicitly or implicitly disparaging women's intellectual capabilities and restricting women's roles in society. Submit the quotation to several transformations to test it and possibly generate some new alternative ideas.

4. A number of "problems" or "crises" have been *defined* by our society:

the drug problem	the welfare problem
the pollution problem or the ecological crisis	the abortion problem
the race problem	the population crisis
the sex problem	the pornography problem
the poverty problem	the Indochina problem
the crime problem	the urban crisis
the unemployment problem	the prison problem
the automation problem	the demonstration problem
the ghetto problem	the old-age problem
	the medical-care problem

The way in which the problem has conventionally been defined determines how we will try to solve that problem. Most of our social problems need to be *redefined* since, if the conventional definitions of the problems were correct, most of these would already have been solved or would be well on the way to solution.

Pick any problem (such as one of those listed above) that interests you and that has been given a conventional definition in our society; question this conventional definition; then redefine the problem in a brief essay.

In preparation for your essay you might ask yourself the following:

a. What is the conventional definition of the "problem"? (State it. Then test and question it using some of the transformations in this chapter.)
b. What assumptions or criteria lie behind the conventional definition and its implied range of solutions?
c. Can you think of better alternative assumptions upon which to construct a new definition of the problem?
d. How would you redefine the problem? (You might use some of the defining paradigms in Chapters 10, 11, and 12 to construct the new definition.)

e. How does your redefinition change the way we perceive that problem and the way we would act in order to solve it?

f. What range of new solutions would you now propose in order to solve the problem as you have redefined it?

For example, the conventional definition of "the drug problem" in the late 1960s and early 1970s in America is that a growing number of criminals are breaking the narcotics laws. Now this definition implies that the way to solve the problem is to stop these criminals by more arrests, which means primarily spending tax money to increase the budgets of the narcotics division of the Justice Department and police forces throughout the country. In spite of such budget increases for the past decade, the problem has not been solved. Perhaps the time is ripe for a redefinition of "the drug problem" so that we can begin to perceive, propose, and try some alternative solutions that might be more effective. The conventional assumption that people who get hooked on drugs are criminals is only beginning to be set aside, and the alternative assumption—that they are in need of medical help rather than penal punishment—is considered by only a minority in our country a possible basis for a redefinition. If the problem were perceived as that of a growing number of people for whom some medical and/or social help is needed, then it would imply that tax money should be going to drug clinics and drug rehabilitation research rather than to the police, courts, and prisons that arrest, sentence, and incarcerate people who are hooked on drugs.

But maybe there are a number of other ways to redefine this problem. Suppose we assume that the real "drug problem" is the several hundred new drugs and chemicals that every year are put directly into our food as sweeteners or preservatives, put indirectly into our food as pesticide or fungicide residue, or injected to speed up the growth of chickens and cows. These substances may be carcinogenic, may add hydrocarbons to our bodies, or even poison us with mercury. After all, such drugs and chemicals affect the health and well-being of everyone in our society. The conscious drug and chemical users can decide whether or not they will use LSD, for instance, and are a small number compared to the *unwitting* users of new drugs and chemicals, who have no choice because they are unaware of what goes into their food and water. If the "drug problem" is not primarily the problem of conscious users of mind-altering drugs and chemicals, but that of all us unaware guinea pigs who are consuming several hundred new drugs and chemicals every year that we never chose or consented to, what is the implied range of new solutions?

Sailing rail car (1878)

20

Generating New Ideas

AN original idea or invention is a new hybrid produced by a cross-structure of two or more older ideas or materials. For example, what we now refer to as the Age of Bronze was brought about by the combination of two metals. Both copper and tin had been used individually before, but had never been melted together in equal parts to produce bronze, which could be used in making tools and implements for which neither copper nor tin alone would serve. The study of chemistry shows us how not just new metals but all the wonderfully varied objects on earth seem to have evolved by successive combinations and recombinations of a few basic elements. According to one theory, even the intricate organization of a living being consists of elaborate patterns which were cross-structured from simpler elements. Slowly, several basic elements combined into other more complex elements, and some of these into molecules, then carbon-containing organic molecules. They, in turn, combined into a variety of macromolecules, then into aggregates that could form elementary structures such as membranes; these cross-structured to form cell organs, then cells, and finally tissues, organs, and organic beings.

This idea, common in mathematics and most sciences—that elaborate complex structures are transformed from more basic

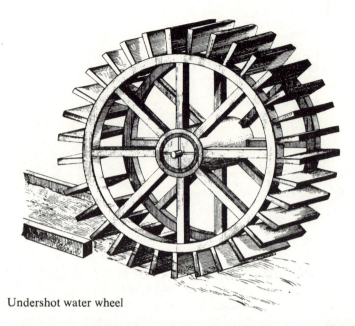

Undershot water wheel

elements according to a set of rules or principles of combining —is known as the concept of *transformation*. And this concept of transformation has been cross-structured in turn with the evolution of language. Some linguists, called transformational grammarians, have theorized that all the complex varieties of sentences ever used can be explained as transformations of basic sentences, according to a set of rules that cross-structures simpler grammatical units into different and more complex ones. Furthermore, the process of cross-structuring seems to be a universal human one. Linguists tell us that even children who have not yet learned to read or write are competent at transforming linguistic elements into original syntactical combinations that have never been spoken or heard before. These newly created sentences can immediately be understood by others who are hearing them for the first time.

We are not, however, often encouraged in school to cross-structure ideas or even to think of ourselves as innovators. On the contrary, education in the past (necessarily more concerned with inculcating a willingness to conform to a traditional culture than with innovative adaptation in a swiftly changing intellectual, social, and ecological environment) encouraged students to memorize and follow the rules and roles of previous generations rather than develop their potential ability to cross-structure and thereby transcend conventions. As a consequence most of us practice and sometimes perfect our combining ability in nonacademic areas. For example, a football player who knows the T formation and the wing formation might easily see, without the coach telling him, how to create another formation, the T-wing, by combining the two formations that he does know. And if he learns the split T formation, he will probably be able to entertain the possi-

Corn-cob column, United States Capitol Building

bility of a split T-wing. New formations and plays in games and sports seem to be created through cross-structuring two or more conventions into some new strategy. Have you ever thought up a new play or tactic in a sport or game? How did the new idea occur to you?

On a nonverbal level, cross-structuring takes place in daily life even when we choose which old blouse to combine with what old skirt or pants to produce a new outfit, or what curtains to combine with which wall paint to produce a distinctive décor. A cook may cross-structure one conventional recipe with another in order to use up what is in the refrigerator and to produce a dish no one has ever tasted before and perhaps never will again.

Now let us begin to discuss verbal cross-structuring. Coining a word is a microcosmic creative act and will provide us with a miniature experience of the same process that all other creative acts are based on. There are numerous ways to invent a word by combining already available words or syllables (even computers can be programmed to combine a relatively small number of nonsense syllables into a new noise like *nylon* or *rayon*). But new words are more often invented by combining vocabularies, borrowing the word we need from another language. For example, English took *bourgeois* from the French vocabulary and introduced it into its own. The Russian word *intelligentsia* was introduced into English by the same method.

We can also derive a new word from a root or stem of an existing word by adding affixes. Recently *mini-, midi-,* and *maxi-* have been affixed to *skirt,* and *-ist* and *-ism* to the root word *sex* to give us several now-common words. Can you invent a new word by combining a root word like *sex* with one of the following prefixes or suffixes: *pan-, para-, -logy, hydro-, octo-, -ary, anti-, astro-, -phobe, trans-, uni-, -phile?*

A new word can be produced by a kind of cross-structure we call a metaphor, where we think and write of one thing (a subject) in terms conventionally related to a quite different context (a reference). For example, *umbilical* is an anatomical reference that astronauts use to stand for a particular subject, namely the cable of wires that attaches the astronaut to his space *ship* or *capsule,* although at the last minute his space mission may be *aborted.* Or maybe we could make up a new word by the process of metonymy. For example, cross a proper name with some characteristic popularly associated with it. (Chauvin was a superpatriot whose name was used to form the word *chauvinist;* an *Edsel,* once an ill-fated variety of Ford automobile, is now a word for any big, new deal that proves a disaster.) We might also cross a word's conventional syntactical function from one part of speech to another. (For example, *jet* can be shifted from a noun function in sentences to a verb function: "It's exciting as well as economical *to jet* across the Atlantic.")

Putting two words together to form a compound word like *housewife* or *male chauvinist* is a very simple and often-used form of cross-structuring. For example, *leopard* is composed of two words, *leo* (lion) + *pard* (panther). *Leopard* is a compound word for a species that exists, but it is just as easy to cross-structure words to create fictional hybrids that exist only in imagination; some, like *mermaid—mer* (sea) + *maid—* serve to charm and delight, while óthers, like *werewolf—wer* (man) + *wolf—*to terrify and obsess. Some compound words record the cross-structuring of two earlier disciplines into a third new field, such as *biochemistry* or *psycholinguistics.* Can you think of any others? Recently the architect, Paolo Soleri, has been so concerned with the total ecology that he coined the new discipline *arcology* to combine the fields of architecture and ecology. Can you make some other possible cross-structures of two or more of the disciplines listed below that might lead to a productive new field of research?

art	physics
history	literature
psychology	medicine
geography	linguistics
physiology	economics
chemistry	politics

mathematics	government
anthropology	biology
sociology	engineering
humanities	law
architecture	ecology
metaphysics	science
philosophy	

Ideas, like words, can be cross-structured in a number of different ways. Remember that E. H. Carr cross-structured opposites (thesis and antithesis) to produce a new synthesis. Such dialectical creativity differs from other cross-structures that begin not with *opposites,* but rather with *analogy.* To become a cross-structure, analogy (i.e., a similarity between two separate ideas) must generate a new idea that is not simply reducible to the sum of its constituents. The difference between an analogy and a cross-structure is like the difference between a simile and a metaphor. The simile and analogy suggest a comparison between one context and another, while the metaphor and cross-structure fuse contexts into something new that could itself become a constituent element of some future cross-structure.

Consider, for example, the following series of cross-structures that begins, but does not end, with an analogy between biology and engineering. Despite the constancy of their reproductive drive the populations of each organic species tend to remain fairly stable. Yet we know that if there were not some restraints to stabilize wild-animal populations, the world could in only a few years be overrun with elephants or rhinoceroses or rabbits. On the other hand, why don't the apparently severe restraints on reproduction steadily diminish each species population to extinction? The check to wild-animal population growth is not a simple restraining mechanism, but a complex kind of control that varies depending on the population density of the species inhabiting a given environment. A diagram of the functioning of such a system to achieve population stability might look like this:

approaching limits of the
available food and space
in the environment

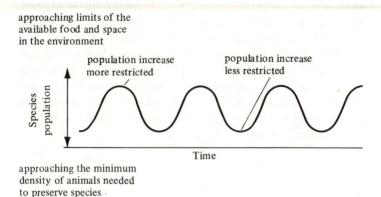

approaching the minimum
density of animals needed
to preserve species

The first step might be an analogy between a thermostat and
the stability of animal populations:

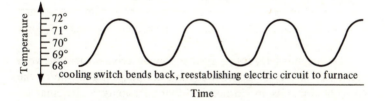

But such an analogy might be turned into a cross-structure
if we could generalize the functions of these two controls.
Each maintains a self-regulating equilibrium controlled by negative feedback so that neither population nor heat can increase
or decrease beyond set limits.

If we were now to cross-structure with physiology this negative-feedback model of control, we might understand in a new
way the approximately 98.6° temperature that our bodies
maintain in summer or winter. If the body could not negate
a rise in temperature by immediate changes in the glands that
cause perspiration and by changes in the rate of metabolism,
positive feedback would occur. Such positive feedback would

mean that as temperature rose, so, too, would metabolic rate, which, in turn, would increase body temperature. The escalation would end in death. Death could also occur at the other extreme. As the body temperature dropped below a certain point, metabolism would slow and further decrease body heat, etc., until positive feedback in the other direction would again lead to the destruction of the organism. Here is the way we might perceive body-temperature stability control using the negative-feedback model:

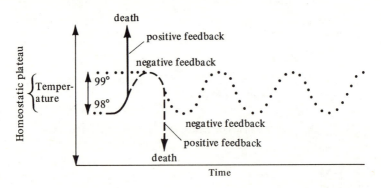

The negative feedback system can be cross-structured with still other concepts. Could we, for example, explain one of the basic fluctuations in economics—that of supply and demand—in terms of negative feedback? Draw your own diagram. Does thinking about economics in terms of cybernetic-equilibrium systems stimulate any new ideas about supply and demand, prices, or profits? Garrett Hardin * shows in discussing negative-feedback systems that within the region of the amplitude of the wave, called the *homeostatic plateau,* stability in the system is maintained, but never without waste. Some fluctuation or waste is always necessary to achieve control and must be considered a normal part of any system.

If this is true, then it would not be desirable, or even possible, to seek an *absolute* standard or constancy in a nega-

* Garrett Hardin, "The Cybernetics of Competition: A Biologist's View of Society," *Perspectives in Biology and Medicine* (autumn, 1963), p. 66.

tive-feedback situation. If we were to think of human ethical behavior in terms of the concept of negative feedback, we could conceive of an alternative ethical system to the absolute standards of the traditional ethics (*A*), where a fall from virtue is not a *normal* fluctuation, but a sin, which produces guilt:

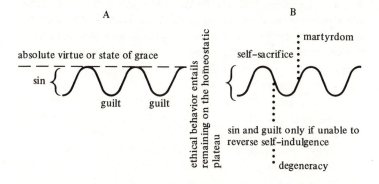

This cross-structure of ideas suggests a possible model of ethical behavior characterized by the absence of guilt, as long as one stayed on the homeostatic plateau. Perhaps *freedom* could be defined according to the negative-feedback system as an extension in the range of the plateau as far as possible without a drift into positive feedback and destruction of the system. Can you imagine a cross-structure of the concept of a negative-feedback system with either toleration of dissent or repression of dissent by government? Draw a diagram and explain your cross-structure and any new ideas it might generate about the relation between the government and the individual citizen. Would you agree with this function of government? What are the limits of a citizen's freedom?

Can you think of other possible societal equilibrium situations to cross-structure with a negative-feedback system?

Though it may seem forbidding at first, cross-structuring ideas will become quite easy with a little practice. The romantic view of creativity as a mysterious gift to a rare elite has conditioned most of us to accept an intellectually passive role in our society—to contribute our genes to biological evolution, but never our own new ideas to the evolution of human culture. The difference between the genius and any other human is not in the possession of this basic skill, but in the *significance* that society attaches to some cross-structures. Too often, however, society does not perceive or has not the means to evaluate the significance of a cross-structure until after the person responsible dies. Often, too, significant cross-structures occur to several people at the same time. Since the ideas or materials from which cross-structures will arise are more than ever before made generally available by books and electronic communication, simultaneous discoveries of the same innovative idea are increasing.

Charles Darwin and Alfred Wallace independently read Thomas Malthus's *Essay on Population* and cross-structured Malthus's theory concerning an equilibrium between human population and available food with their independent studies of animal populations in order to discover the key to how nature's system of selection functions. Darwin combined Malthus's theory of the necessity for high infant mortality to keep the human species from multiplying exponentially, thus preventing famines, with his own speculations on the intense struggle for survival among the young that keeps each animal population fairly constant. This insures that only the best adapted will survive and pass on their adaptive characteristics to effect the process of evolution. Darwin and Wallace published separate papers on the new theory of evolution in the *Journal of the Proceedings of the Linnean Society* (1859). Darwin's publication of a full-book version of the theory in 1859 made him, rather than Wallace, the more famous. Ironically, Darwin's theories in his *Origin of Species,* in which he did not even discuss *human* evolution, were soon cross-structured again with the human species and the cultural environment to produce new social and economic theories. Social Darwinists, such as Carnegie, cross-structuring laissez-faire economics and the concept of the survival of the fittest, ignored the many ways that individual organisms depend upon one another to promote the general welfare of the species, and emphasized instead the competitive struggle for existence. Poor people who had lost out in the economic struggle were thus considered obviously inferior members of the human species, and the wealthy were obviously superior genetically and deserved to survive. Another group of social Darwinists, among whom was Thomas Huxley, considered this ruthlessly competitive model offensive to the higher moral sensibilities that civilized man had evolved. Their point was that civilized man had transcended his animal origins and, therefore, should never want to turn society back into a competitive jungle. They assumed that people had evolved ethical qualities of mercy and benevolence toward their fellows and must co-operate to create a society as far as possible from the ruth-lessness of a competitive jungle. These two very different cross-structures of the theory of evolution with modern human society still clash whenever people debate social reforms, such as a guaranteed income for all citizens.

Some assumptions seem to lend themselves to, or even provoke, many different kinds of cross-structuring. Darwin's theories in one form or another were, in the late nineteenth and early twentieth centuries and perhaps even now, a fertile source for cross-structuring with other ideas. For example, the historian J. B. Bury wrote an essay entitled "Darwinism and History" in his *Selected Essays* (1930) in which he cross-struc-tured the assumptions of evolution with a set of assumptions about history. Bury set himself the problem of reconciling the large sociological movements of history with the obvious part that chance and unusual individuals play in the course of history. His solution was to cross-structure the course of human history with biological evolution. Great individuals and chance actions that change the course of history need no longer be ignored or looked on as embarrassing exceptions to so-ciological generalizations, according to Bury, but can be ac-counted for rather neatly as kinds of historical variations or mutations that were selected for and, therefore, helped de-termine the overall evolution of history.

Can you cross-structure the concept of evolution with some other idea in one of the following fields: literature, art, music, law, government, economics, religion, education?

The kinds of cross-structures produced in an historical pe-riod reflect the occupations and preoccupations of that time.

Some earlier cross-structures were made between areas that are today very far apart—writing and farming, for instance, as in the following example. In the ancient Mediterranean world, when languages were commonly written from right to left, the Greeks began to write in the opposite direction—the way we still do—from left to right. The Greeks did not make the change suddenly, for we can see from inscriptions preserved from the sixth, seventh, and even eighth centuries B.C.

MANOEOS:AIOOY:EY
:ITƎ:IIᐊ:IƎTᴙIᴙAX
MIKƎI ᴦENTAOꟻOY:
ꟻOᐊIAᴒ

Ancient Greek inscription cut into marble in boustrophedon fashion (seventh–sixth century B.C.).

many examples during this transition period of letters and words running either from right to left or from left to right, alternately changing direction from line to line. Such writing was known as *βουστροφηδον—boustrophedon* —which means "ox-turn." Apparently the conventional style of writing was being cross-structured with the equally conventional style of plowing a field. An ox plowed first in one direction, and then the *ox* was *turned* at the end of the field and started back in the opposite direction, and so on.

A cross-structure between the pattern of writing lines and

the pattern of plowed furrows was much more obvious in a primitive agrarian society, where the traditional pattern of plowing fields may have seemed to be a kind of magic spell or ritual to assure survival, not unlike the pattern of written words that are so often regarded in primitive societies as a kind of magic spell. It may seem weird to us that so unlikely a cross-structure as boustrophedon was ever made between two such seemingly unrelated areas, and yet we probably owe our own convention of writing from left to right to this Greek cross-structure of the seventh or eighth century B.C.

On the other hand, some cross-structures that we might find likely in our culture would certainly have seemed incomprehensible to the ancient Greeks. For example, it does not surprise us that we could cross-structure a convention of the writing medium with a technique from the film medium. Since we are so used to moving our eyes from left to right when we read, movie directors can take advantage of this reading convention by having an actor whom they wish to characterize as strong, forceful, or unconventional enter our field of vision from right to left. An actor or action that moves from stage left to stage right apparently does not surprise our eyes and therefore is less likely to challenge our conventional expectations.

Many other techniques of writing are used by film makers. The modern film technique of introducing a new sound sequence before the old visual context has faded (called "overlapping sound") was achieved much earlier in writing. T. S. Eliot, for instance, in "The Love Song of J. Alfred Prufrock" (1917), evokes a waterfront-slum scene in a large city, and without warning breaks into that scene with the following words:

> In the room the women come and go
> Talking of Michelangelo.

It is not until several lines later that he evokes the new and very different context into which these two lines fit: an upper-class drawing room in another part of the city, where the "cultured" guests are quite insulated from the indigent slum dwellers.

It would be easy enough for a modern writer to cross-structure the effect of the film technique of overlapping sound with, for example, a traditional stanza form (or, in prose, chapter organization) by ending one stanza (or chapter) with words that do not quite make sense until the reader begins the next stanza (or chapter).

Many modern writers, like Ernest Hemingway, Gertrude Stein, and F. Scott Fitzgerald, attempted to cross-structure music and writing. They occasionally tried to write prose that combined 1920s jazz or swing rhythms with the rhythms of

---

Easter Wings
(16)

Lord, who createdst man in wealth and store,
Though foolishly he lost the same,
Decaying more and more,
Till he became
Most poore:
With thee
O let me rise
As larks, harmoniously,
And sing this day thy victories:
Then shall the fall further the flight in me.

My tender age in sorrow did beginne:
And still with sicknesses and shame
Thou didst so punish sinne,
That I became
Most thinne.
With thee
Let me combine
And feel this day thy victorie:
For, if I imp my wing on thine,
Affliction shall advance the flight in me.

—George Herbert

their syntax and sentence structure. Some modern writers and artists seek to cross-structure high-brow culture with the forms and techniques of pop culture. Mixed media have become important in almost all art forms. A "painting" may now be more than line and color; it may incorporate words, moving parts, music, several textures, and even several odors. Films may mix black and white still slides with color motion. An ancient technique, called "acrostic poetry," combines poetry with some visual form. This technique, popular once again, is now called "concrete poetry."

from *Flowers in Concrete*
 (1966)

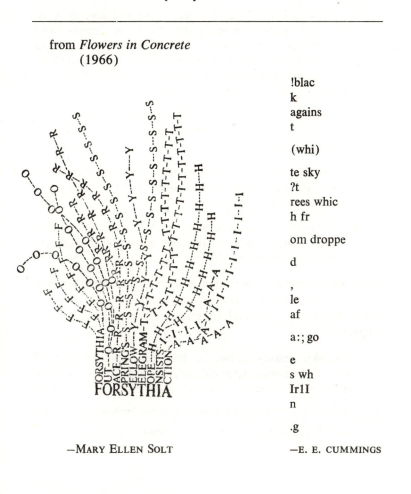

—MARY ELLEN SOLT

!blac
k
agains
t

(whi)

te sky
?t
rees whic
h fr

om droppe

d

,
le
af

a:; go

e
s wh
Ir1I
n

·g

—E. E. CUMMINGS

In "!blac," by e. e. cummings, how are the verse form, its visual image on the page, the sound, and the subject matter combined to enhance meaning? Can you think of a way to cross-structure several words or lines with a shape so as to produce an original "concrete poem"?

In this chapter we have seen how many new ideas were formulated from cross-structures between conventional concepts in disparate fields not previously thought to bear any relation to each other. A noted scientist, Harvey Brooks, recently stated it this way:

> . . . laws and principles that are simple and general in one domain of science frequently turn out to be "unreasonably" applicable in other domains of science—domains having only the remotest connection with the original inquiry that first led to their formation. This happens to an almost uncanny degree. . . .*

Jean Piaget, in his book *Structuralism* (1970), explains how a number of important modern concepts in science were the result of cross-structures:

> . . . Gestalt psychologists believed they could discern immediate wholes in primary perception comparable to the field effects that figure in electromagnetism. . . .**

> . . . Lewin very early conceived of the idea of applying Gestalt structures to social relations and for this generalized the notion of "field." †

And here is Piaget's description of the complex cross-structure that resulted in Noam Chomsky's celebrated theory of syntax (this theory has generated enormous amounts of research in linguistics):

> Chomsky actually arrived at [his] conception of linguistic structure by combining mathematico-logical concepts and techniques of formalization (algorithms, recursive devices, abstract

---

* Harvey Brooks, "Can Science Survive in the Modern Age?" *Science*, 174/4004 (Oct. 1, 1971), p. 27.
** Jean Piaget, *Structuralism* (New York, 1970), p. 8.
† *Ibid.*, p. 99.

calculi, and especially the algebraic concept of the monoid or semigroup) with ideas taken from general linguistics on the one hand (especially the conception of syntax as "creative") and from psycholinguistics on the other (for example, the idea of the speaker-hearer's "competence" in his own language).*

Exercises

1. List on one sheet of paper for each of the courses you are taking this semester several key concepts that you have read about or heard about in class or informal discussions (for example, the concept of "conditioning" in psychology, or "genetic programming" in biology, or "ethnocentricity" in anthropology, or "the process of reperception" in composition). Next, try to develop, in a paragraph each, as many cross-structures as you can between any two or more of these ideas or concepts which until now you may have considered only in isolation from one another. Remember that although a cross-structure can begin to be developed from an analogy or an opposition between two ideas, it must end in a new, third idea.

2. People often suppose that the way to become creative is to avoid learning any traditional structures or conventions. But provided we are adept at cross-structuring, the more conventions from different areas of knowledge that we have available for combination, the more likely we are to come up with original ideas and assumptions that can help us adapt to changes in the present and future. Learning conventional structures and concepts can lead us into a possible dead end only if we are not also taught the process of generating new alternatives by cross-structuring. If you are not already familiar with the following modern concepts, well known enough in their respective fields to be considered conventional, look them up in a general or scientific encyclopedia:

* *Ibid.*, p. 84.

negative-feedback system   communication theory
dialectical thinking   concept of ethnocentrism in
evolution   anthropology
Gestalt psychology   concept of the model
behavioral conditioning   ecology
field theory (concept of field,   determinism
    wave, particle)   structuralism
concept of vectors   computer programming (binary
Freudian or Jungian psycho-   opposition)
    analysis   history of ideas
transformational grammar   humanism

Choose a field of study, perhaps the one in which you are thinking of majoring, and pick some specific problem within that field which interests you. Now try to think of your problem in terms of each of the conventional concepts above. Develop one of the combined ways of thinking into a cross-structure that can stand on its own. In a page or two write a clear explanation of your new idea. You will have to develop a half-playful and half-determined attitude to seek relations between domains that never before seemed compatible and be ready to take advantage of unexpected insights and implications.

3. Here are four conventional assumptions about how society functions:

   a. The *mechanical* convention encourages the perception of society as a supermachine, with government providing the necessary checks and balances to keep the machine running smoothly. The larger units of society are perceived as aggregates of smaller units, consisting of separate individuals or cogs. These larger units (or "pressure groups") can exert considerable force against the inertia of the whole system to change its linear direction or "get it back on the right track."

   b. The *hydraulic* convention encourages the perception of society as dammed-up water or a head of steam. The irrational emotions and energies of society must be controlled by "diverting" them in one direction or another. If one of society's normal outlets is dammed up or "repressed" the energy will build up pressure until it overflows or breaks out of its proper "channels" and "sweeps all before it." Sometimes individuals attempt to "turn the tide" or "pull against the tide" and at other times we must try "to change the course" of events, though such attempts seem to defy nature. The easiest course for the individual is to be swept along in the wake of events.

c. The *electromagnetic* convention encourages the perception of society as a kind of magnetic field in which individuals are perceived as unit charges under magnetic leaders, attracted into groups that repel each other and eventually become "polarized." This process will continue in spite of any moderate group's attempt to insulate against it until the whole magnetic field is polarized into opposite sides. One side will win and society will at last be neutralized, and then a new issue will start the polarization process again.

d. The *organic* convention encourages the perception of society as a growing organism. The whole being of society is perceived as "vital" and something more than the sum of its individual parts. Nothing in society can be viewed properly in isolation from its other parts and organs. Society is constantly in the process of growing or "evolving," and yet it must always be on guard against ideological weeds or cancers, which must be "rooted" or "cut" out. The chief executive is the "head" of society, and to help him he has "the strong right arm of the law." It is a terrible thing for society to "lack conscience" or "be without a heart."

Question each of the four conventions and generate, by cross-structuring, some fifth, new alternative assumption about the function of society. How would your new cross-structure change our way of perceiving society? Would it be a better way of perceiving society than the other four? In what way or ways?

4. We are usually unaware of how most new concepts were cross-structured, because once a new idea is born we have a tendency to forget the fact that it was a cross-structure, even when the evidence is fairly obvious or easy to ascertain. Such habitual forgetfulness may give us some insight into the way the human mind functions. For example, when we speak of "round ice*cubes*" or "green *black*boards," we apparently are so used to thinking of the compound as a *whole* entity that we are not normally aware of the glaring inconsistency. Biological cross-

structures between species such as that between horses and donkeys end in sterile hybrids like mules, whereas cultural cross-structures can themselves quickly become constituents in new cross-structures—over and over again. In a brief essay discuss how this "limitation" of the human mind serves to make the process of cultural evolution much more rapid than biological evolution and what this might mean for the future of our species.

5. Consider a few modern ideas or inventions that you are interested in. Did they originate as cross-structures? How? What were their constituents? Write a brief essay explaining how one of these ideas or inventions was combined from earlier ideas or materials.

21

Evaluating and Recommending Original Ideas

WHEN two or more ideas are crossed to produce a new hybrid, a creative act has taken place, however small or insignificant. The difference between a student composing an original metaphor and Charles Darwin cross-structuring Malthus's *Essay on the Principle of Population* with his own work on animal populations is not a difference in cognitive process. We need not assume that the genius's mind functions in a way basically foreign to the normal run of men. The difference between a genius's cross-structuring and the cross-structurings that all of us perform daily lies in the degree of significance that we attribute to the product of cross-structuring. And this depends on the criterion of relevance with which we verify or evaluate a new concept. Some innovators go undiscovered by their own generation because contemporaries cannot perceive significance in their new ideas or assumptions. Such ideas are disparaged as "eccentric," which means that though they are original their originality seems at the moment "out of the mainstream." If a new idea or assumption sooner or later cannot satisfy some acceptable criterion of relevance and contribute to the stream of culture as one of the components of further cross-structurings, then it will die without progeny like a sterile hybrid.

Anyone can learn to originate ideas, but judging the rele-

vance of new ideas—separating the significant from the insignificant—may be a problem until we relate what was said
in Chapter 15 on criteria of relevance to cross-structuring.
Cross-structures divorced from any criteria are mere novelties.
And few novelties are better than the conventions they are
intended to replace. In order to evaluate the products of our
cross-structuring we will have to accept some specific criterion
of relevance or perhaps a combination of criteria.

Let us look at some examples of cross-structuring and
consider in each case the criterion, or criteria, according to
which the new idea was verified or evaluated. A cross-structuring of two almost antithetical ideas into one, "militant nonviolence," was used most notably in this country by Martin
Luther King. Many thinkers find it a very significant alternative way of bringing about social reform. But according to what
criterion could militant nonviolence be evaluated? For the
most part, a *pragmatic* criterion was used to judge its significance. It has been said that before Dr. King was assassinated
in 1968 he managed, by using militant nonviolence, to bring
about in a few short years a more rapid series of civil-rights
reforms than had occurred over the past hundred years, except
in the immediate wake of the Civil War. Do you think that
Dr. King's militant nonviolence was a more practical way of
getting social reforms put into law and actually enforced than
any method of social action since his death? What recent ideas
or inventions could you recommend in terms of their practical effects?

Cross-structuring literary forms and genres is a practice
as old as literature itself. For example, Shakespeare has
Polonius remind us humorously of the complex cross-structures,
of questionable aesthetic significance, that became widespread
in drama around 1600. He calls the traveling players that have
come to Denmark "the best actors in the world, either for
tragedy, comedy, history, pastoral, pastoral-comical, historical-
pastoral-tragical-historical, tragical-comical-historical-pastoral"
(*Hamlet,* II, ii).

Here is the Italian Renaissance literary theorist, Guarini,
in 1599 defending the significance of a new dramatic cross-
structure called "tragicomedy." Tragicomedy is the most sig-

nificant dramatic form, according to Guarini, because it stays closer to the Aristotelian mean between extremes than either of the earlier excessive forms, tragedy or comedy, from which it was composed. Let us follow Guarini's actual description and evaluation:

> . . . [I] am content to hand over to tragedy kings, serious actions, the terrible, and the piteous; to comedy I assign private affairs, laughter, and jests; in these things are the specific differences between the two. I wish for the present to concede that one may not enter into the jurisdiction of the other. Will it follow from this that, since they are of diverse species, they cannot be united to make up a third poem? Certainly it cannot be said that this is in opposition to the practice of nature, and much less to that of art.

> Speaking first of nature, are not the horse and the ass two distinct species? Certainly, and yet of the two is made a third, the mule, which is neither one nor the other. . . .

> He who composes tragicomedy takes from tragedy its great persons but not its great action, its verisimilar plot but not its true one, its movement of the feelings but not its disturbance of them, its pleasure but not its sadness, its danger but not its death; from comedy it takes laughter that is not excessive, modest amusement, feigned difficulty, happy reversal, and above all the comic order, of which we shall speak in its place. These components, thus managed, can stand together in a single story. . . .

> But it would be possible here to raise a new question, namely, what actually is such a mixture as tragicomedy? I answer that it is the mingling of tragic and comic pleasure, which does not allow hearers to fall into excessive tragic melancholy or comic relaxation. From this results a poem of the most excellent form and composition . . . much more noble than simple tragedy or simple comedy, as that which does not inflict on us atrocious events and horrible and in‧ humane sights, such as blood and deaths, and which, on the other hand, does not cause us to be so relaxed in laughter that we sin against the modesty and decorum of a well-bred man. And truly if today men understood well how to compose tragicomedy (for it is not an easy thing to do), no other

drama should be put on the stage, for tragicomedy is able
to include all the good qualities of dramatic poetry and to
reject all the bad ones; it can delight all dispositions, all ages,
and all tastes—something that is not true of the other two,
tragedy and comedy, which are at fault because they go to
excess.

To recommend art forms because they do not go to excess
must seem strange to our ears since we are rather fond
of excess in all its forms. To recommend the middle of the road
is to recommend a time-hallowed criterion; but is the mean
always to be preferred over the extremes? What do you think
is the significance of some of our own newer cross-structured
forms or genres, such as op art or mixed media? What different criteria could you use to judge their significance?

Here is a case where evaluating the significance of a cross-
structure can become quite complex, since the evaluation depends on how the cross-structure was used. In the English
Renaissance, dramas were customarily conceived in five parts
or acts rather than in three (or sometimes one act) as they
are at present. In some cases this seems to have been simply
a convention that playwrights or printers honored by making
arbitrary divisions into five more or less equal groups of
scenes. In other cases, however, we can see writers patterning
their scenes more carefully into a cohesive, five-part structure.*
This tradition of the five-act structure, which lasted for centuries in Western dramatic literature, was the result of a cross-
structure between law-court procedure and literary form in-
novated by classical rhetoricians. The kind of rhetoric that
was studied by aspiring writers in classical times and in the
Renaissance was concerned not only with literary style but,
more practically, with teaching a lawyer or public figure how
best to persuade judges in a formal court of law.

Ancient law courts (and even today's) display a kind of

---

* Such quintpartite construction might or might not be printed as five
acts. For instance, some of Shakespeare's plays are printed in five-act divisions
during his lifetime, and later printed in the First Folio as a sequence of
scenes with no division into acts. But it is not the printer's habits we are concerned with here, but the custom among many Renaissance playwrights of
conceiving a drama in five steps or stages.

five-part pattern of development. First, the object of the proceedings and all parties to the proceedings are identified; the opposing sides—defense and prosecution—introduce themselves; the charges are read; and the plea recorded. Second, there are preliminary statements by both the opposing sides (the right to make these preliminary statements is usually waived by both prosecution and defense in a modern trial). Third, one side (prosecution) presents its full case against the other. Fourth, the opposite side (defense) has its day in court. Finally come the summations, and a judgment is made in favor of one side or the other.

This five-part pattern, when related to drama, produced a play that was not only structured into five acts, but was typically slow in starting and then very heavy in plot-counterplot exchanges between opposed sides. Consider Shakespeare's *Hamlet*. In Act I the main characters are all introduced, and the opposing interests and objectives of the protagonists made clear. In Act II the first tentative sparring or preliminary skirmishes occur between the opposed sides—Hamlet versus King Claudius. It is not until Act III that Hamlet sets up the play within a play and catches "the conscience of the King." Though Hamlet seems to have won this act, the king, in Act IV, quickly takes the initiative away by counterplotting to have Hamlet sent to England and beheaded. In Act V, Hamlet and Claudius have their last contest, and justice is served by turning Claudius's final plot against Hamlet onto his own head. Horatio is left to justify the verdict "to the yet unknowing world."

In another play of Shakespeare's, the conventional relation, apparently taken for granted by his audience, between the five divisions of a legal trial and the five-part structure of a drama seems purposely ignored. But as we shall see, even *ignoring* a conventional structural relation that most people have learned to expect can grant a kind of significance to the conventional cross-structure. Unlike the usual plot-counterplot between opposing sides in Renaissance drama, Shakespeare's *King Lear* begins with one side plotting and winning and continuing to grow in evil and prosper against the better side act after act,

until the very end of Act V. Then, at last, a judgment in trial
by combat is meted out to the guilty, but not before the life
of an innocent has been taken. Much of the play concerns
the concept of justice, and the characters in the play are continually calling justice into question, asking the gods when a
long-overdue justice will ever be served. To a Renaissance
playgoer who was at all familiar with the traditional plot-
counterplot structure of five-act dramas, the purposefully lop-
sided structure of Shakespeare's *King Lear* would have seemed
to question justice. Using the aesthetic criterion that structure
or form should be related congruently with subject we see that
Shakespeare's warping of the convention apparently adds significance to *Lear*.

But Shakespeare's unconventional use of the five-act structure reveals something else of interest that is not simply aesthetic. The conventional five-act structure must have seemed
relevant for philosophic reasons, because it apparently fit current ideas, before *Lear,* about the essential justice of divine
providence. The relation between literary form and law-court
procedure implied a fairly orderly exchange of plot and counterplot between worthy opponents—who seem to have been
guaranteed equal time—and administration of final justice by
Providence. In ignoring the convention in *Lear,* Shakespeare
is making a significant statement about justice in the world
after 1600, which could not have been made unless the five-
act structure had earlier seemed relevant enough to current
ideas about social justice to have become conventional. With
Lear, Shakespeare not only verifies the earlier significance of
conventional five-act structure, but makes a new statement
that the convention no longer fits the world after *Lear,* in
which the judgments of Divine Providence are apparently
considerably more ambiguous than they were thought to have
been.

An interesting recent novel called *Hopscotch,* by Julio
Cortázar, has been written in such a way that a reader is
encouraged to ignore the conventional sequence of chapters
and play organizational hopscotch, reading the chapters in

various sequences. The reader who plays along finds more than one story in *Hopscotch*. By encouraging his audience to participate in organizing the novel, Cortázar may have achieved a significant innovation from a seemingly trivial cross-structure between the form of a novel and a game of hopscotch. What criteria might you use to judge such a novel's significance?

The traditional corporate model is structured hierarchically —that is, it makes large distinctions in status, pay, privilege, and responsibility among its employees. Orders are made and carried down from the top executives, and there is a high rate of turnover at the lower ranks, maybe due to boredom with a job that offers insignificant responsibilities, alienation from decision making, or frustration at very slow advance. But there is presently a new corporate model operating in a few growing businesses. Here is a list of its characteristics:

1. No vita, recommendations, or specific educational requirements for any job in the firm. Decisions made in a series of interviews, followed by six months probationary period. Decision to grant permanent employment based on how you can fit into a community that is adapting and changing. Tenure (almost complete job security) granted after first six months with firm.
2. No formality in office—all on first-name terms.
3. Important decisions made in committees elected by all segments of employees.
4. All personnel are encouraged to serve on whatever committees interest them.
5. Profits are shared equally in company from president to maintenance men.
6. Mail-order cost cutting and high morale due to community cooperation and profit sharing decrease corporate costs and increase profits.

Where do you think some of these new ideas or procedures come from? That is, how was this new corporate model cross-structured? How could you judge its significance?

Some corporations that enjoy a monopoly and want to continue to serve the public without growing sluggish and obsolete have created and given power to a research and development branch. This branch generates products or ideas and makes periodic reports recommending new products so that the company can be motivated, though not in competition with other firms, to realize its own future capabilities. Suppose the United States, in a corporate cross-structure, were now to create a fourth branch of government empowered to investigate and report to the people our future capabilities.

Science and technology are moving much faster than seemed possible when the founding fathers set up the three branches of government (executive, legislative, judicial) to check and balance each other. The present governmental dilemma is the possibility and even the necessity of living up to our increasing technological potential to solve social and environmental problems, while at the same time there is a growing tendency of the chief executive and Congress to follow polls that beat the well-worn path of comfortable convention, instead of *leading* the country into the future.

The chief executive could not simply maintain the status quo nor as easily ignore the power of the recommendations of a fourth branch of government as he often now ignores or buries reports of future capabilities from his own cabinet or appointed special committees. Instead of having to await the judgment of history, the performance of a president or Congress could be measured in terms of how much their years in office accomplished of what the country was capable of doing. What might be the significance of this possible cross-structure? How could you evaluate it?

Cross-structuring in science is not different from cross-structuring in any other field. But the unique contribution of science to human creativity lies in a standardized criterion of relevance, to which any new hypothesis must be submitted to judge its significance—i.e., *the new hypothesis must be shown to have some advantage in predicting events in nature, and the alleged predictive advantage must usually be submitted to an objective test before its significance is verified.*

Jet-propelled space ship for flying to the sun, proposed in 1656 by Cyrano de Bergerac—poet, swordsman, and science-fiction writer. Heated air escaping from top of ship would supposedly pull the ship upward. Right idea, wrong direction!

However, science will often accept tentatively, before it can be verified, a set of assumptions forming a new model of nature if it meets other criteria. These criteria include being able to explain previously inexplicable events; providing a more elegant—i.e., more economical—explanation of events than was possible before; being capable of generating new research that may potentially yield some future predictive

The Macrocosm, the Microcosm, and the Winds (ca. A.D. 1200).

advantage. These criteria of evaluation are fairly well established for all scientists. Yet the process of discovery is purposely left open since there appears to be no one proper method of pursuing scientific innovation. Throughout history scientists have stumbled on cross-structures for various and strange reasons. What is most important is not the method of discovery but the scientist's willingness to evaluate it by objectively testing its predictive advantage. William Harvey was a great scientist who displayed exemplary patience and care in evaluating his new model of the human circulatory system, although his cross-structure itself may seem quaint to modern students.

Harvey's discovery of the circulation of the blood was a very complex interaction between hypothesis and experimental evidence. In order to explain his discovery he likens the human heart to the sun of the solar system and the circulation of blood to the continuous circling of planets always in the same direction and, by another cross-structure, to the circulation of the wind and clouds around the earth. It was possible for Harvey to make these cross-structures between the individual (the microcosm) and the larger universe (the macrocosm) because the microcosm-macrocosm analogy was a convention during the early seventeenth century when Harvey was writing.

Most conventional analogies do not produce significant cross-structures. But in this case Harvey sees and tests empirically the significance of a particular kind of cross-structure between the human being and the universe. In the dedication to his 1620 treatise on the circulation of the blood, Harvey seems to be using the cross-structure as an extravagant compliment to royalty, and its significance seems here mainly aesthetic:

TO
THE MOST SERENE AND PUISSANT
CHARLES
KING OF GREAT BRITAIN, FRANCE, AND IRELAND
DEFENDER OF THE FAITH

Most Serene King!

The animal's heart is the basis of its life, its chief member, the sun of its microcosm; on the heart all its activity depends, from the heart all its liveliness and strength arise. Equally is the king the basis of his kingdoms, the sun of his microcosm, the heart of the state; from him all power arises and all grace stems. In offering your Majesty—in the fashion of the time—this account of the heart's movement, I have been encouraged by the fact that almost all our concepts of humanity are modelled on our knowledge of man himself, and several of our concepts of royalty on our knowledge of the heart. An understanding of his heart is thus of service to the king as being a very special portrayal, if on a more modest level, of his own functioning.*

But in this excerpt from his treatise what may have appeared at first as only a loose analogy seems to be elaborated seriously beyond a point where we can disregard its significance as a cross-structure:

We have as much right to call this movement of the blood circular as Aristotle had to say the air and rain emulate the circular movement of the heavenly bodies. The moist earth, he wrote, is warmed by the sun and gives off vapours which condense as they are carried up aloft and in their condensed form fall again as rain and remoisten the earth, so producing successions of fresh life from it. In similar fashion the circular movement of the sun, that is to say, its approach and recession, give rise to storms and atmospheric phenomena.

It may very well happen thus in the body with the movement of the blood. All parts may be nourished, warmed, and activated by the hotter, perfect, vaporous, spirituous and, so to speak, nutritious blood. On the other hand, in parts the blood may be cooled, coagulated, and be figuratively worn out. From such parts it returns to its starting-point, namely, the heart, as if to its source or to the centre of the body's economy, to be restored to its erstwhile state of perfection. Therein, by the natural, powerful, fiery heat, a sort of store of life, it is re-liquefied and becomes impregnated with spirits and (if I may so style it) sweetness. From the heart it is

* William Harvey, *The Circulation of the Blood and Other Writings*, trans. Kenneth J. Franklin (London, 1963), p. 3.

redistributed. And all these happenings are dependent upon the pulsatile movement of the heart.

This organ deserves to be styled the starting point of life and the sun of our microcosm just as much as the sun deserves to be styled the heart of the world. For it is by the heart's vigorous beat that the blood is moved, perfected, activated, and protected from injury and coagulation. The heart is the tutelary deity of the body, the basis of life, the source of all things, carrying out its function of nourishing, warming, and activating the body as a whole. But we shall more fittingly speak of these matters when we consider the final cause of this kind of movement.*

Could Harvey have managed to perceive what others before him had not because of his new cross-structure between the continuous one-way circulation of the planets of the macrocosm and the human body's microcosmic system? Harvey affirms this:

In consequence, I began privately to consider if it had a movement, as it were, in a circle. This hypothesis I subsequently verified, finding that the pulsation of the left ventricle of the heart forces the blood out of it and propels it through the arteries into all parts of the body's system in exactly the same way as the pulsation of the right ventricle forces the blood out of that chamber and propels it through the artery-like vein into the lungs. . . .**

As Harvey continues his new alternative assumptions, their significance can be evaluated by two criteria: that of predictive advantage, and that of generating fruitful new research. One area of new research was begun by Harvey himself in physiology and comparative anatomy because his new assumptions made obvious an important link between the functioning of human bodies and those of other animals. The position and precise functioning of heart, lungs, veins, and arteries in various animals could now be compared and contrasted.

Not only in science but in general the process of evaluating the cross-structure is just as important as making the cross-

* *Ibid.*, pp. 58–59.
** *Ibid.*, p. 58.

structure. The application of a specific criterion to an example of cross-structuring will often do more than simply help to assess its relevance with respect to that criterion. It may very likely imply ways of modifying the new concept to render it more significant than it originally seemed. At first this process of cross-structuring and then judging and discarding until you produce a significant new idea will seem slow. However, as you develop more skill at it, you may find that cross-structures and an initial evaluation of them are beginning to happen preconsciously. The preconscious mind can apparently cross-structure and even eliminate insignificant cross-structures very rapidly, and nominate as a candidate for consciousness only the most relevant combinations as though originality were happening intuitively. Anyone can achieve this "intuitive" originality who is willing to keep practicing cross-structures and evaluating them according to some specific set of criteria until the process becomes habitual. Occasionally a cross-structure will seem to happen almost by accident, but may be no less valuable than those more laboriously generated.

Exercises

1. Refer to exercise 1 of Chapter 20, in which you were asked to make as many cross-structures as you could among the major ideas presented in your courses this semester. Now pick out what you think is the most significant of all the cross-structures you have been able to make so far and develop it into an essay. This search for the *most significant* new cross-structure rather than the first one that pops into our heads usually has an important effect on our thinking. It may encourage us to *relate* much of the disparate knowledge from various courses and sources during a college term that would otherwise have remained fragmented and soon forgotten. Finally, add a paragraph or two to your essay to explain the significance of your

cross-structure according to some criterion of relevance or some combination of criteria. Here, for example, are some alternative criteria with which you might judge the significance of your cross-structure:

a. it is the simplest (most "elegant") possible solution to a problem;

b. it constitutes a hypothesis to explain what has never been explained;

c. it is likely to generate much fruitful new research;

d. it poses a new problem or asks an important new question;

e. it clarifies or makes measurable or more rigorous an issue, event, or phenomenon that until now seemed vague or shallow;

f. it postulates a model of the subject or a hypothesis from which predictions about future events or issues can be made and submitted to objective test in order to validate that model or hypothesis;

g. it frames in a new and more useful perspective an issue, phenomenon, or problem we have taken for granted—it allows us to reperceive a part of our experience that has become blunted by convention;

h. it shows its apparently isolated subject to be part of a larger system or ecology by revealing a relation or interdependency that had not previously been noticed;

i. it poses the most economically efficient solution or decision;

j. it constitutes the most humane or compassionate solution or decision;

k. it combines several of the above criteria (such as efficiency and compassion) or two or more criteria of your own (such as careful research together with lively imagination) to form a compound criteria for judging significance.

2. Here is a list of some inventions that Herman Kahn and Anthony J. Wiener * say are likely or at least possible within the next two or three decades:

a. multiple applications of lasers and masers for sensing, measuring, communication, cutting, heating, welding, power transmission, illumination, destructive (defensive), and other purposes;

b. more reliable and longer-range weather forecasting;

   c. major reduction in hereditary and congenital defects;

   d. new techniques and institutions for adult education;

   e. inexpensive design and procurement of "one of a kind" items through use of computerized analysis and automated production;

   f. new or improved uses of the oceans (mining, extraction of minerals, controlled "farming," source of energy, and the like);

   g. new and more reliable "education" and propaganda techniques for affecting human behavior—public and private;

   h. new techniques for very cheap, convenient, and reliable birth control;

   i. new, more varied, and more reliable drugs for control of fatigue, relaxation, alertness, mood, personality, perceptions, fantasies, and other psychobiological states;

   j. general and substantial increase in life expectancy, postponement of aging, and limited rejuvenation;

   k. "high quality" medical care for undeveloped areas (e.g., use of medical aides and technicians, referral hospitals, broad spectrum antibiotics, and artificial blood plasma);

   l. physically nonharmful methods of overindulging;

  m. extensive use of robots and machines "slaved" to humans;

   n. automated universal (real time) credit, audit, and banking systems;

   o. chemical methods for improving memory and learning;

   p. improved chemical control of some mental illnesses and some aspects of senility;

   q. mechanical and chemical methods for improving human analytical ability more or less directly;

   r. new techniques for keeping physically fit and/or acquiring physical skills;

   s. inexpensive high-capacity world-wide, regional, and local (home and business) communication (perhaps using satellites, lasers, and light pipes);

   t. individual flying platforms;

   u. practical large-scale desalinization;

   v. home education via video and computerized and programmed learning;

   w. stimulated and planned and perhaps programmed dreams;

* From Herman Kahn and Anthony J. Wiener, *The Year 2000: A Framework for Speculation on the Next Thirty-three Years* (New York: Macmillan, 1967), pp. 51–58.

   x. flexible penology without necessarily using prisons (by use
      of modern methods of surveillance, monitoring, and control);
   y. inexpensive world-wide transportation of humans and cargo.

   Obviously these inventions will not be equally significant,
though the list makes no distinctions among them. Which do
you suppose will be *most* significant? How do you decide this?
You could, for example, extrapolate the likely implications or
consequences of each invention and develop a set of criteria
to assess the importance of these implications.

3. We can examine a painting, for example, *A Hunt in a Forest*
   by Paolo Uccello (Ashmolean Museum, Oxford) and possibly
   abstract some criteria that may have governed the artist in its
   composition. (See cover and title page.)
      It is immediately obvious that Uccello was not working ac-
   cording to the conventional criterion that aims to individualize
   human character, for all his men have the same body and
   facial structures. Only their stance and the color or surface
   characteristics of their garments differ. All dogs are also cut
   from the same pattern, as are the horses and trees. If he is not
   interested in individualization he does seem interested in the
   total pattern of the hunt, which spatially relates the species man,
   dog, horse, tree. One of his criteria, then, may be the aim of
   forming various species into a colorful pattern of activity, where
   the total composition of active forms and colors is considered
   much more important than any individualization within a species.
      See if you can discover some of the possible criteria or aims
   of the artists who created each of the following works:

EDVARD MUNCH *The Cry.* 1895

African mask,
Akan region.

Edvard Munch, *The Cry* (1895).
National Gallery of Art, Washington, D.C.
Rosenwald collection.

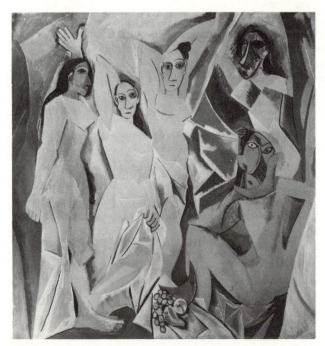

Pablo Picasso,
*Les Demoiselles
d'Avignon* (1907).
Collection,
The Museum of
Modern Art,
New York.

William Blake,
*Beatrice
Addressing Dante
from the Car*
(*Purgatorio,*
Canto XXIX)
(The Tate Gallery,
London)

William S. Mount,
*The Power of
Music* (Century
Association,
New York)

Pablo Picasso, *Guernica* (the Museum of Modern Art, New York)

Salvador Dali,
*The Persistence
of Memory*
(Collection, the
Museum of
Modern Art,
New York)

Egyptian Musicians
(Metropolitan
Museum of Art,
New York)

Salvador Dali,
*Soft Construction
with Boiled Beans:
Premonition of
Civil War* (1936).

Index